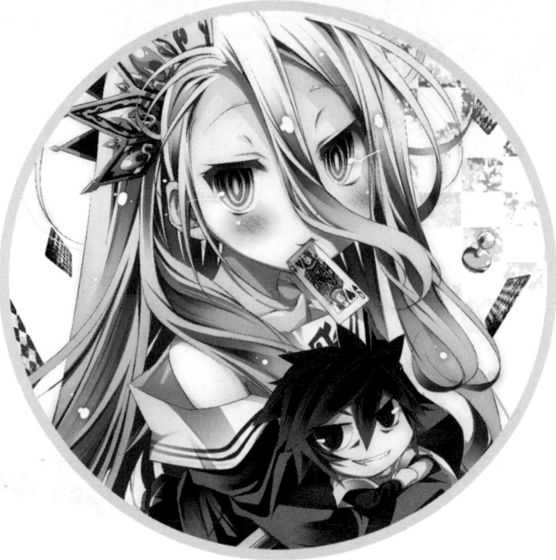

NO GAME NO LIFE

01

Art:
Mashiro Hiiragi & Yuu Kamiya

Original Story/Character Designs:
Yuu Kamiya

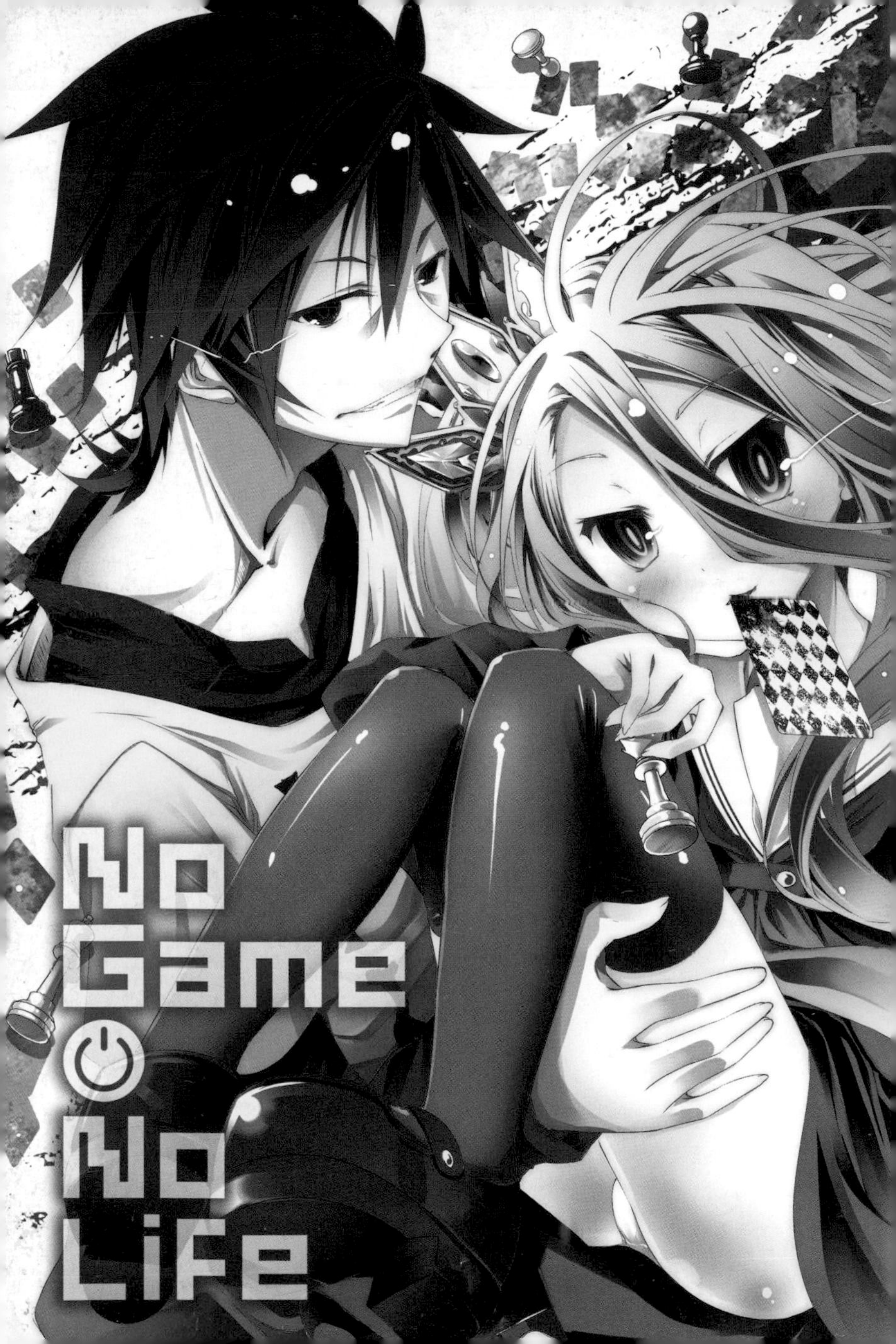
No Game No Life

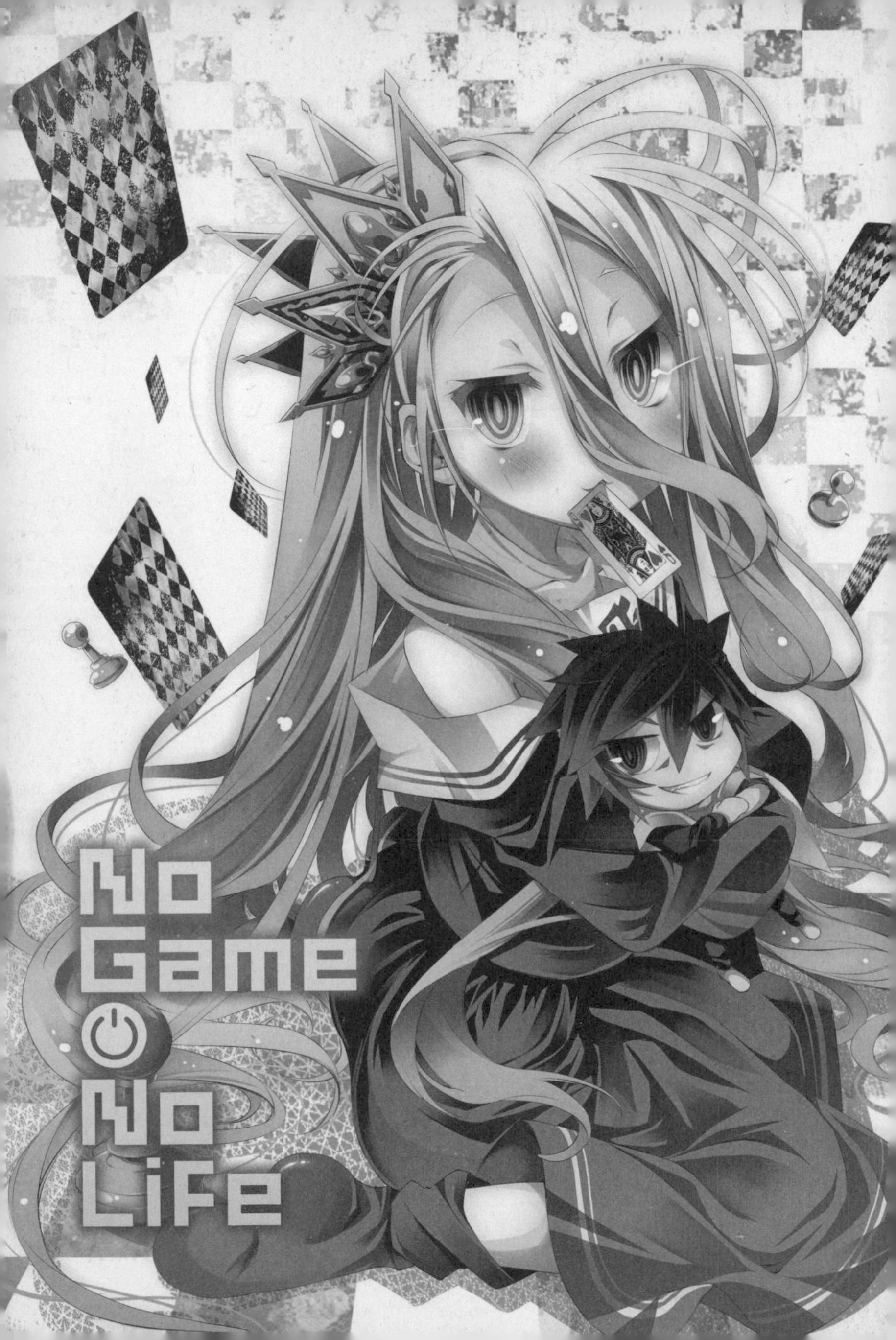
No Game No Life

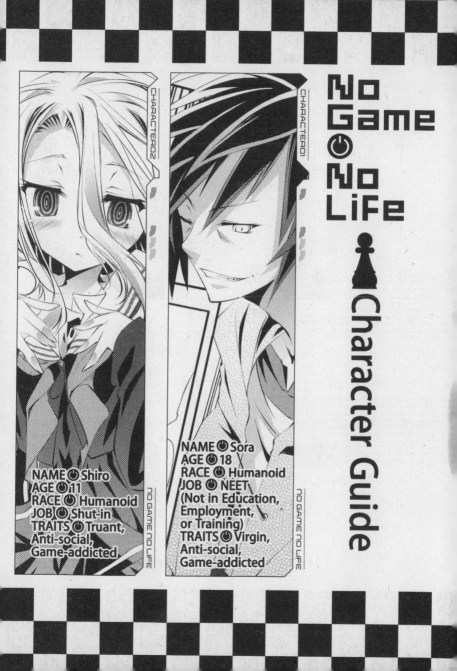

No Game No Life

Character Guide

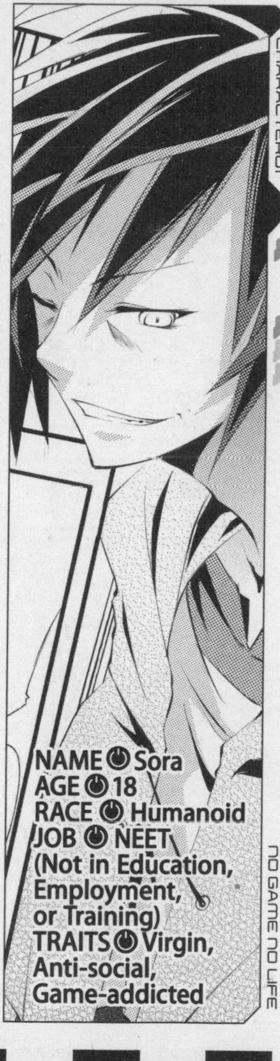

CHARACTER01
NAME Sora
AGE 18
RACE Humanoid
JOB NEET (Not in Education, Employment, or Training)
TRAITS Virgin, Anti-social, Game-addicted
NO GAME NO LIFE

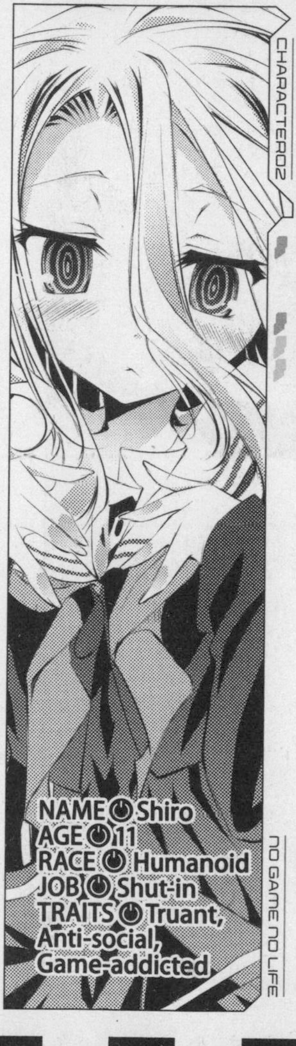

CHARACTER02
NAME Shiro
AGE 11
RACE Humanoid
JOB Shut-in
TRAITS Truant, Anti-social, Game-addicted
NO GAME NO LIFE

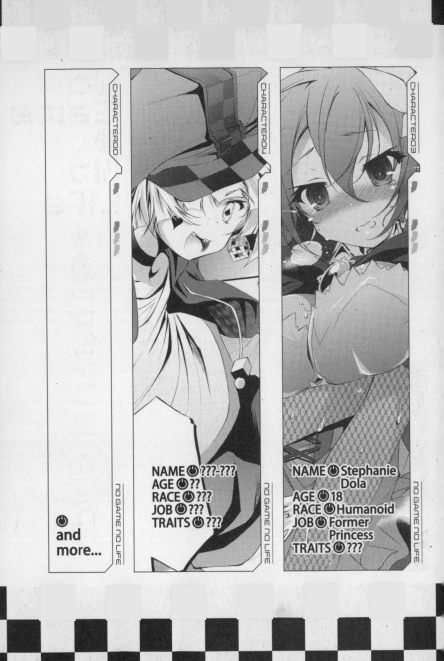

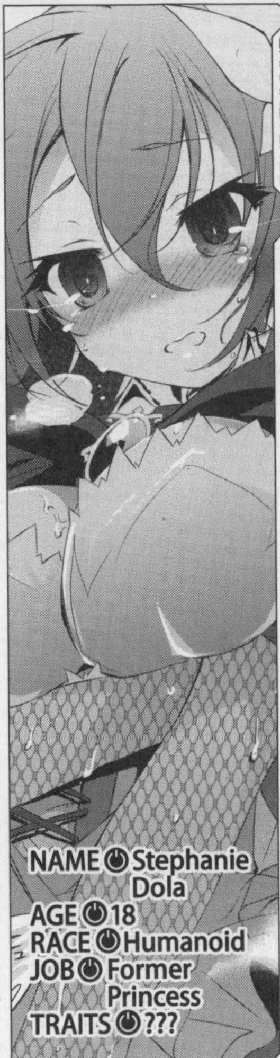
CHARACTER03
NAME Stephanie Dola
AGE 18
RACE Humanoid
JOB Former Princess
TRAITS ???
NO GAME NO LIFE

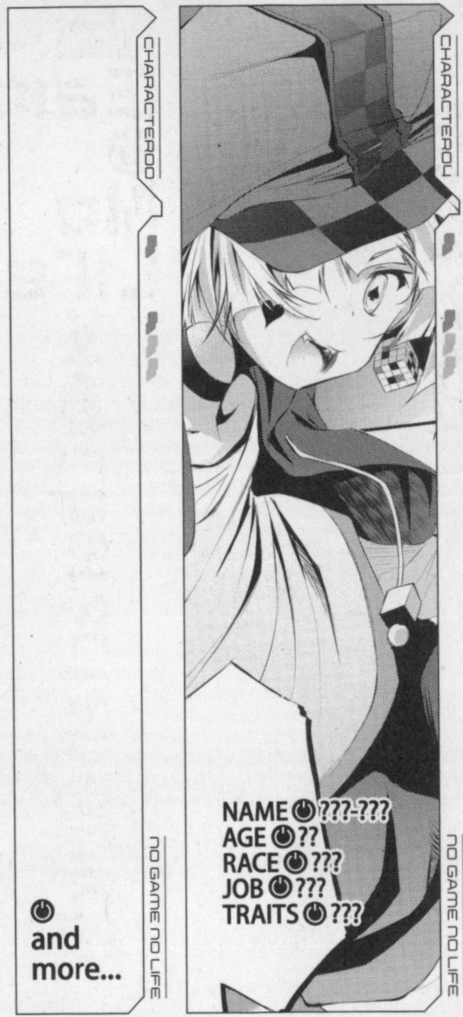
CHARACTER04
NAME ???-???
AGE ??
RACE ???
JOB ???
TRAITS ???
NO GAME NO LIFE

CHARACTER00

and more...

NO GAME NO LIFE

SEVEN SEAS ENTERTAINMENT PRESENTS

No Game No Life

story by YUU KAMIYA / art by MASHIRO HIIRAGI & YUU KAMIYA

VOLUME 1

TRANSLATION
Ryan Peterson
Adrienne Beck

ADAPTATION
Danielle King

COPY EDITOR
Lee Otter

LETTERING
Roland Amago

LAYOUT
Bambi Eloriaga-Amago

LOGO DESIGN
Courtney Williams

COVER DESIGN
Nicky Lim

MANAGING EDITOR
Adam Arnold

PUBLISHER
Jason DeAngelis

NO GAME NO LIFE VOL. 1

Edited by MEDIA FACTORY.
First published in Japan in 2013 by KADOKAWA CORPORATION, Tokyo.

ISBN: 978-1-626920-79-8

Printed in Canada

First Printing: October 2014

10 9 8 7 6 5 4 3 2

FOLLOW US ONLINE: ***www.gomanga.com***

READING DIRECTIONS

This book reads from ***right to left***, Japanese style. If this is your first time reading manga, you start reading from the top right panel on each page and take it from there. If you get lost, just follow the numbered diagram here. It may seem backwards at first, but you'll get the hang of it! Have fun!!

1
2
3
4
5
6
7
8
9

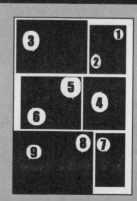

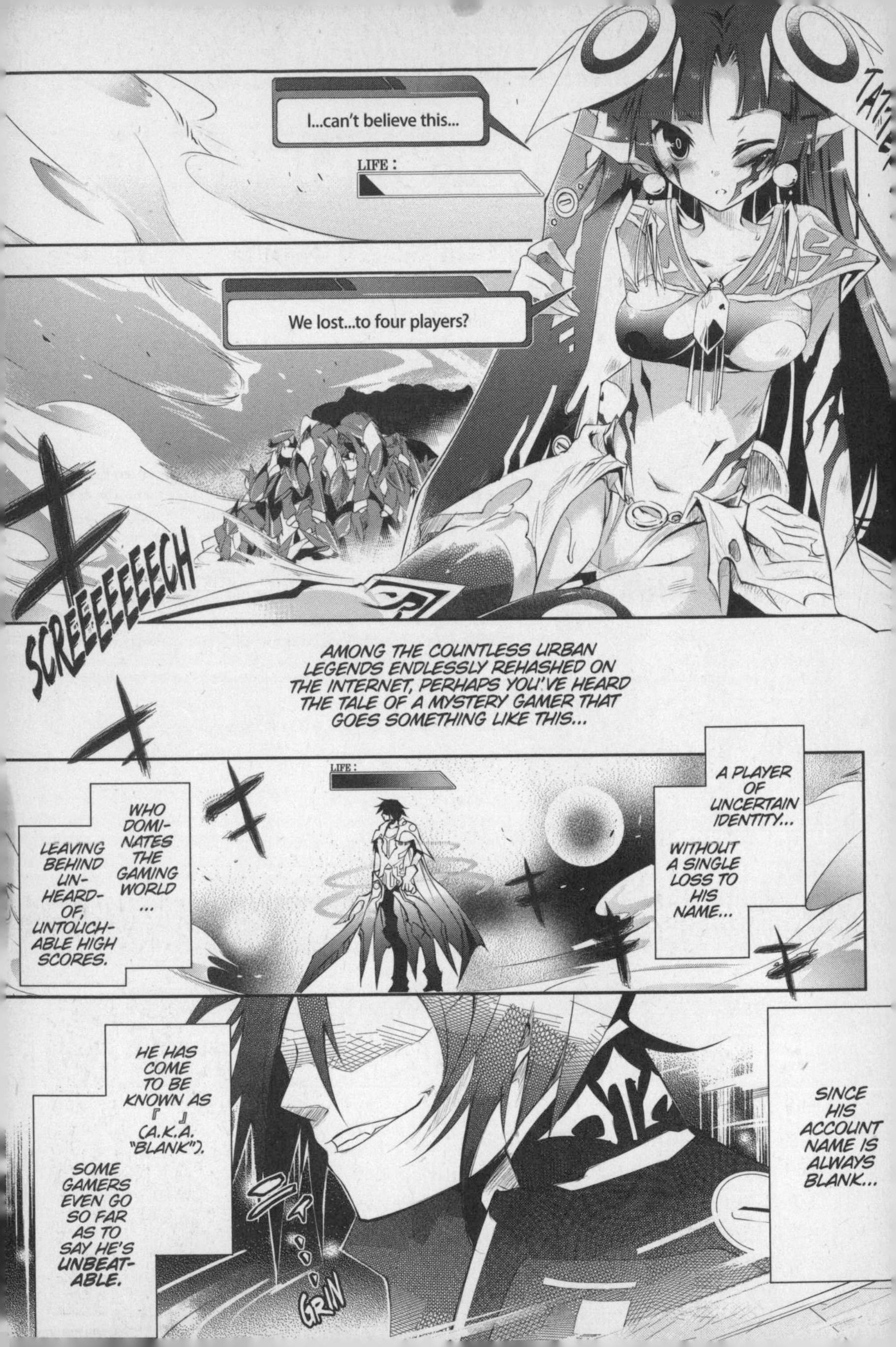
I...can't believe this...
LIFE:
We lost...to four players?
SCREEEEEEEECH
AMONG THE COUNTLESS URBAN LEGENDS ENDLESSLY REHASHED ON THE INTERNET, PERHAPS YOU'VE HEARD THE TALE OF A MYSTERY GAMER THAT GOES SOMETHING LIKE THIS...
A PLAYER OF UNCERTAIN IDENTITY...
WITHOUT A SINGLE LOSS TO HIS NAME...
LIFE:
WHO DOMINATES THE GAMING WORLD...
LEAVING BEHIND UNHEARD-OF, UNTOUCHABLE HIGH SCORES.
SINCE HIS ACCOUNT NAME IS ALWAYS BLANK...
HE HAS COME TO BE KNOWN AS 『 』 (A.K.A. "BLANK").
SOME GAMERS EVEN GO SO FAR AS TO SAY HE'S UNBEATABLE.
GRIN

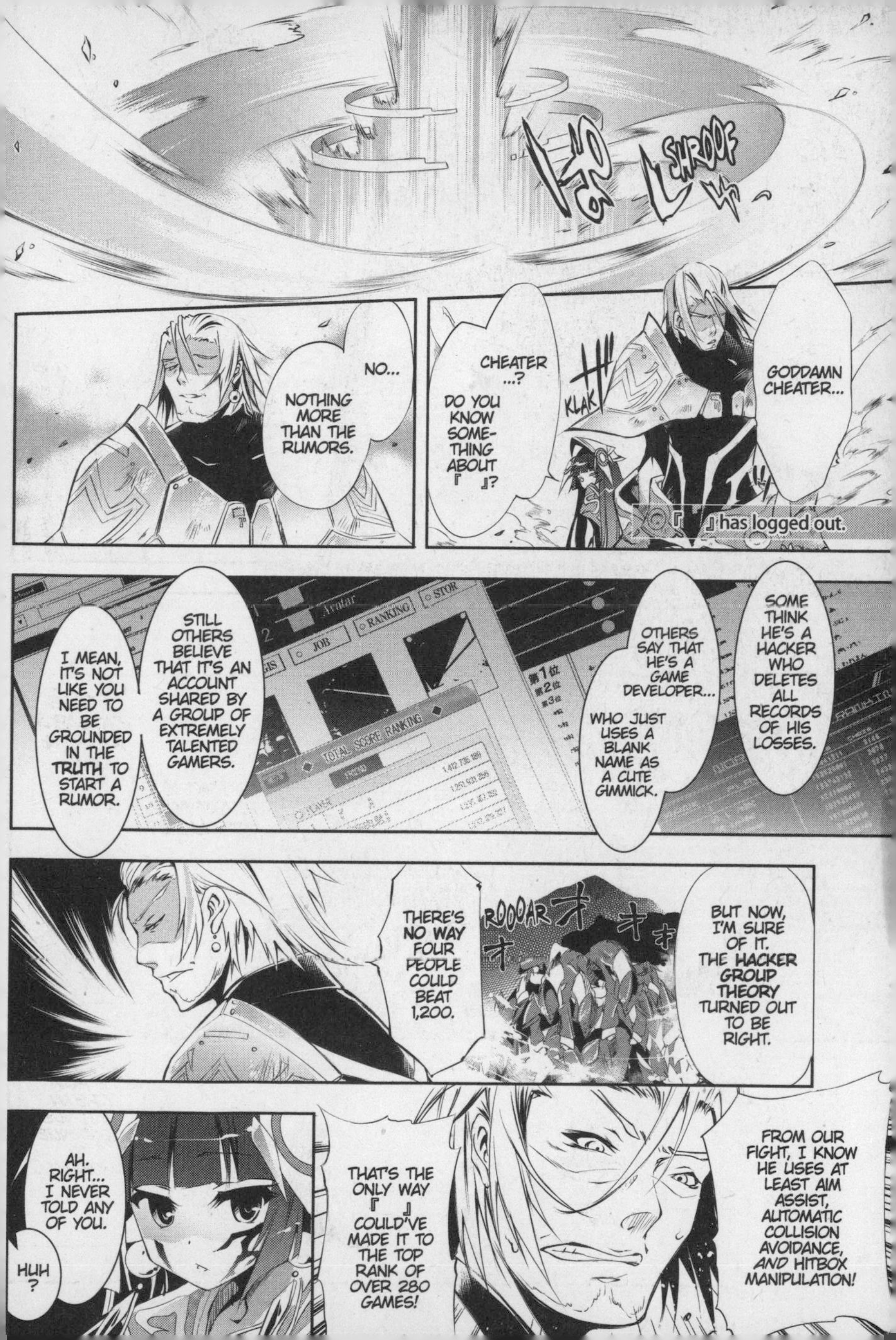
SHROOF
GODDAMN CHEATER...
『 』has logged out.
KLAK
CHEATER ...? DO YOU KNOW SOMETHING ABOUT 『 』?
NO... NOTHING MORE THAN THE RUMORS.
SOME THINK HE'S A HACKER WHO DELETES ALL RECORDS OF HIS LOSSES.
OTHERS SAY THAT HE'S A GAME DEVELOPER...
WHO JUST USES A BLANK NAME AS A CUTE GIMMICK.
RANKING
JOB
TOTAL SCORE RANKING
STILL OTHERS BELIEVE THAT IT'S AN ACCOUNT SHARED BY A GROUP OF EXTREMELY TALENTED GAMERS.
I MEAN, IT'S NOT LIKE YOU NEED TO BE GROUNDED IN THE TRUTH TO START A RUMOR.
BUT NOW, I'M SURE OF IT. THE HACKER GROUP THEORY TURNED OUT TO BE RIGHT.
ROOOAR
THERE'S NO WAY FOUR PEOPLE COULD BEAT 1,200.
FROM OUR FIGHT, I KNOW HE USES AT LEAST AIM ASSIST, AUTOMATIC COLLISION AVOIDANCE, AND HITBOX MANIPULATION!
THAT'S THE ONLY WAY 『 』 COULD'VE MADE IT TO THE TOP RANK OF OVER 280 GAMES!
AH. RIGHT... I NEVER TOLD ANY OF YOU.
HUH?

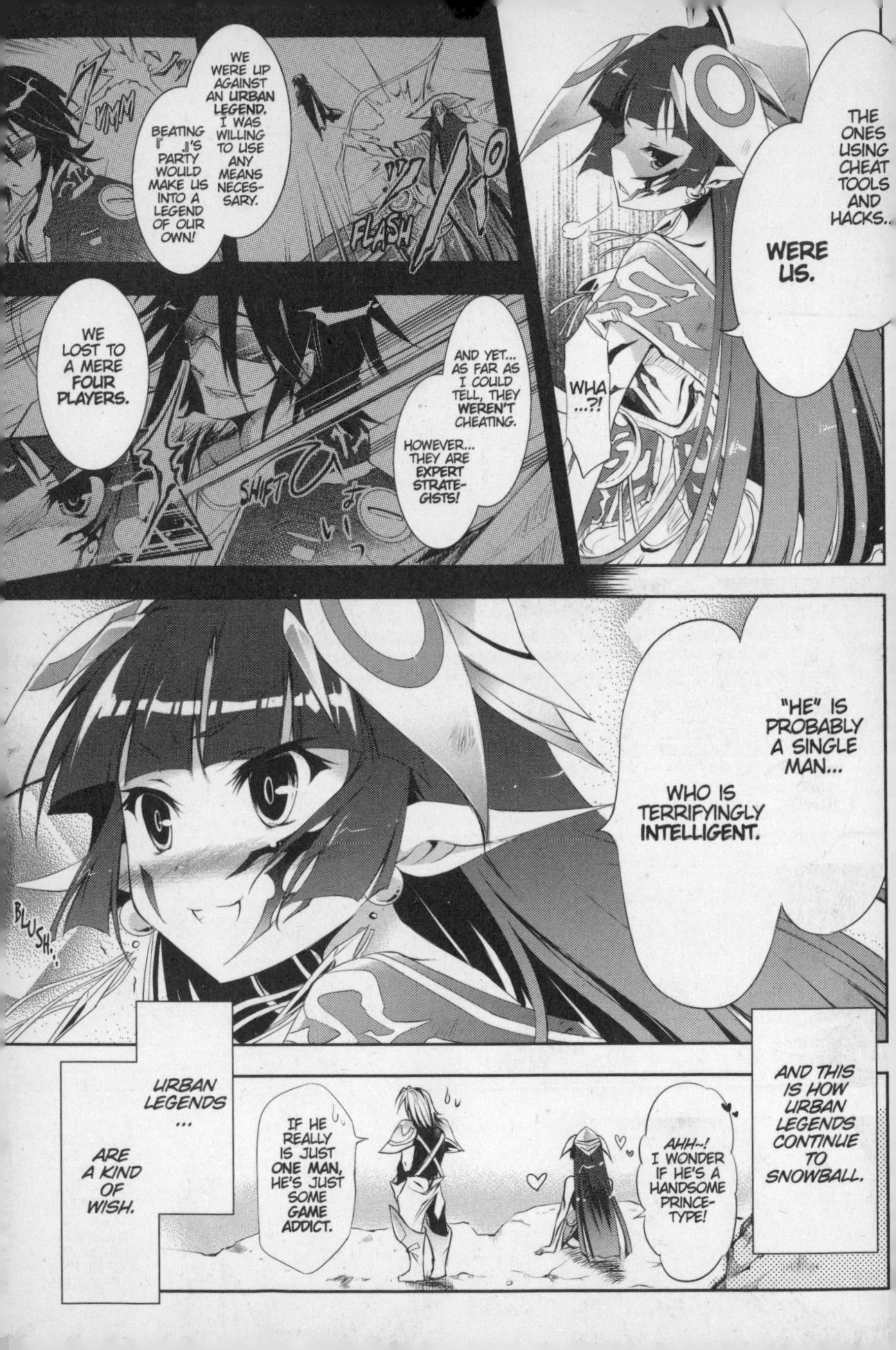
THE ONES USING CHEAT TOOLS AND HACKS..
WERE US.
WHA ...?!
WE WERE UP AGAINST AN URBAN LEGEND. I WAS WILLING TO USE ANY MEANS NECES-SARY.
BEATING 『 』'S PARTY WOULD MAKE US INTO A LEGEND OF OUR OWN!
VMM
FLASH
AND YET... AS FAR AS I COULD TELL, THEY WEREN'T CHEATING.
HOWEVER... THEY ARE EXPERT STRATE-GISTS!
WE LOST TO A MERE FOUR PLAYERS.
SHIFT
"HE" IS PROBABLY A SINGLE MAN...
WHO IS TERRIFYINGLY INTELLIGENT.
BLUSH
AND THIS IS HOW URBAN LEGENDS CONTINUE TO SNOWBALL.
AHH~! I WONDER IF HE'S A HANDSOME PRINCE-TYPE!
IF HE REALLY IS JUST ONE MAN, HE'S JUST SOME GAME ADDICT.
URBAN LEGENDS ...
ARE A KIND OF WISH.

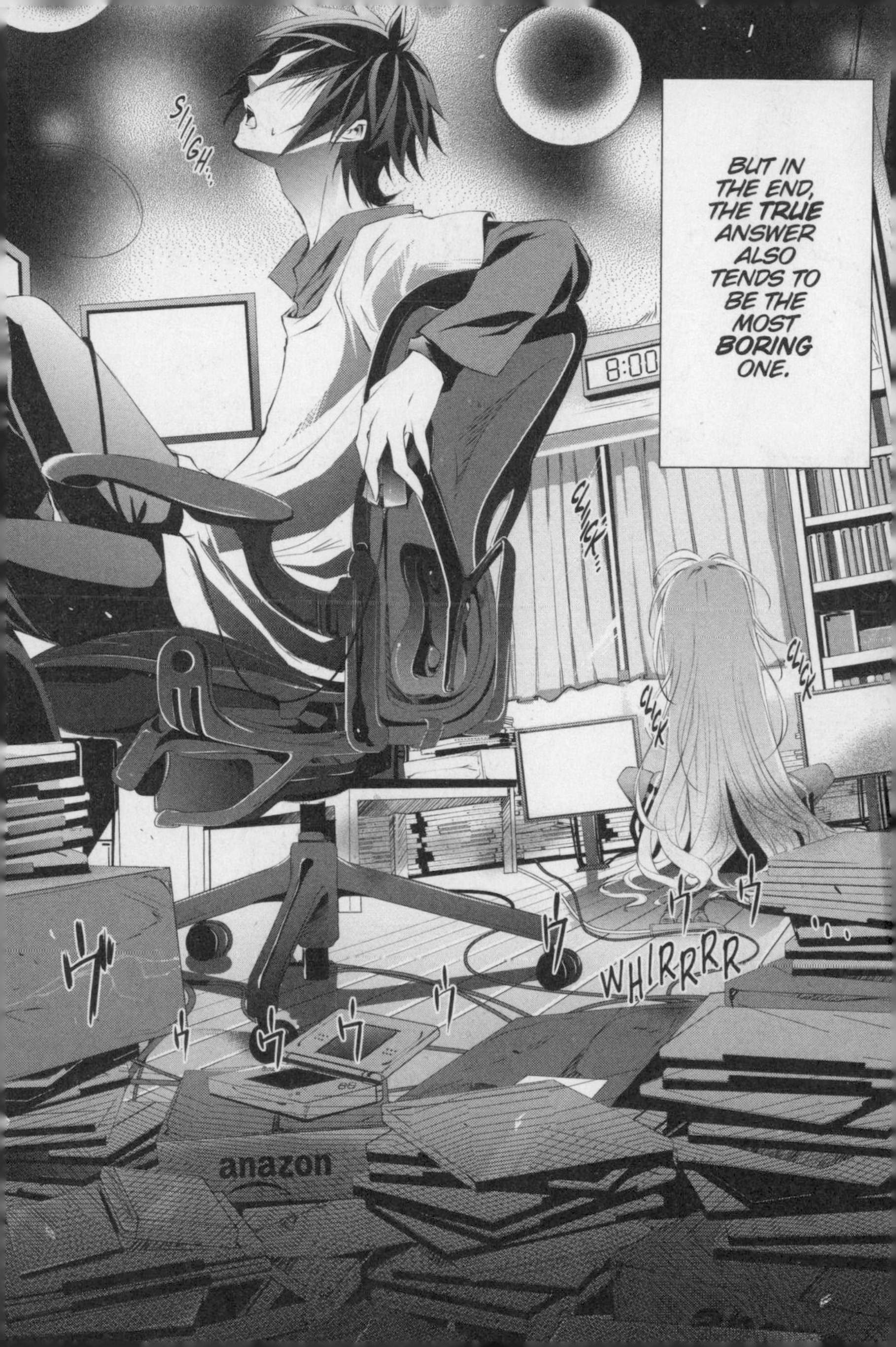
BUT IN THE END, THE TRUE ANSWER ALSO TENDS TO BE THE MOST BORING ONE.
SIIIGH...
CLICK...
CLICK
CLICK
...
WHIRRRR
anazon

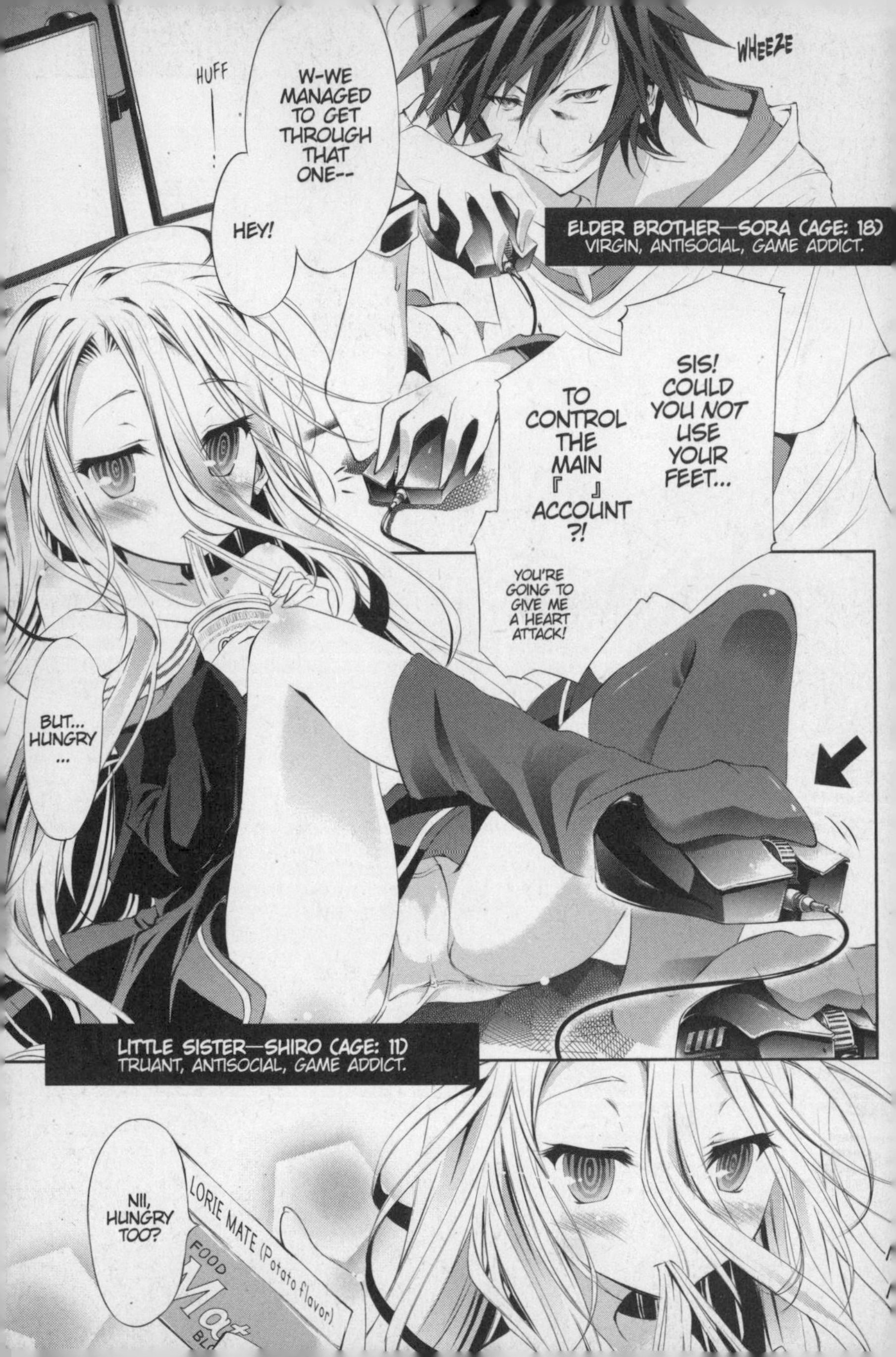
WHEEZE
ELDER BROTHER—SORA (AGE: 18)
VIRGIN, ANTISOCIAL, GAME ADDICT.
HUFF
W-WE MANAGED TO GET THROUGH THAT ONE--
HEY!
SIS! COULD YOU NOT USE YOUR FEET...
TO CONTROL THE MAIN『 』ACCOUNT ?!
YOU'RE GOING TO GIVE ME A HEART ATTACK!
BUT... HUNGRY ...
LITTLE SISTER—SHIRO (AGE: 11)
TRUANT, ANTISOCIAL, GAME ADDICT.
LORIE MATE (Potato flavor)
NII, HUNGRY TOO?

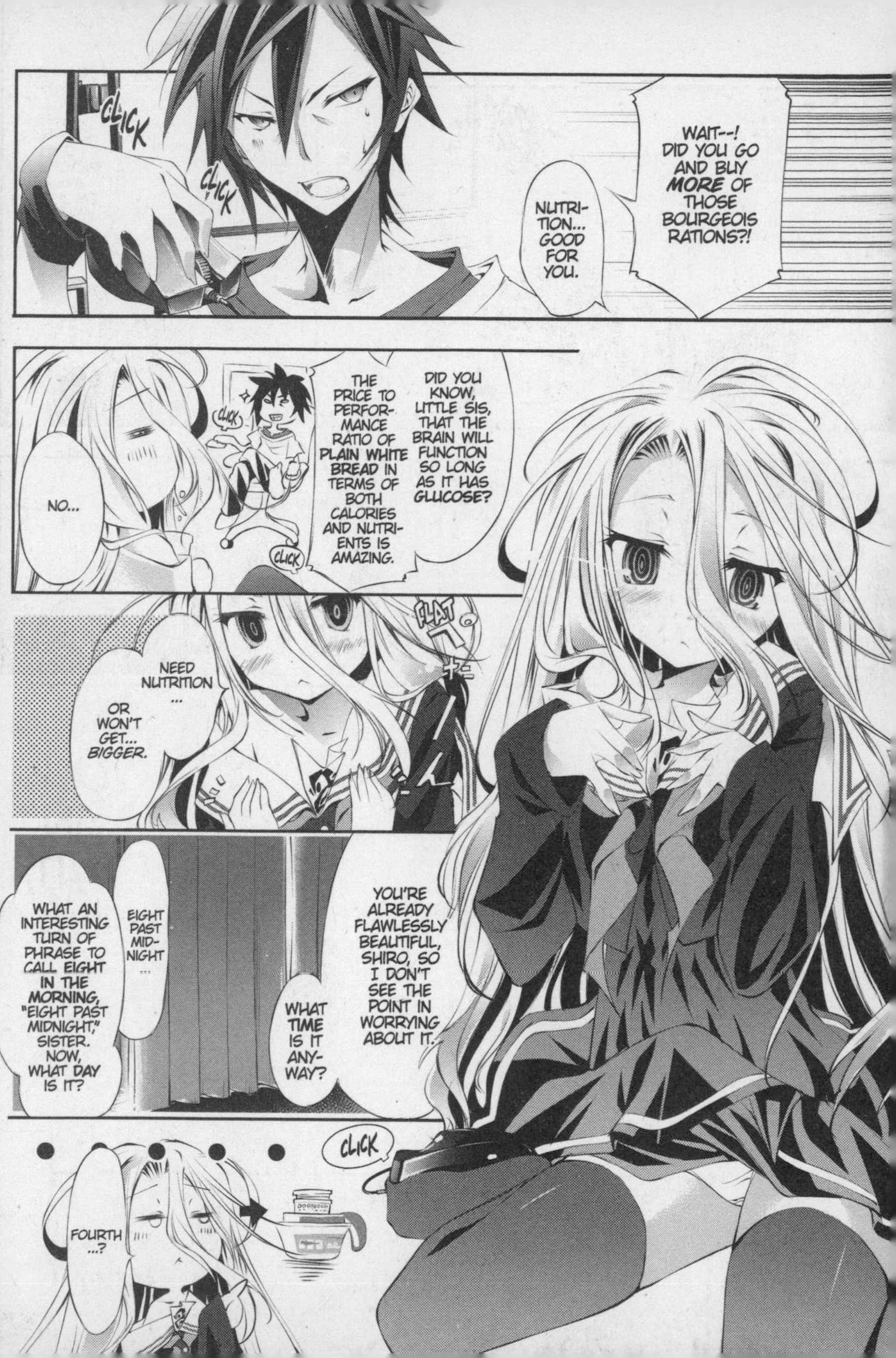
WAIT--! DID YOU GO AND BUY MORE OF THOSE BOURGEOIS RATIONS?!
NUTRITION... GOOD FOR YOU.
CLICK
CLICK
DID YOU KNOW, LITTLE SIS, THAT THE BRAIN WILL FUNCTION SO LONG AS IT HAS GLUCOSE?
THE PRICE TO PERFORMANCE RATIO OF PLAIN WHITE BREAD IN TERMS OF BOTH CALORIES AND NUTRITENTS IS AMAZING.
CLICK
CLICK
NO...
FLAT
NEED NUTRITION ...
OR WON'T GET... BIGGER.
YOU'RE ALREADY FLAWLESSLY BEAUTIFUL, SHIRO, SO I DON'T SEE THE POINT IN WORRYING ABOUT IT.
WHAT TIME IS IT ANYWAY?
EIGHT PAST MIDNIGHT ...
WHAT AN INTERESTING TURN OF PHRASE TO CALL EIGHT IN THE MORNING, "EIGHT PAST MIDNIGHT," SISTER. NOW, WHAT DAY IS IT?
CLICK
FOURTH ...?

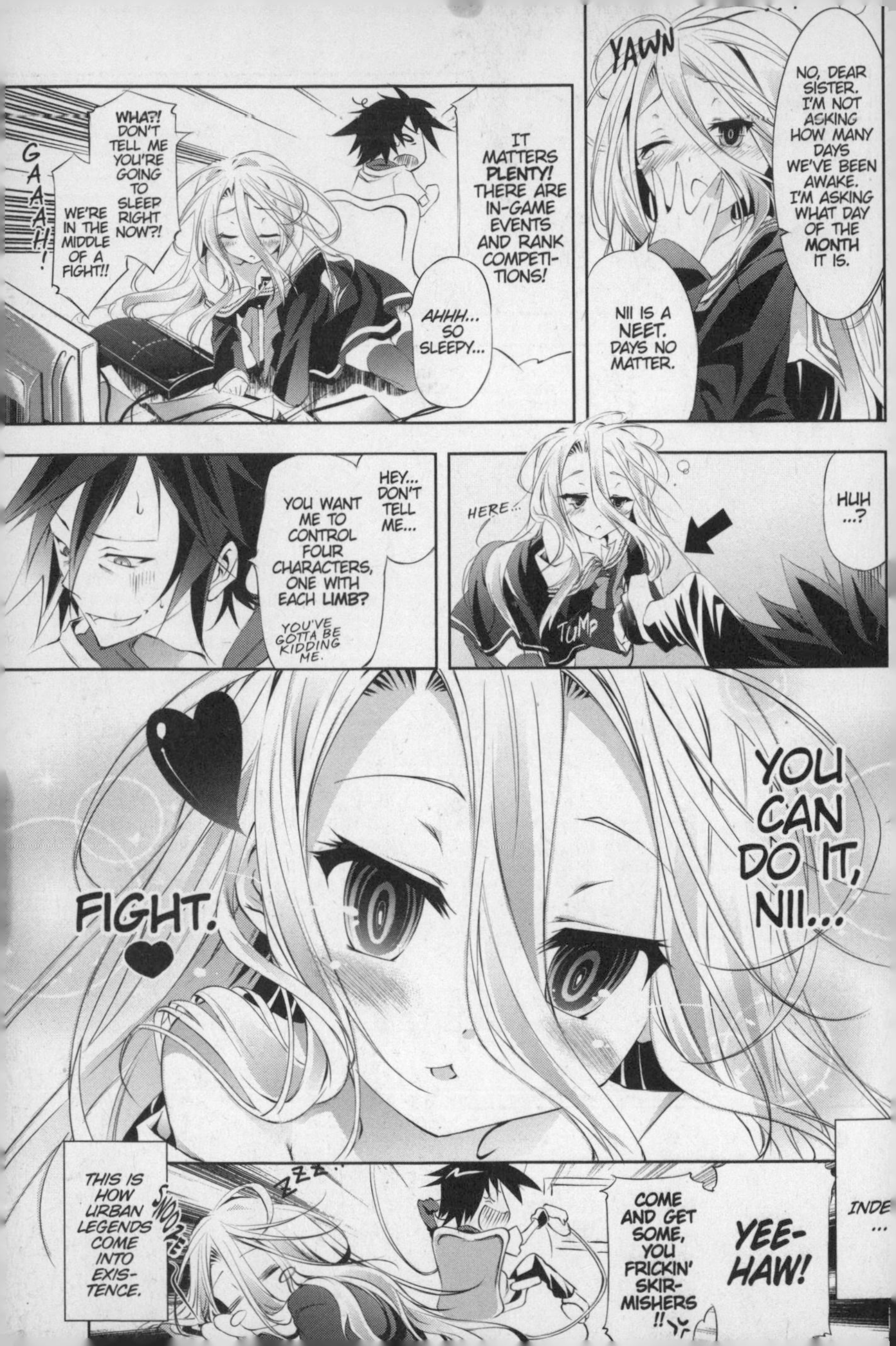
YAWN
NO, DEAR SISTER. I'M NOT ASKING HOW MANY DAYS WE'VE BEEN AWAKE. I'M ASKING WHAT DAY OF THE MONTH IT IS.
NII IS A NEET. DAYS NO MATTER.
IT MATTERS PLENTY! THERE ARE IN-GAME EVENTS AND RANK COMPETI-TIONS!
AHHH... SO SLEEPY...
WHAT?! DON'T TELL ME YOU'RE GOING TO SLEEP RIGHT NOW?!
WE'RE IN THE MIDDLE OF A FIGHT!!
GAAAH!
HUH ...?
HERE...
TUMP
HEY... DON'T TELL ME...
YOU WANT ME TO CONTROL FOUR CHARACTERS, ONE WITH EACH LIMB?
YOU'VE GOTTA BE KIDDING ME.
YOU CAN DO IT, NII...
FIGHT.
INDE ...
YEE-HAW!
COME AND GET SOME, YOU FRICKIN' SKIR-MISHERS!!
ZZZ
SNOOZE
THIS IS HOW URBAN LEGENDS COME INTO EXIS-TENCE.

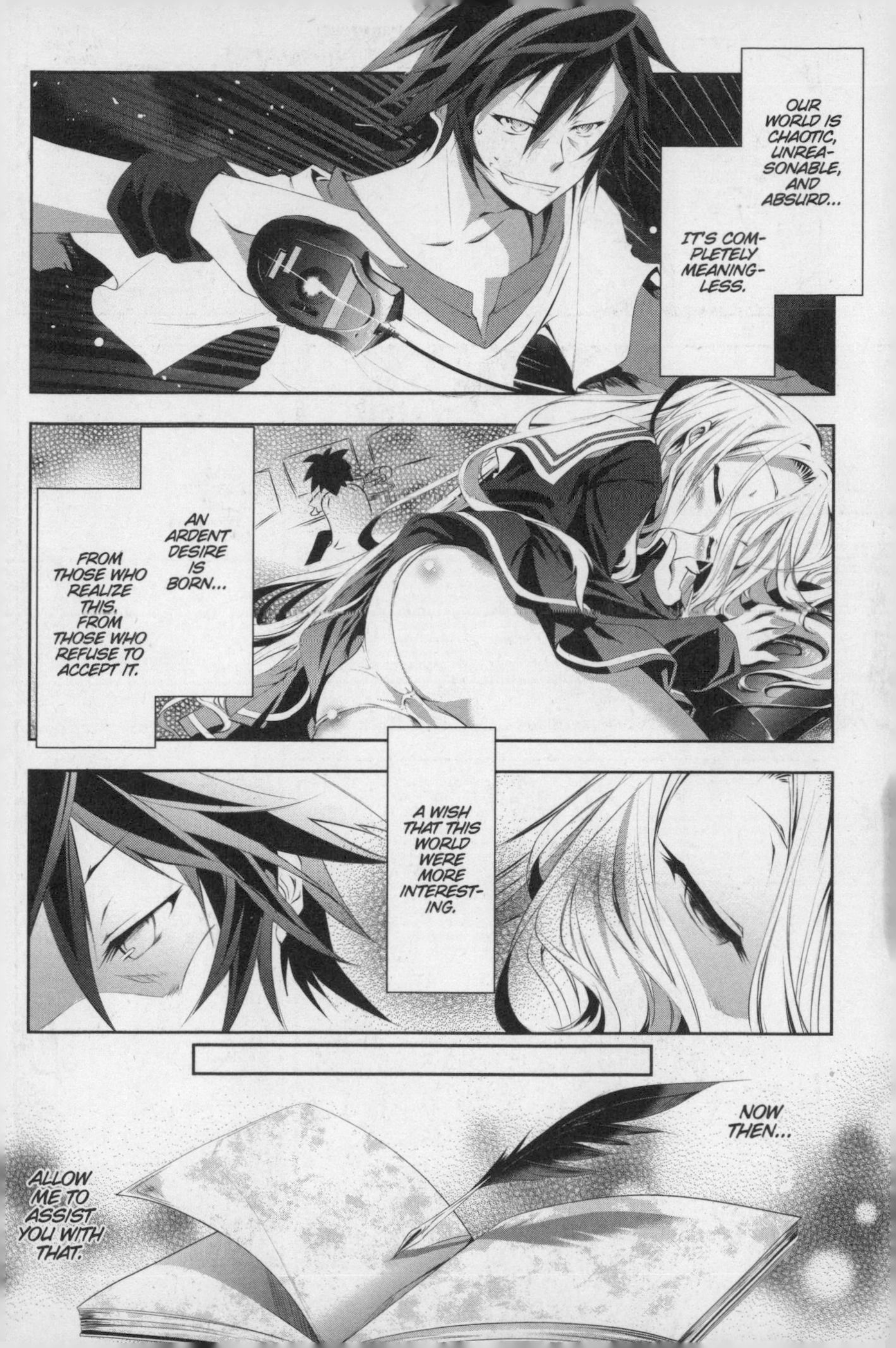
OUR WORLD IS CHAOTIC, UNREASONABLE, AND ABSURD...
IT'S COMPLETELY MEANINGLESS.
AN ARDENT DESIRE IS BORN...
FROM THOSE WHO REALIZE THIS, FROM THOSE WHO REFUSE TO ACCEPT IT.
A WISH THAT THIS WORLD WERE MORE INTERESTING.
NOW THEN...
ALLOW ME TO ASSIST YOU WITH THAT.

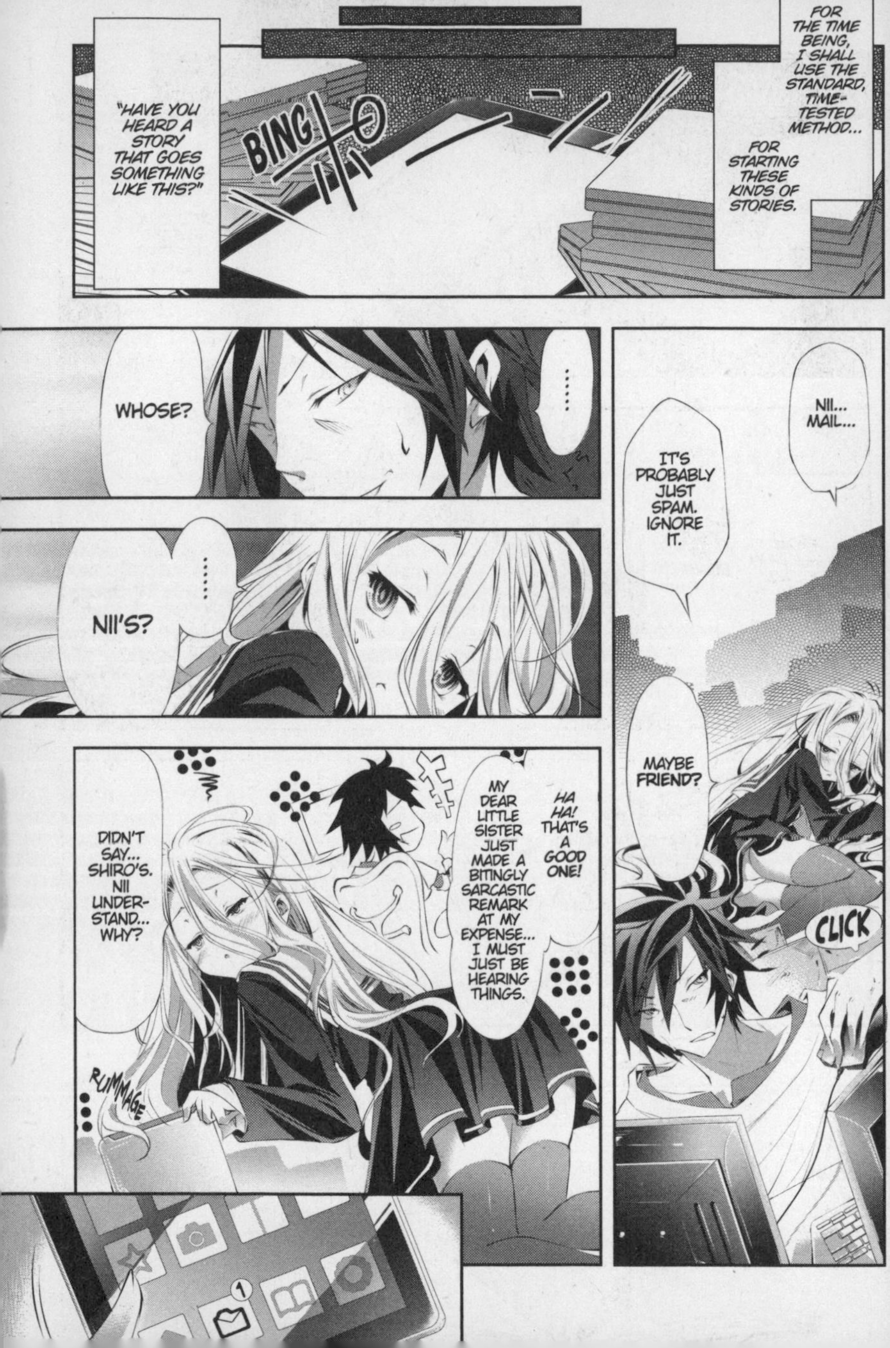
FOR THE TIME BEING, I SHALL USE THE STANDARD, TIME-TESTED METHOD...
FOR STARTING THESE KINDS OF STORIES.
BING
"HAVE YOU HEARD A STORY THAT GOES SOMETHING LIKE THIS?"
NII... MAIL...
IT'S PROBABLY JUST SPAM. IGNORE IT.
MAYBE FRIEND?
CLICK
......
WHOSE?
......
NII'S?
HA HA! THAT'S A GOOD ONE!
MY DEAR LITTLE SISTER JUST MADE A BITINGLY SARCASTIC REMARK AT MY EXPENSE... I MUST JUST BE HEARING THINGS.
DIDN'T SAY... SHIRO'S. NII UNDER-STAND... WHY?
RUMMAGE

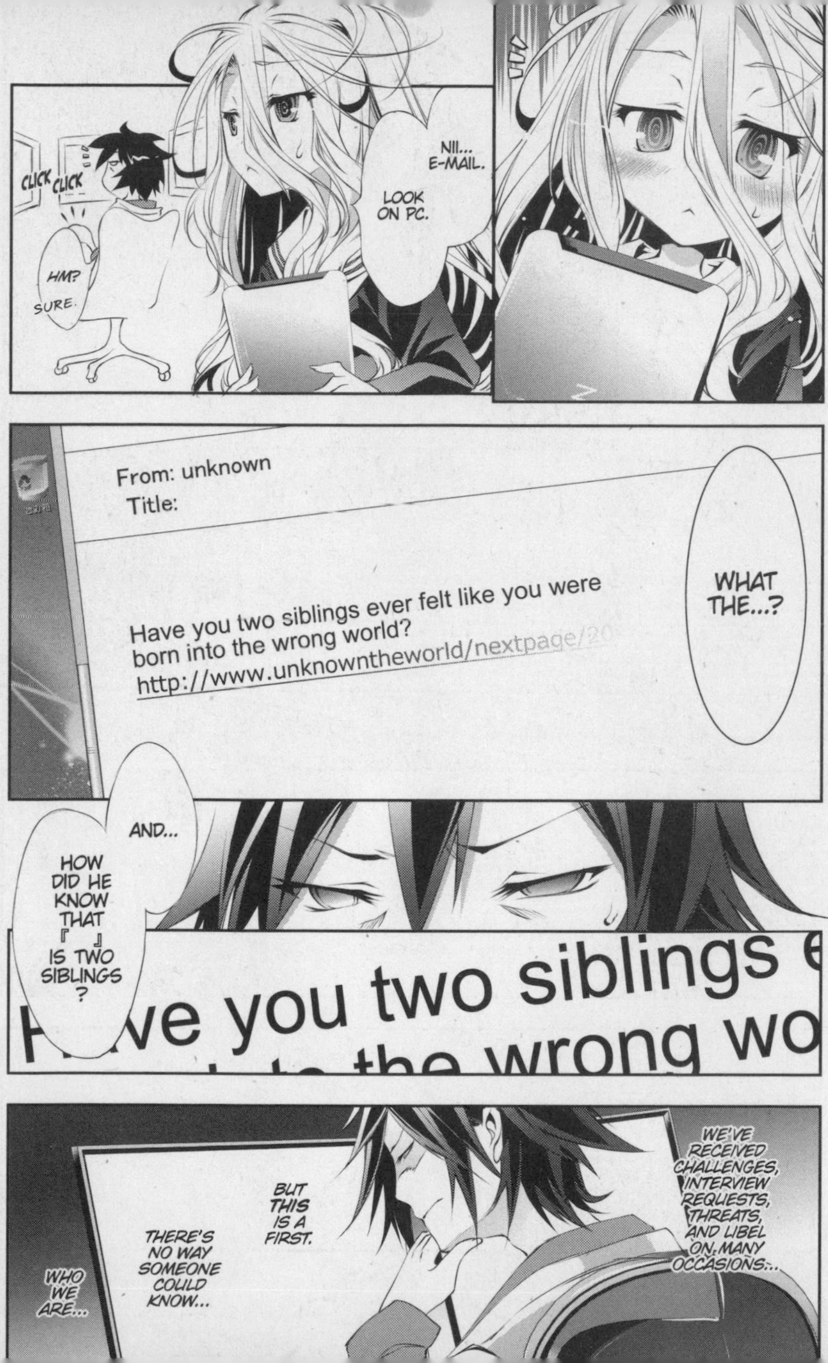
NII... E-MAIL.
LOOK ON PC.
CLICK CLICK
HM? SURE.
From: unknown
Title:
Have you two siblings ever felt like you were born into the wrong world?
http://www.unknowntheworld/nextpage/20
WHAT THE...?
AND...
HOW DID HE KNOW THAT 『 』 IS TWO SIBLINGS?
ve you two siblings
the wrong wo
WE'VE RECEIVED CHALLENGES, INTERVIEW REQUESTS, THREATS, AND LIBEL ON MANY OCCASIONS...
BUT THIS IS A FIRST.
THERE'S NO WAY SOMEONE COULD KNOW...
WHO WE ARE...

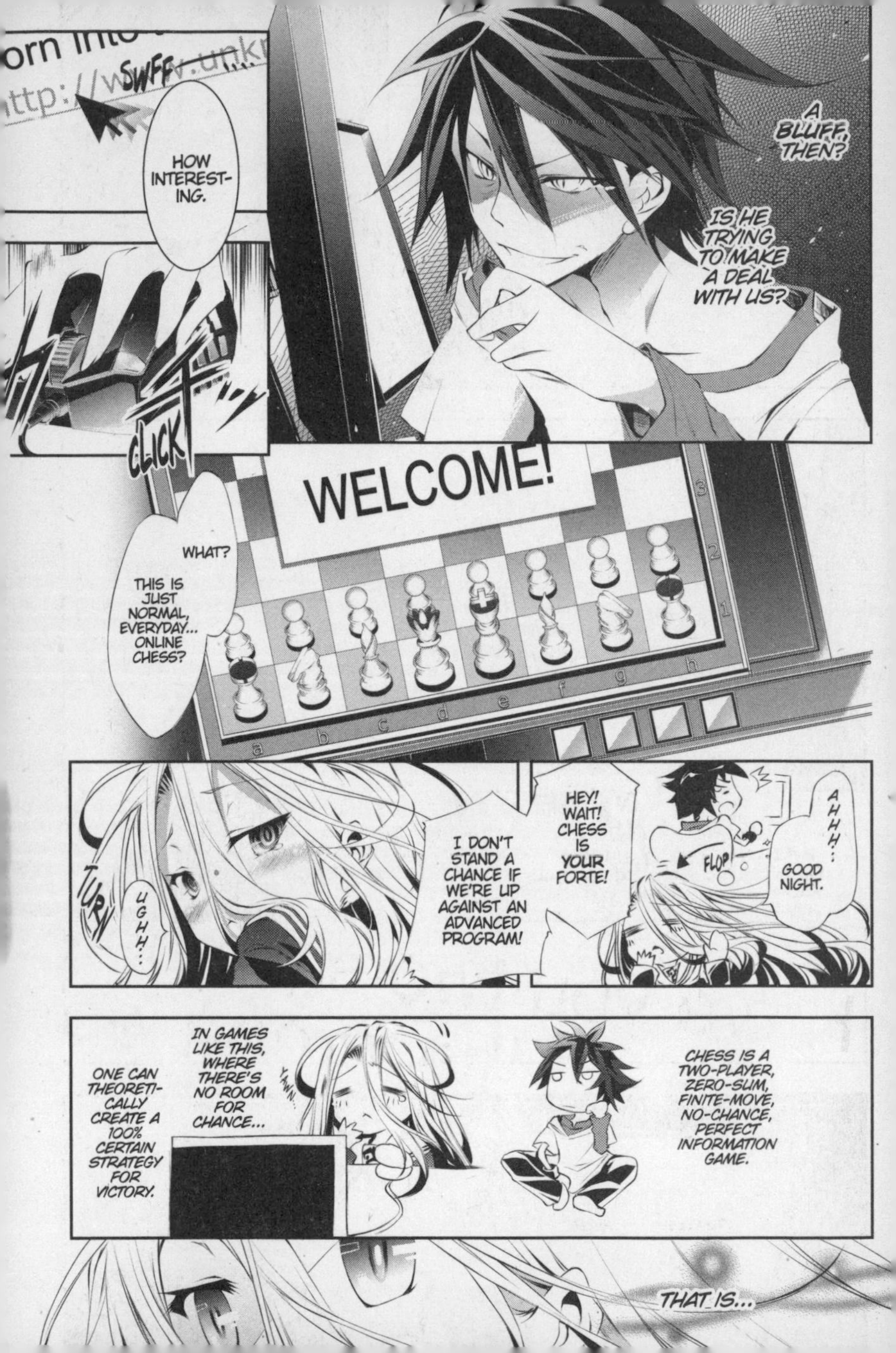
A BLUFF, THEN?
IS HE TRYING TO MAKE A DEAL WITH US?
SWFF
HOW INTEREST-ING.
CLICK
WELCOME!
WHAT?
THIS IS JUST NORMAL, EVERYDAY... ONLINE CHESS?
AHHH...
GOOD NIGHT.
FLOP
HEY! WAIT! CHESS IS YOUR FORTE!
I DON'T STAND A CHANCE IF WE'RE UP AGAINST AN ADVANCED PROGRAM!
UGHH...
TURN
CHESS IS A TWO-PLAYER, ZERO-SUM, FINITE-MOVE, NO-CHANCE, PERFECT INFORMATION GAME.
YAWN
IN GAMES LIKE THIS, WHERE THERE'S NO ROOM FOR CHANCE...
ONE CAN THEORETI-CALLY CREATE A 100% CERTAIN STRATEGY FOR VICTORY.
THAT IS...

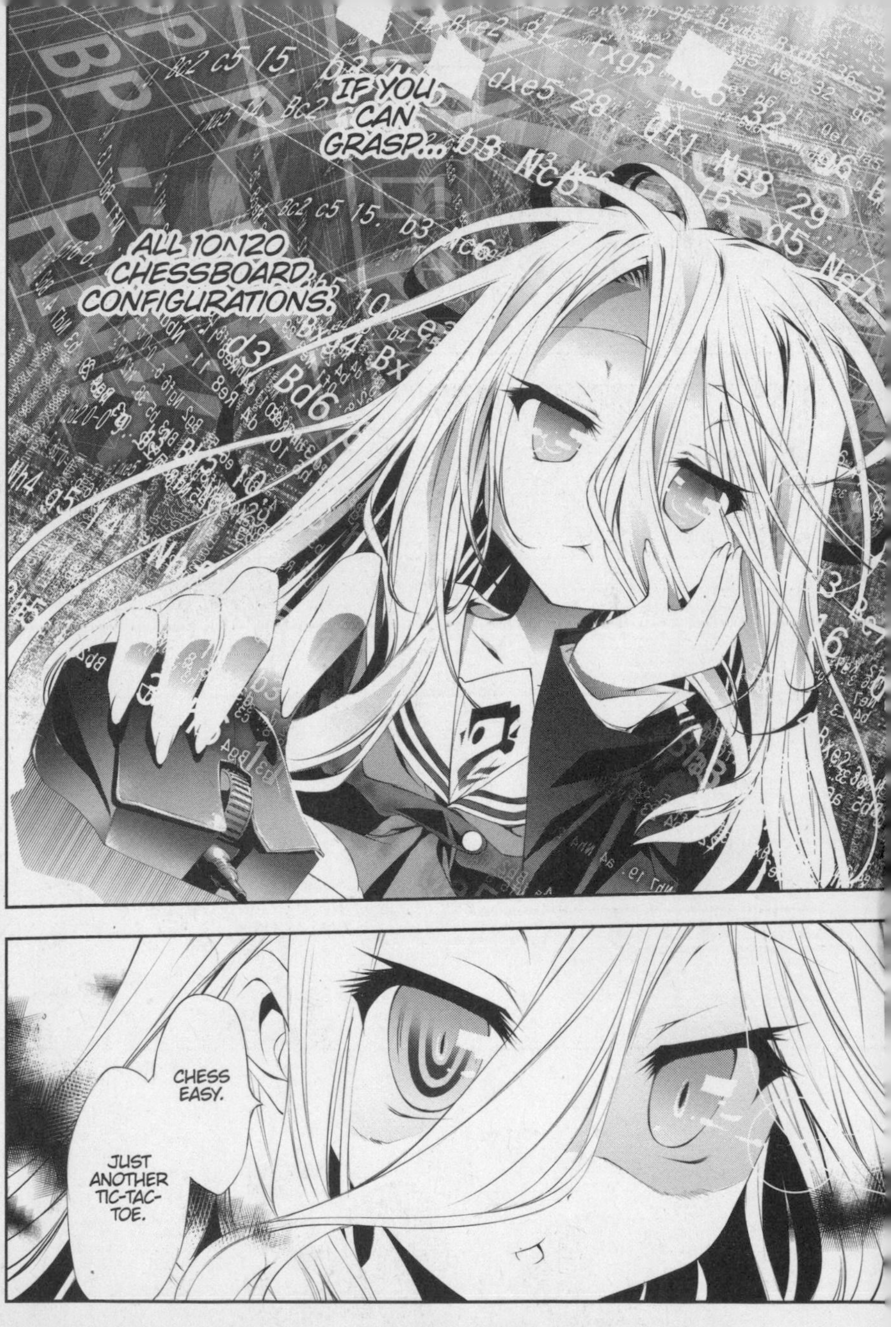
IF YOU CAN GRASP...
ALL 10^120 CHESSBOARD CONFIGURATIONS.
CHESS EASY.
JUST ANOTHER TIC-TAC-TOE.

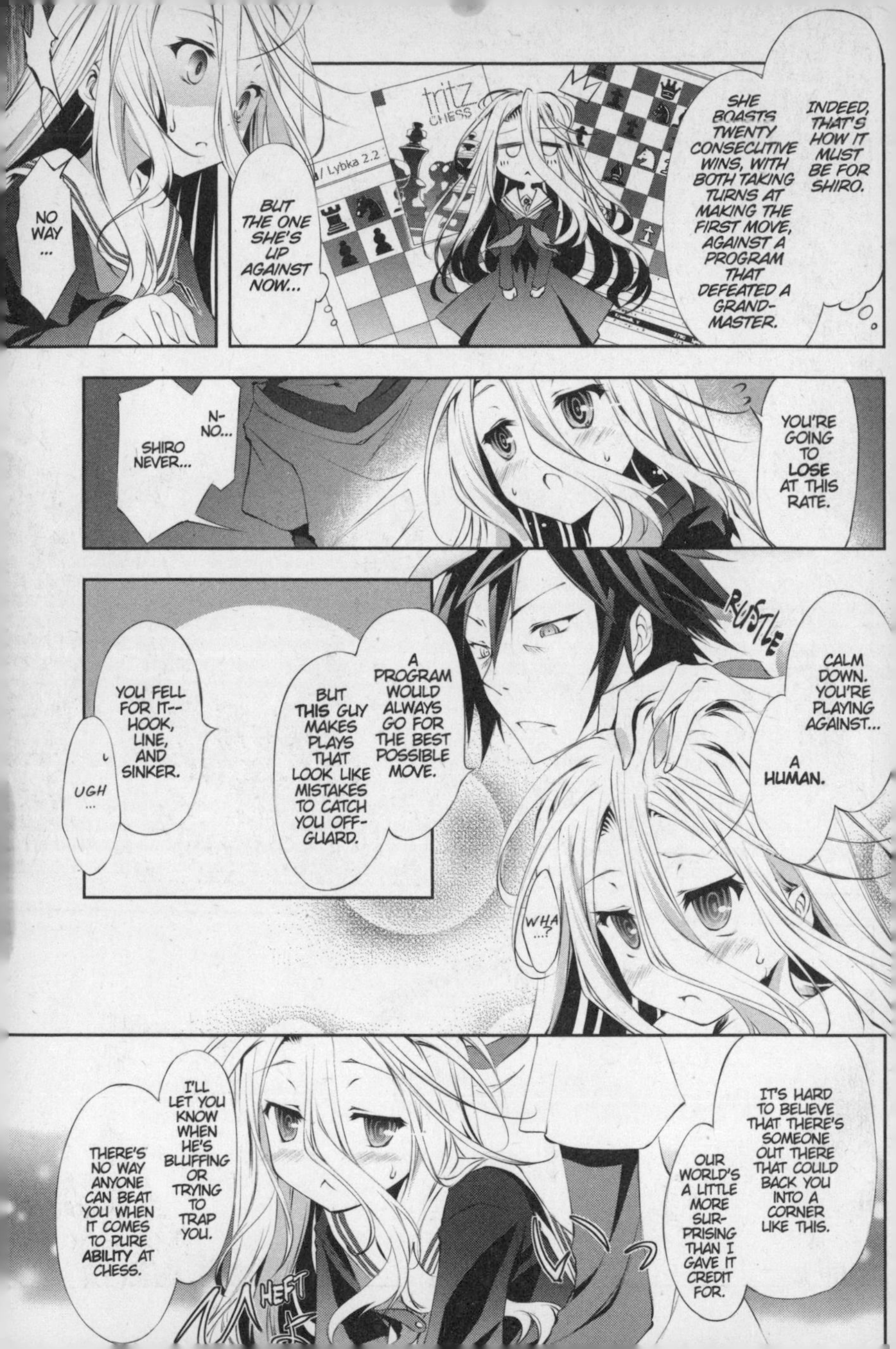
INDEED, THAT'S HOW IT MUST BE FOR SHIRO.
SHE BOASTS TWENTY CONSECUTIVE WINS, WITH BOTH TAKING TURNS AT MAKING THE FIRST MOVE, AGAINST A PROGRAM THAT DEFEATED A GRAND-MASTER.
tritz CHESS
BUT THE ONE SHE'S UP AGAINST NOW...
NO WAY ...
YOU'RE GOING TO LOSE AT THIS RATE.
N-NO... SHIRO NEVER...
RUSTLE
CALM DOWN. YOU'RE PLAYING AGAINST...
A HUMAN.
A PROGRAM WOULD ALWAYS GO FOR THE BEST POSSIBLE MOVE.
BUT THIS GUY MAKES PLAYS THAT LOOK LIKE MISTAKES TO CATCH YOU OFF-GUARD.
YOU FELL FOR IT--HOOK, LINE, AND SINKER.
UGH ...
WHA ...?
IT'S HARD TO BELIEVE THAT THERE'S SOMEONE OUT THERE THAT COULD BACK YOU INTO A CORNER LIKE THIS.
OUR WORLD'S A LITTLE MORE SUR-PRISING THAN I GAVE IT CREDIT FOR.
I'LL LET YOU KNOW WHEN HE'S BLUFFING OR TRYING TO TRAP YOU.
THERE'S NO WAY ANYONE CAN BEAT YOU WHEN IT COMES TO PURE ABILITY AT CHESS.
HEFT

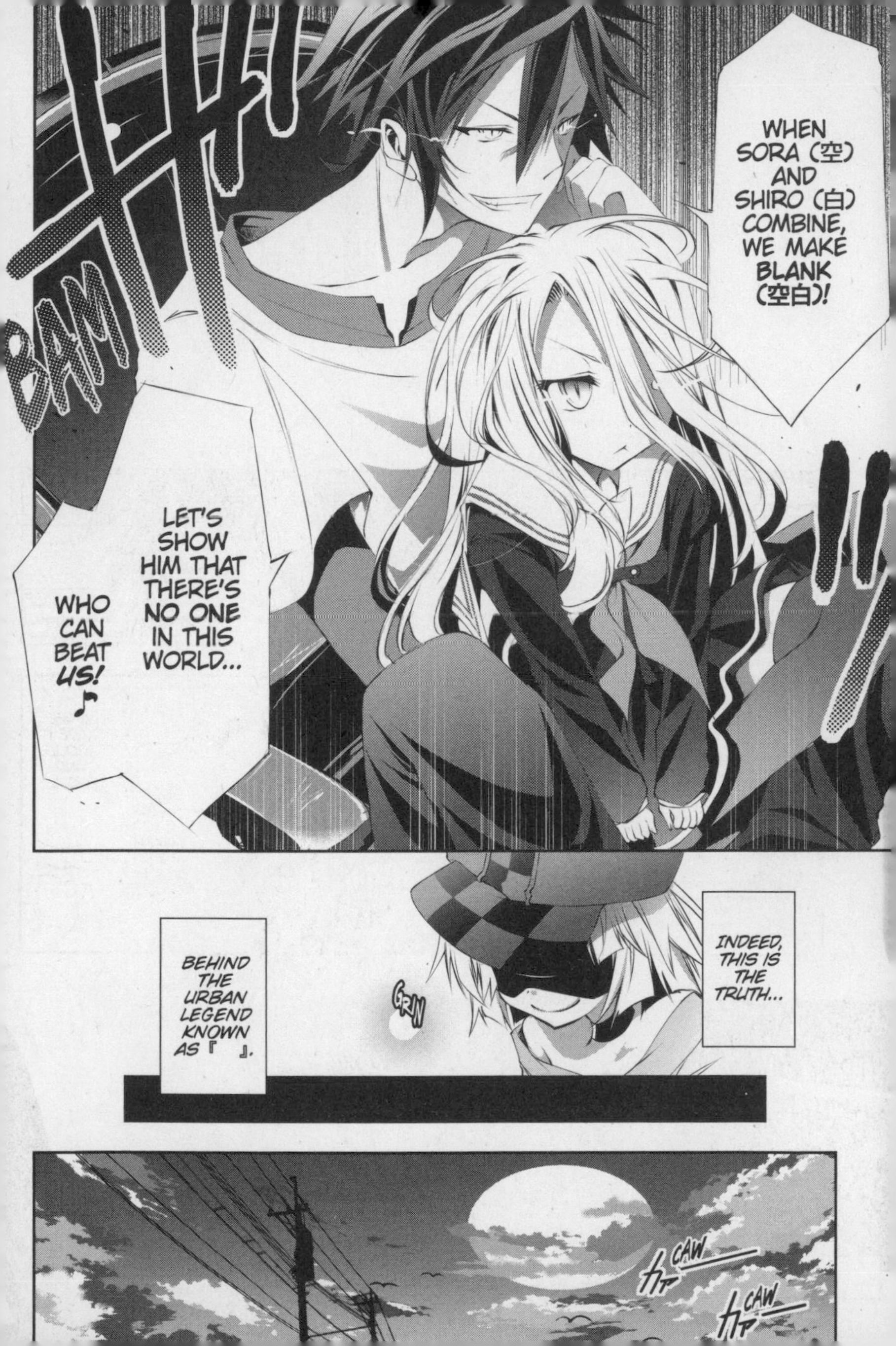
WHEN SORA (空) AND SHIRO (白) COMBINE, WE MAKE BLANK (空白)!
LET'S SHOW HIM THAT THERE'S NO ONE IN THIS WORLD...
WHO CAN BEAT US! ♪
BAM
INDEED, THIS IS THE TRUTH...
GRIN
BEHIND THE URBAN LEGEND KNOWN AS『 』.
CAW
CAW

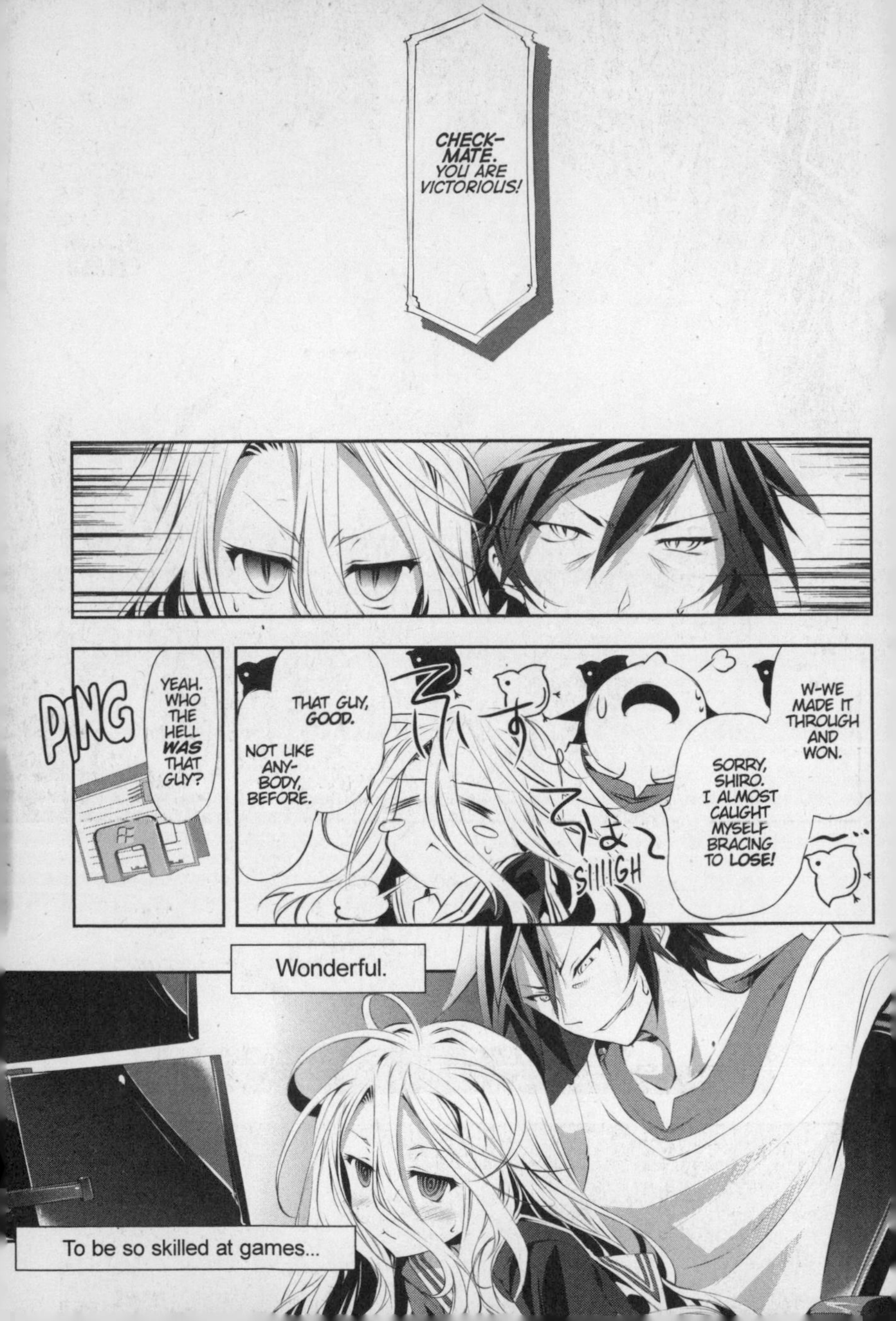
CHECK-MATE. YOU ARE VICTORIOUS!
W-WE MADE IT THROUGH AND WON.
SORRY, SHIRO. I ALMOST CAUGHT MYSELF BRACING TO LOSE!
SIIIGH
THAT GUY, GOOD.
NOT LIKE ANY-BODY, BEFORE.
YEAH. WHO THE HELL *WAS* THAT GUY?
PING
Wonderful.
To be so skilled at games...

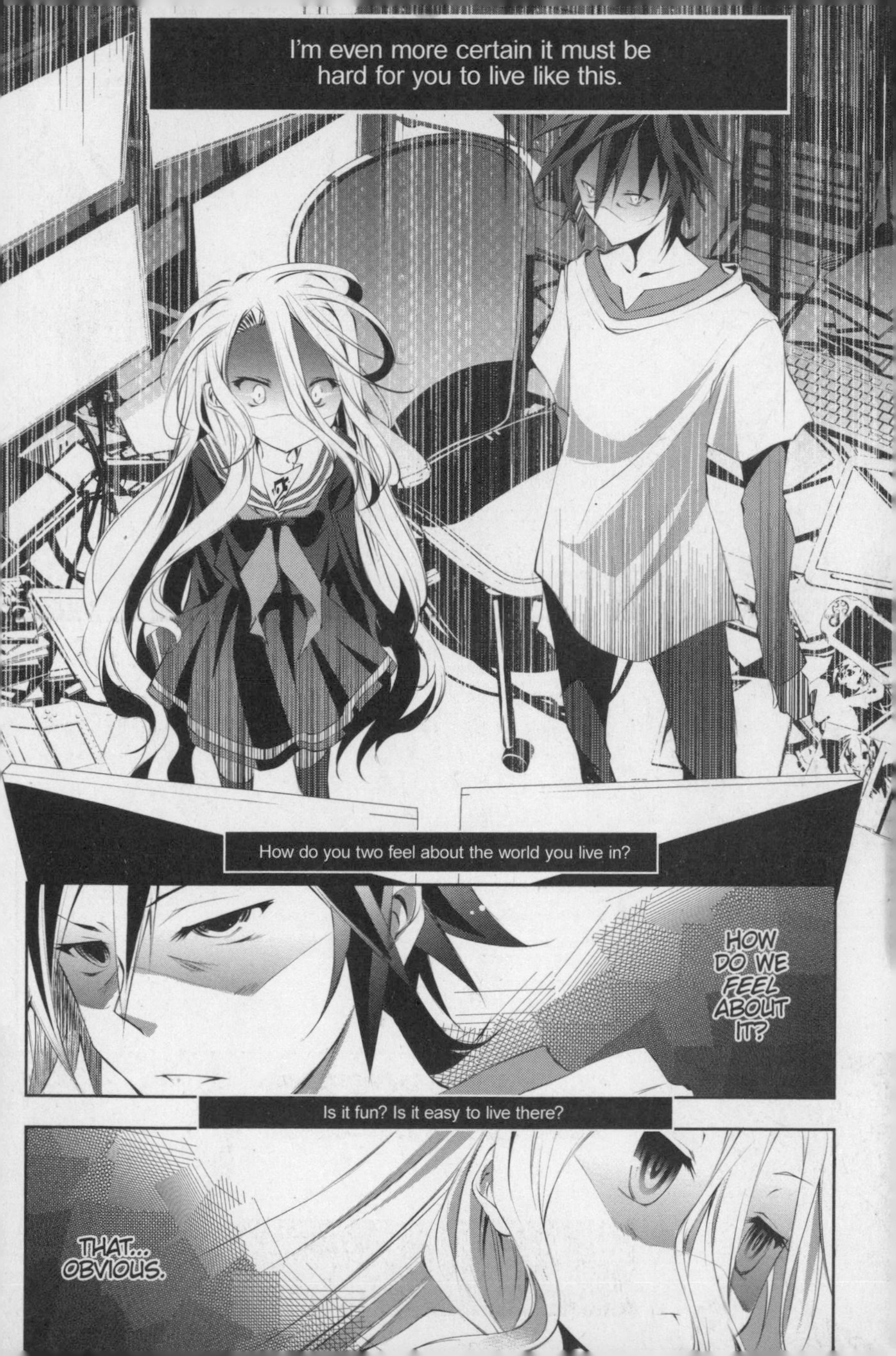
I'm even more certain it must be hard for you to live like this.
How do you two feel about the world you live in?
HOW DO WE FEEL ABOUT IT?
Is it fun? Is it easy to live there?
THAT... OBVIOUS.

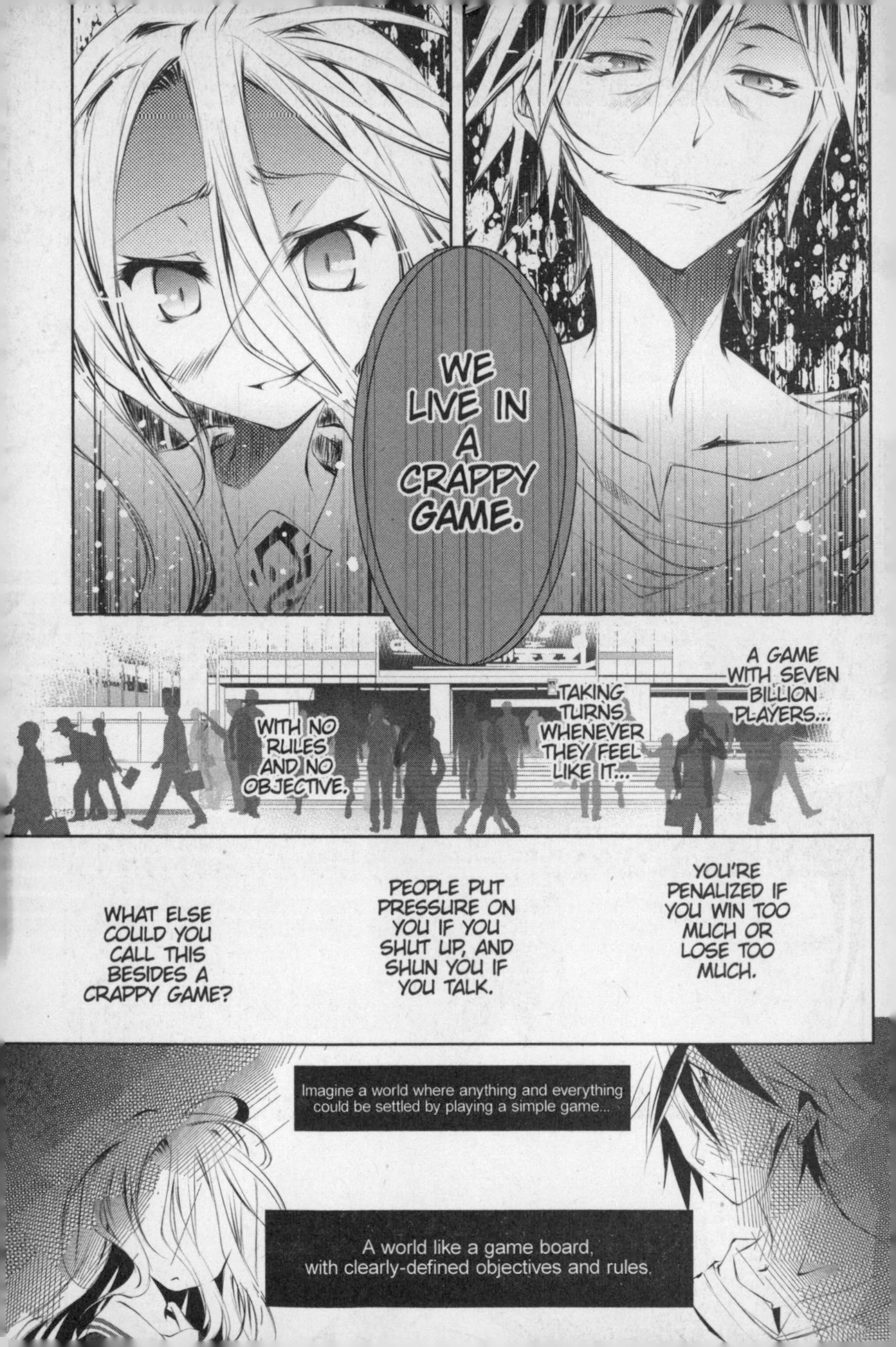
WE LIVE IN A CRAPPY GAME.
A GAME WITH SEVEN BILLION PLAYERS...
TAKING TURNS WHENEVER THEY FEEL LIKE IT...
WITH NO RULES AND NO OBJECTIVE.
YOU'RE PENALIZED IF YOU WIN TOO MUCH OR LOSE TOO MUCH.
PEOPLE PUT PRESSURE ON YOU IF YOU SHUT UP, AND SHUN YOU IF YOU TALK.
WHAT ELSE COULD YOU CALL THIS BESIDES A CRAPPY GAME?
Imagine a world where anything and everything could be settled by playing a simple game...
A world like a game board, with clearly-defined objectives and rules.

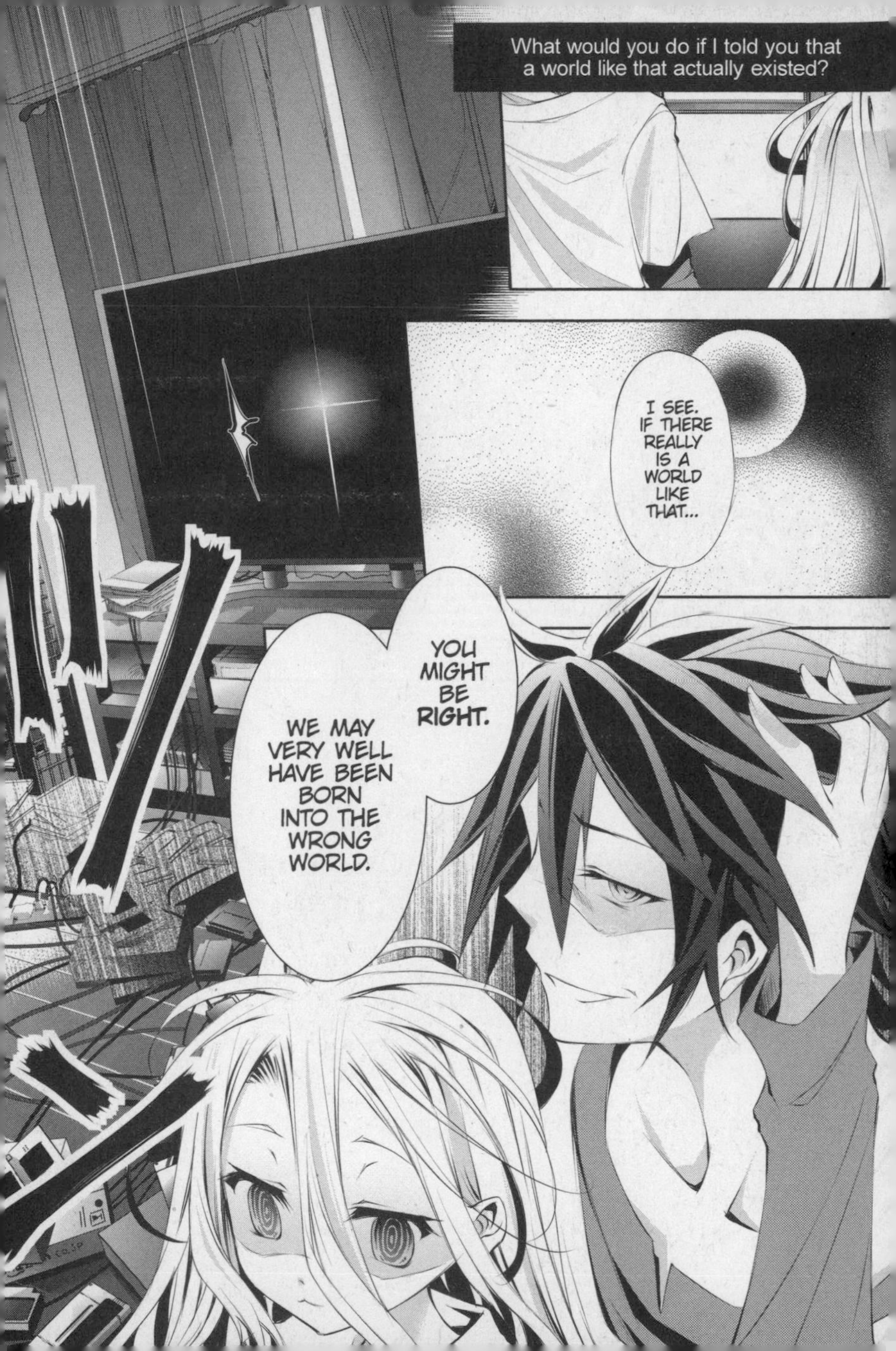

What would you do if I told you that a world like that actually existed?
I SEE. IF THERE REALLY IS A WORLD LIKE THAT...
YOU MIGHT BE RIGHT.
WE MAY VERY WELL HAVE BEEN BORN INTO THE WRONG WORLD.

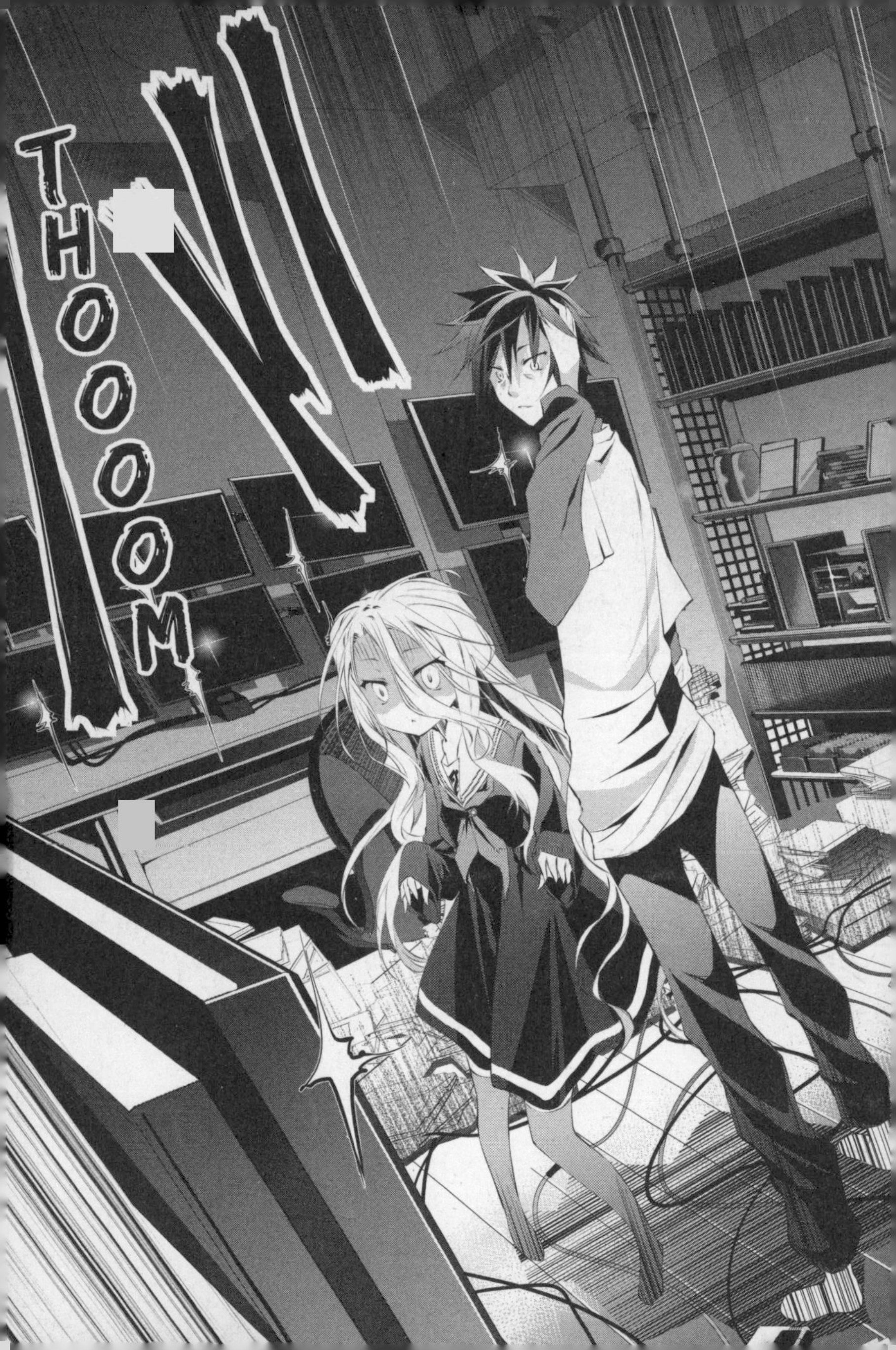
THOOOOM

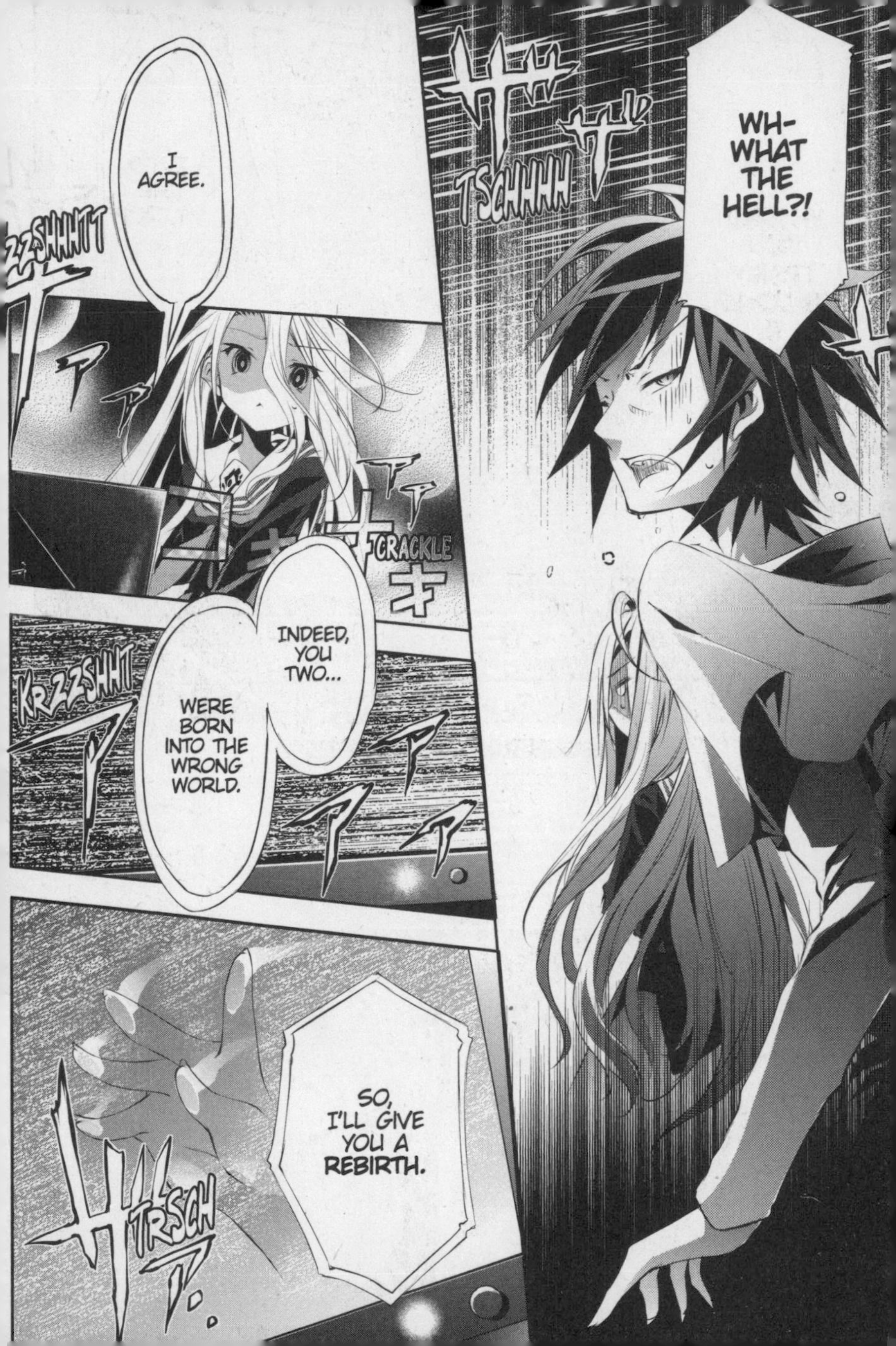
WH-WHAT THE HELL?!
TSCHHHH
I AGREE.
ZZSHHTT
CRACKLE
INDEED, YOU TWO...
WERE BORN INTO THE WRONG WORLD.
KRZZSHHT
SO, I'LL GIVE YOU A REBIRTH.
TRSCH

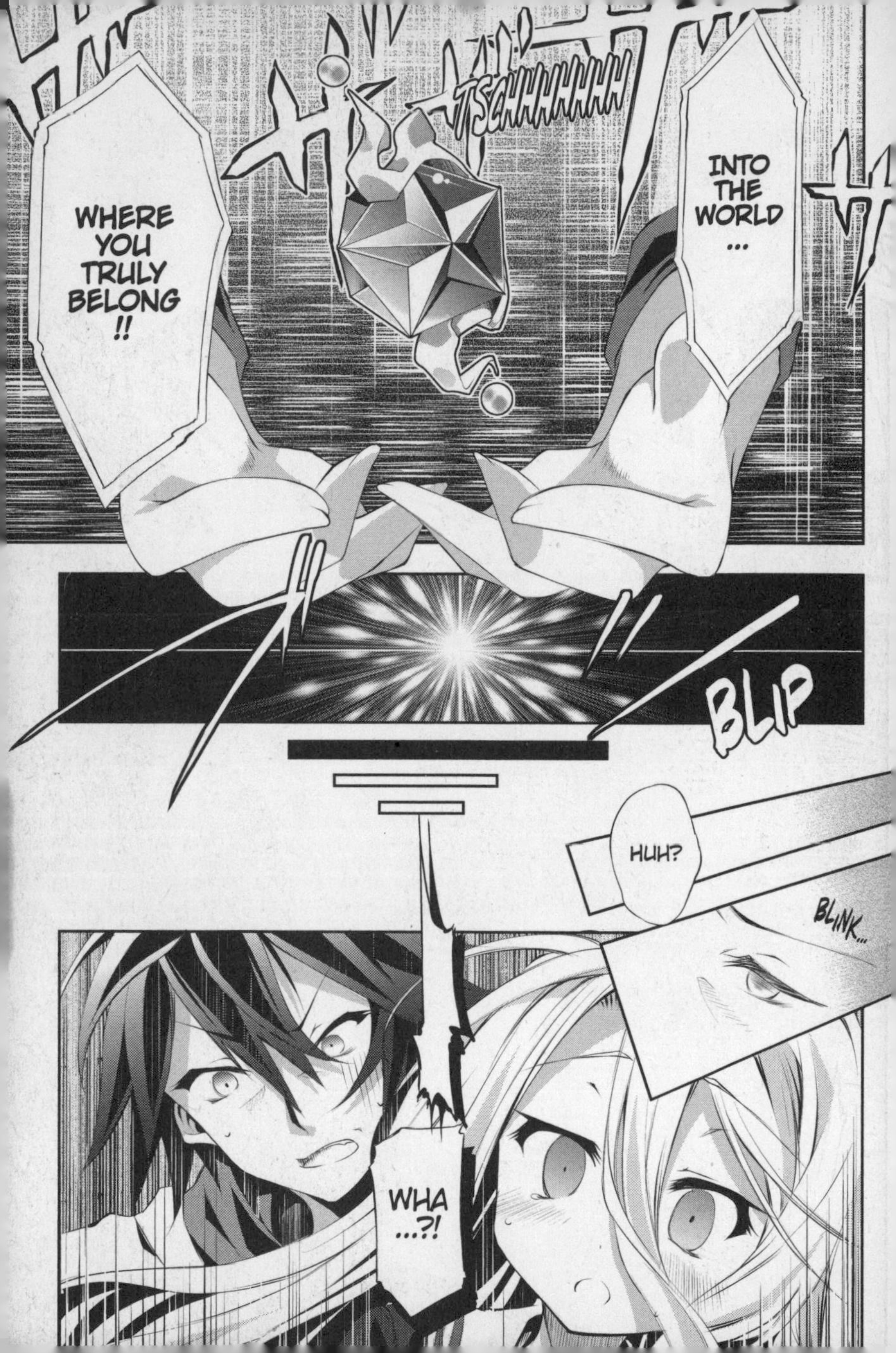
INTO THE WORLD ...
WHERE YOU TRULY BELONG!!
TSCHHHHHHH
BLIP
HUH?
BLINK...
WHA ...?!

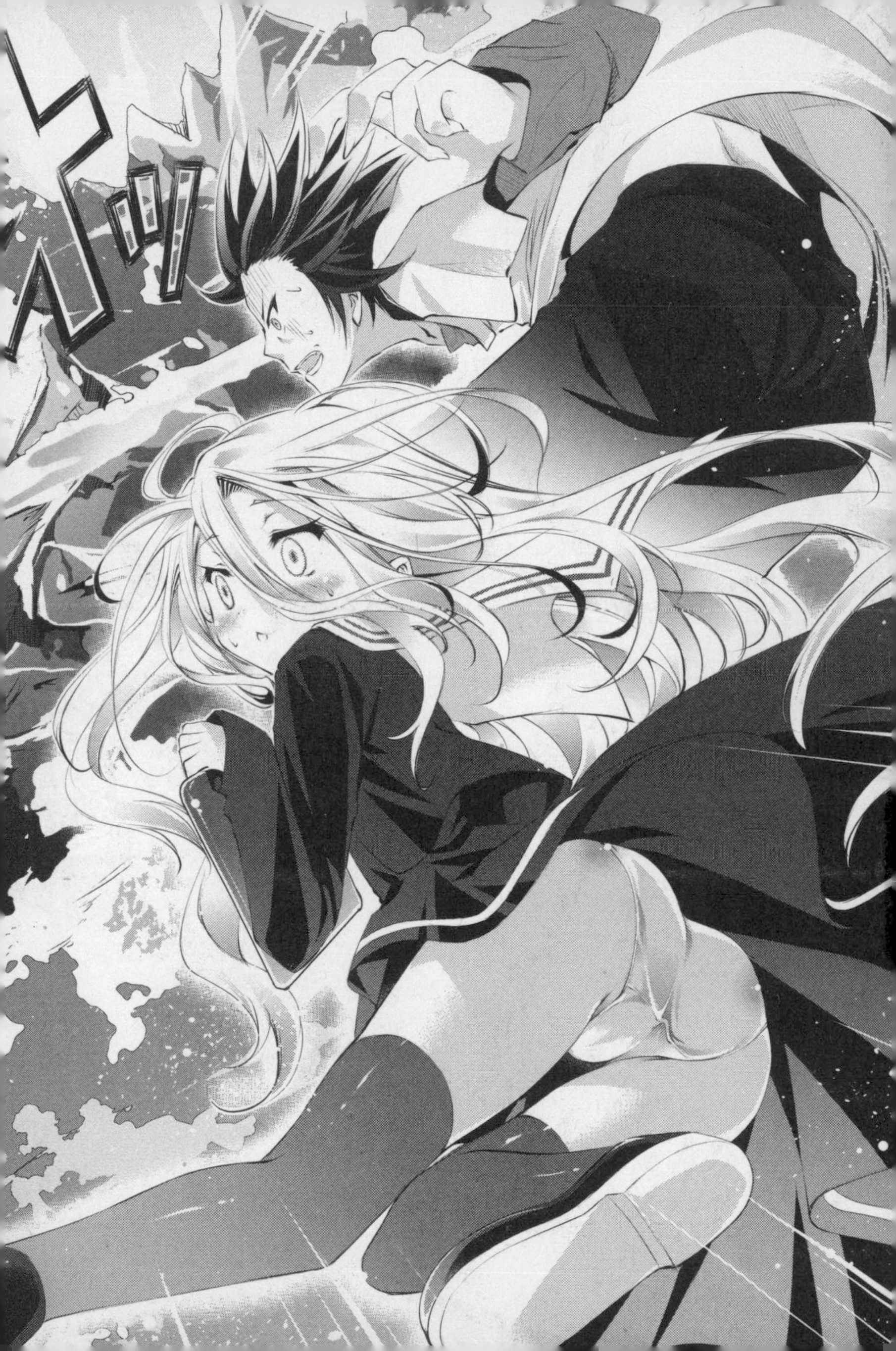

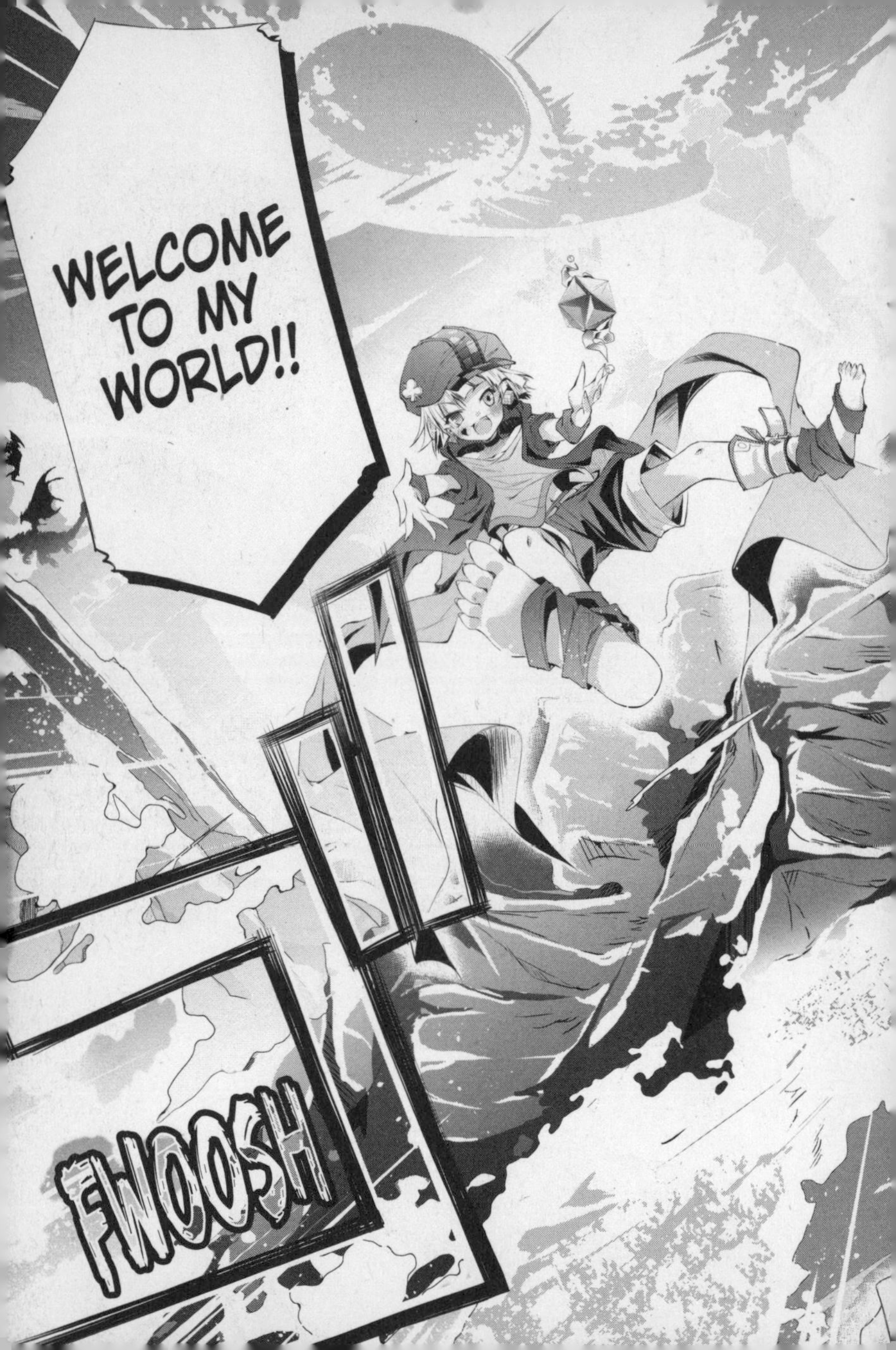
WELCOME TO MY WORLD!!
FWOOSH

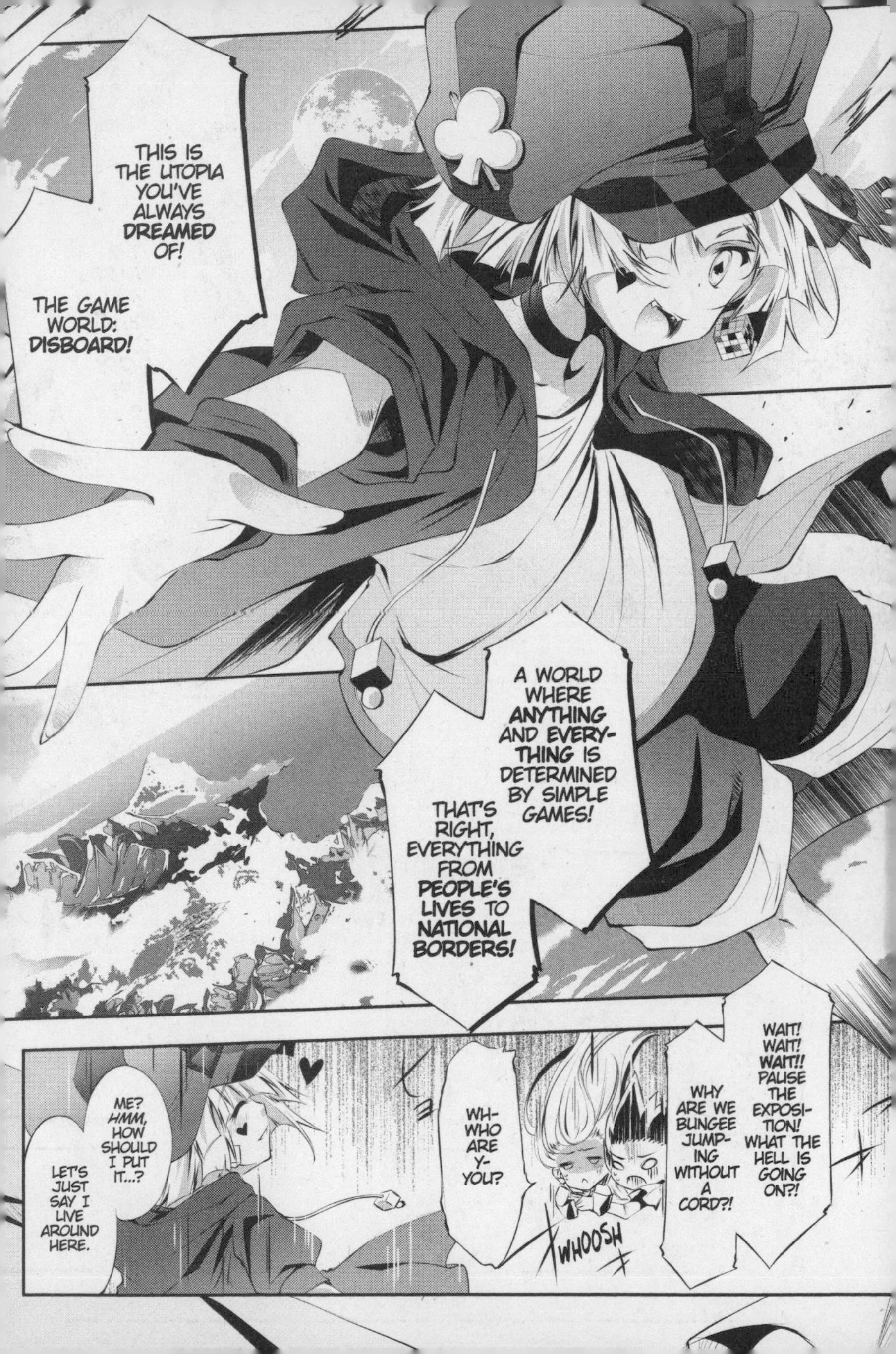
THIS IS THE UTOPIA YOU'VE ALWAYS DREAMED OF!
THE GAME WORLD: DISBOARD!
A WORLD WHERE ANYTHING AND EVERY-THING IS DETERMINED BY SIMPLE GAMES!
THAT'S RIGHT, EVERYTHING FROM PEOPLE'S LIVES TO NATIONAL BORDERS!
WAIT! WAIT! WAIT!! PAUSE THE EXPOSI-TION! WHAT THE HELL IS GOING ON?!
WHY ARE WE BUNGEE JUMP-ING WITHOUT A CORD?!
WHOOSH
WH-WHO ARE Y-YOU?
ME? HMM, HOW SHOULD I PUT IT...?
LET'S JUST SAY I LIVE AROUND HERE.

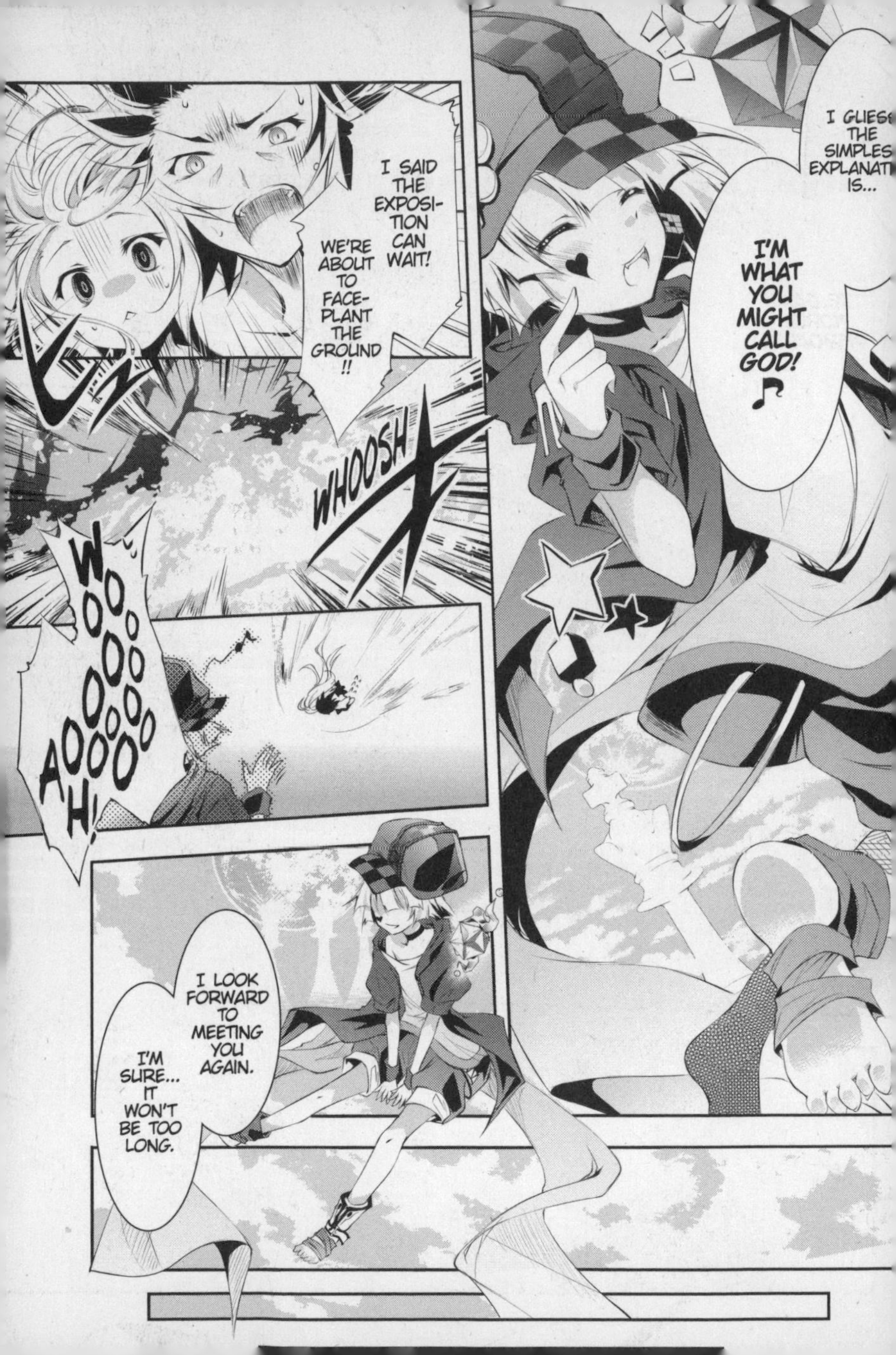
I GUESS THE SIMPLES EXPLANATI IS...
I'M WHAT YOU MIGHT CALL GOD! ♪
I SAID THE EXPOSITION CAN WAIT!
WE'RE ABOUT TO FACE-PLANT THE GROUND!!
WHOOSH
WOOOOOOOOOOOOAAAAH!
I LOOK FORWARD TO MEETING YOU AGAIN.
I'M SURE... IT WON'T BE TOO LONG.

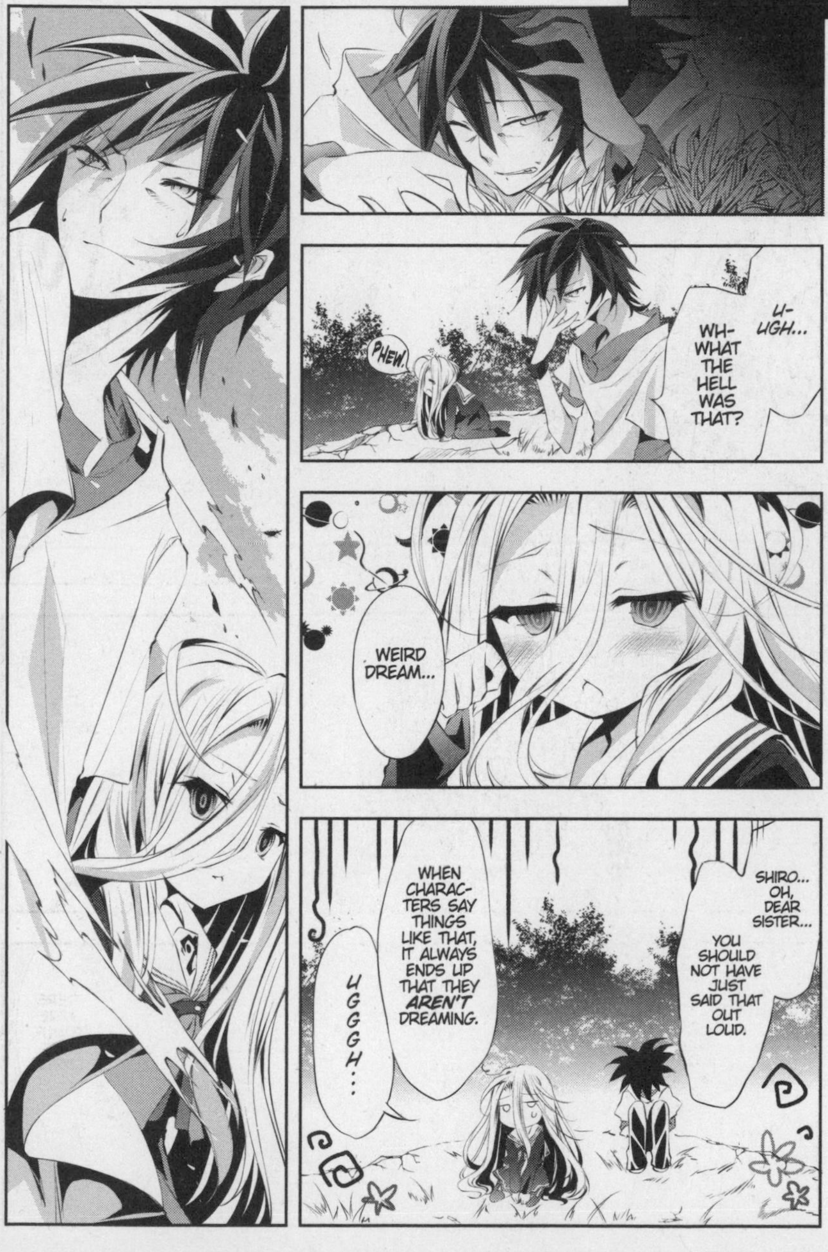
U-UGH...
WH-WHAT THE HELL WAS THAT?
PHEW.
WEIRD DREAM...
SHIRO... OH, DEAR SISTER...
YOU SHOULD NOT HAVE JUST SAID THAT OUT LOUD.
WHEN CHARACTERS SAY THINGS LIKE THAT, IT ALWAYS ENDS UP THAT THEY *AREN'T* DREAMING.
UGGGH...

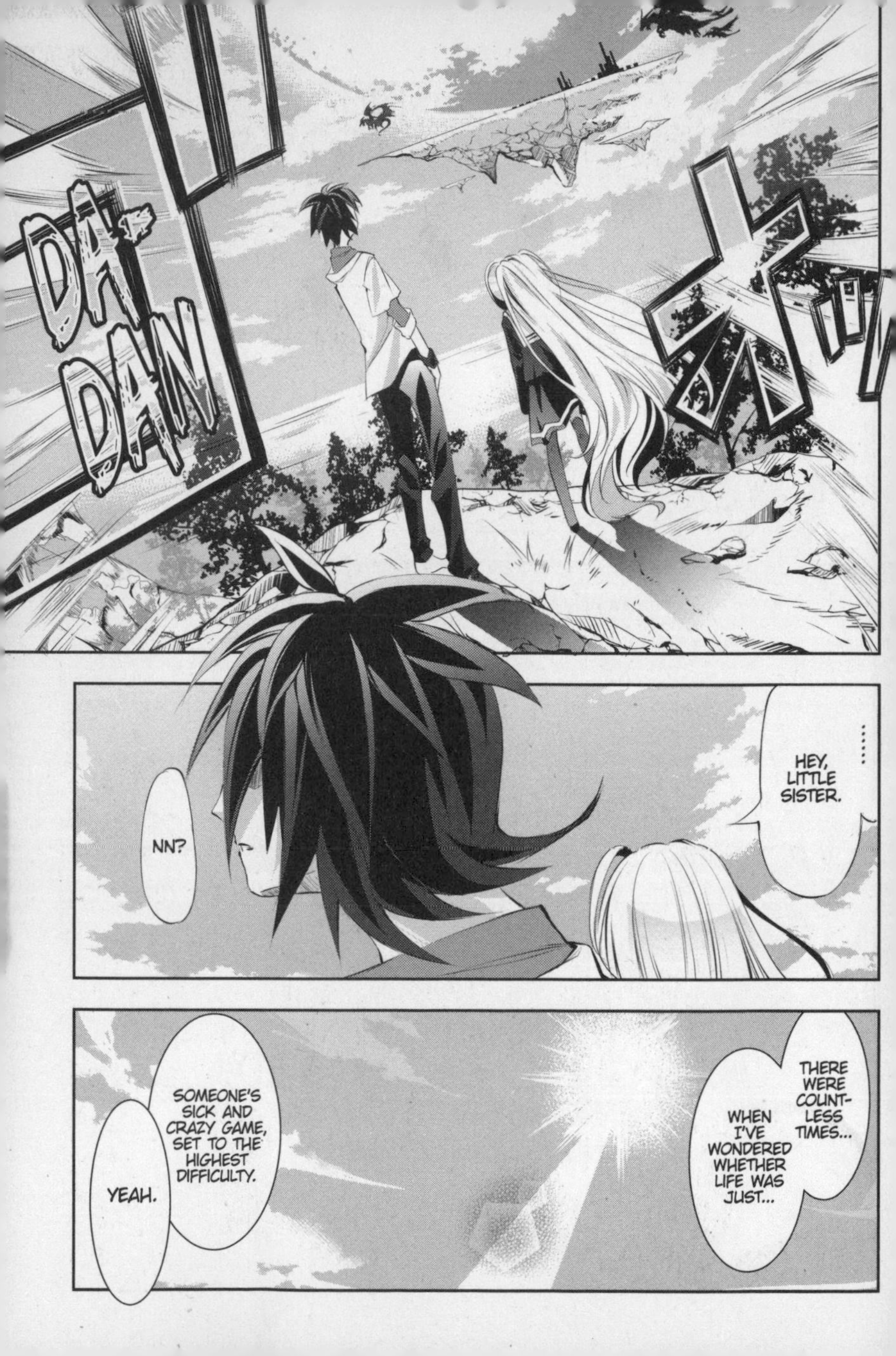
DA DAN
......
HEY, LITTLE SISTER.
NN?
THERE WERE COUNTLESS TIMES...
WHEN I'VE WONDERED WHETHER LIFE WAS JUST...
SOMEONE'S SICK AND CRAZY GAME, SET TO THE HIGHEST DIFFICULTY.
YEAH.

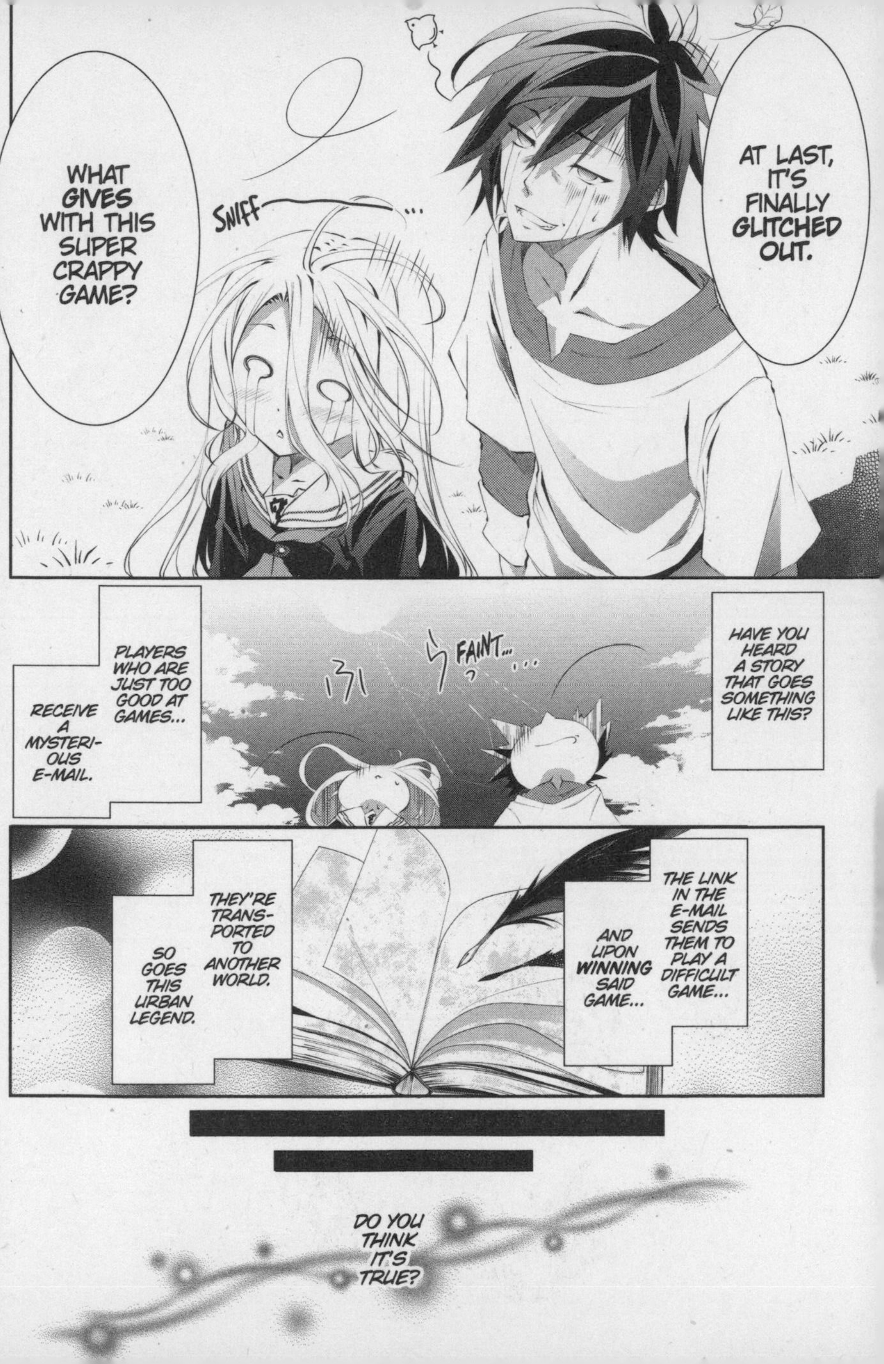
AT LAST, IT'S FINALLY GLITCHED OUT.
SNIFF...
WHAT GIVES WITH THIS SUPER CRAPPY GAME?
HAVE YOU HEARD A STORY THAT GOES SOMETHING LIKE THIS?
FAINT...
PLAYERS WHO ARE JUST TOO GOOD AT GAMES...
RECEIVE A MYSTERIOUS E-MAIL.
THE LINK IN THE E-MAIL SENDS THEM TO PLAY A DIFFICULT GAME...
AND UPON WINNING SAID GAME...
THEY'RE TRANSPORTED TO ANOTHER WORLD.
SO GOES THIS URBAN LEGEND.
DO YOU THINK IT'S TRUE?

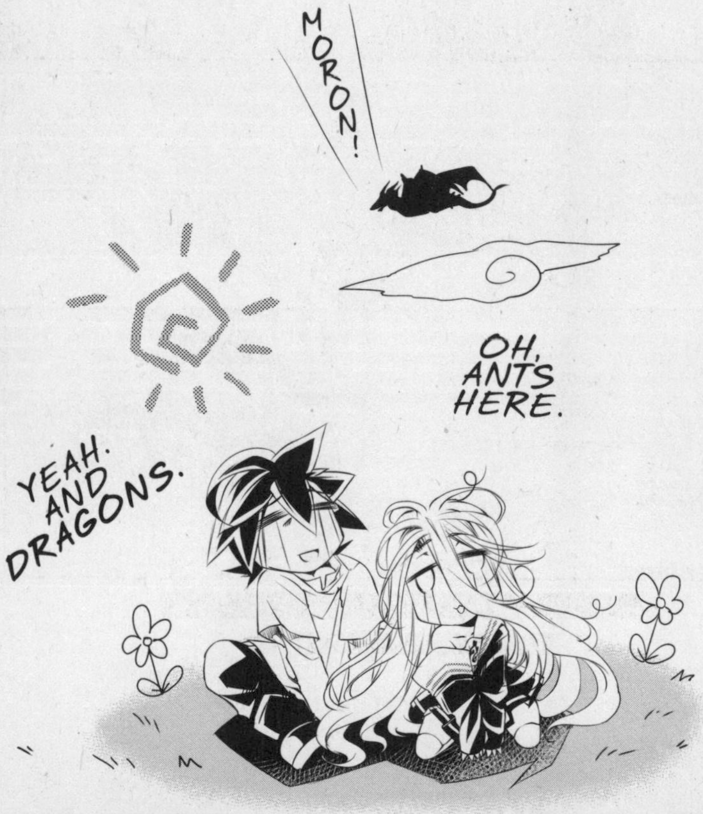
MORON!
OH, ANTS HERE.
YEAH. AND DRAGONS.

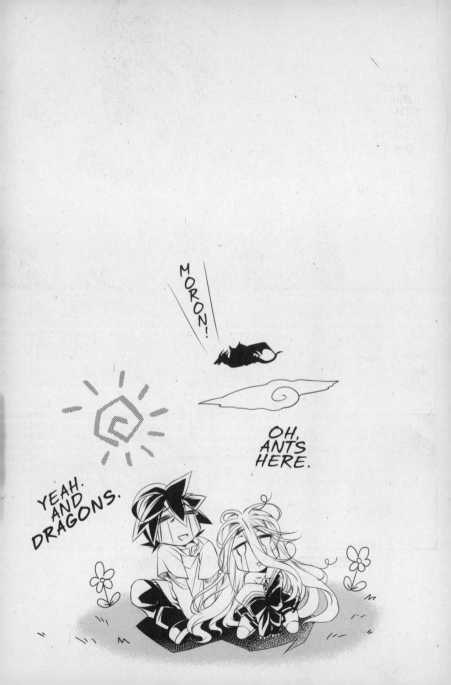

No Game No Life

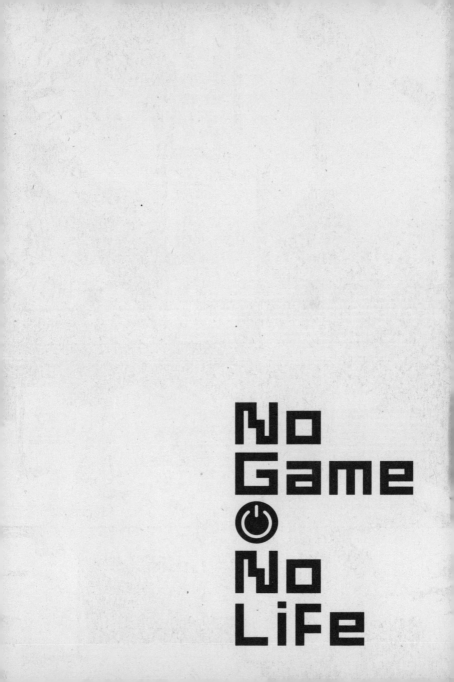

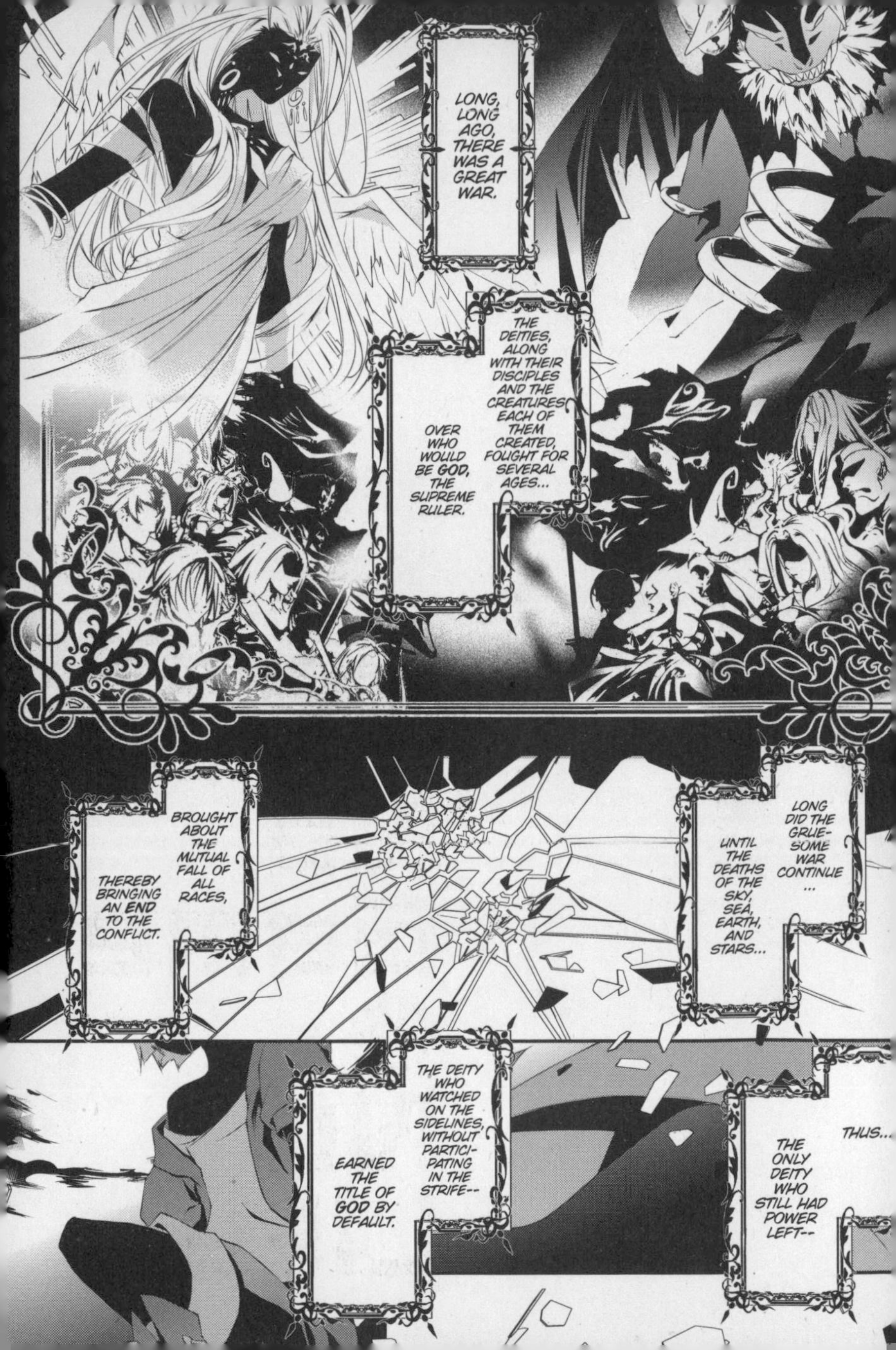
LONG, LONG AGO, THERE WAS A GREAT WAR.
THE DEITIES, ALONG WITH THEIR DISCIPLES AND THE CREATURES EACH OF THEM CREATED, FOUGHT FOR SEVERAL AGES...
OVER WHO WOULD BE GOD, THE SUPREME RULER.
LONG DID THE GRUE-SOME WAR CONTINUE...
UNTIL THE DEATHS OF THE SKY, SEA, EARTH, AND STARS...
BROUGHT ABOUT THE MUTUAL FALL OF ALL RACES,
THEREBY BRINGING AN END TO THE CONFLICT.
THUS...
THE ONLY DEITY WHO STILL HAD POWER LEFT--
THE DEITY WHO WATCHED ON THE SIDELINES, WITHOUT PARTICI-PATING IN THE STRIFE--
EARNED THE TITLE OF GOD BY DEFAULT.

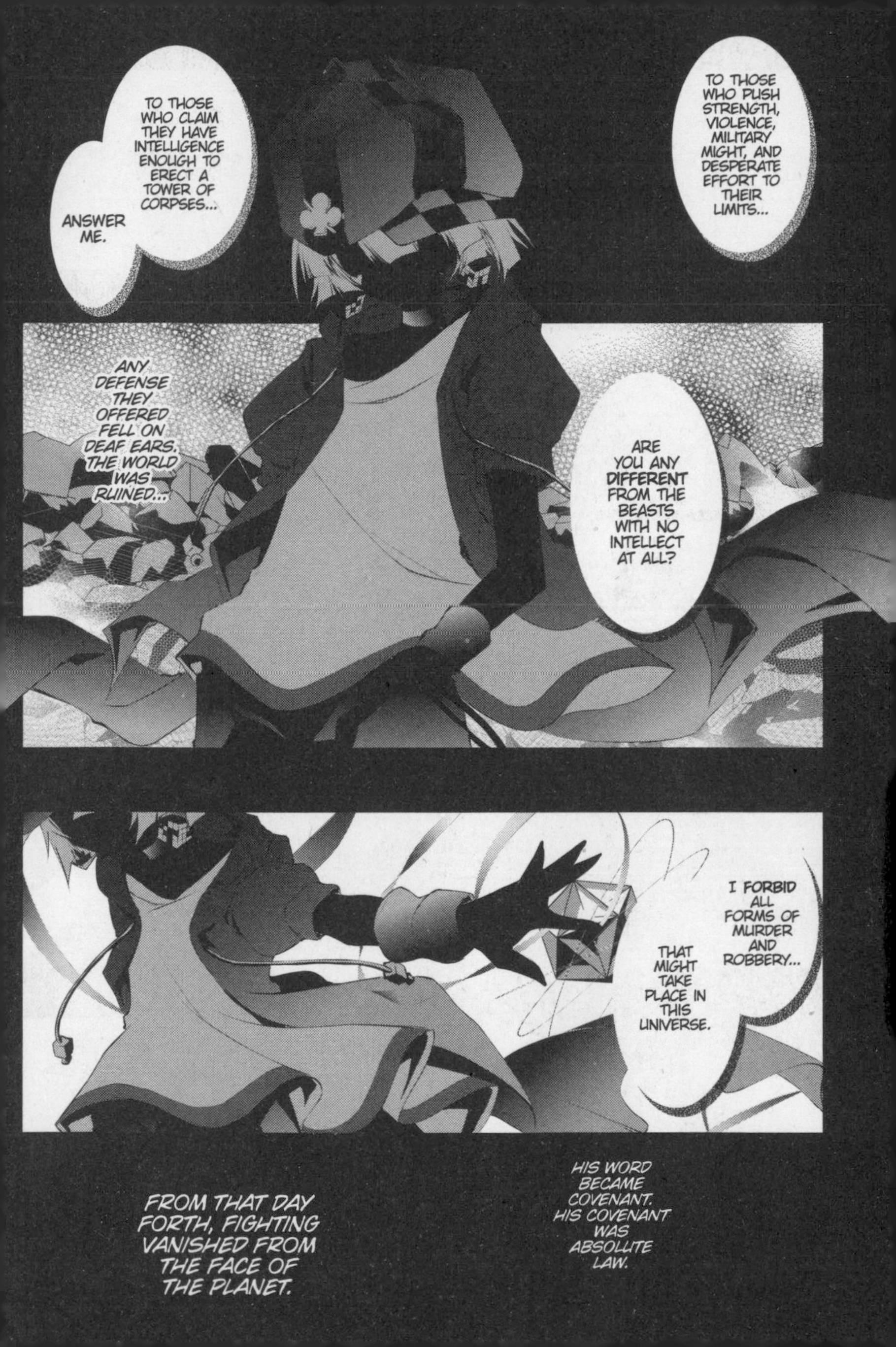
TO THOSE WHO PUSH STRENGTH, VIOLENCE, MILITARY MIGHT, AND DESPERATE EFFORT TO THEIR LIMITS...
TO THOSE WHO CLAIM THEY HAVE INTELLIGENCE ENOUGH TO ERECT A TOWER OF CORPSES...
ANSWER ME.
ARE YOU ANY DIFFERENT FROM THE BEASTS WITH NO INTELLECT AT ALL?
ANY DEFENSE THEY OFFERED FELL ON DEAF EARS. THE WORLD WAS RUINED...
I FORBID ALL FORMS OF MURDER AND ROBBERY...
THAT MIGHT TAKE PLACE IN THIS UNIVERSE.
HIS WORD BECAME COVENANT. HIS COVENANT WAS ABSOLUTE LAW.
FROM THAT DAY FORTH, FIGHTING VANISHED FROM THE FACE OF THE PLANET.

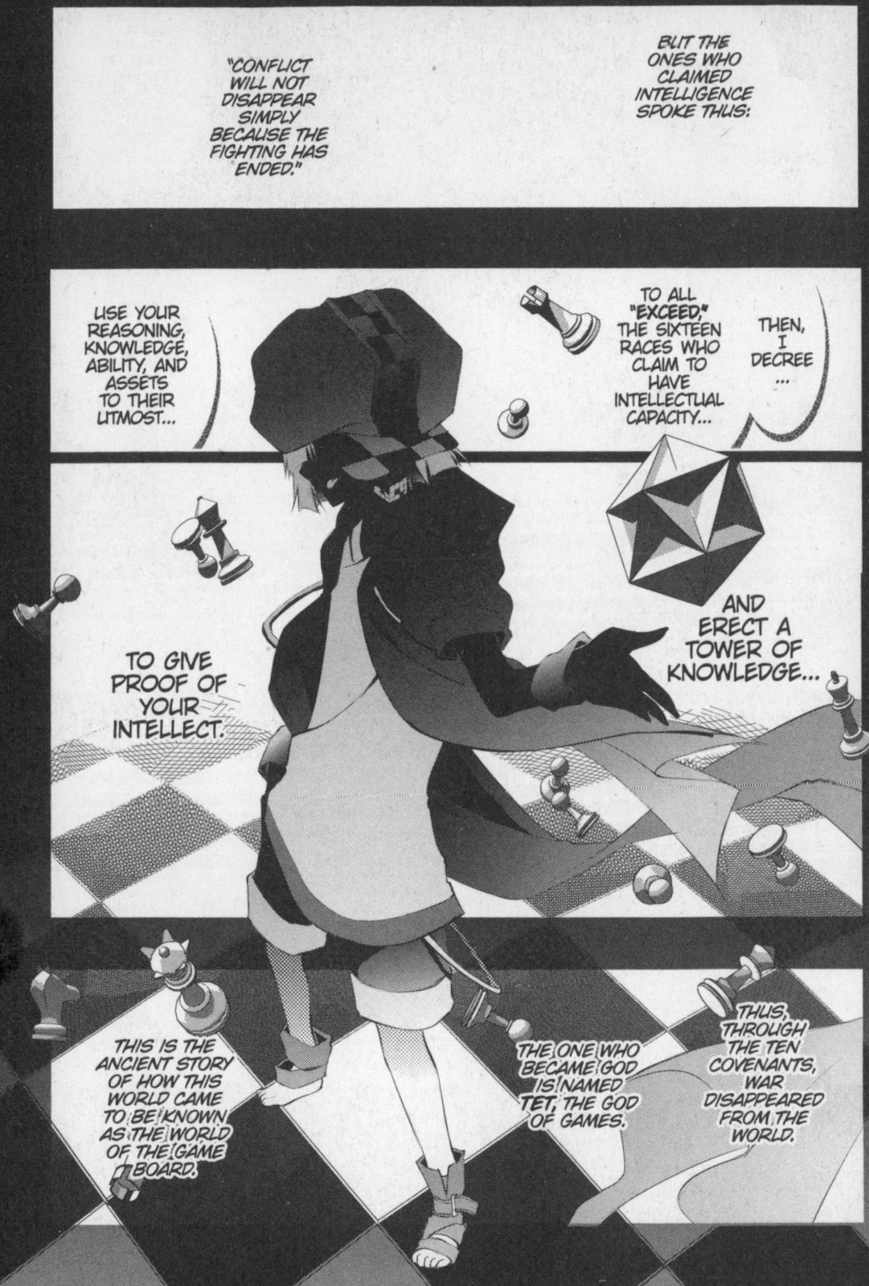
BUT THE ONES WHO CLAIMED INTELLIGENCE SPOKE THUS:
"CONFLICT WILL NOT DISAPPEAR SIMPLY BECAUSE THE FIGHTING HAS ENDED."
THEN, I DECREE...
TO ALL "EXCEED," THE SIXTEEN RACES WHO CLAIM TO HAVE INTELLECTUAL CAPACITY...
USE YOUR REASONING, KNOWLEDGE, ABILITY, AND ASSETS TO THEIR UTMOST...
AND ERECT A TOWER OF KNOWLEDGE...
TO GIVE PROOF OF YOUR INTELLECT.
THUS, THROUGH THE TEN COVENANTS, WAR DISAPPEARED FROM THE WORLD.
THE ONE WHO BECAME GOD IS NAMED TET, THE GOD OF GAMES.
THIS IS THE ANCIENT STORY OF HOW THIS WORLD CAME TO BE KNOWN AS THE WORLD OF THE GAME BOARD.

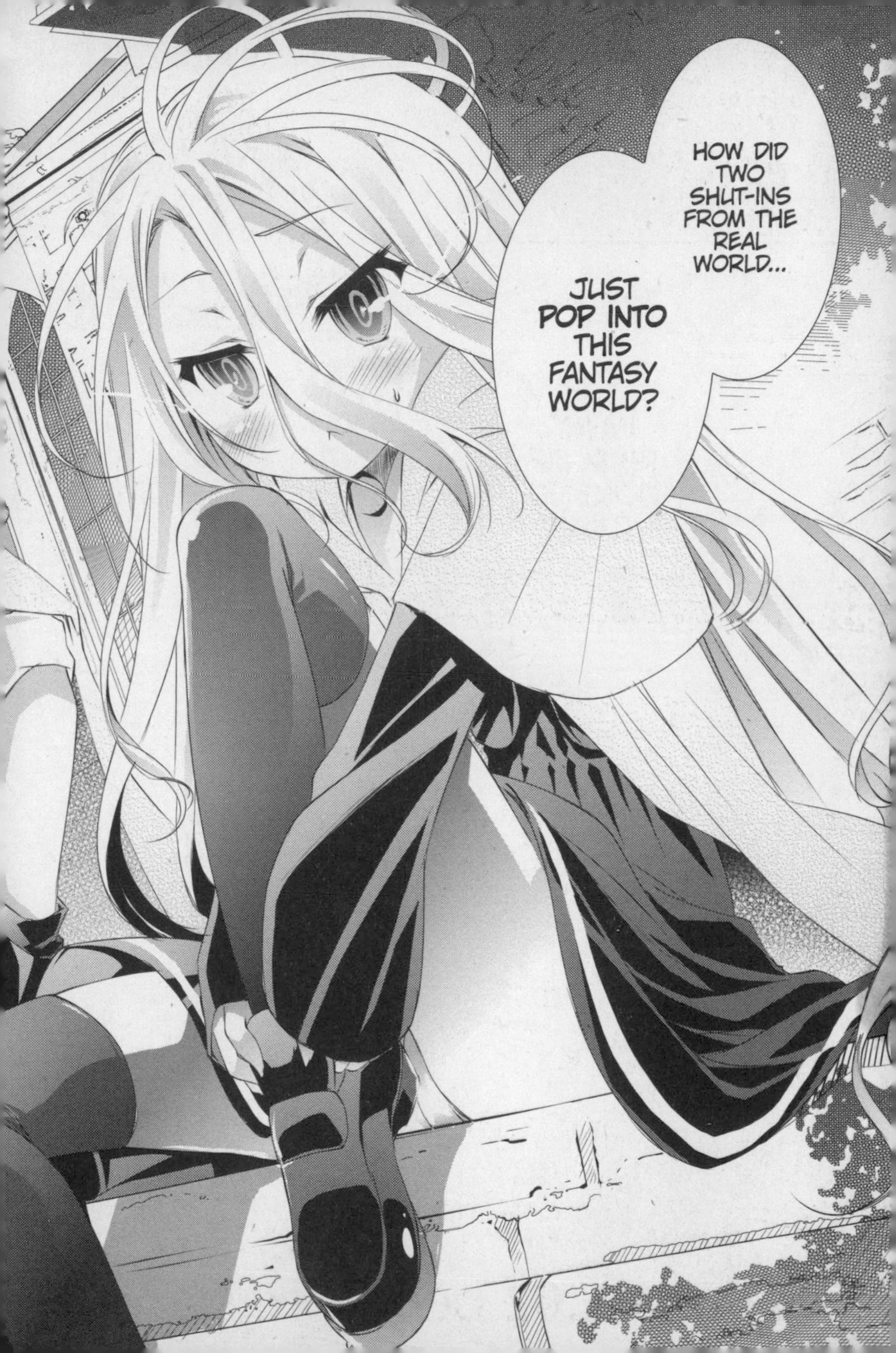
HOW DID TWO SHUT-INS FROM THE REAL WORLD...
JUST POP INTO THIS FANTASY WORLD?

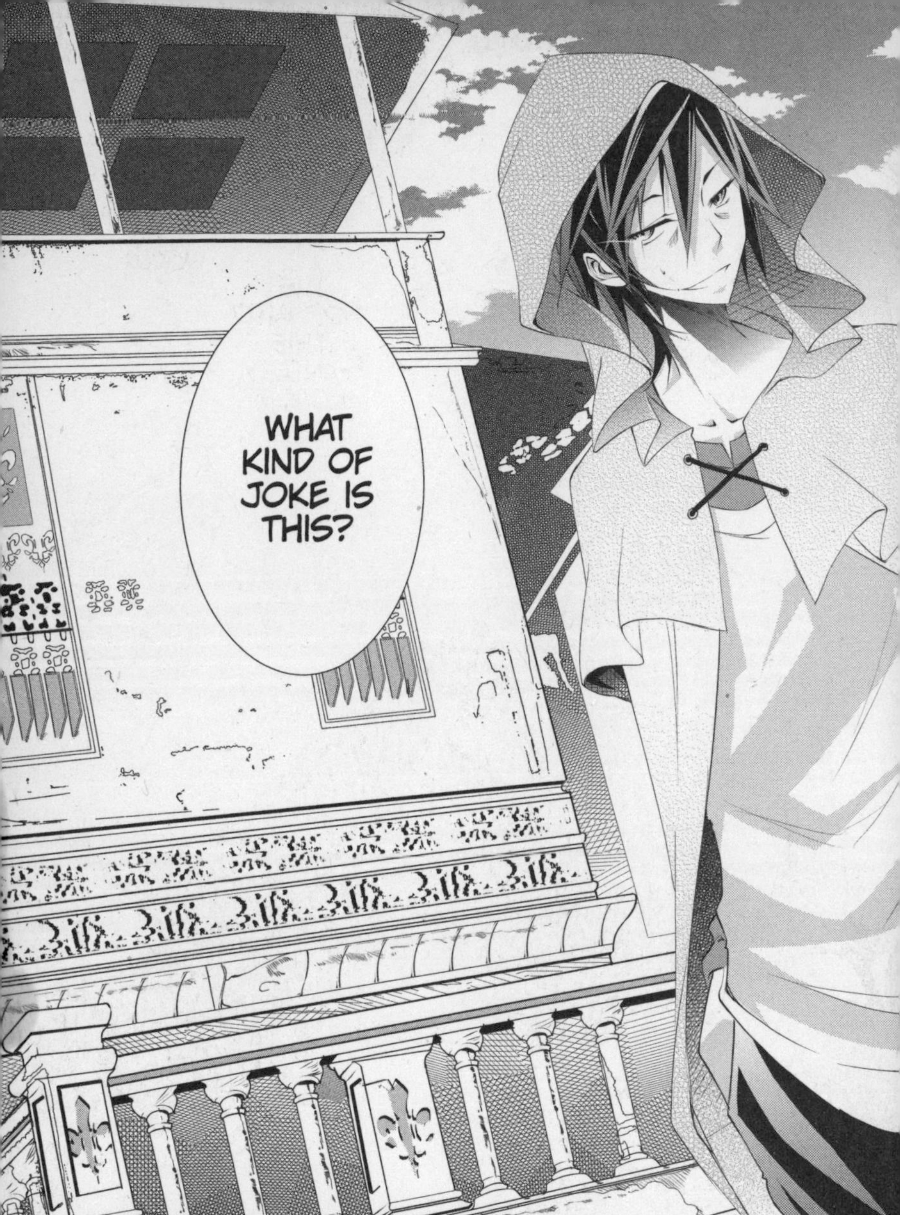
WHAT KIND OF JOKE IS THIS?

GAME.02 beginner: stage 1

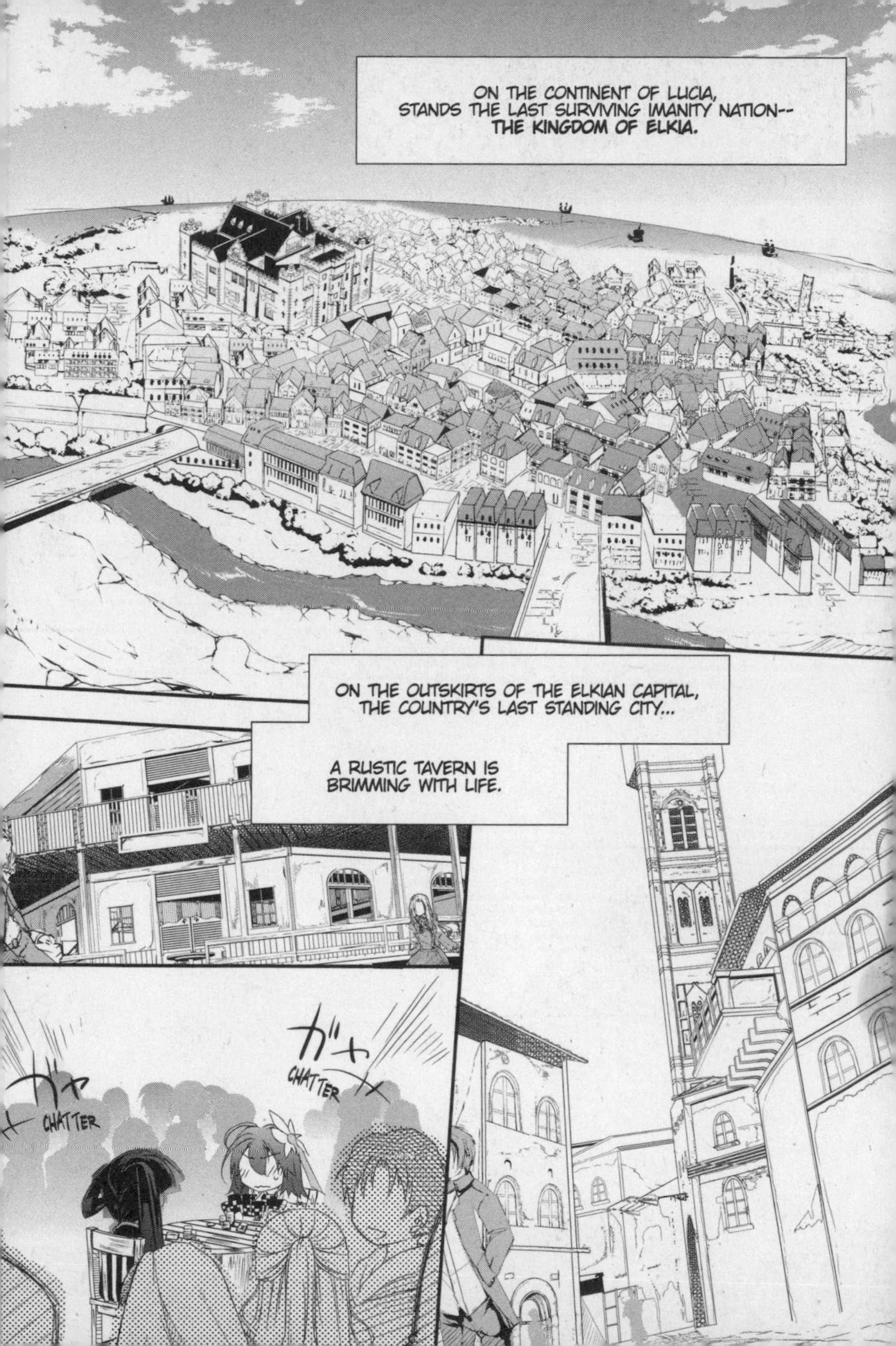
ON THE CONTINENT OF LUCIA, STANDS THE LAST SURVIVING IMANITY NATION-- THE KINGDOM OF ELKIA.
ON THE OUTSKIRTS OF THE ELKIAN CAPITAL, THE COUNTRY'S LAST STANDING CITY...
A RUSTIC TAVERN IS BRIMMING WITH LIFE.
ガヤ
CHATTER
ガヤ
CHATTER

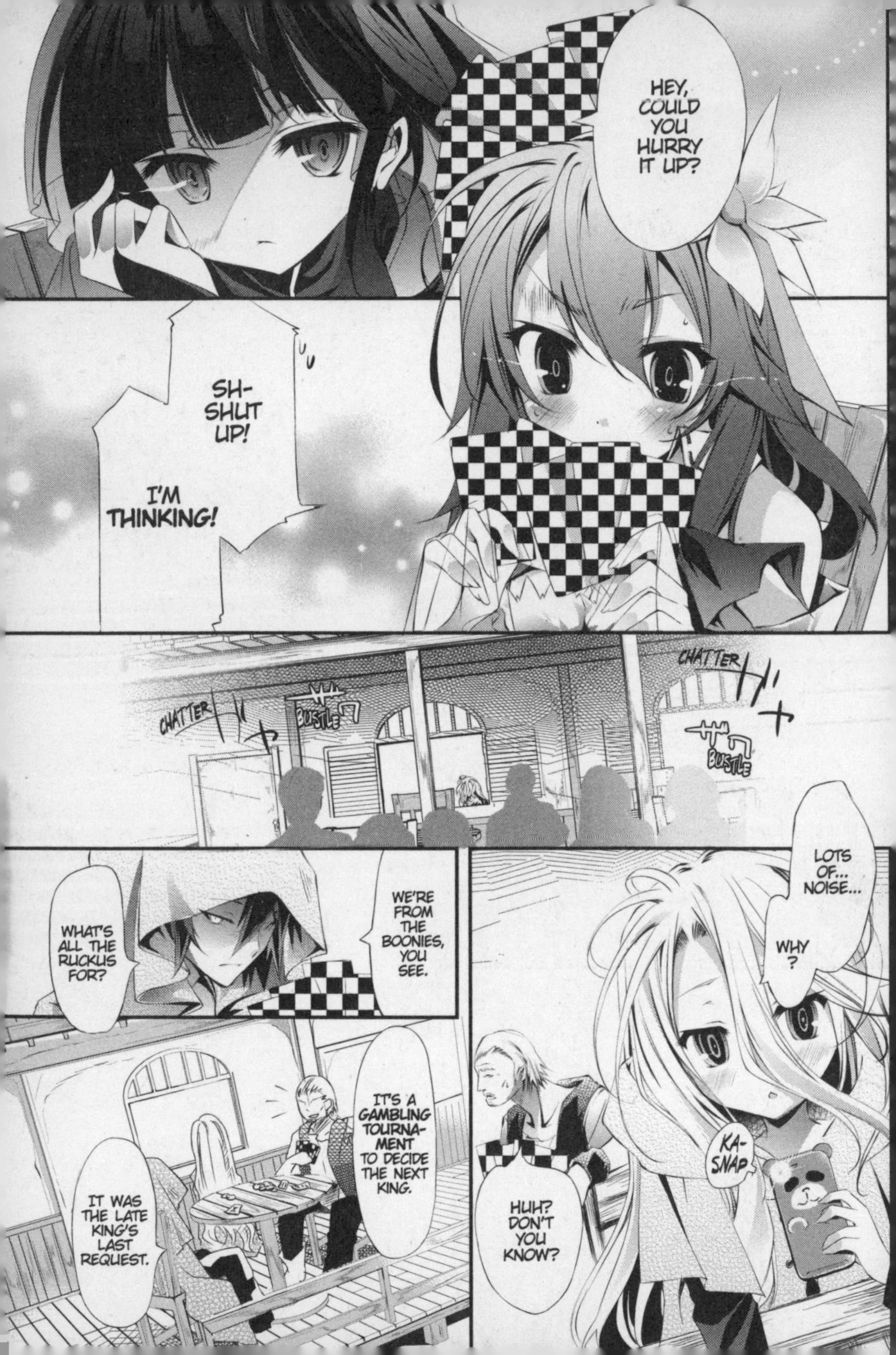
HEY, COULD YOU HURRY IT UP?
SH- SHUT UP!
I'M THINKING!
CHATTER
BUSTLE
CHATTER
BUSTLE
LOTS OF... NOISE...
WHY?
KA-SNAP
HUH? DON'T YOU KNOW?
WE'RE FROM THE BOONIES, YOU SEE.
WHAT'S ALL THE RUCKUS FOR?
IT'S A GAMBLING TOURNAMENT TO DECIDE THE NEXT KING.
IT WAS THE LATE KING'S LAST REQUEST.

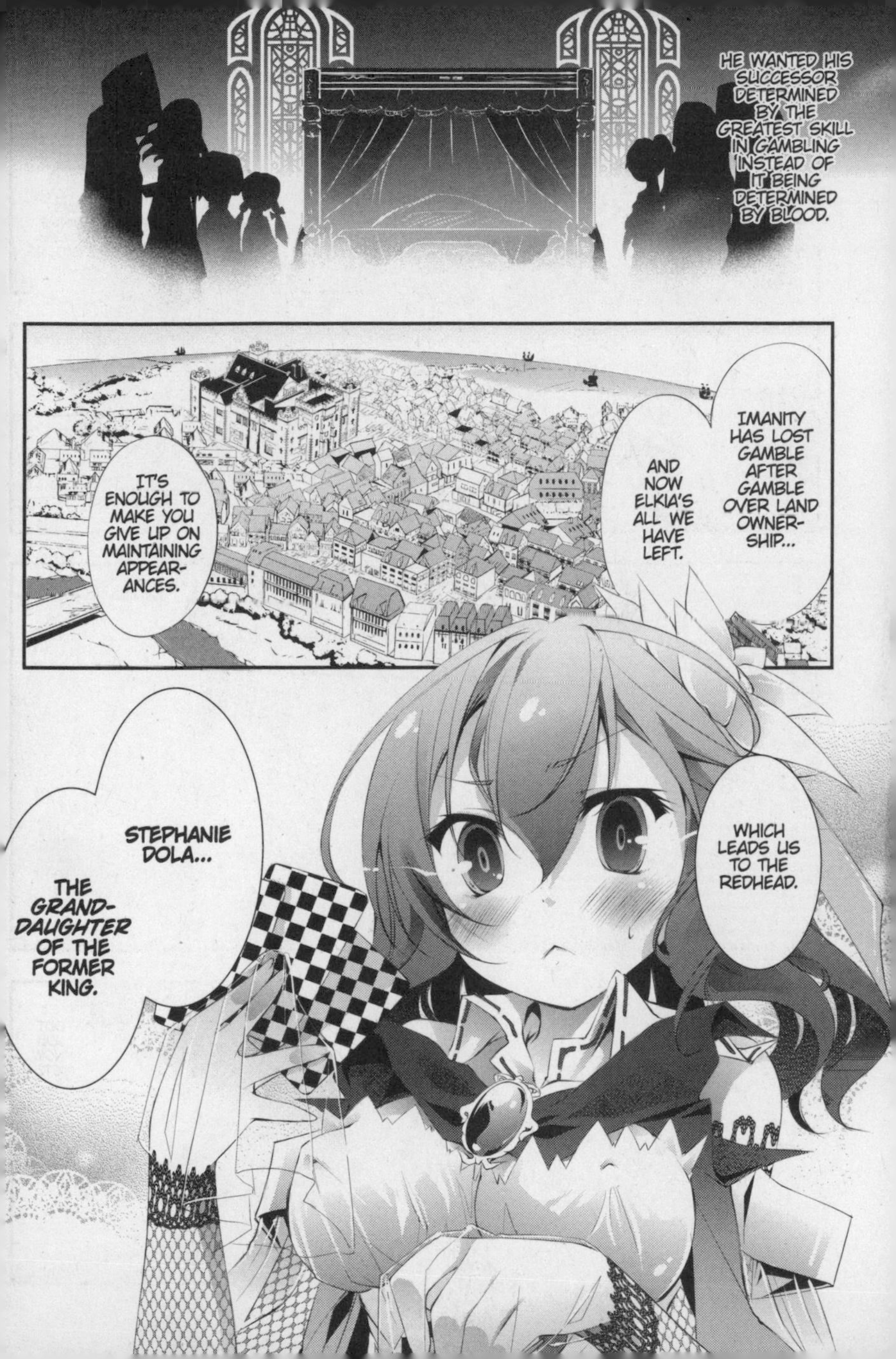
HE WANTED HIS SUCCESSOR DETERMINED BY THE GREATEST SKILL IN GAMBLING INSTEAD OF IT BEING DETERMINED BY BLOOD.
IMANITY HAS LOST GAMBLE AFTER GAMBLE OVER LAND OWNERSHIP...
AND NOW ELKIA'S ALL WE HAVE LEFT.
IT'S ENOUGH TO MAKE YOU GIVE UP ON MAINTAINING APPEARANCES.
WHICH LEADS US TO THE REDHEAD.
STEPHANIE DOLA...
THE GRANDDAUGHTER OF THE FORMER KING.

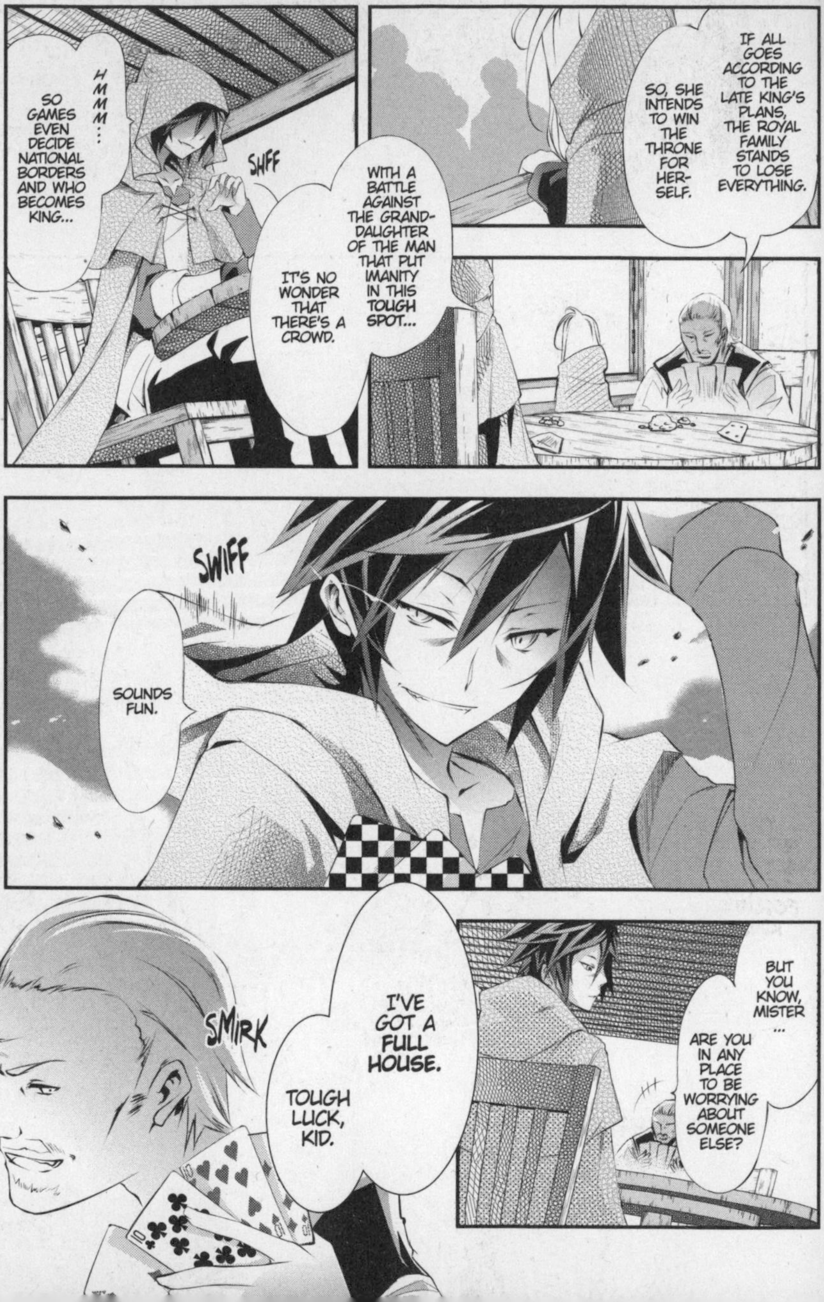
IF ALL GOES ACCORDING TO THE LATE KING'S PLANS, THE ROYAL FAMILY STANDS TO LOSE EVERYTHING.
SO, SHE INTENDS TO WIN THE THRONE FOR HER-SELF.
WITH A BATTLE AGAINST THE GRAND-DAUGHTER OF THE MAN THAT PUT IMANITY IN THIS TOUGH SPOT...
IT'S NO WONDER THAT THERE'S A CROWD.
SHFF
HMMM...
SO GAMES EVEN DECIDE NATIONAL BORDERS AND WHO BECOMES KING...
SWIFF
SOUNDS FUN.
BUT YOU KNOW, MISTER...
ARE YOU IN ANY PLACE TO BE WORRYING ABOUT SOMEONE ELSE?
I'VE GOT A FULL HOUSE.
TOUGH LUCK, KID.
SMIRK

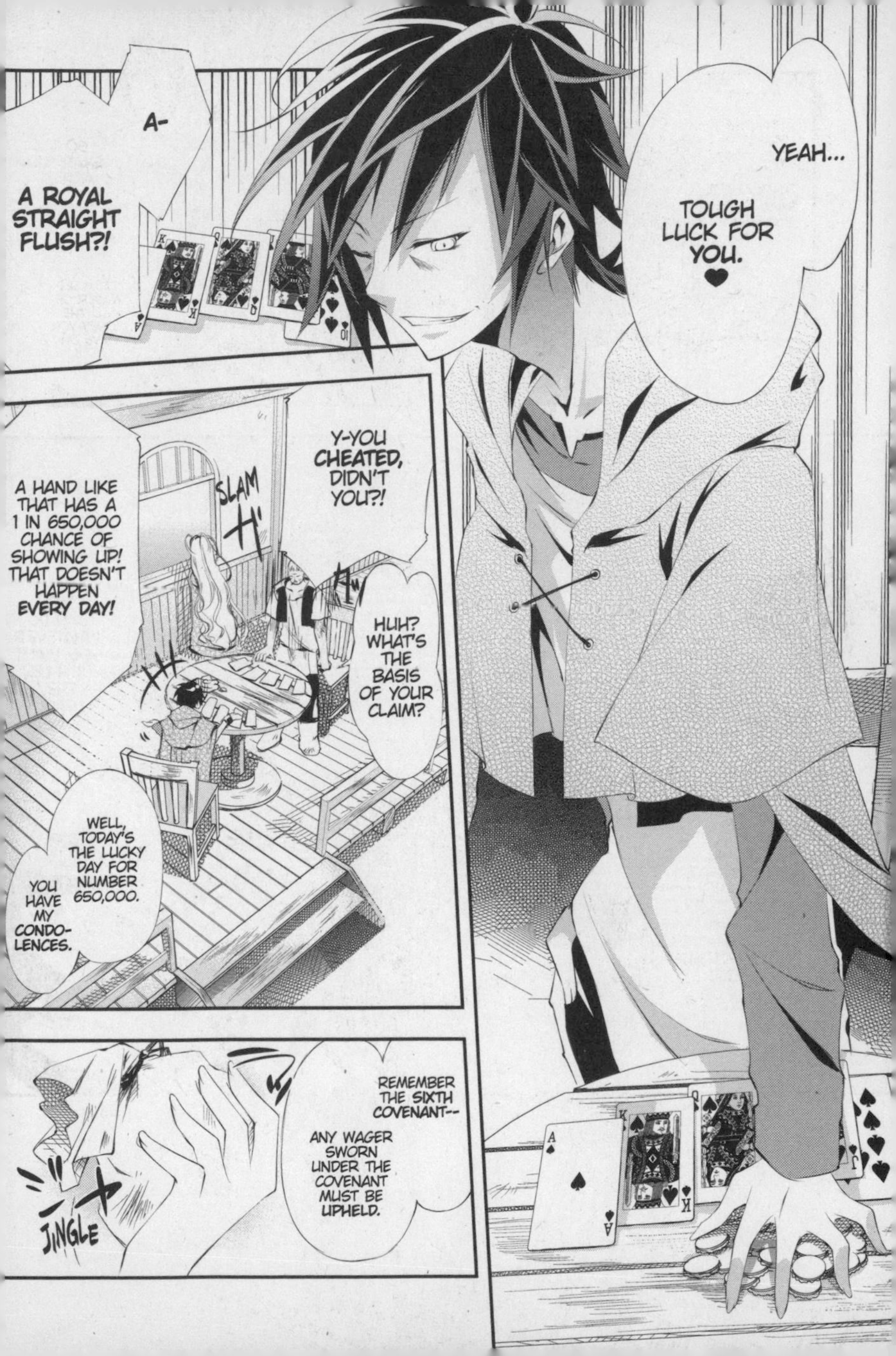

YEAH...
TOUGH LUCK FOR YOU. ♥
A-
A ROYAL STRAIGHT FLUSH?!
Y-YOU CHEATED, DIDN'T YOU?!
SLAM
A HAND LIKE THAT HAS A 1 IN 650,000 CHANCE OF SHOWING UP! THAT DOESN'T HAPPEN EVERY DAY!
HUH? WHAT'S THE BASIS OF YOUR CLAIM?
WELL, TODAY'S THE LUCKY DAY FOR NUMBER 650,000.
YOU HAVE MY CONDO-LENCES.
REMEMBER THE SIXTH COVENANT--
ANY WAGER SWORN UNDER THE COVENANT MUST BE UPHELD.
JINGLE

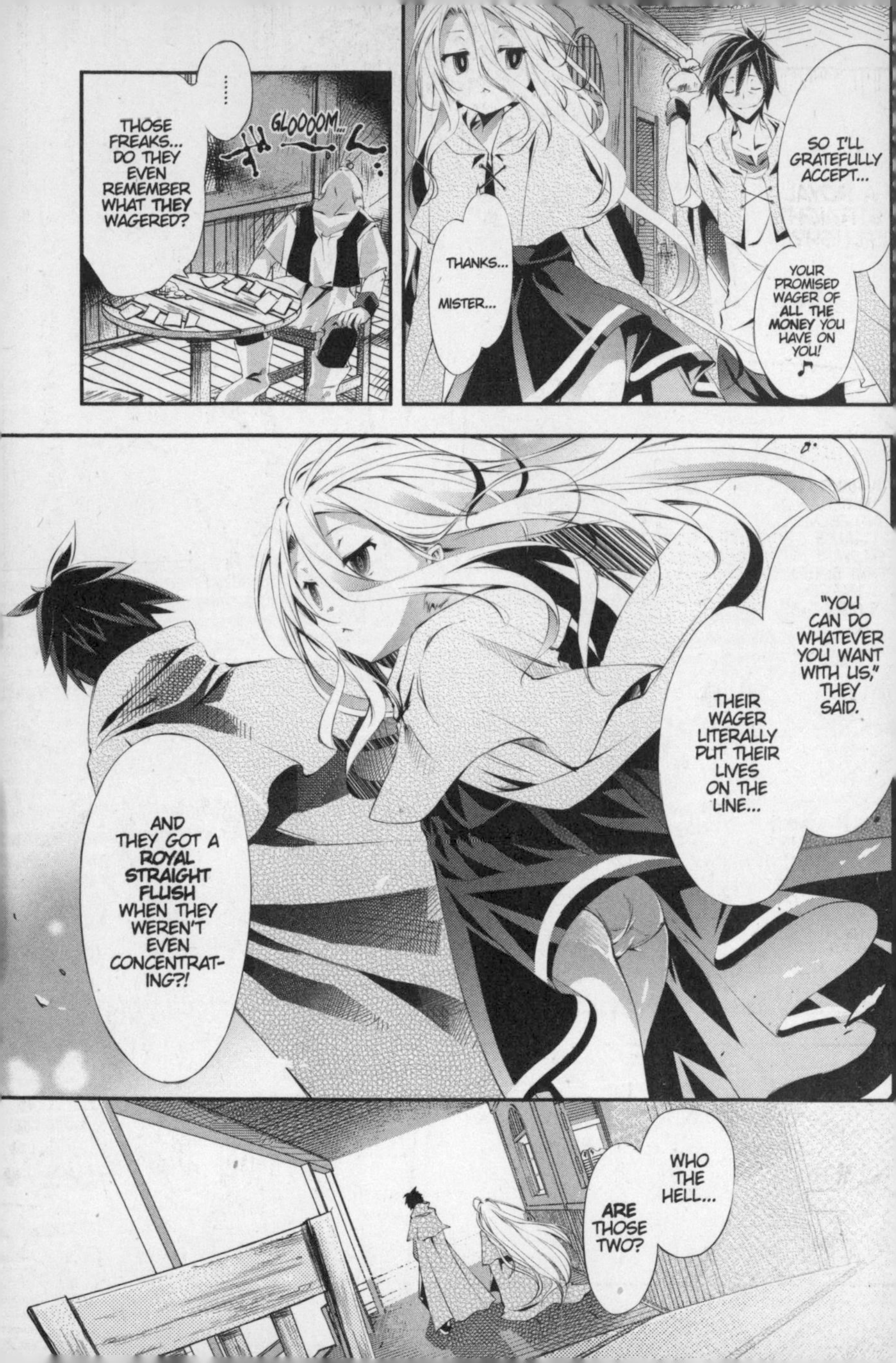

SO I'LL GRATEFULLY ACCEPT...
YOUR PROMISED WAGER OF ALL THE MONEY YOU HAVE ON YOU! ♪
THANKS...
MISTER...
......
GLOOOOM...
THOSE FREAKS... DO THEY EVEN REMEMBER WHAT THEY WAGERED?
"YOU CAN DO WHATEVER YOU WANT WITH US," THEY SAID.
THEIR WAGER LITERALLY PUT THEIR LIVES ON THE LINE...
AND THEY GOT A ROYAL STRAIGHT FLUSH WHEN THEY WEREN'T EVEN CONCENTRATING?!
WHO THE HELL...
ARE THOSE TWO?

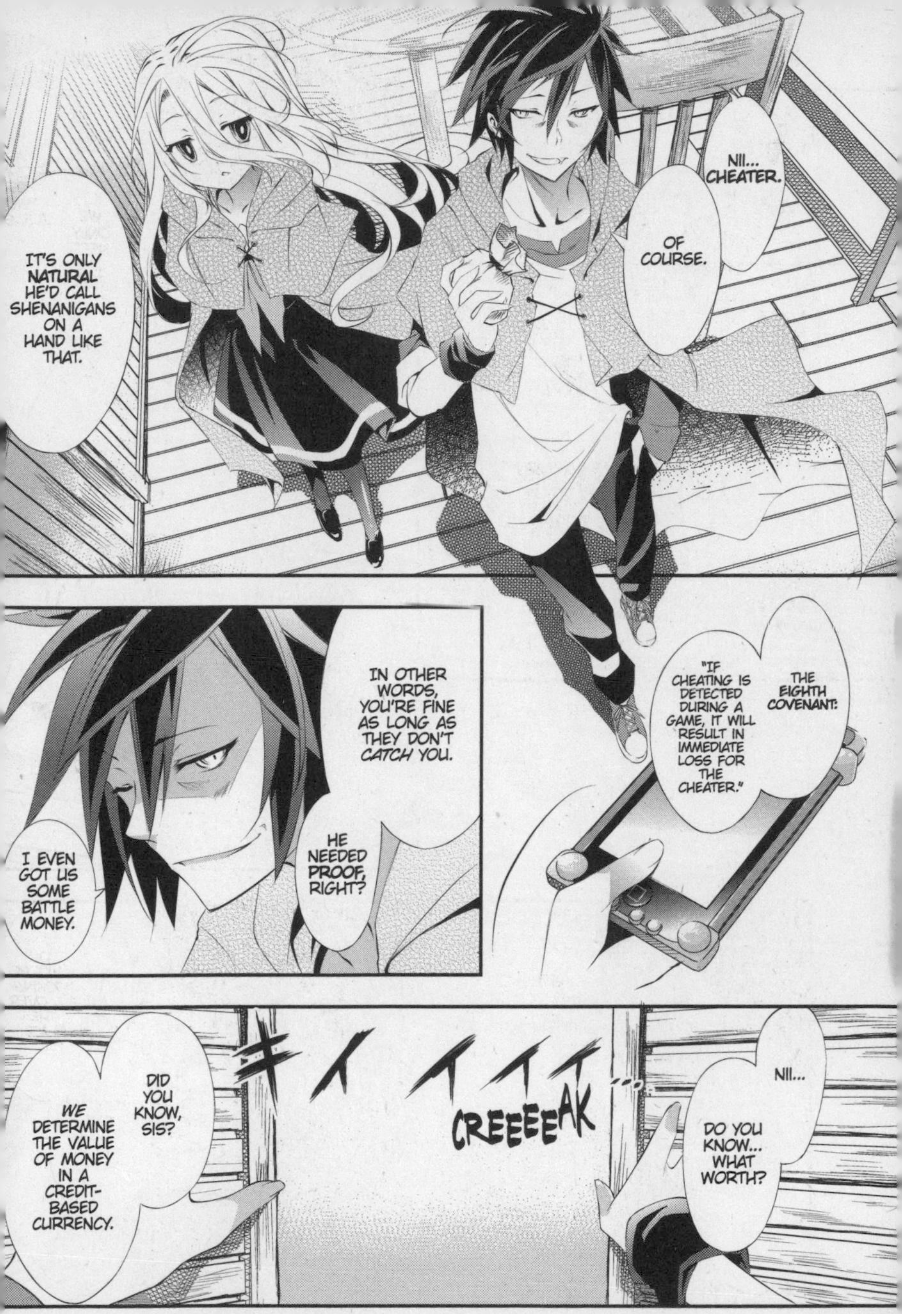
NII... CHEATER.
OF COURSE.
IT'S ONLY NATURAL HE'D CALL SHENANIGANS ON A HAND LIKE THAT.
THE EIGHTH COVENANT:
"IF CHEATING IS DETECTED DURING A GAME, IT WILL RESULT IN IMMEDIATE LOSS FOR THE CHEATER."
IN OTHER WORDS, YOU'RE FINE AS LONG AS THEY DON'T *CATCH* YOU.
HE NEEDED PROOF, RIGHT?
I EVEN GOT US SOME BATTLE MONEY.
NII...
DO YOU KNOW... WHAT WORTH?
CREEEEAK
DID YOU KNOW, SIS?
WE DETERMINE THE VALUE OF MONEY IN A CREDIT-BASED CURRENCY.

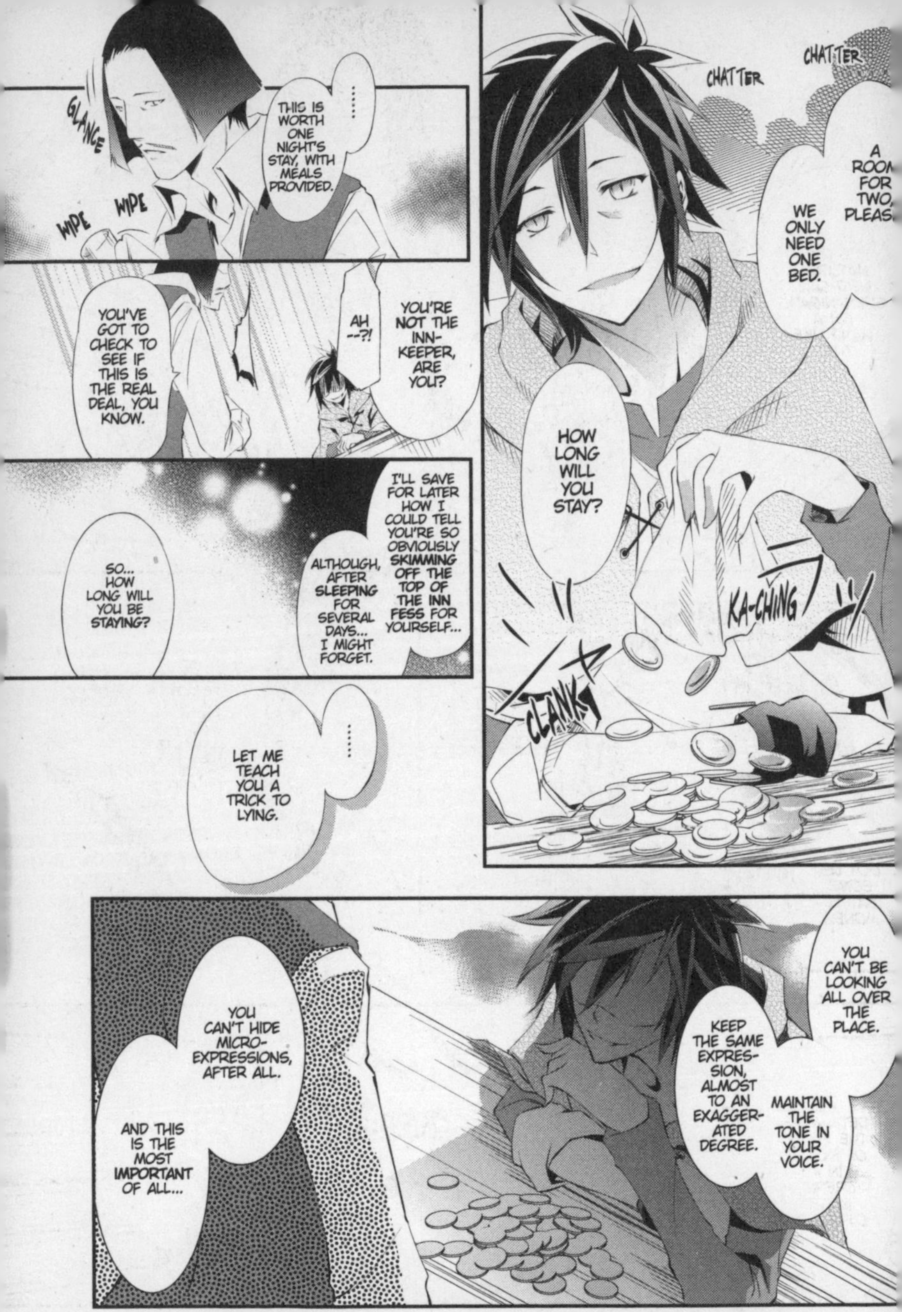
CHATTER CHATTER
A ROOM FOR TWO, PLEAS
WE ONLY NEED ONE BED.
HOW LONG WILL YOU STAY?
KA-CHING
CLANK
......
THIS IS WORTH ONE NIGHT'S STAY, WITH MEALS PROVIDED.
GLANCE
WIPE WIPE
YOU'RE NOT THE INN-KEEPER, ARE YOU?
AH --?!
YOU'VE GOT TO CHECK TO SEE IF THIS IS THE REAL DEAL, YOU KNOW.
I'LL SAVE FOR LATER HOW I COULD TELL YOU'RE SO OBVIOUSLY SKIMMING OFF THE TOP OF THE INN FESS FOR YOURSELF...
ALTHOUGH, AFTER SLEEPING FOR SEVERAL DAYS... I MIGHT FORGET.
SO... HOW LONG WILL YOU BE STAYING?
......
LET ME TEACH YOU A TRICK TO LYING.
YOU CAN'T BE LOOKING ALL OVER THE PLACE.
KEEP THE SAME EXPRESSION, ALMOST TO AN EXAGGERATED DEGREE.
MAINTAIN THE TONE IN YOUR VOICE.
YOU CAN'T HIDE MICRO-EXPRESSIONS, AFTER ALL.
AND THIS IS THE MOST IMPORTANT OF ALL...

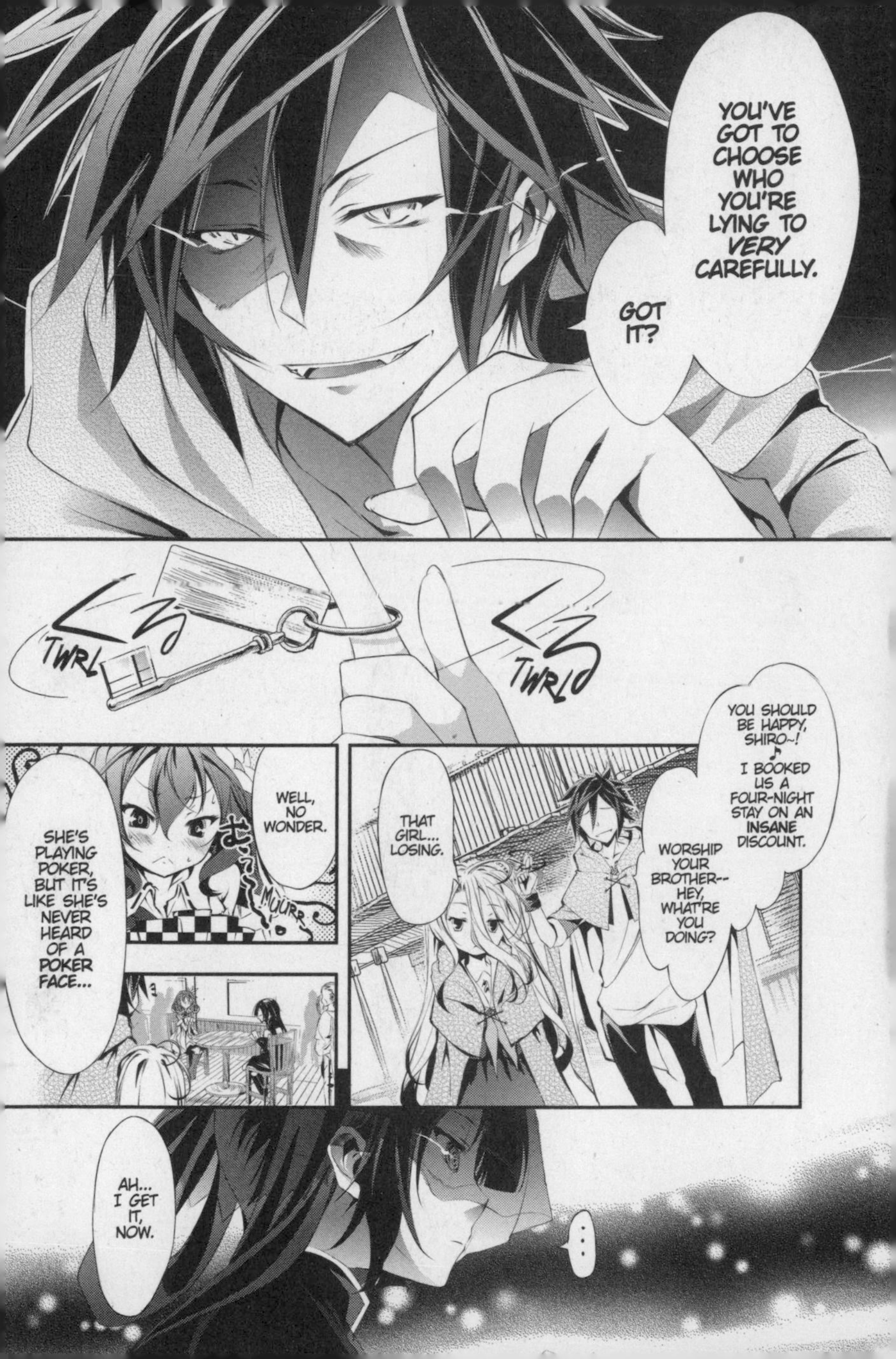
YOU'VE GOT TO CHOOSE WHO YOU'RE LYING TO *VERY* CAREFULLY.
GOT IT?
TWRL
TWRL
YOU SHOULD BE HAPPY, SHIRO~! ♪ I BOOKED US A FOUR-NIGHT STAY ON AN INSANE DISCOUNT.
WORSHIP YOUR BROTHER-- HEY, WHAT'RE YOU DOING?
THAT GIRL... LOSING.
WELL, NO WONDER.
MUURR
SHE'S PLAYING POKER, BUT IT'S LIKE SHE'S NEVER HEARD OF A POKER FACE...
...
AH... I GET IT, NOW.

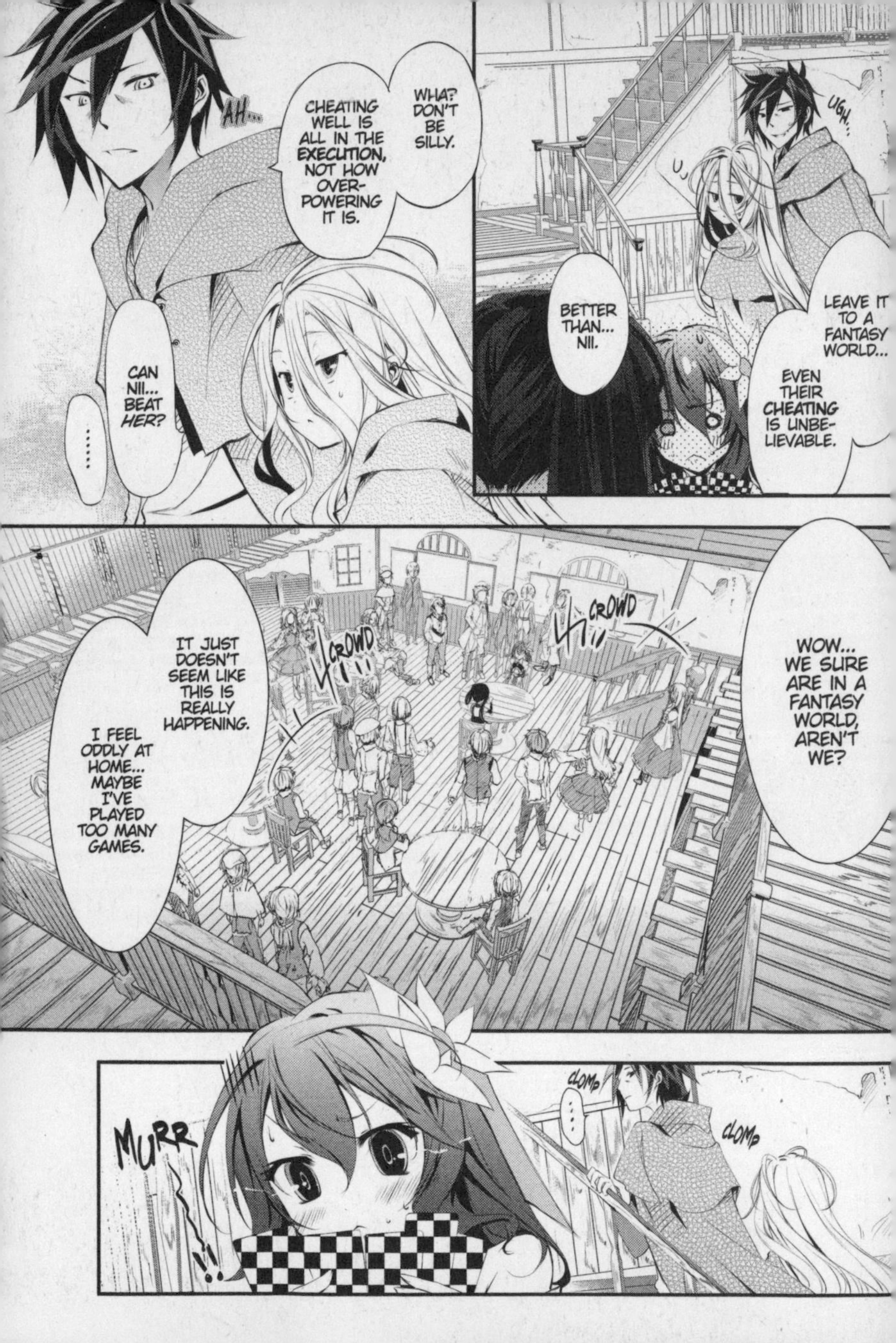
UGH...
LEAVE IT TO A FANTASY WORLD...
EVEN THEIR CHEATING IS UNBE-LIEVABLE.
BETTER THAN... NII.
WHA? DON'T BE SILLY.
CHEATING WELL IS ALL IN THE EXECUTION, NOT HOW OVER-POWERING IT IS.
AH...
CAN NII... BEAT HER?
......
WOW... WE SURE ARE IN A FANTASY WORLD, AREN'T WE?
CROWD
CROWD
IT JUST DOESN'T SEEM LIKE THIS IS REALLY HAPPENING.
I FEEL ODDLY AT HOME... MAYBE I'VE PLAYED TOO MANY GAMES.
CLOMP
CLOMP
...
MURR

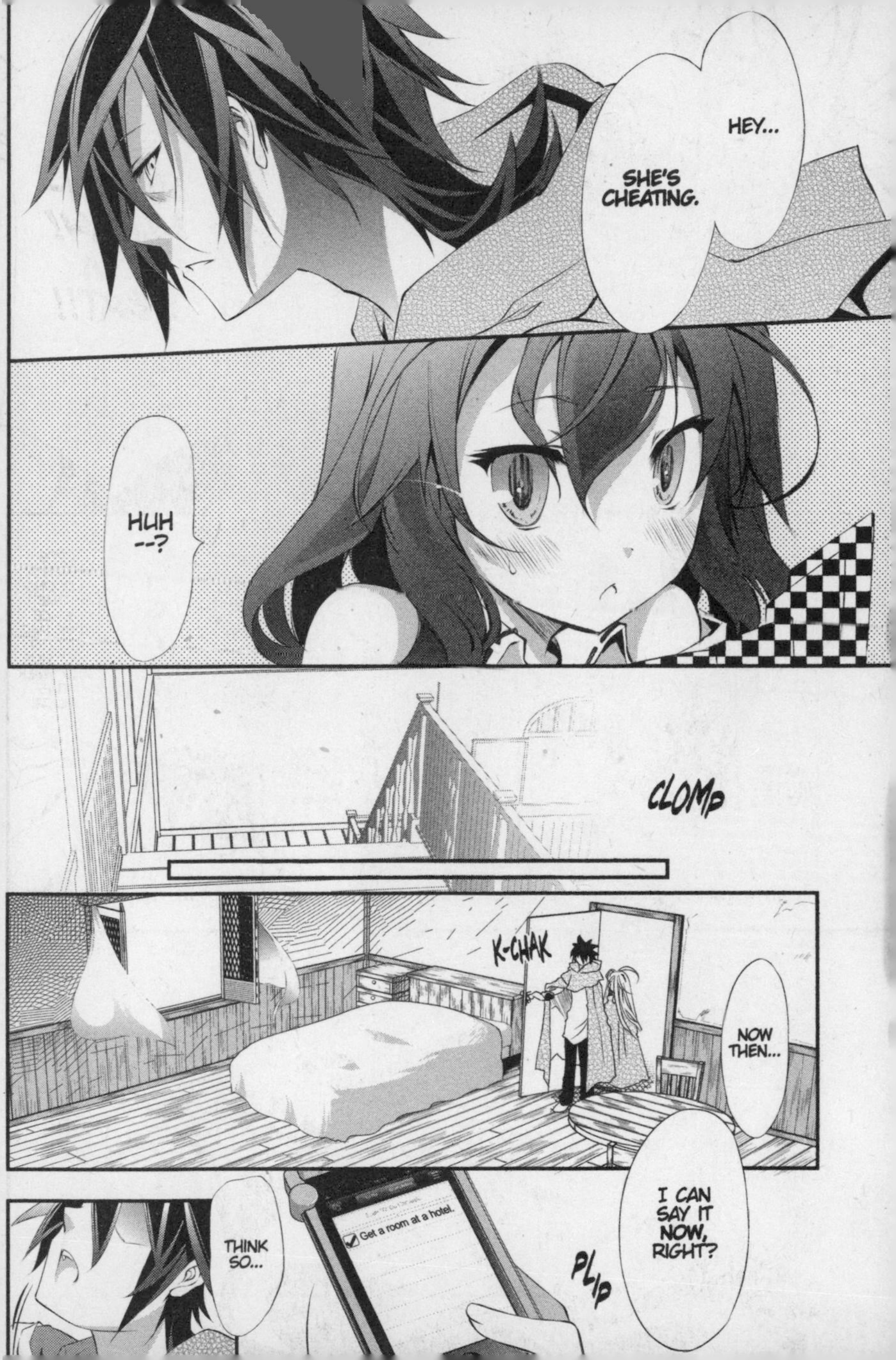
HEY...
SHE'S CHEATING.
HUH --?
CLOMP
NOW THEN...
K-CHAK
I CAN SAY IT NOW, RIGHT?
PLIP
Get a room at a hotel.
THINK SO...

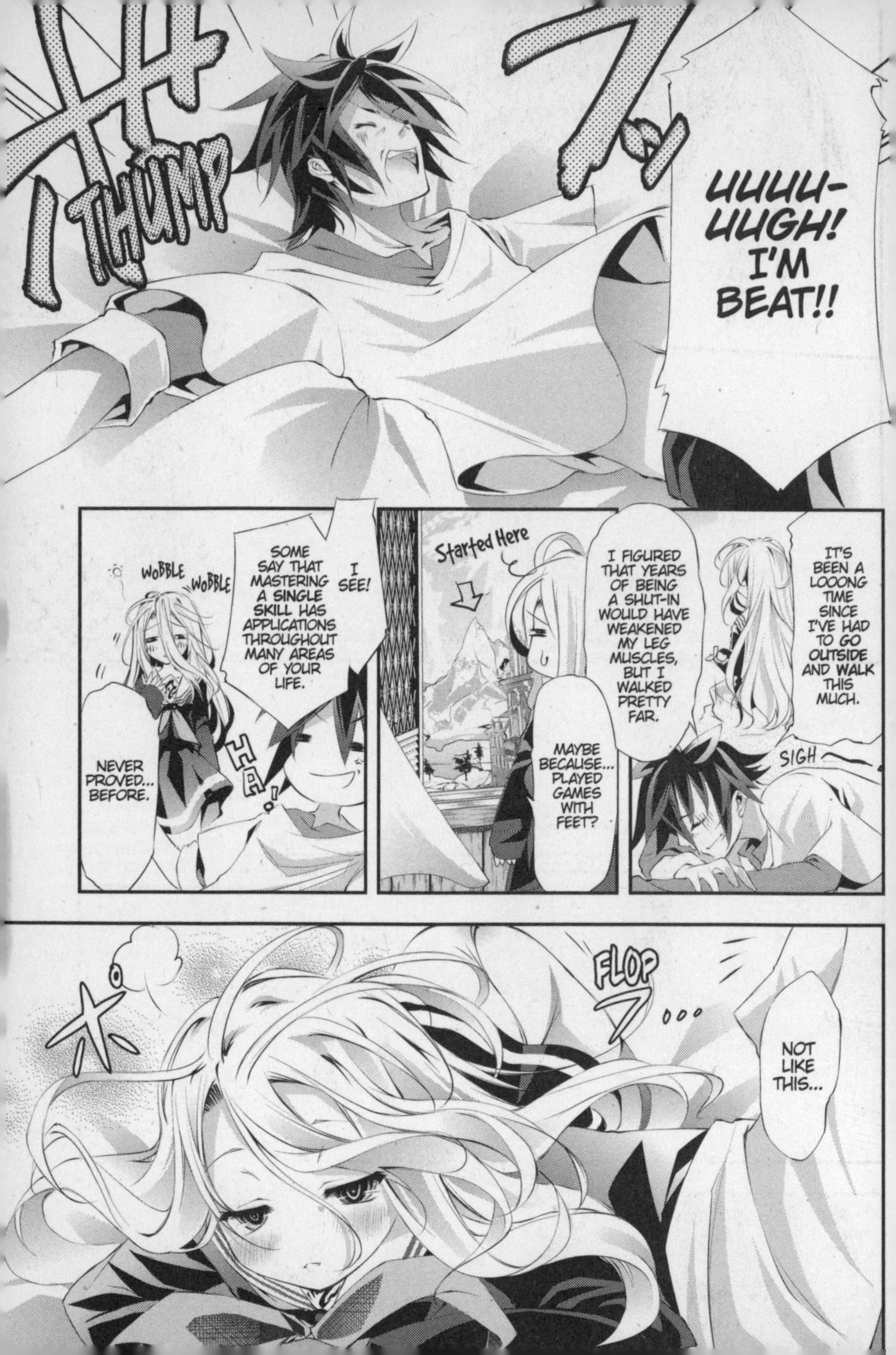
UUUU-UUGH! I'M BEAT!!
THUMP
IT'S BEEN A LOOONG TIME SINCE I'VE HAD TO GO OUTSIDE AND WALK THIS MUCH.
SIGH
I FIGURED THAT YEARS OF BEING A SHUT-IN WOULD HAVE WEAKENED MY LEG MUSCLES, BUT I WALKED PRETTY FAR.
Started Here
MAYBE BECAUSE... PLAYED GAMES WITH FEET?
I SEE!
SOME SAY THAT MASTERING A SINGLE SKILL HAS APPLICATIONS THROUGHOUT MANY AREAS OF YOUR LIFE.
WOBBLE WOBBLE
HA!
NEVER PROVED... BEFORE.
NOT LIKE THIS...
FLOP

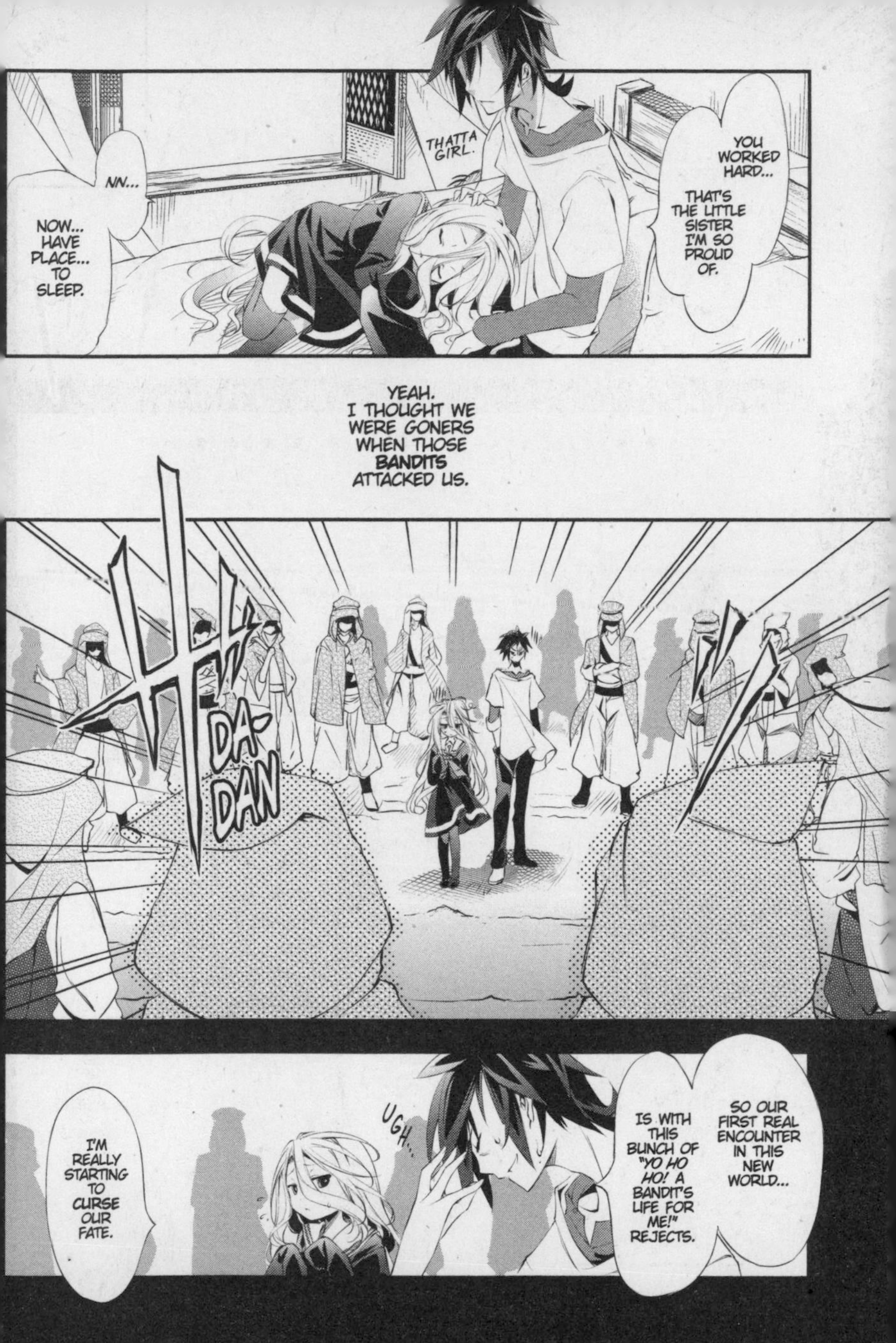
YOU WORKED HARD... THAT'S THE LITTLE SISTER I'M SO PROUD OF.
THATTA GIRL.
NN...
NOW... HAVE PLACE... TO SLEEP.
YEAH. I THOUGHT WE WERE GONERS WHEN THOSE BANDITS ATTACKED US.
DA-DAN
SO OUR FIRST REAL ENCOUNTER IN THIS NEW WORLD...
IS WITH THIS BUNCH OF "YO HO HO! A BANDIT'S LIFE FOR ME!" REJECTS.
UGH...
I'M REALLY STARTING TO CURSE OUR FATE.

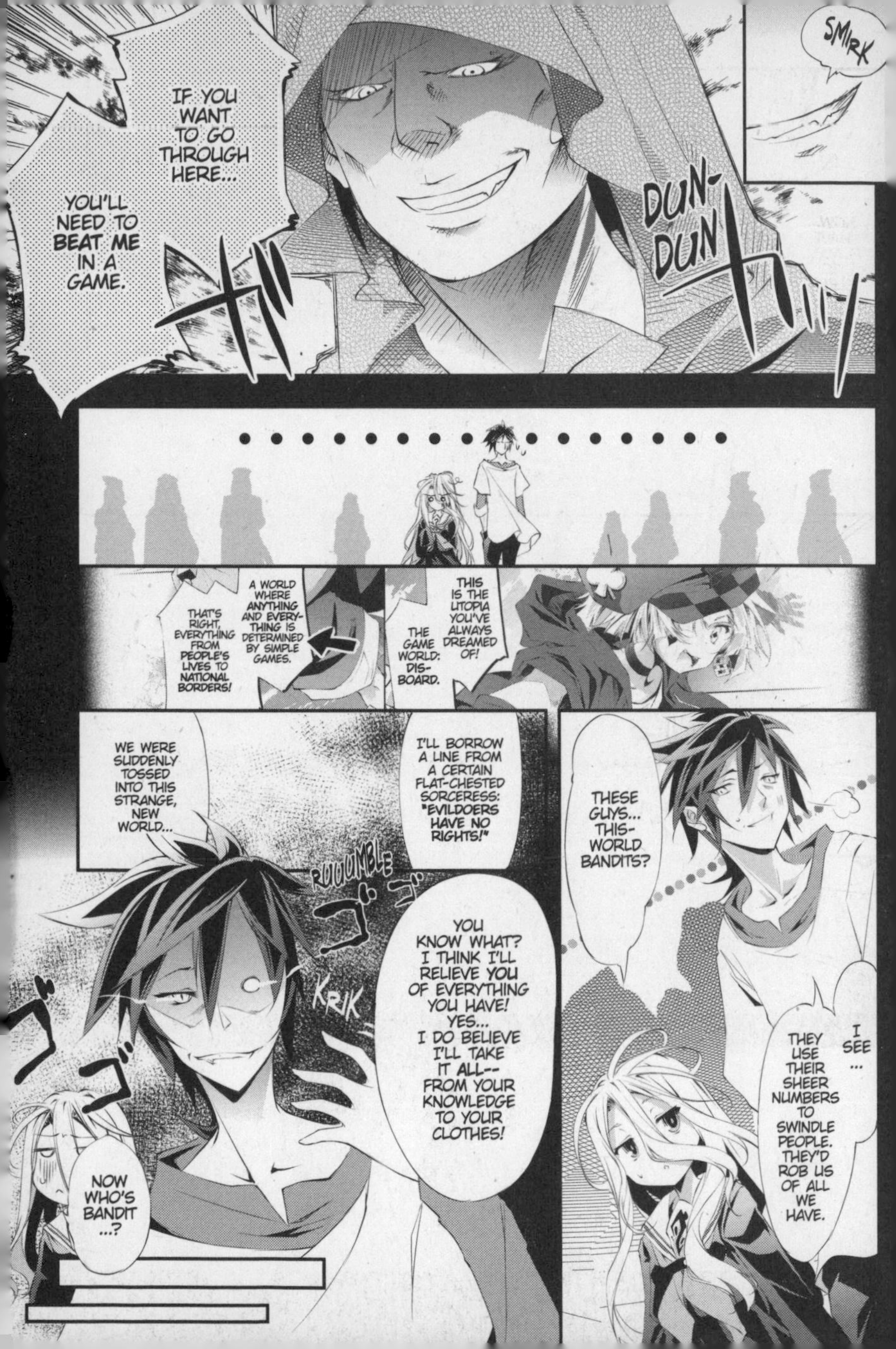
SMIRK
DUN-DUN
IF YOU WANT TO GO THROUGH HERE...
YOU'LL NEED TO BEAT ME IN A GAME.
THIS IS THE UTOPIA YOU'VE ALWAYS DREAMED OF!
THE GAME WORLD: DIS-BOARD.
A WORLD WHERE ANYTHING AND EVERY-THING IS DETERMINED BY SIMPLE GAMES.
THAT'S RIGHT, EVERYTHING FROM PEOPLE'S LIVES TO NATIONAL BORDERS!
THESE GUYS... THIS-WORLD BANDITS?
I SEE...
THEY USE THEIR SHEER NUMBERS TO SWINDLE PEOPLE. THEY'D ROB US OF ALL WE HAVE.
WE WERE SUDDENLY TOSSED INTO THIS STRANGE, NEW WORLD...
I'LL BORROW A LINE FROM A CERTAIN FLAT-CHESTED SORCERESS: "EVILDOERS HAVE NO RIGHTS!"
RUUUMBLE
KRIK
YOU KNOW WHAT? I THINK I'LL RELIEVE YOU OF EVERYTHING YOU HAVE! YES... I DO BELIEVE I'LL TAKE IT ALL-- FROM YOUR KNOWLEDGE TO YOUR CLOTHES!
NOW WHO'S BANDIT ...?

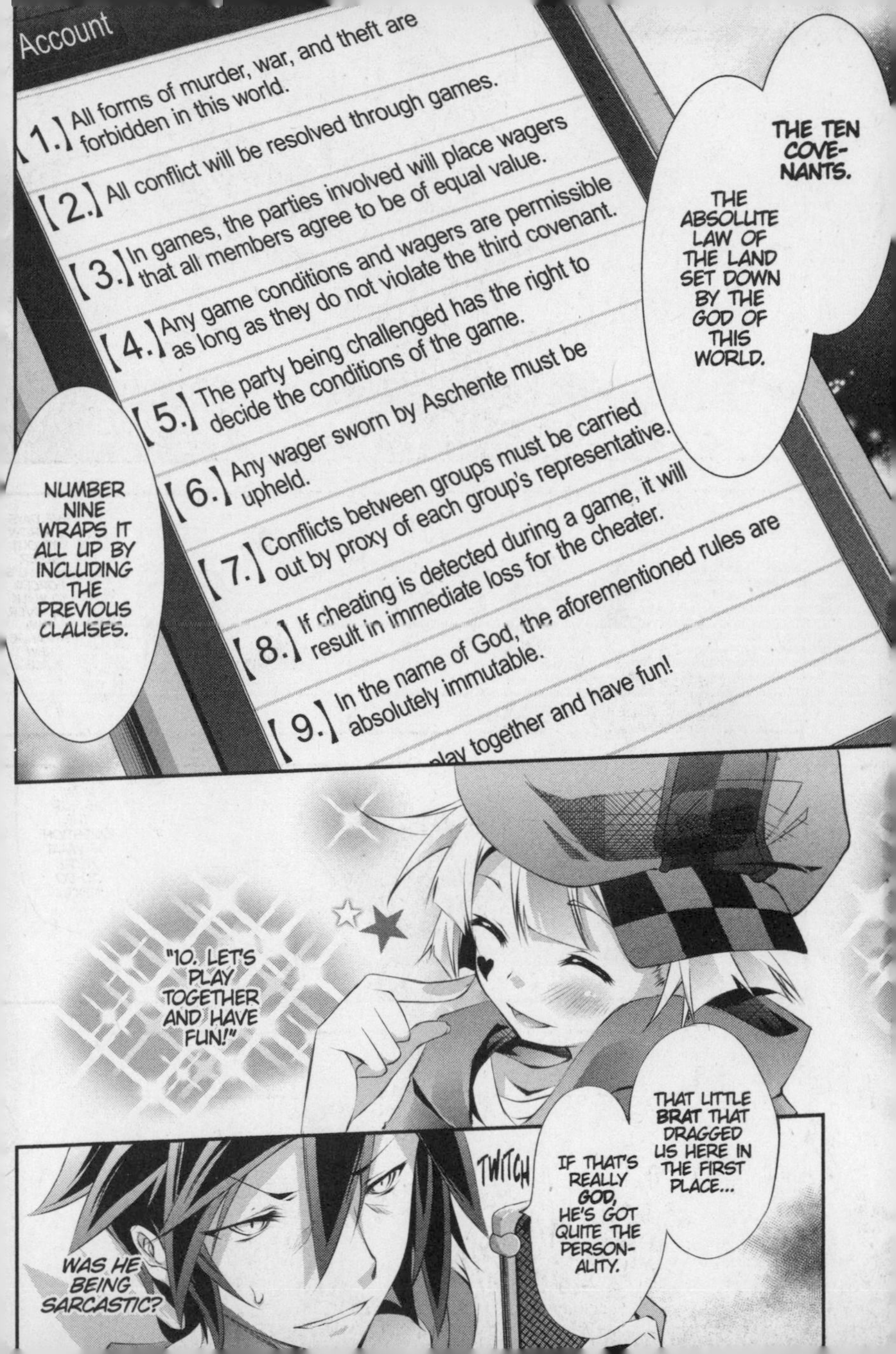
THE TEN COVENANTS.
THE ABSOLUTE LAW OF THE LAND SET DOWN BY THE GOD OF THIS WORLD.
Account
【1.】All forms of murder, war, and theft are forbidden in this world.
【2.】All conflict will be resolved through games.
【3.】In games, the parties involved will place wagers that all members agree to be of equal value.
【4.】Any game conditions and wagers are permissible as long as they do not violate the third covenant.
【5.】The party being challenged has the right to decide the conditions of the game.
【6.】Any wager sworn by Aschente must be upheld.
【7.】Conflicts between groups must be carried out by proxy of each group's representative.
【8.】If cheating is detected during a game, it will result in immediate loss for the cheater.
【9.】In the name of God, the aforementioned rules are absolutely immutable.
lay together and have fun!
NUMBER NINE WRAPS IT ALL UP BY INCLUDING THE PREVIOUS CLAUSES.
"10. LET'S PLAY TOGETHER AND HAVE FUN!"
THAT LITTLE BRAT THAT DRAGGED US HERE IN THE FIRST PLACE...
IF THAT'S REALLY GOD, HE'S GOT QUITE THE PERSONALITY.
TWITCH
WAS HE BEING SARCASTIC?

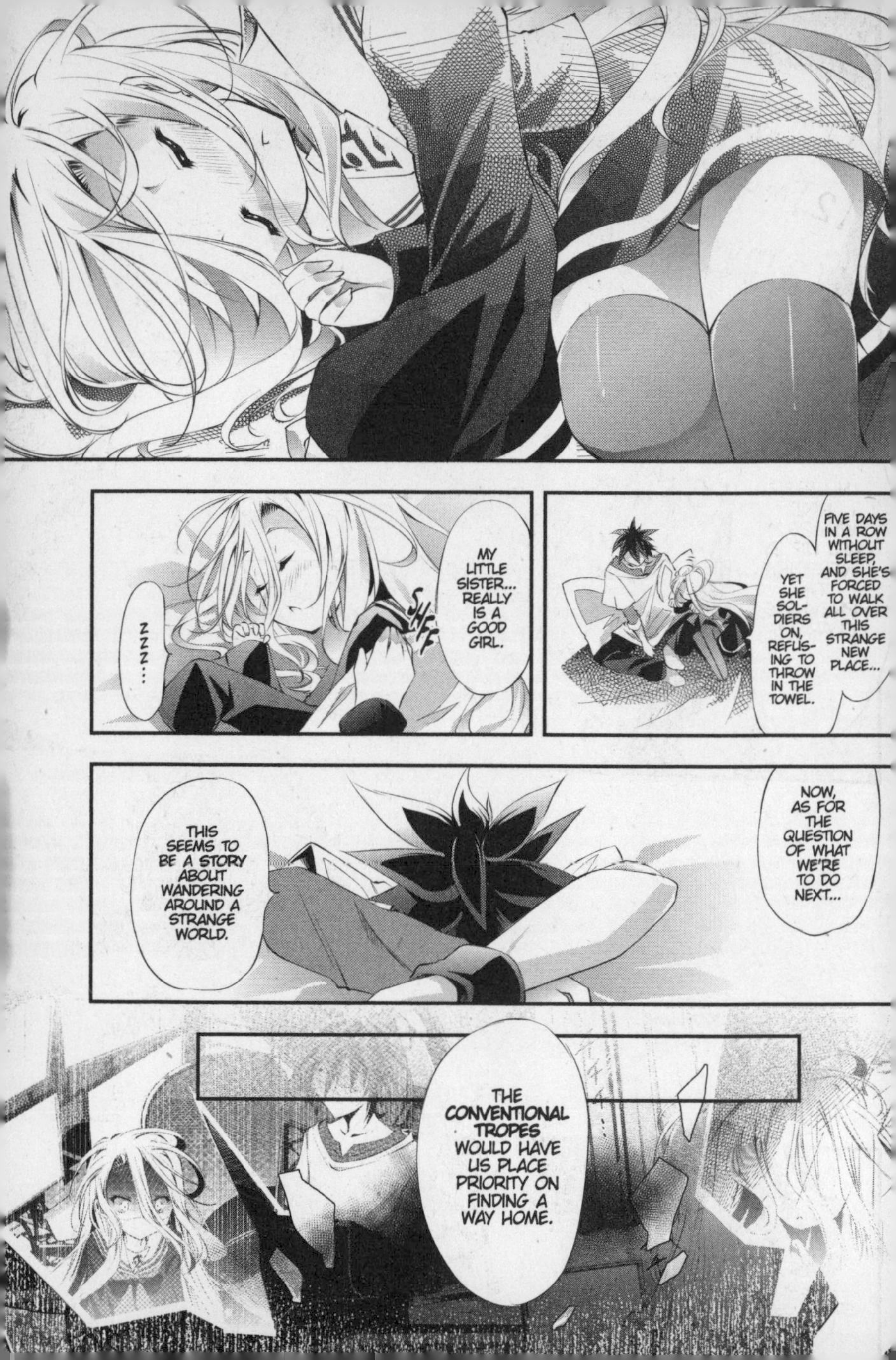
FIVE DAYS IN A ROW WITHOUT SLEEP, AND SHE'S FORCED TO WALK ALL OVER THIS STRANGE NEW PLACE...
YET SHE SOLDIERS ON, REFUSING TO THROW IN THE TOWEL.
MY LITTLE SISTER... REALLY IS A GOOD GIRL.
SHFF
ZZZ...
NOW, AS FOR THE QUESTION OF WHAT WE'RE TO DO NEXT...
THIS SEEMS TO BE A STORY ABOUT WANDERING AROUND A STRANGE WORLD.
THE CONVENTIONAL TROPES WOULD HAVE US PLACE PRIORITY ON FINDING A WAY HOME.

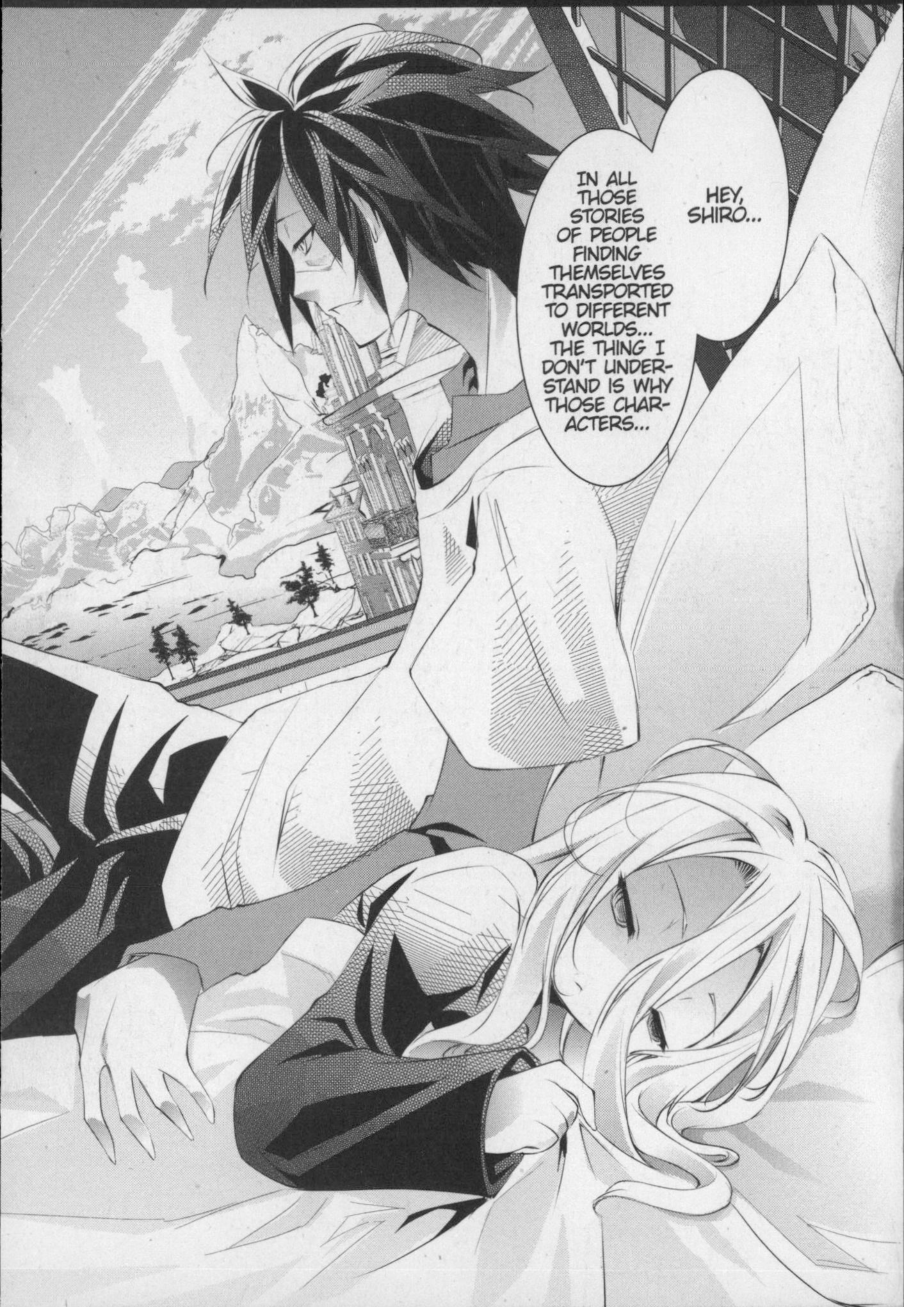
HEY, SHIRO...
IN ALL THOSE STORIES OF PEOPLE FINDING THEMSELVES TRANSPORTED TO DIFFERENT WORLDS... THE THING I DON'T UNDER-STAND IS WHY THOSE CHAR-ACTERS...

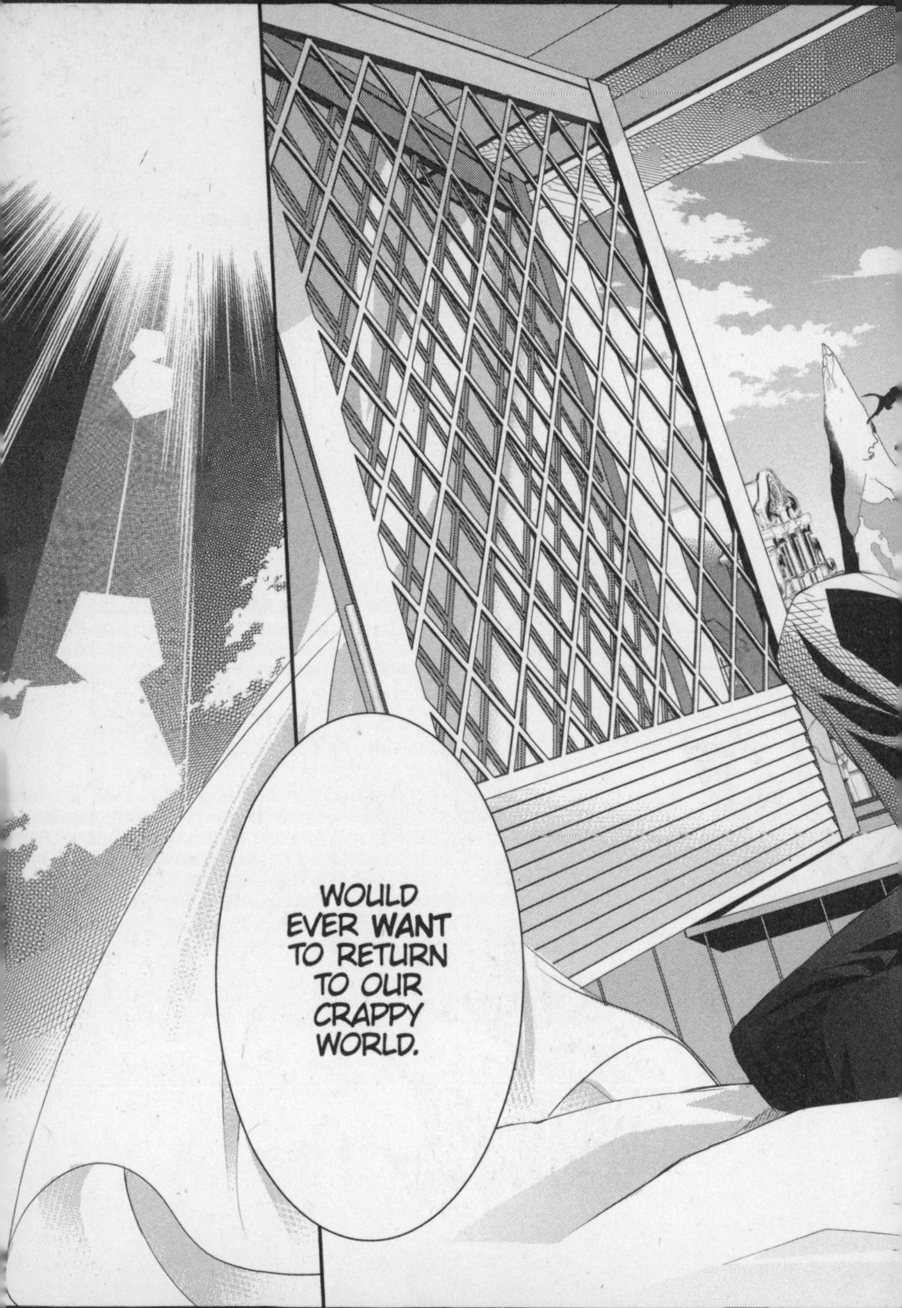
WOULD EVER WANT TO RETURN TO OUR CRAPPY WORLD.

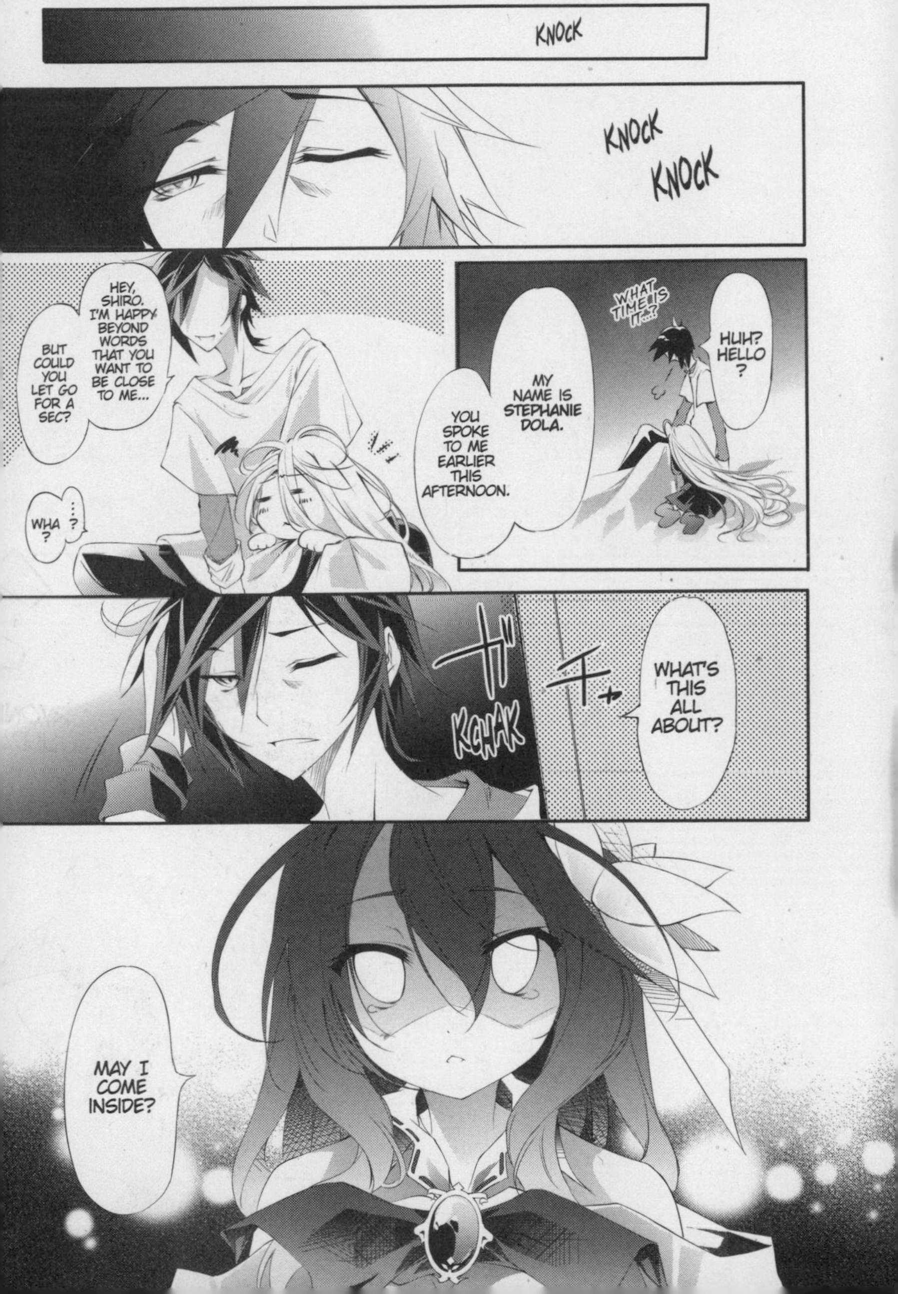
KNOCK
KNOCK
KNOCK
HUH? HELLO?
WHAT TIME IS IT...?
MY NAME IS STEPHANIE DOLA.
YOU SPOKE TO ME EARLIER THIS AFTERNOON.
HEY, SHIRO. I'M HAPPY BEYOND WORDS THAT YOU WANT TO BE CLOSE TO ME...
BUT COULD YOU LET GO FOR A SEC?
...WHA?
WHAT'S THIS ALL ABOUT?
KCHAK
MAY I COME INSIDE?

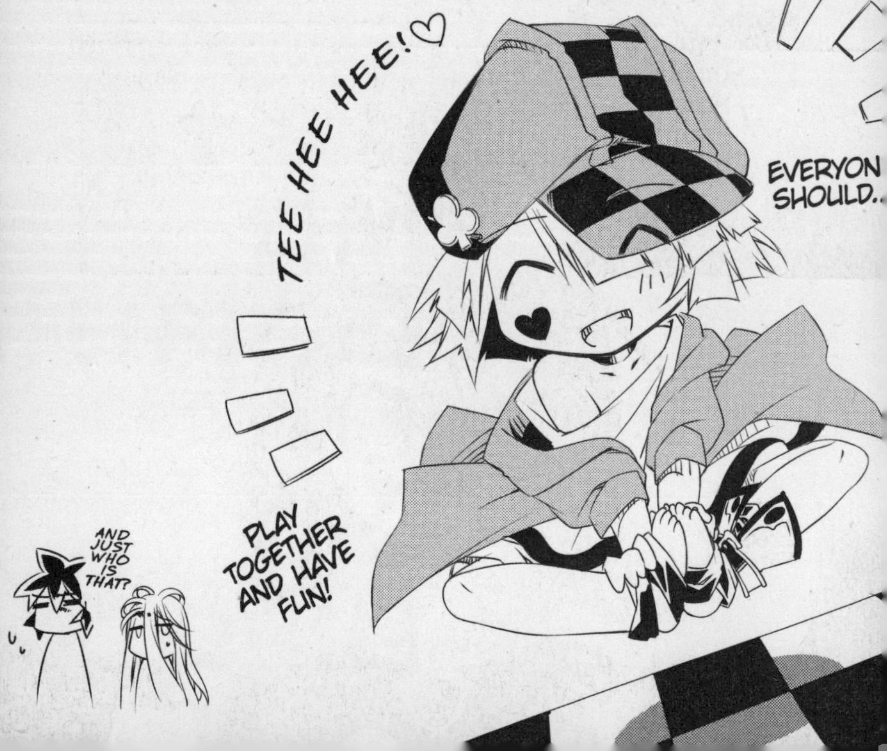
EVERYON SHOULD..
PLAY TOGETHER AND HAVE FUN!
TEE HEE HEE! ♡
AND JUST WHO IS THAT?

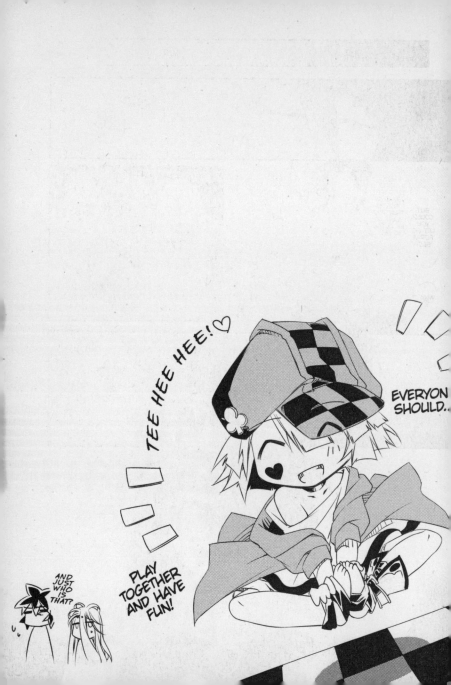

No
Game
No
Life

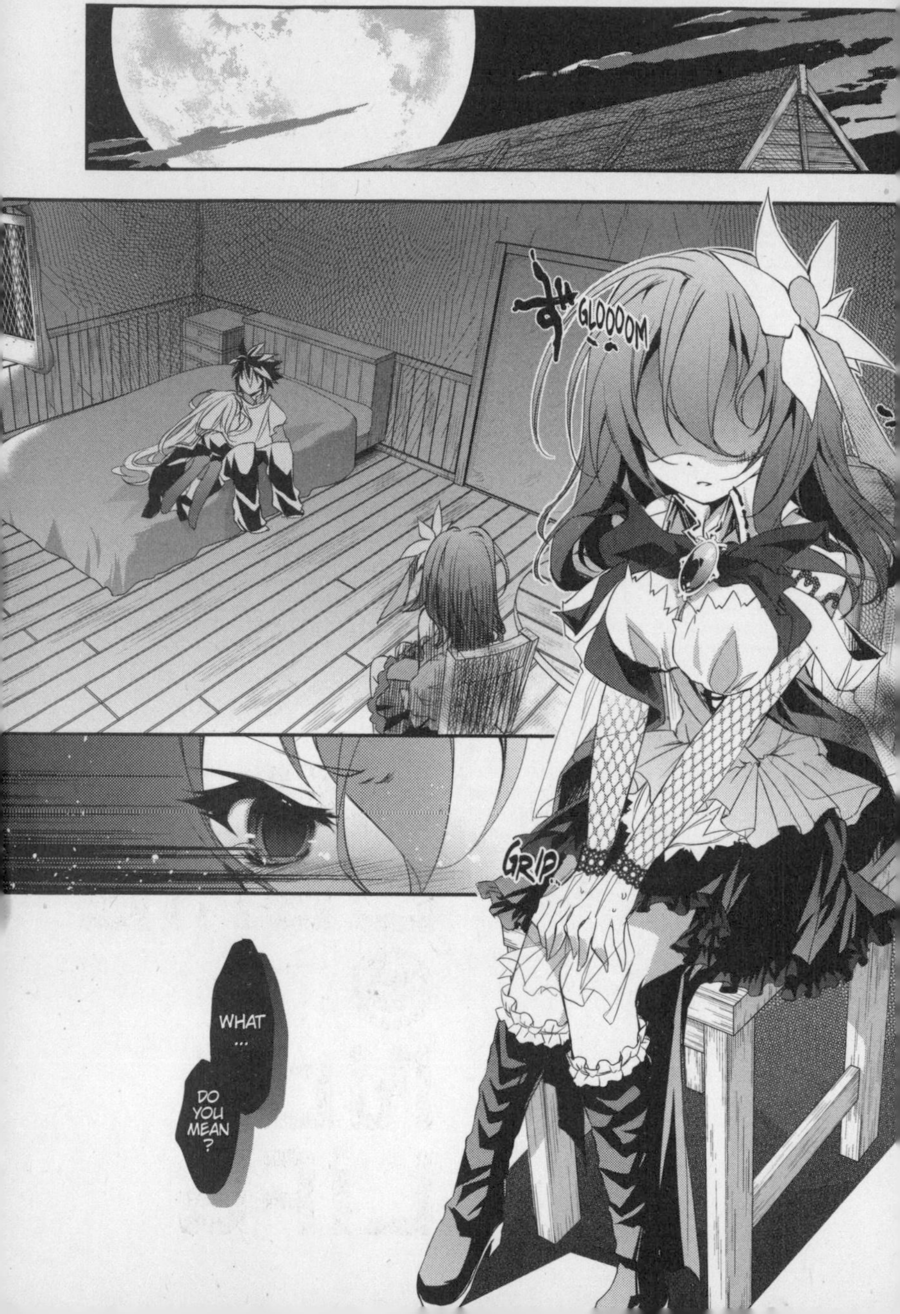
ず
GLOOOOM
GRIP
WHAT ...
DO YOU MEAN ?

GAME.03 beginner: stage 2

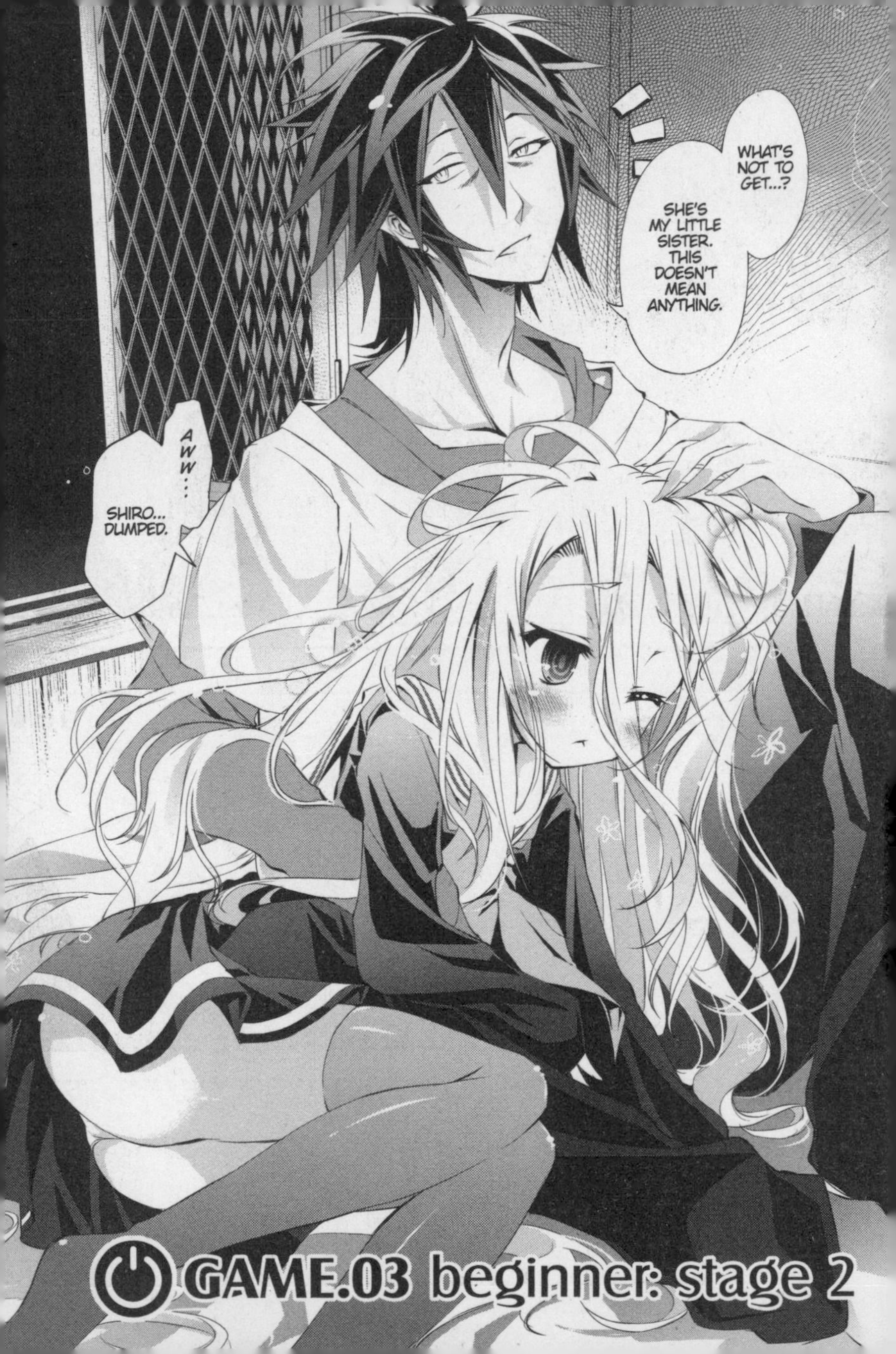
WHAT'S NOT TO GET...?
SHE'S MY LITTLE SISTER. THIS DOESN'T MEAN ANYTHING.
AWW...
SHIRO... DUMPED.

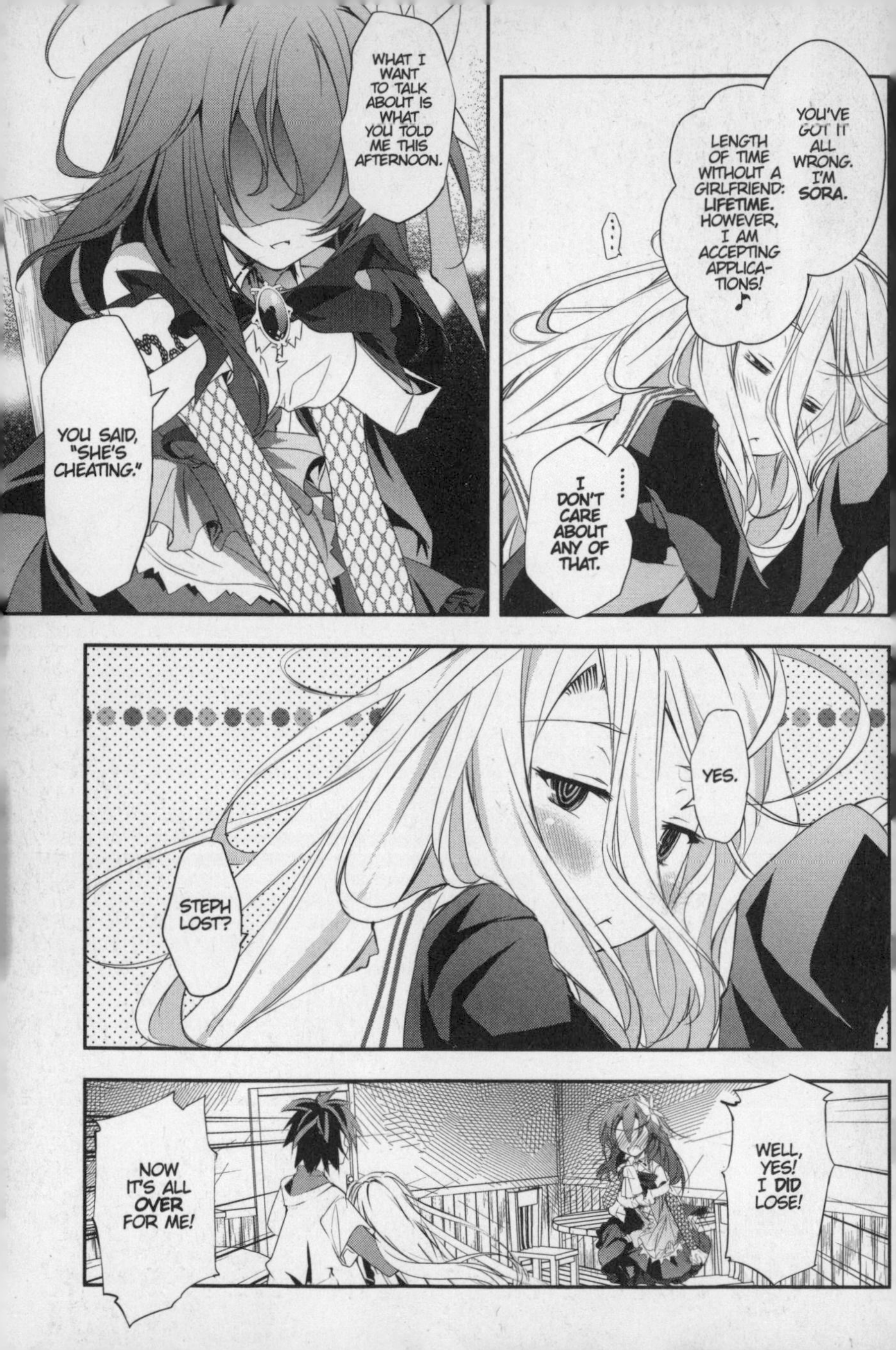
YOU'VE GOT IT ALL WRONG. I'M SORA.
LENGTH OF TIME WITHOUT A GIRLFRIEND: LIFETIME. HOWEVER, I AM ACCEPTING APPLICA-TIONS! ♪
...
...... I DON'T CARE ABOUT ANY OF THAT.
WHAT I WANT TO TALK ABOUT IS WHAT YOU TOLD ME THIS AFTERNOON.
YOU SAID, "SHE'S CHEATING."
YES.
STEPH LOST?
WELL, YES! I DID LOSE!
NOW IT'S ALL OVER FOR ME!

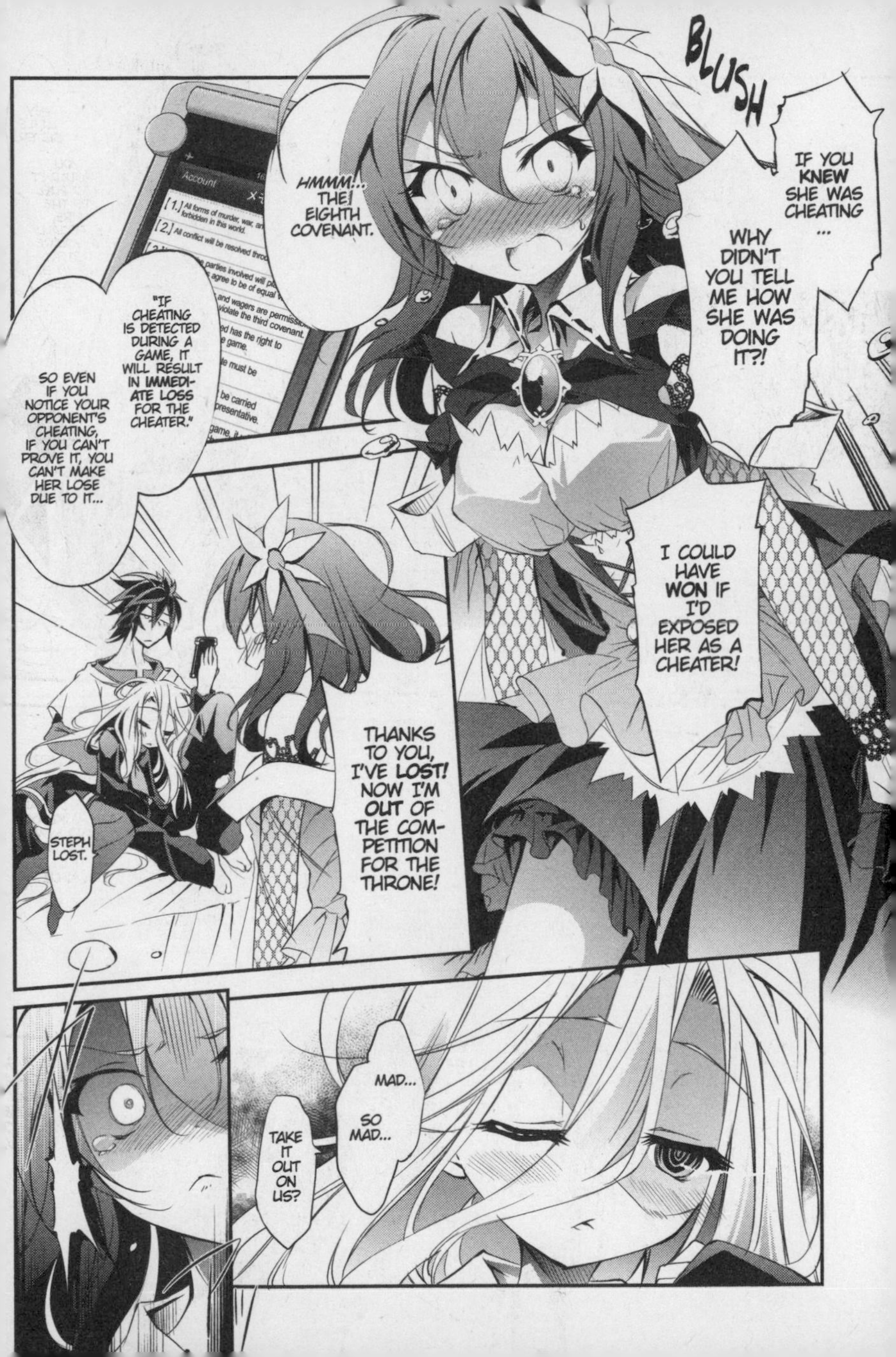
BLUSH
IF YOU KNEW SHE WAS CHEATING ...
WHY DIDN'T YOU TELL ME HOW SHE WAS DOING IT?!
HMMM... THE EIGHTH COVENANT.
Account
"IF CHEATING IS DETECTED DURING A GAME, IT WILL RESULT IN IMMEDIATE LOSS FOR THE CHEATER."
SO EVEN IF YOU NOTICE YOUR OPPONENT'S CHEATING, IF YOU CAN'T PROVE IT, YOU CAN'T MAKE HER LOSE DUE TO IT...
I COULD HAVE WON IF I'D EXPOSED HER AS A CHEATER!
THANKS TO YOU, I'VE LOST! NOW I'M OUT OF THE COMPETITION FOR THE THRONE!
STEPH LOST.
MAD...
SO MAD...
TAKE IT OUT ON US?

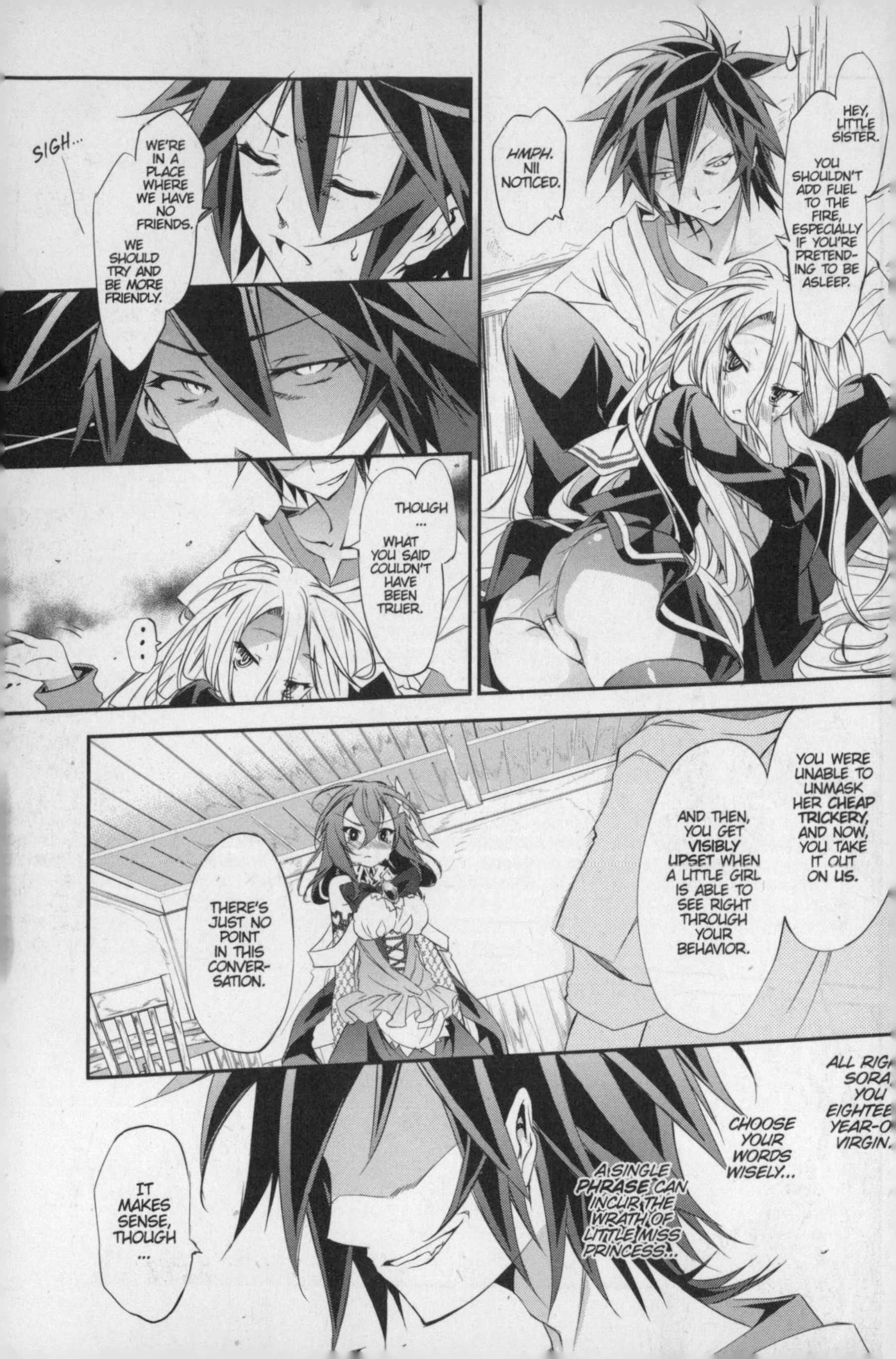
HEY, LITTLE SISTER. YOU SHOULDN'T ADD FUEL TO THE FIRE, ESPECIALLY IF YOU'RE PRETENDING TO BE ASLEEP.
HMPH. NII NOTICED.
WE'RE IN A PLACE WHERE WE HAVE NO FRIENDS. WE SHOULD TRY AND BE MORE FRIENDLY.
SIGH...
THOUGH ... WHAT YOU SAID COULDN'T HAVE BEEN TRUER.
...
YOU WERE UNABLE TO UNMASK HER CHEAP TRICKERY, AND NOW, YOU TAKE IT OUT ON US.
AND THEN, YOU GET VISIBLY UPSET WHEN A LITTLE GIRL IS ABLE TO SEE RIGHT THROUGH YOUR BEHAVIOR.
THERE'S JUST NO POINT IN THIS CONVERSATION.
ALL RIG SORA, YOU EIGHTEE YEAR-O VIRGIN.
CHOOSE YOUR WORDS WISELY...
A SINGLE PHRASE CAN INCUR THE WRATH OF LITTLE MISS PRINCESS...
IT MAKES SENSE, THOUGH ...

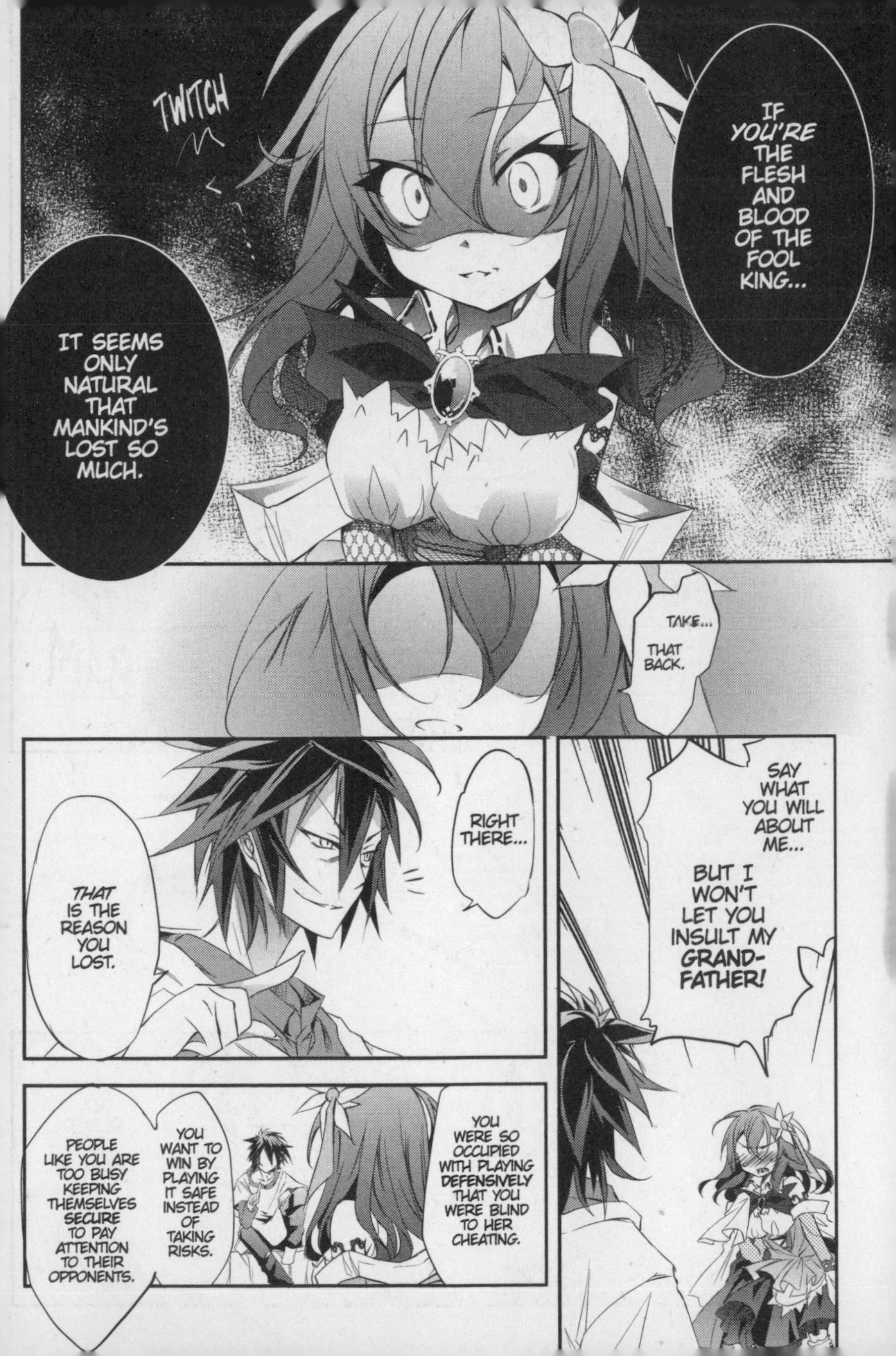
IF YOU'RE THE FLESH AND BLOOD OF THE FOOL KING...
TWITCH
IT SEEMS ONLY NATURAL THAT MANKIND'S LOST SO MUCH.
TAKE... THAT BACK.
SAY WHAT YOU WILL ABOUT ME...
BUT I WON'T LET YOU INSULT MY GRANDFATHER!
RIGHT THERE...
THAT IS THE REASON YOU LOST.
YOU WERE SO OCCUPIED WITH PLAYING DEFENSIVELY THAT YOU WERE BLIND TO HER CHEATING.
YOU WANT TO WIN BY PLAYING IT SAFE INSTEAD OF TAKING RISKS.
PEOPLE LIKE YOU ARE TOO BUSY KEEPING THEMSELVES SECURE TO PAY ATTENTION TO THEIR OPPONENTS.

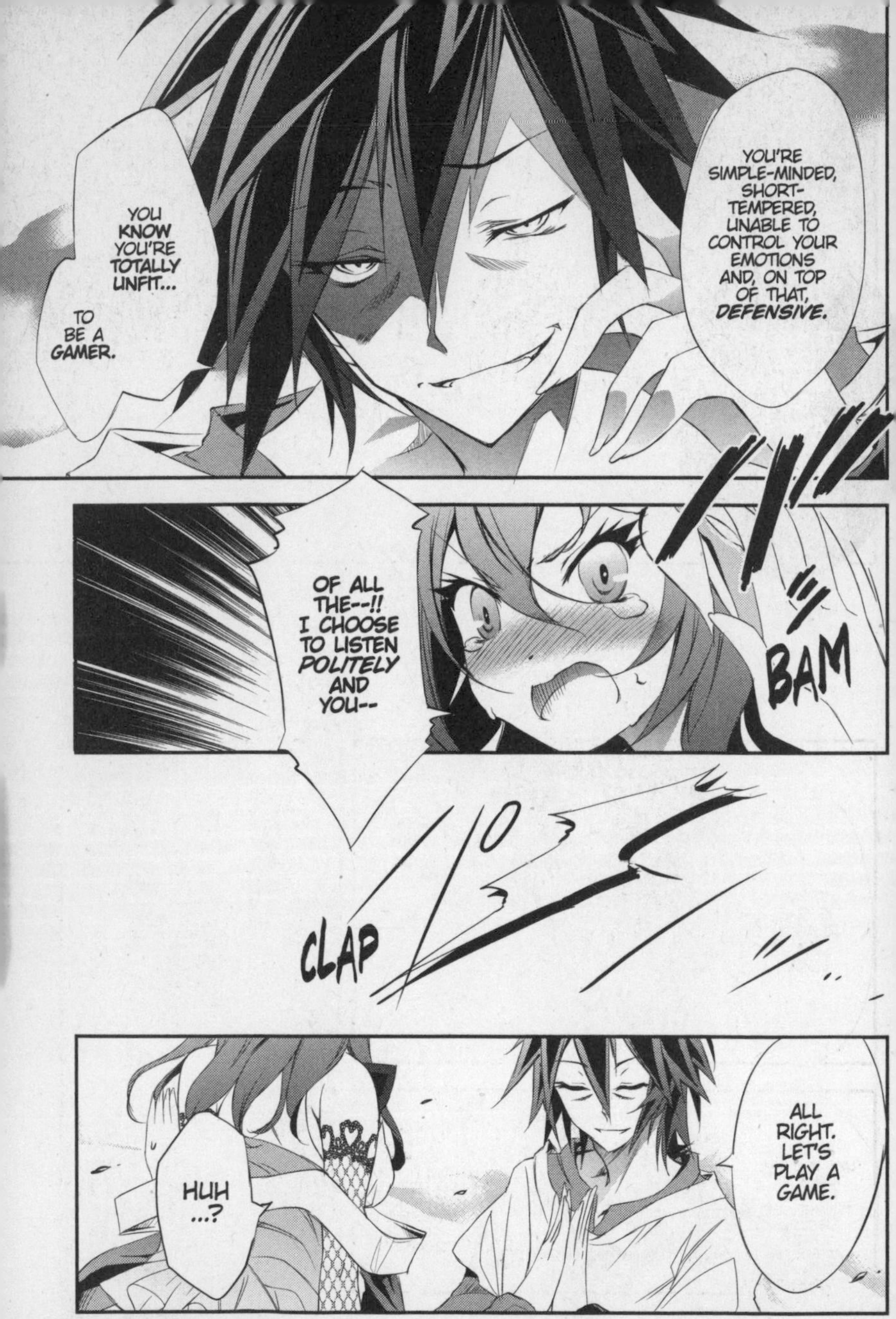
YOU'RE SIMPLE-MINDED, SHORT-TEMPERED, UNABLE TO CONTROL YOUR EMOTIONS AND, ON TOP OF THAT, *DEFENSIVE.*
YOU KNOW YOU'RE TOTALLY UNFIT...
TO BE A GAMER.
BAM
OF ALL THE--!! I CHOOSE TO LISTEN *POLITELY* AND YOU--
CLAP
ALL RIGHT. LET'S PLAY A GAME.
HUH ...?

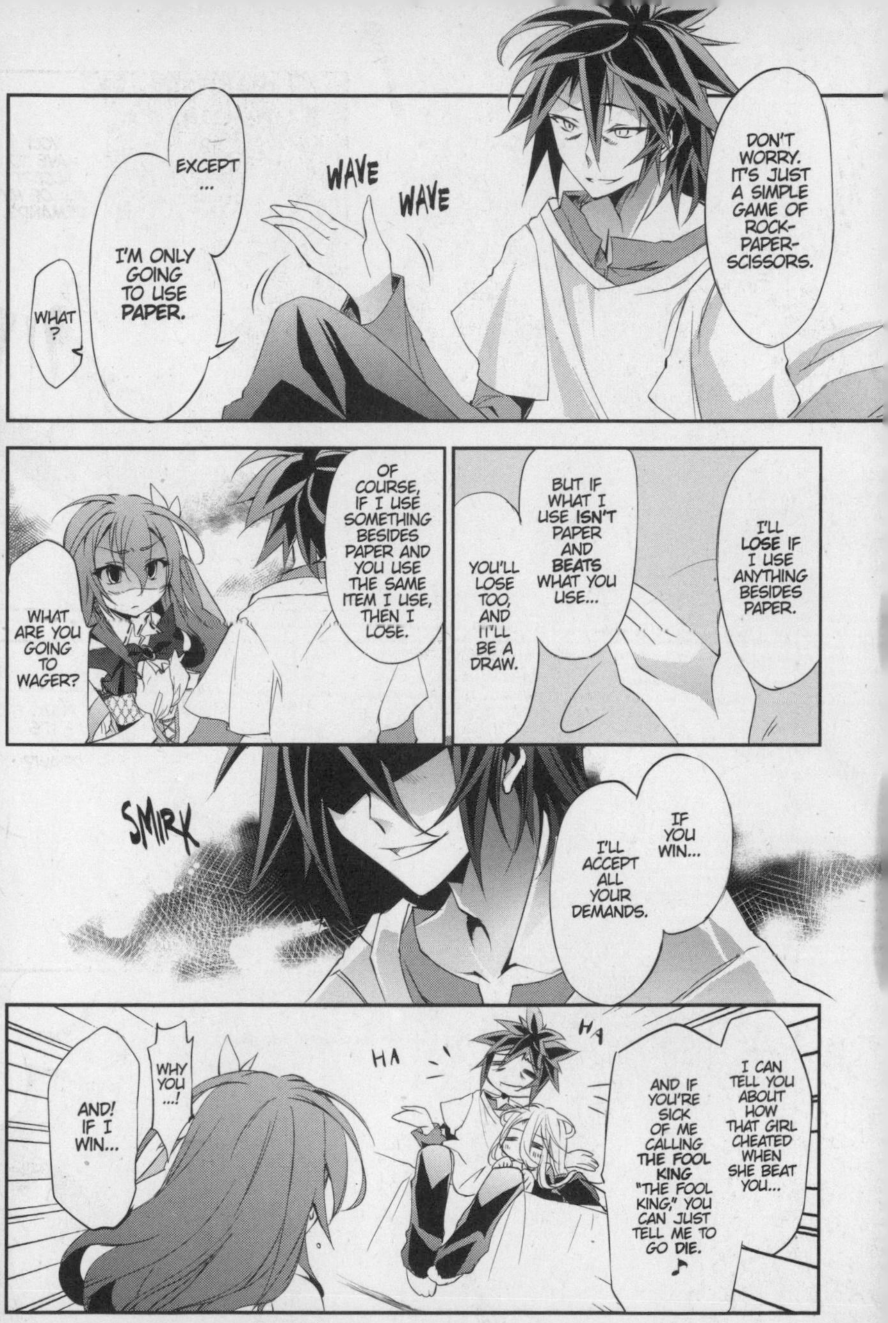
DON'T WORRY. IT'S JUST A SIMPLE GAME OF ROCK-PAPER-SCISSORS.
WAVE
WAVE
EXCEPT...
I'M ONLY GOING TO USE PAPER.
WHAT?
I'LL LOSE IF I USE ANYTHING BESIDES PAPER.
BUT IF WHAT I USE ISN'T PAPER AND BEATS WHAT YOU USE...
YOU'LL LOSE TOO, AND IT'LL BE A DRAW.
OF COURSE, IF I USE SOMETHING BESIDES PAPER AND YOU USE THE SAME ITEM I USE, THEN I LOSE.
WHAT ARE YOU GOING TO WAGER?
IF YOU WIN...
I'LL ACCEPT ALL YOUR DEMANDS.
SMIRK
I CAN TELL YOU ABOUT HOW THAT GIRL CHEATED WHEN SHE BEAT YOU...
AND IF YOU'RE SICK OF ME CALLING THE FOOL KING "THE FOOL KING," YOU CAN JUST TELL ME TO GO DIE. ♪
HA
HA
WHY YOU...!
AND! IF I WIN...

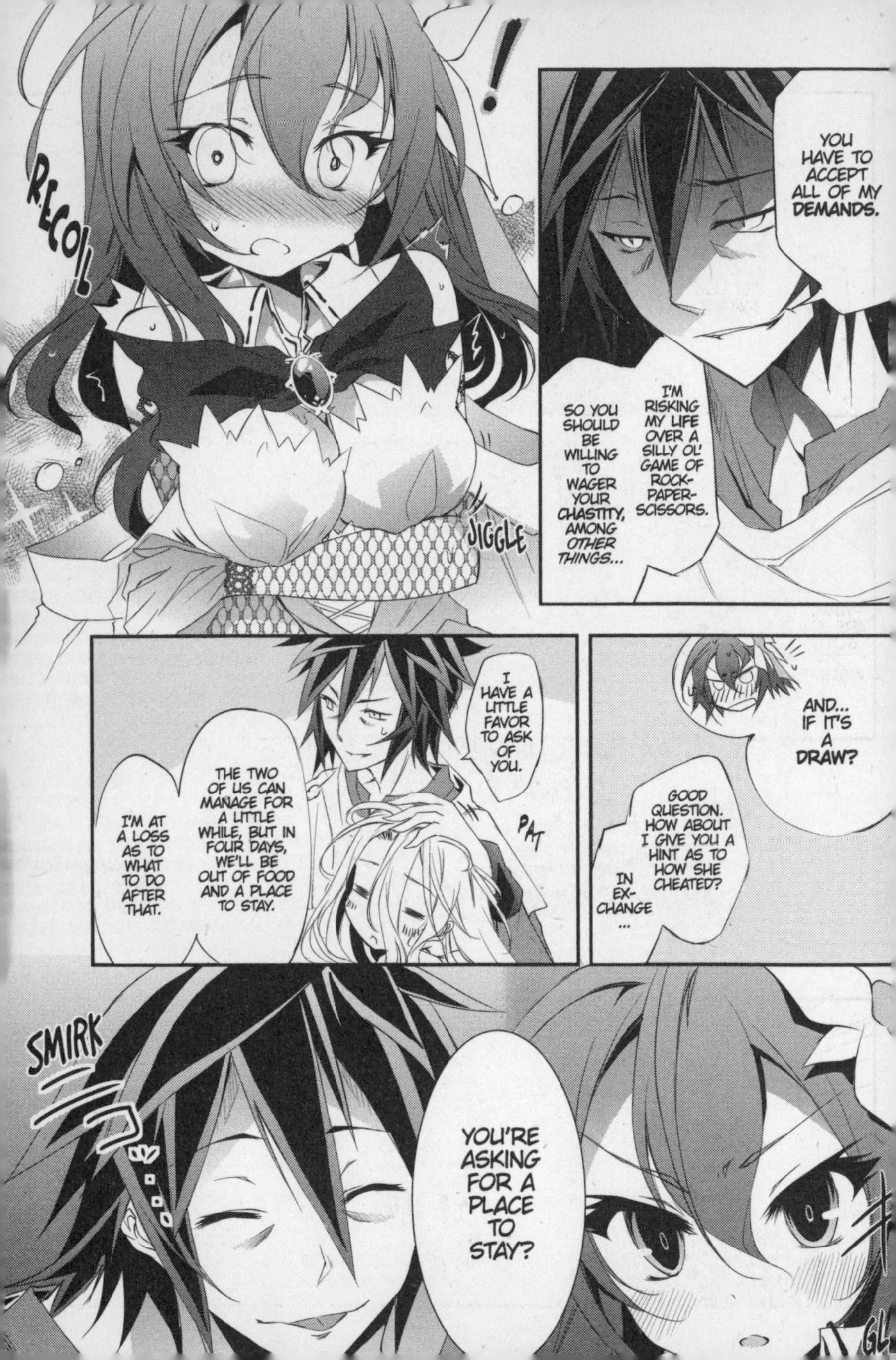
YOU HAVE TO ACCEPT ALL OF MY DEMANDS.
I'M RISKING MY LIFE OVER A SILLY OL' GAME OF ROCK-PAPER-SCISSORS.
SO YOU SHOULD BE WILLING TO WAGER YOUR CHASTITY, AMONG OTHER THINGS...
!
RECOIL
JIGGLE
AND... IF IT'S A DRAW?
GOOD QUESTION. HOW ABOUT I GIVE YOU A HINT AS TO HOW SHE CHEATED?
IN EX-CHANGE...
I HAVE A LITTLE FAVOR TO ASK OF YOU.
PAT
THE TWO OF US CAN MANAGE FOR A LITTLE WHILE, BUT IN FOUR DAYS, WE'LL BE OUT OF FOOD AND A PLACE TO STAY.
I'M AT A LOSS AS TO WHAT TO DO AFTER THAT.
YOU'RE ASKING FOR A PLACE TO STAY?
SMIRK

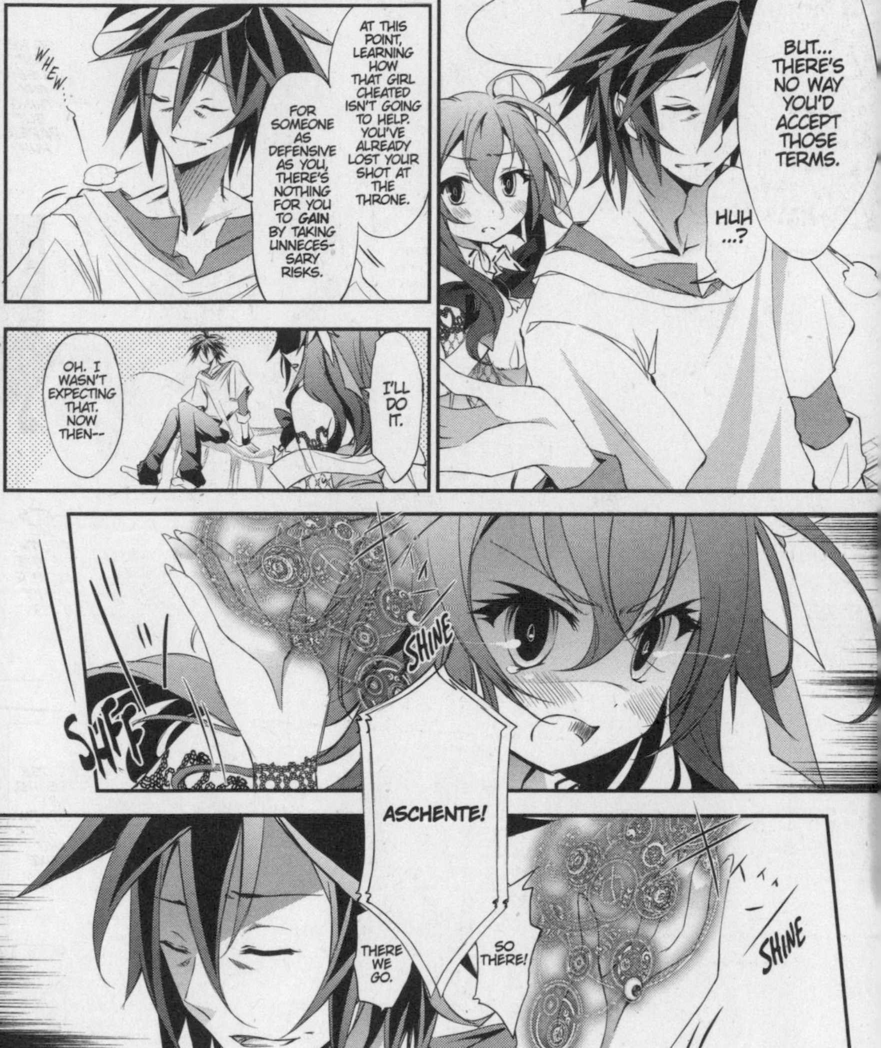
BUT... THERE'S NO WAY YOU'D ACCEPT THOSE TERMS.
HUH ...?
AT THIS POINT, LEARNING HOW THAT GIRL CHEATED ISN'T GOING TO HELP. YOU'VE ALREADY LOST YOUR SHOT AT THE THRONE.
FOR SOMEONE AS DEFENSIVE AS YOU, THERE'S NOTHING FOR YOU TO GAIN BY TAKING UNNECESSARY RISKS.
WHEW...
I'LL DO IT.
OH. I WASN'T EXPECTING THAT. NOW THEN--
SHINE
SHFF
ASCHENTE!
SHINE
SO THERE!
THERE WE GO.

"ASCHENTE.
A DECLARATION OF INTENTION WHEN MAKING A WAGER THAT ABSOLUTELY MUST BE UPHELD, PER THE TEN COVENANTS, BY SWEARING TO GOD."

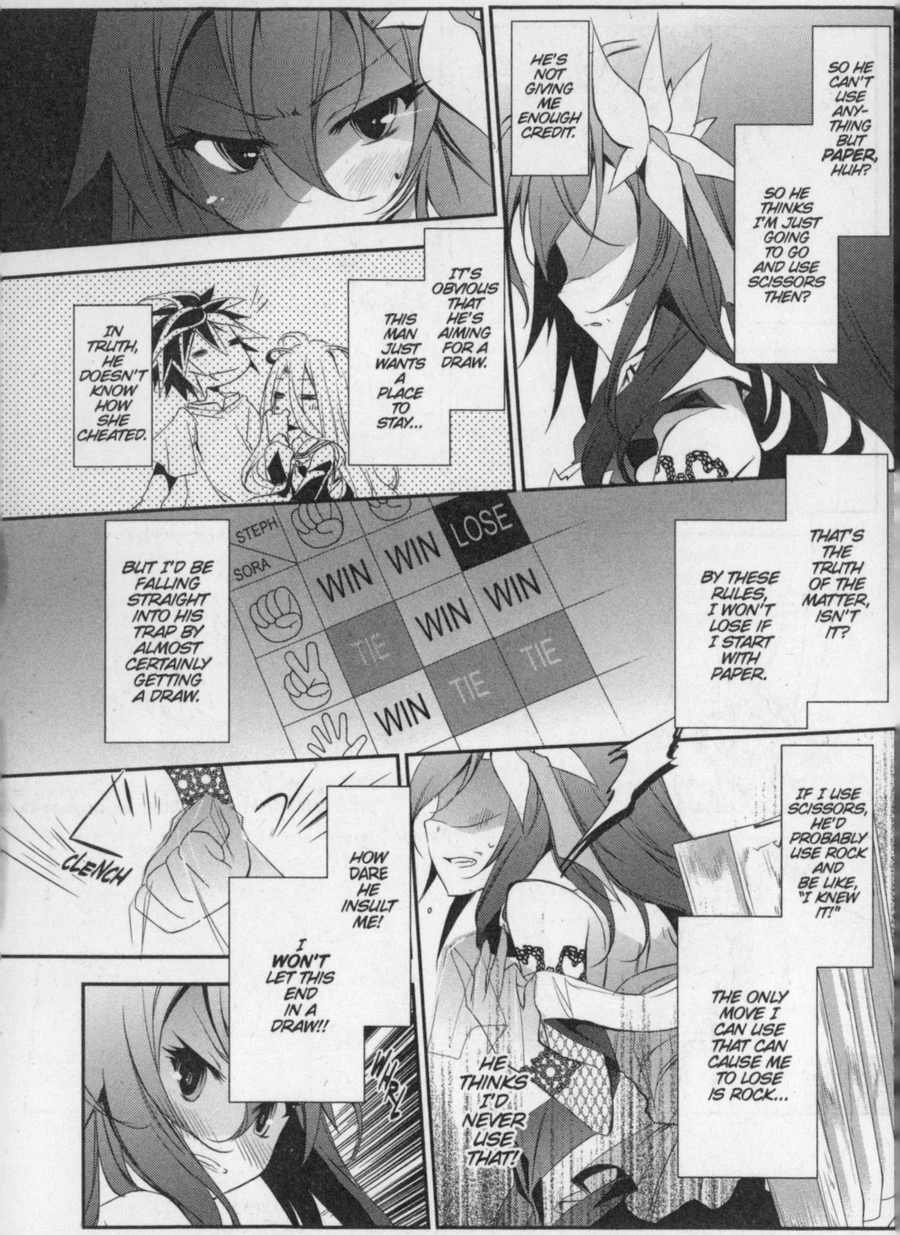
SO HE CAN'T USE ANYTHING BUT PAPER, HUH?
SO HE THINKS I'M JUST GOING TO GO AND USE SCISSORS THEN?
HE'S NOT GIVING ME ENOUGH CREDIT.
IT'S OBVIOUS THAT HE'S AIMING FOR A DRAW.
THIS MAN JUST WANTS A PLACE TO STAY...
IN TRUTH, HE DOESN'T KNOW HOW SHE CHEATED.
THAT'S THE TRUTH OF THE MATTER, ISN'T IT?
BY THESE RULES, I WON'T LOSE IF I START WITH PAPER.
STEPH
SORA
WIN WIN LOSE
WIN WIN WIN
TIE WIN
TIE TIE
WIN
BUT I'D BE FALLING STRAIGHT INTO HIS TRAP BY ALMOST CERTAINLY GETTING A DRAW.
IF I USE SCISSORS, HE'D PROBABLY USE ROCK AND BE LIKE, "I KNEW IT!"
THE ONLY MOVE I CAN USE THAT CAN CAUSE ME TO LOSE IS ROCK...
HE THINKS I'D NEVER USE THAT!
HOW DARE HE INSULT ME!
CLENCH
I WON'T LET THIS END IN A DRAW!!
WHRL

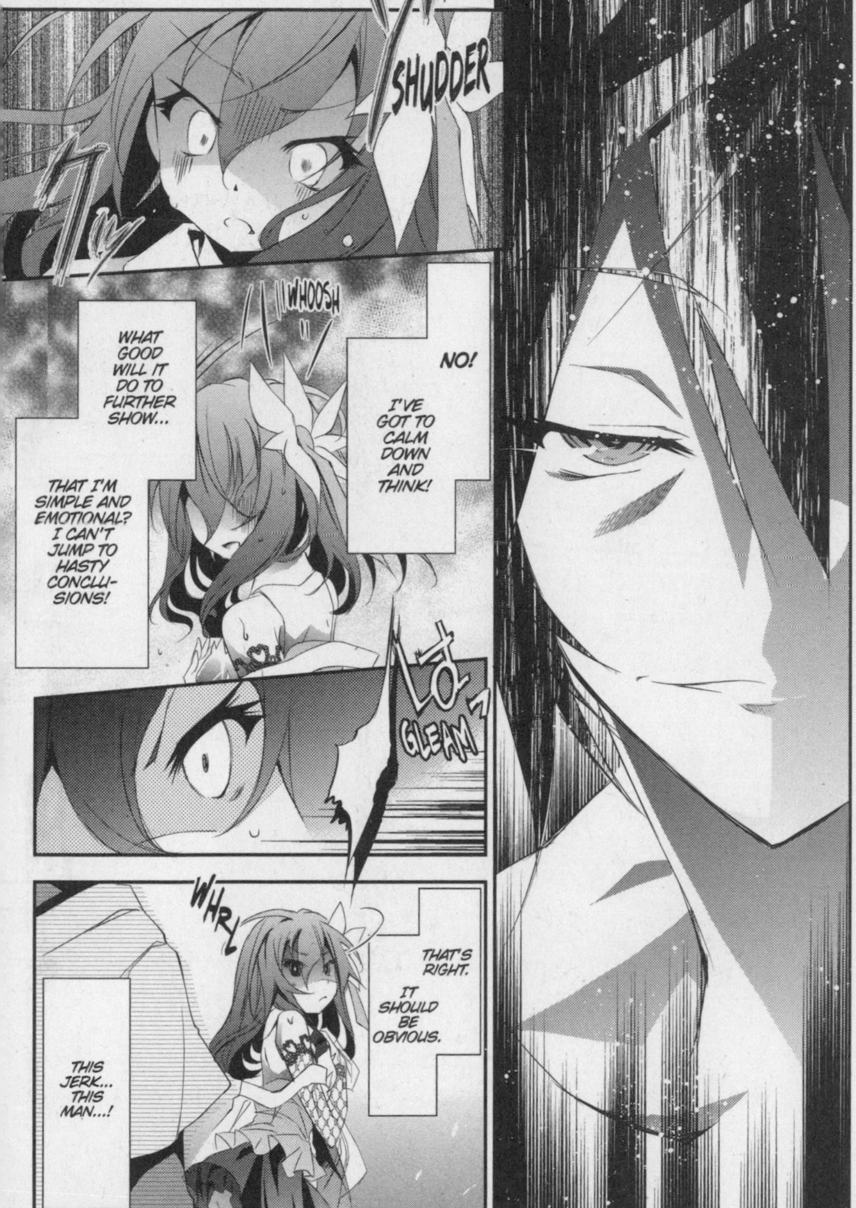
SHUDDER
WHOOSH
NO!
I'VE GOT TO CALM DOWN AND THINK!
WHAT GOOD WILL IT DO TO FURTHER SHOW...
THAT I'M SIMPLE AND EMOTIONAL? I CAN'T JUMP TO HASTY CONCLUSIONS!
GLEAM
WHRL
THAT'S RIGHT.
IT SHOULD BE OBVIOUS.
THIS JERK... THIS MAN...!

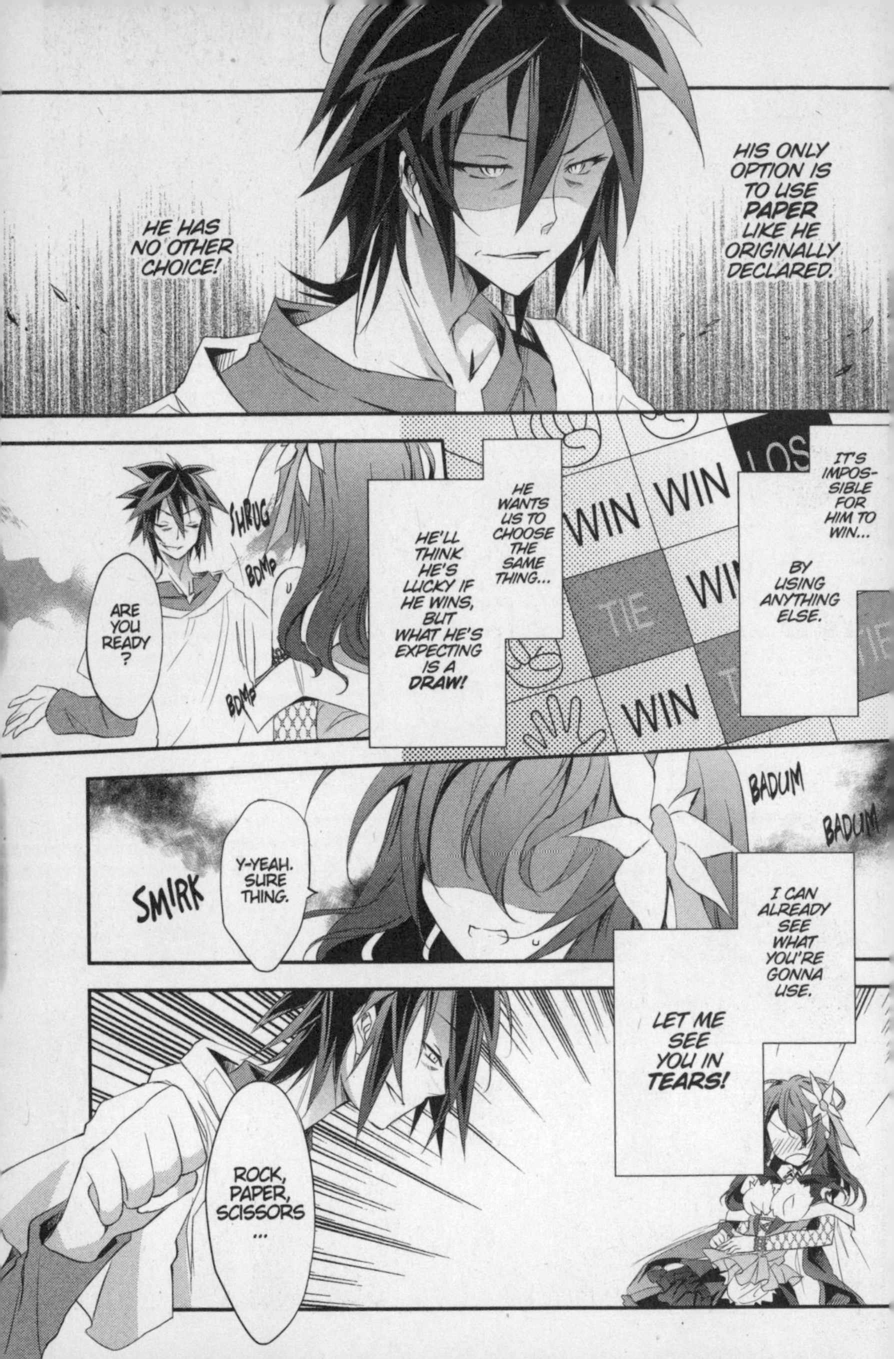
HIS ONLY OPTION IS TO USE PAPER LIKE HE ORIGINALLY DECLARED.
HE HAS NO OTHER CHOICE!
IT'S IMPOSSIBLE FOR HIM TO WIN...
BY USING ANYTHING ELSE.
WIN
WIN
TIE
WIN
HE WANTS US TO CHOOSE THE SAME THING...
HE'LL THINK HE'S LUCKY IF HE WINS, BUT WHAT HE'S EXPECTING IS A DRAW!
SHRUG
BDMP
BDMP
ARE YOU READY?
BADUM
BADUM
I CAN ALREADY SEE WHAT YOU'RE GONNA USE.
Y-YEAH. SURE THING.
SMIRK
LET ME SEE YOU IN TEARS!
ROCK, PAPER, SCISSORS...

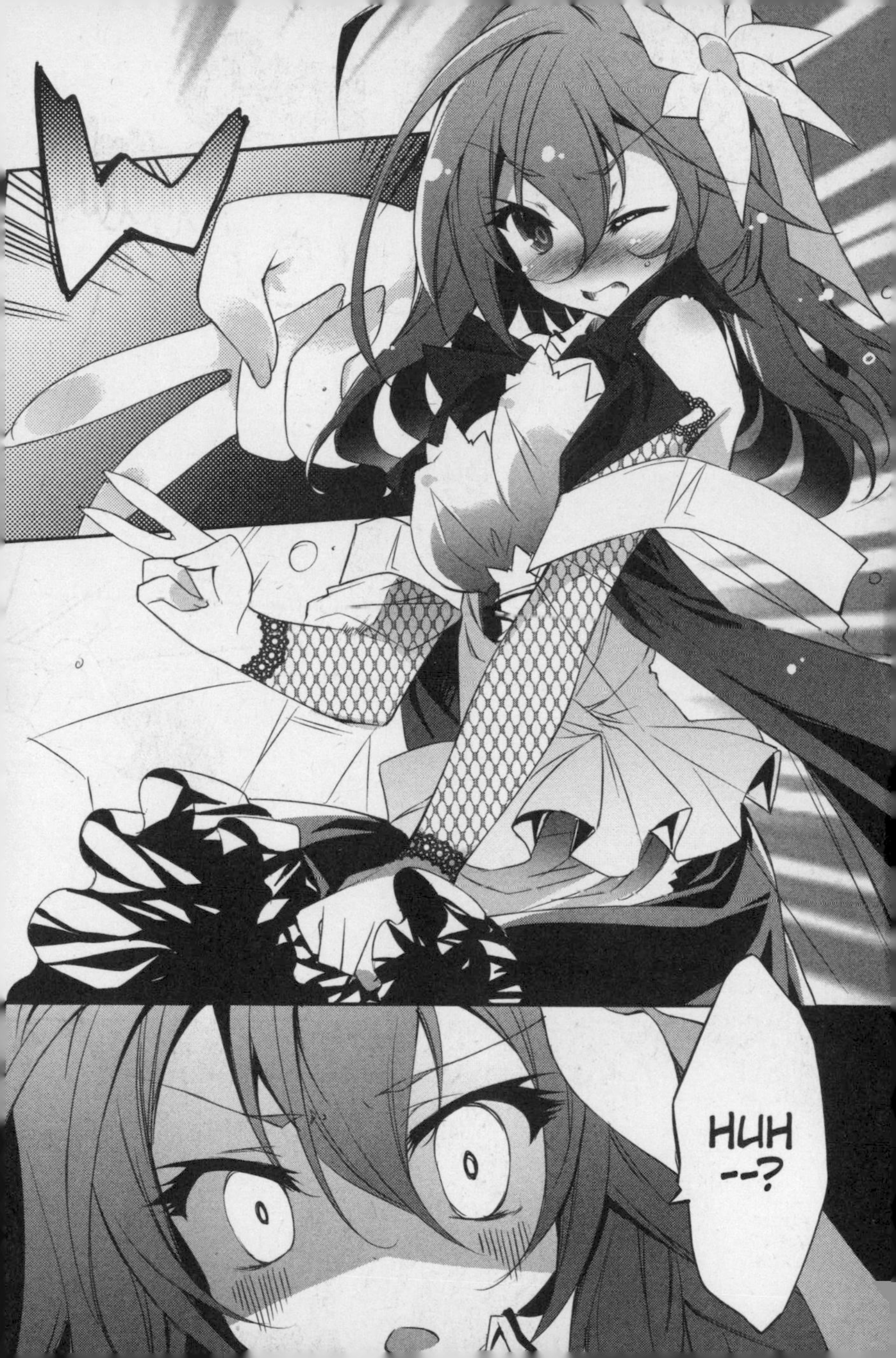
HUH --?

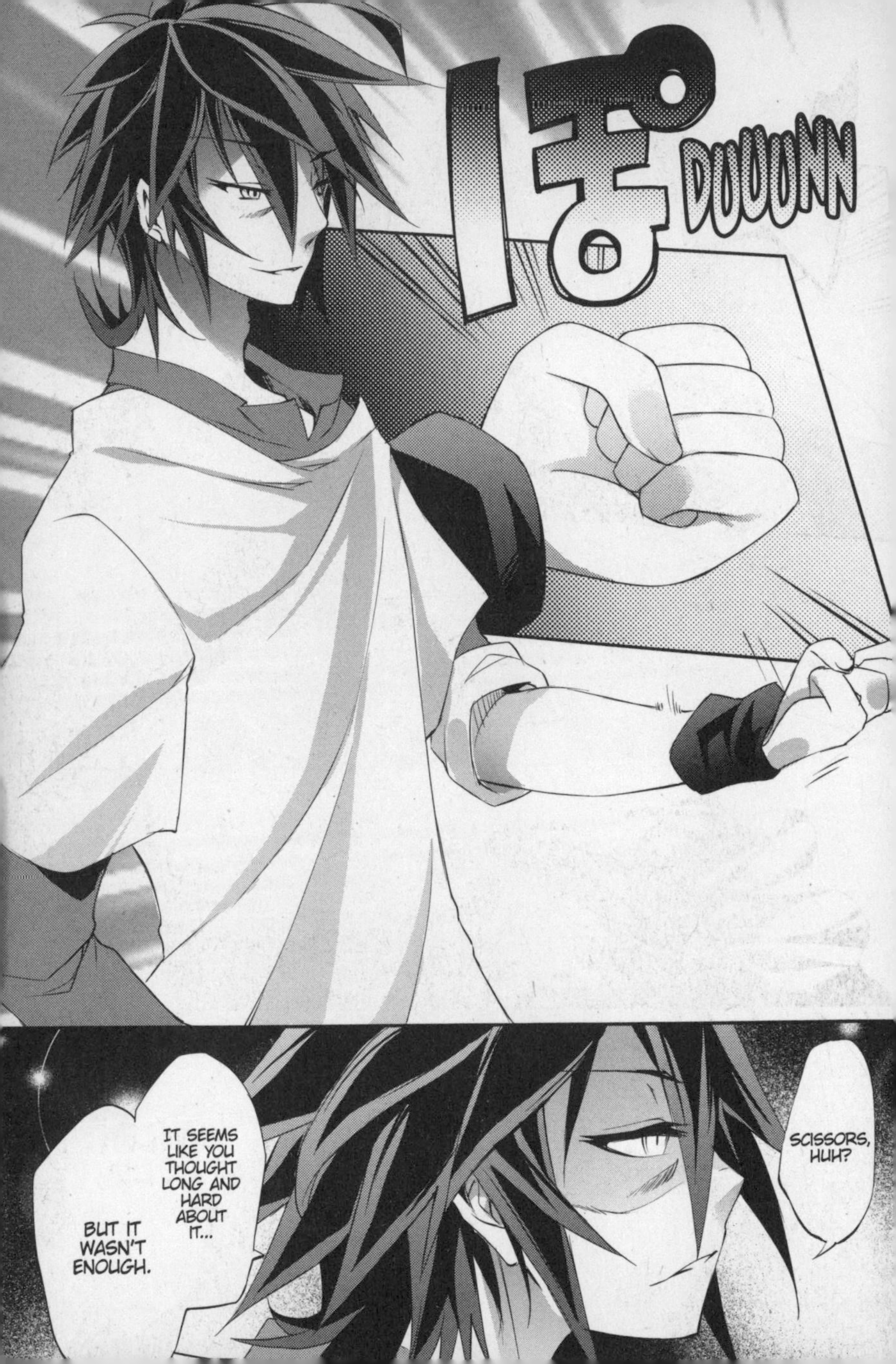
ぽ
DUUUNN
SCISSORS, HUH?
IT SEEMS LIKE YOU THOUGHT LONG AND HARD ABOUT IT...
BUT IT WASN'T ENOUGH.

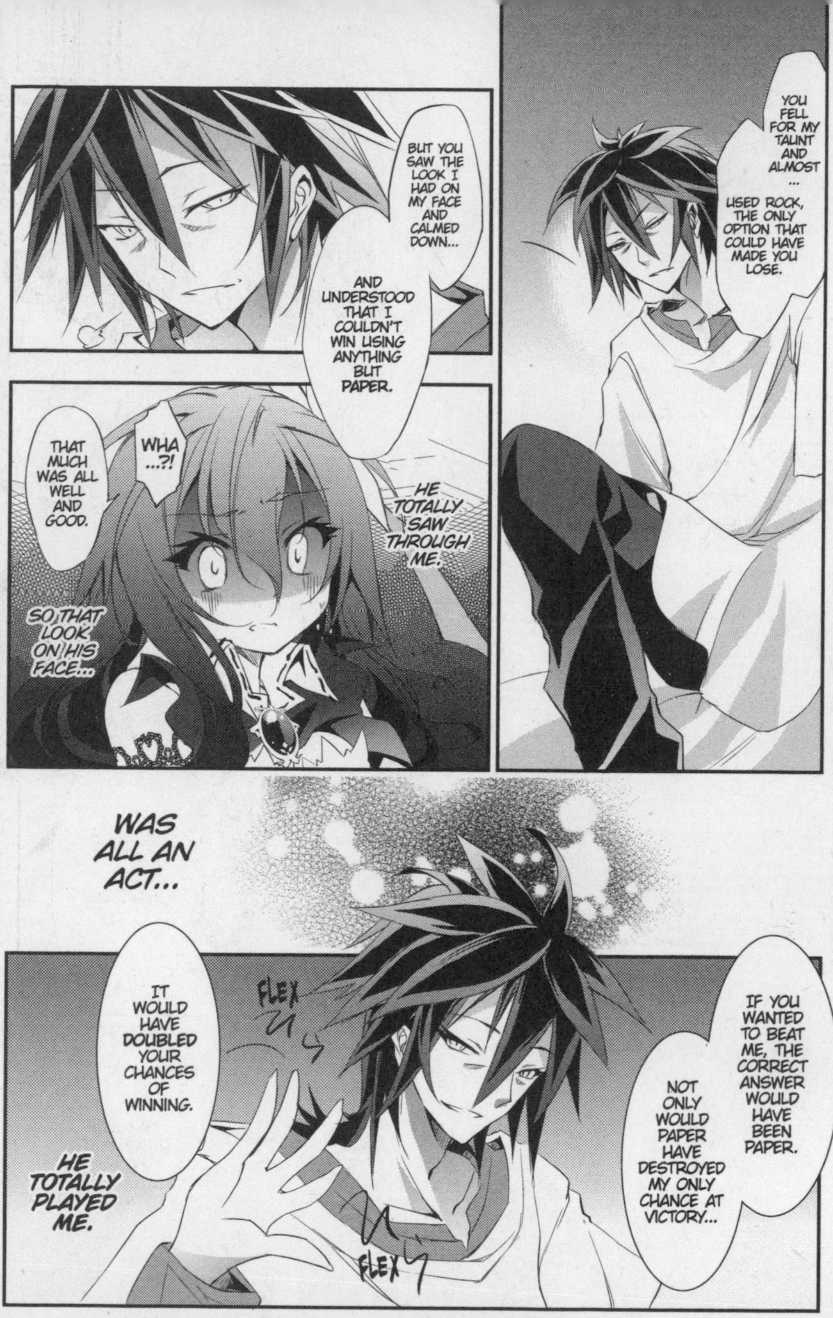
YOU FELL FOR MY TAUNT AND ALMOST ...
USED ROCK, THE ONLY OPTION THAT COULD HAVE MADE YOU LOSE.
BUT YOU SAW THE LOOK I HAD ON MY FACE AND CALMED DOWN...
AND UNDERSTOOD THAT I COULDN'T WIN USING ANYTHING BUT PAPER.
WHA ...?!
THAT MUCH WAS ALL WELL AND GOOD.
HE TOTALLY SAW THROUGH ME.
SO THAT LOOK ON HIS FACE...
WAS ALL AN ACT...
IF YOU WANTED TO BEAT ME, THE CORRECT ANSWER WOULD HAVE BEEN PAPER.
NOT ONLY WOULD PAPER HAVE DESTROYED MY ONLY CHANCE AT VICTORY...
FLEX
IT WOULD HAVE DOUBLED YOUR CHANCES OF WINNING.
HE TOTALLY PLAYED ME.
FLEX

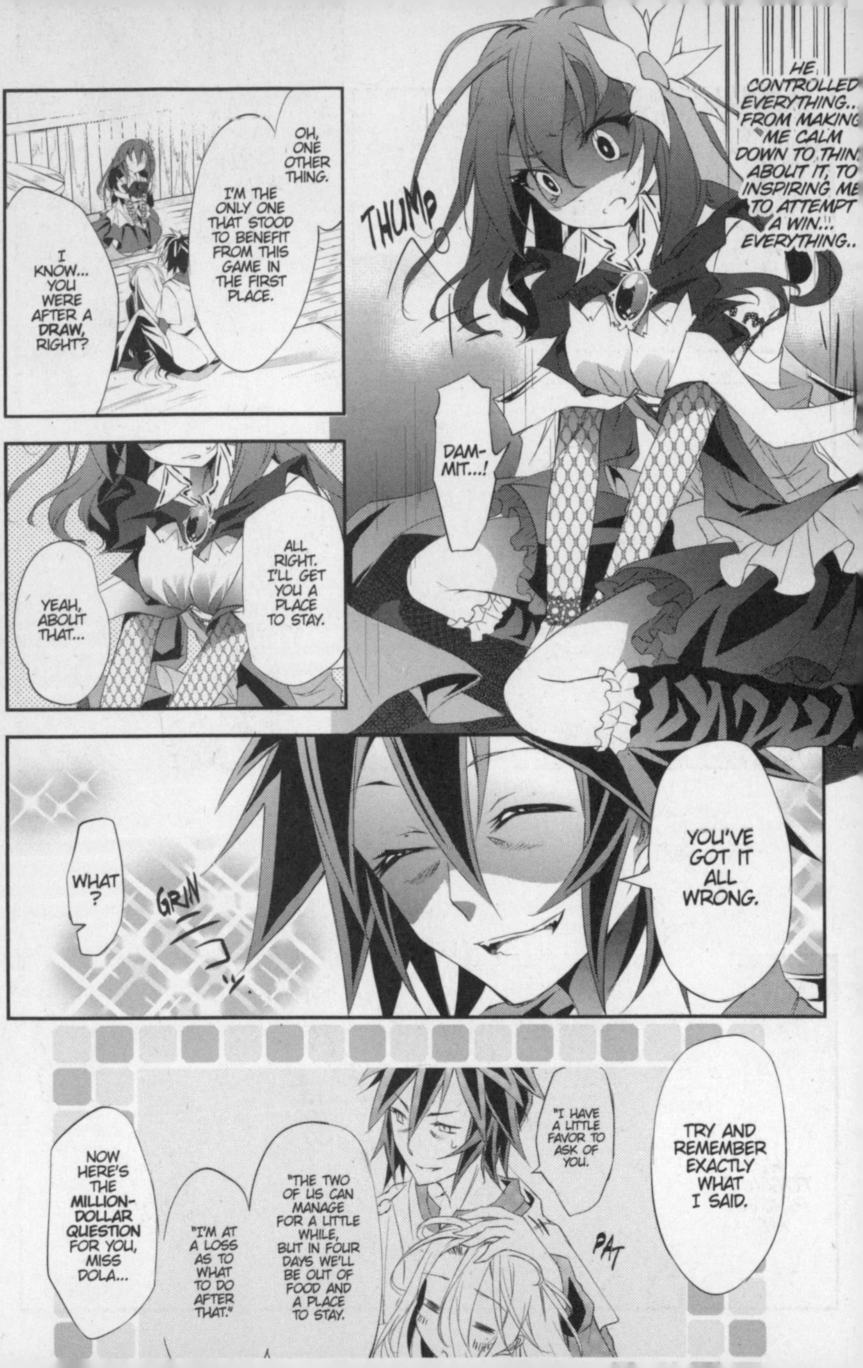
OH, ONE OTHER THING.
I'M THE ONLY ONE THAT STOOD TO BENEFIT FROM THIS GAME IN THE FIRST PLACE.
I KNOW... YOU WERE AFTER A DRAW, RIGHT?
HE CONTROLLED EVERYTHING... FROM MAKING ME CALM DOWN TO THINK ABOUT IT, TO INSPIRING ME TO ATTEMPT A WIN... EVERYTHING...
THUMP
DAM-MIT...!
ALL RIGHT. I'LL GET YOU A PLACE TO STAY.
YEAH, ABOUT THAT...
YOU'VE GOT IT ALL WRONG.
GRIN
WHAT?
TRY AND REMEMBER EXACTLY WHAT I SAID.
PAT
"I HAVE A LITTLE FAVOR TO ASK OF YOU.
"THE TWO OF US CAN MANAGE FOR A LITTLE WHILE, BUT IN FOUR DAYS WE'LL BE OUT OF FOOD AND A PLACE TO STAY.
"I'M AT A LOSS AS TO WHAT TO DO AFTER THAT."
NOW HERE'S THE MILLION-DOLLAR QUESTION FOR YOU, MISS DOLA...

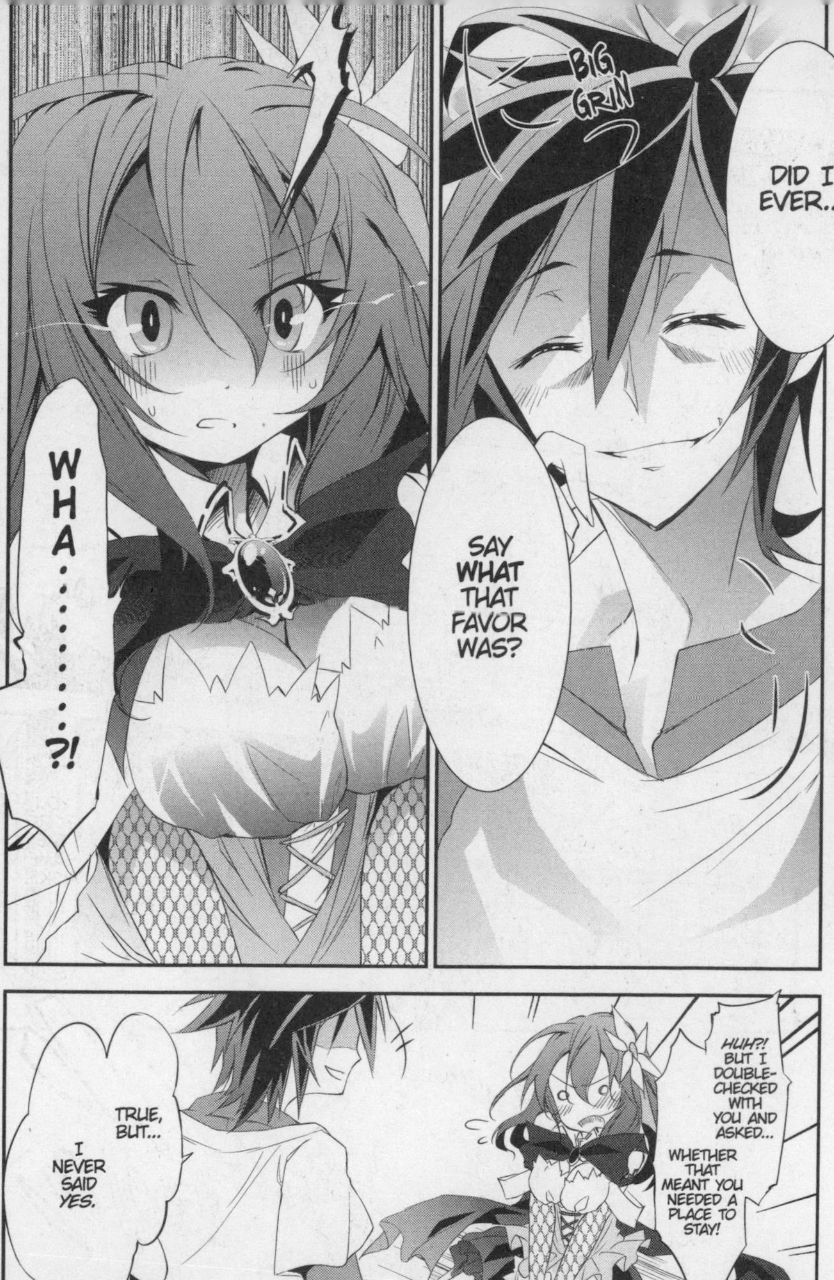
BIG GRIN
DID I EVER...
SAY WHAT THAT FAVOR WAS?
WHA.........?!
HUH?! BUT I DOUBLE-CHECKED WITH YOU AND ASKED...
WHETHER THAT MEANT YOU NEEDED A PLACE TO STAY!
TRUE, BUT...
I NEVER SAID YES.

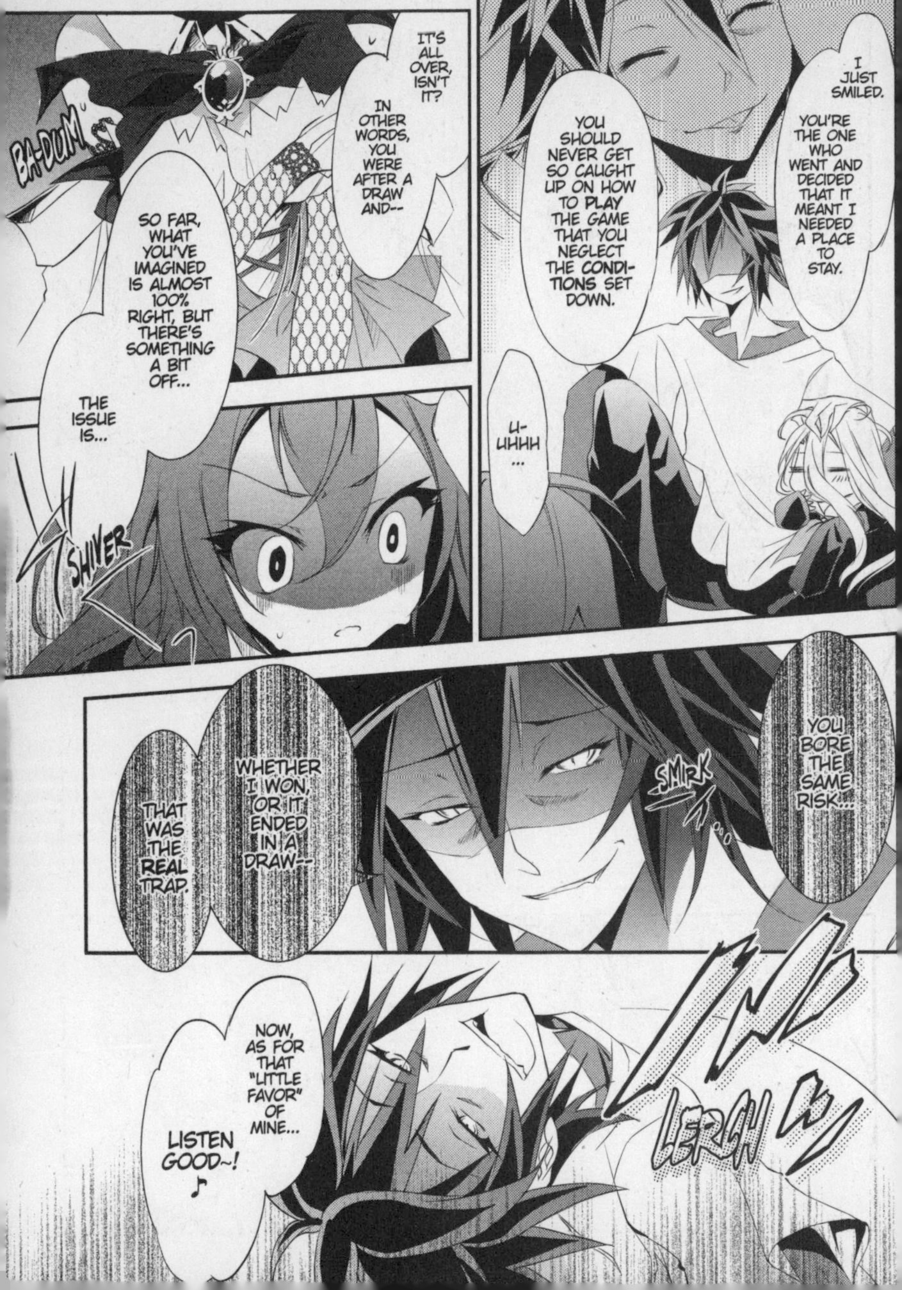
I JUST SMILED.
YOU'RE THE ONE WHO WENT AND DECIDED THAT IT MEANT I NEEDED A PLACE TO STAY.
YOU SHOULD NEVER GET SO CAUGHT UP ON HOW TO PLAY THE GAME THAT YOU NEGLECT THE CONDITIONS SET DOWN.
U-UHHH...
IT'S ALL OVER, ISN'T IT?
IN OTHER WORDS, YOU WERE AFTER A DRAW AND--
BA-DUM
SO FAR, WHAT YOU'VE IMAGINED IS ALMOST 100% RIGHT, BUT THERE'S SOMETHING A BIT OFF...
THE ISSUE IS...
SHIVER
YOU BORE THE SAME RISK...
SMIRK
WHETHER I WON, OR IT ENDED IN A DRAW--
THAT WAS THE REAL TRAP.
LERCH
NOW, AS FOR THAT "LITTLE FAVOR" OF MINE...
LISTEN GOOD~! ♪

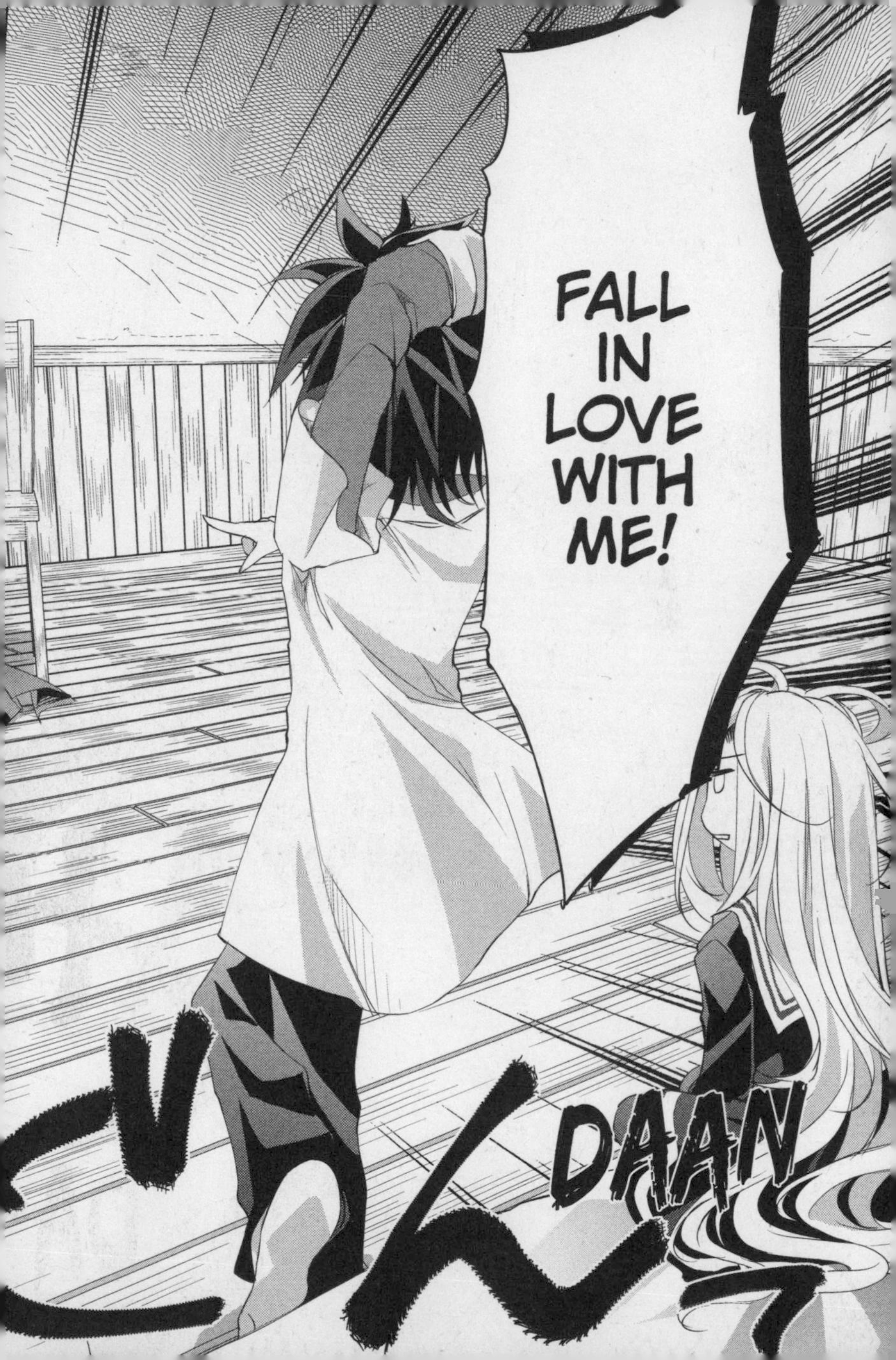
FALL IN LOVE WITH ME!
DAAN

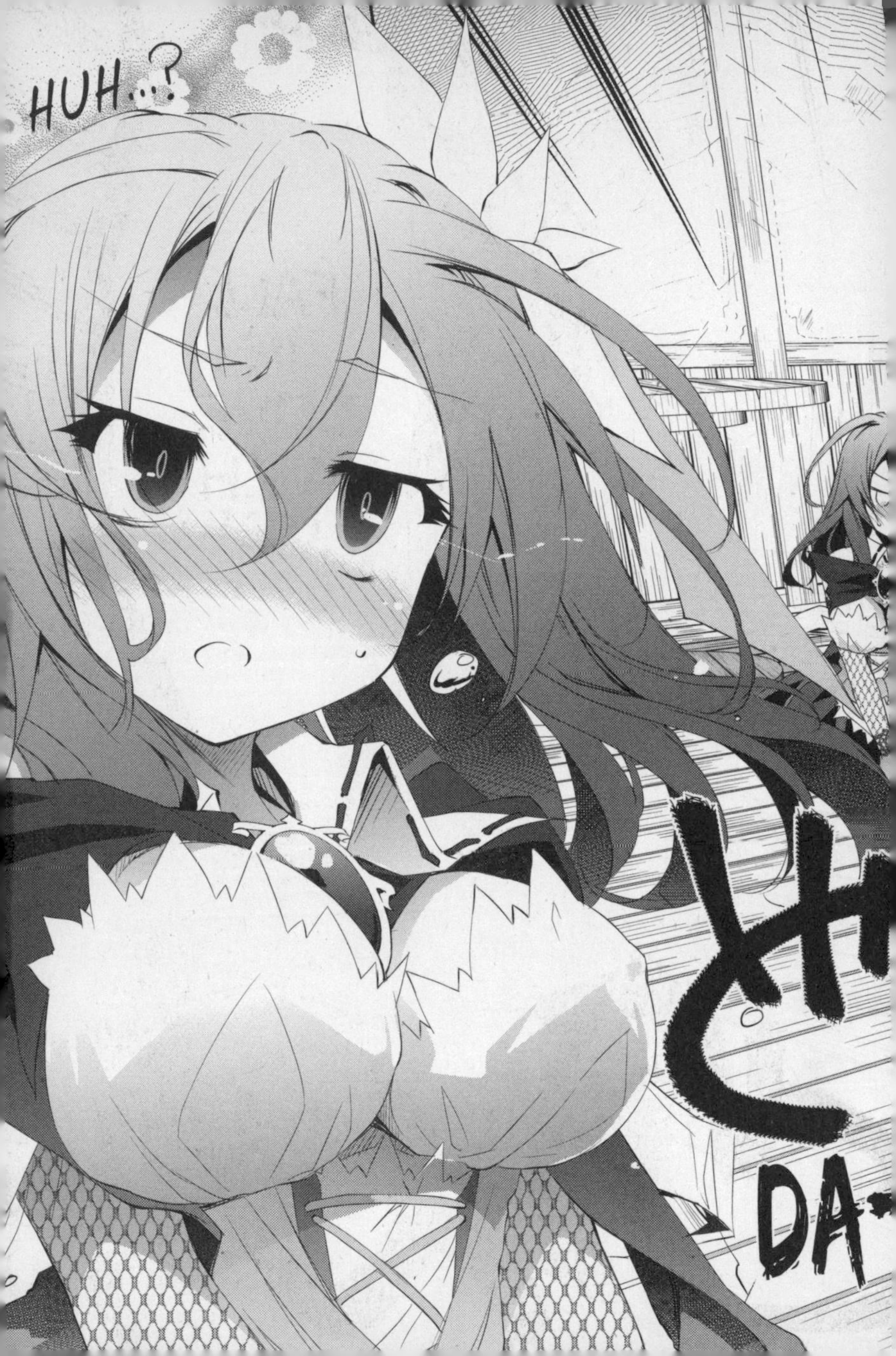
HUH...?
DA

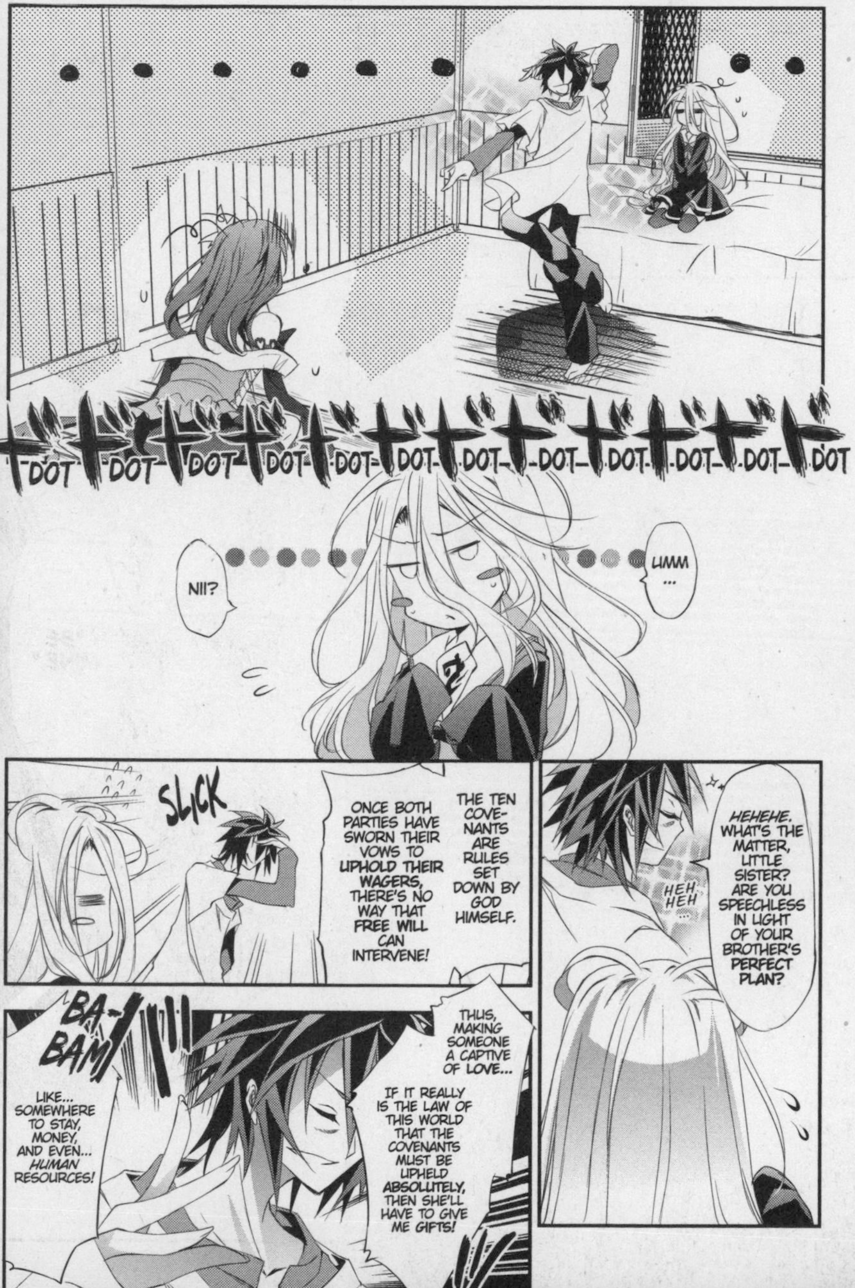
DOT-DOT-DOT-DOT-DOT-DOT-DOT-DOT-DOT-DOT-DOT-DOT
UMM ...
NII?
HEHEHE. WHAT'S THE MATTER, LITTLE SISTER? ARE YOU SPEECHLESS IN LIGHT OF YOUR BROTHER'S PERFECT PLAN?
HEH HEH ...
THE TEN COVENANTS ARE RULES SET DOWN BY GOD HIMSELF.
ONCE BOTH PARTIES HAVE SWORN THEIR VOWS TO UPHOLD THEIR WAGERS, THERE'S NO WAY THAT FREE WILL CAN INTERVENE!
SLICK
THUS, MAKING SOMEONE A CAPTIVE OF LOVE...
IF IT REALLY IS THE LAW OF THIS WORLD THAT THE COVENANTS MUST BE UPHELD ABSOLUTELY, THEN SHE'LL HAVE TO GIVE ME GIFTS!
BA-BAM
LIKE... SOMEWHERE TO STAY, MONEY, AND EVEN... *HUMAN RESOURCES!*

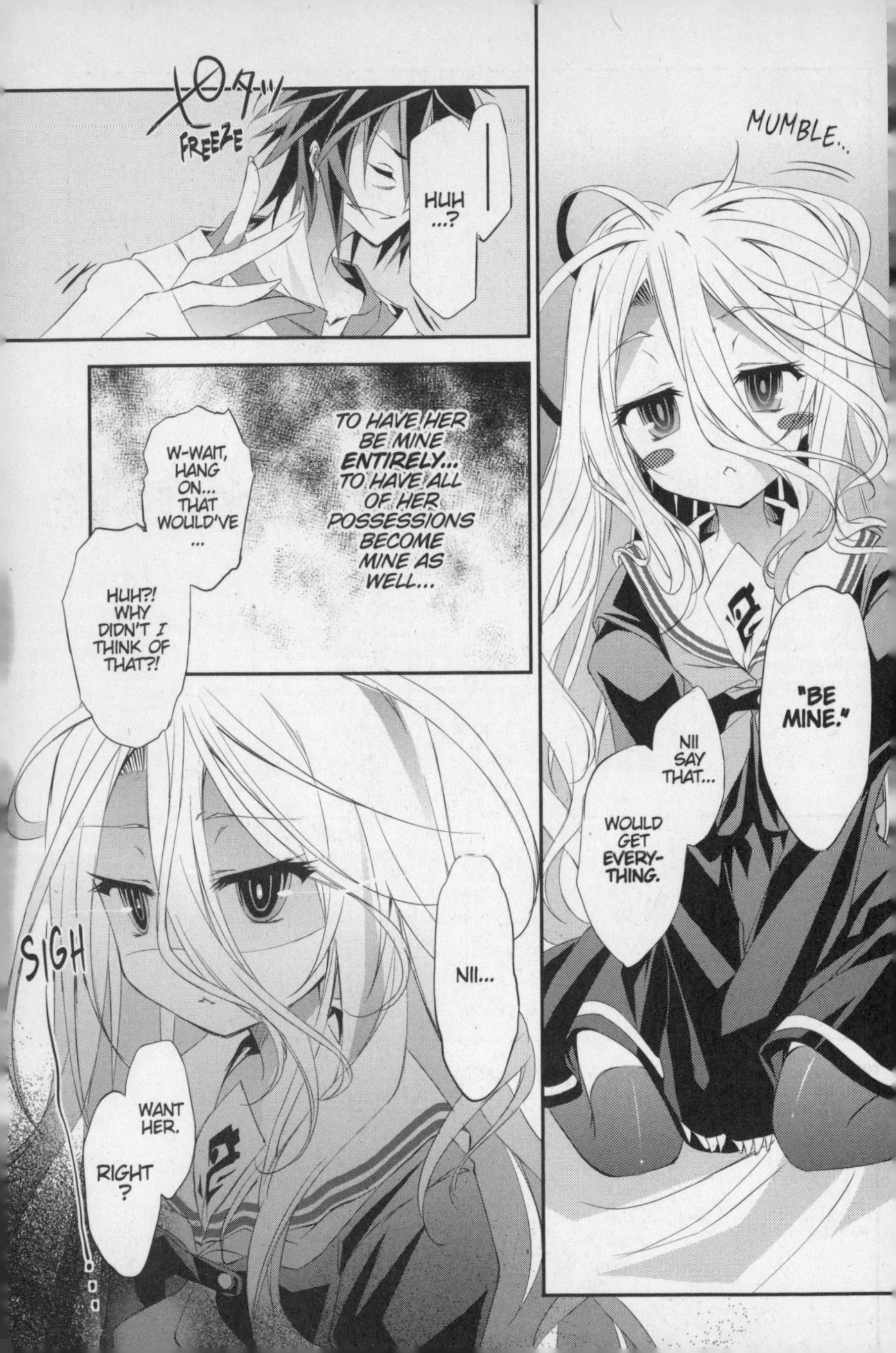
MUMBLE...
"BE MINE."
NII SAY THAT...
WOULD GET EVERY-THING.
HUH ...?
FREEZE
TO HAVE HER BE MINE ENTIRELY... TO HAVE ALL OF HER POSSESSIONS BECOME MINE AS WELL...
W-WAIT, HANG ON... THAT WOULD'VE ...
HUH?! WHY DIDN'T I THINK OF THAT?!
NII...
SIGH
WANT HER.
RIGHT ?

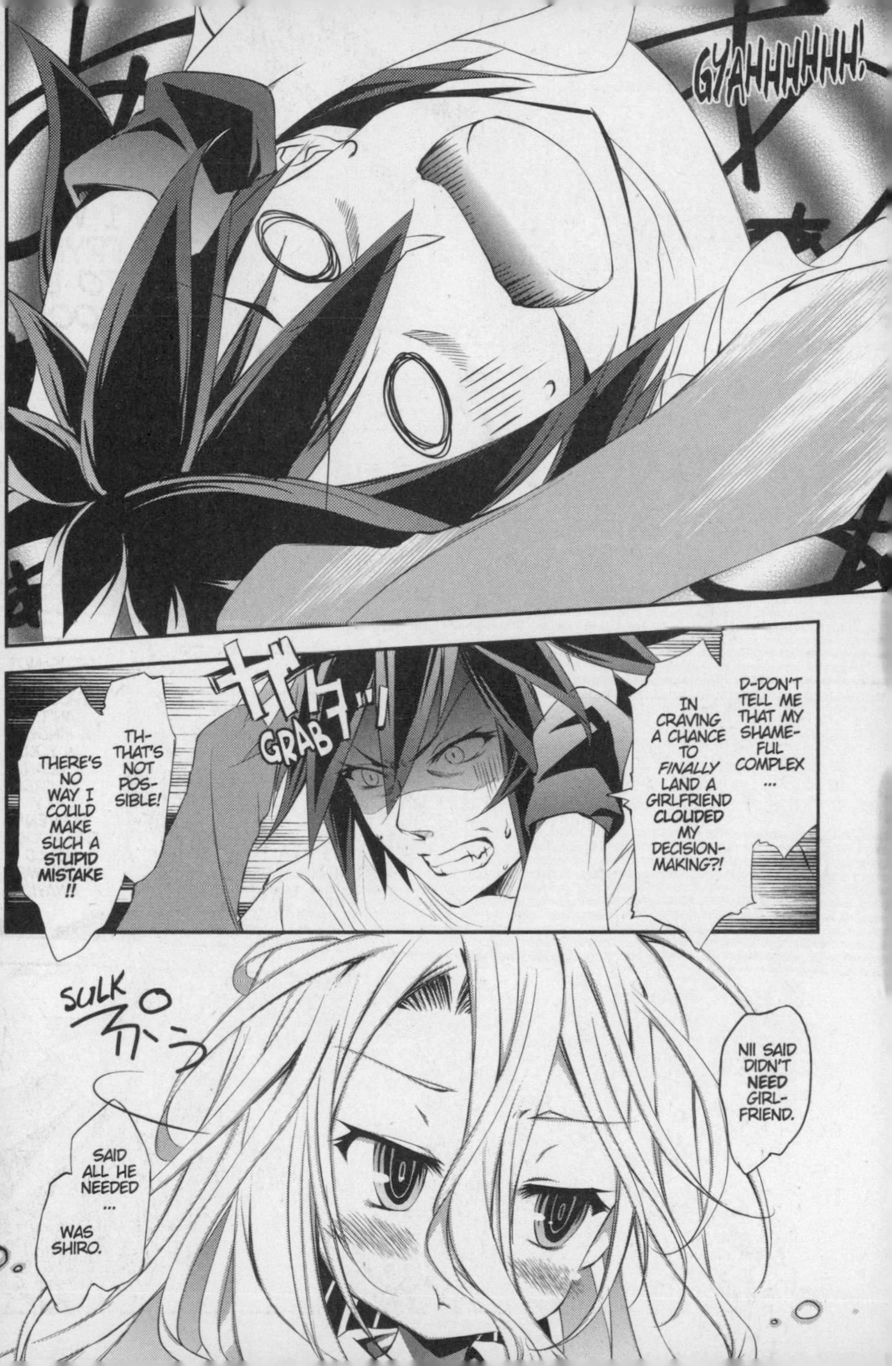
GYAHHHHHH!
D-DON'T TELL ME THAT MY SHAME-FUL COMPLEX ...
IN CRAVING A CHANCE TO FINALLY LAND A GIRLFRIEND CLOUDED MY DECISION-MAKING?!
GRAB
TH-THAT'S NOT POS-SIBLE!
THERE'S NO WAY I COULD MAKE SUCH A STUPID MISTAKE !!
NII SAID DIDN'T NEED GIRL-FRIEND.
SULK
SAID ALL HE NEEDED ... WAS SHIRO.

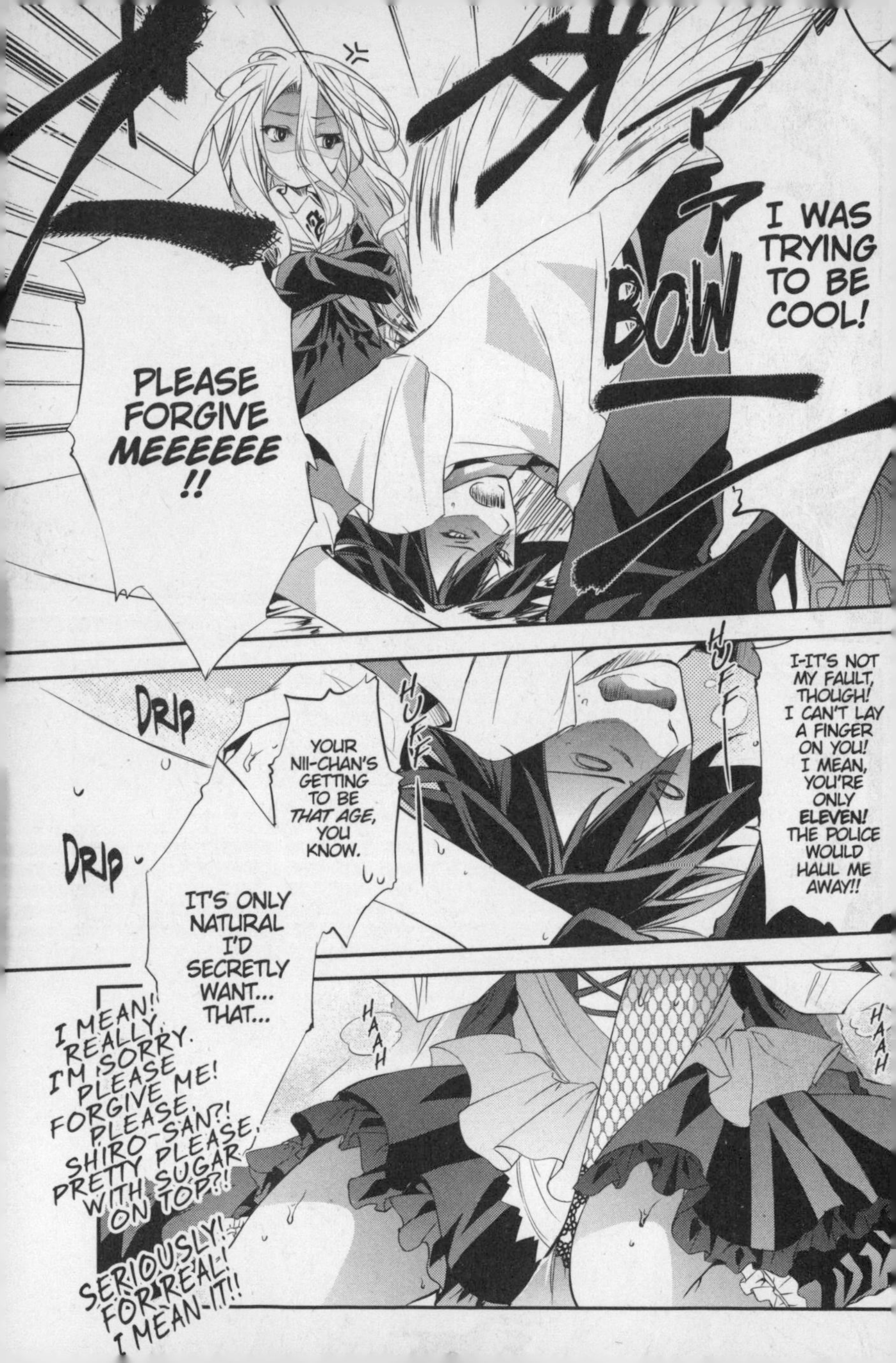

I WAS TRYING TO BE COOL!
BOW
PLEASE FORGIVE MEEEEEE!!
I-IT'S NOT MY FAULT, THOUGH! I CAN'T LAY A FINGER ON YOU! I MEAN, YOU'RE ONLY ELEVEN! THE POLICE WOULD HAUL ME AWAY!!
HUFF
HUFF
YOUR NII-CHAN'S GETTING TO BE THAT AGE, YOU KNOW.
Drip
Drip
IT'S ONLY NATURAL I'D SECRETLY WANT... THAT...
HAAH
HAAH
I MEAN! REALLY. I'M SORRY. PLEASE FORGIVE ME! PLEASE, SHIRO-SAN?! PRETTY PLEASE, WITH SUGAR ON TOP?!
SERIOUSLY! FOR REAL! I MEAN IT!!

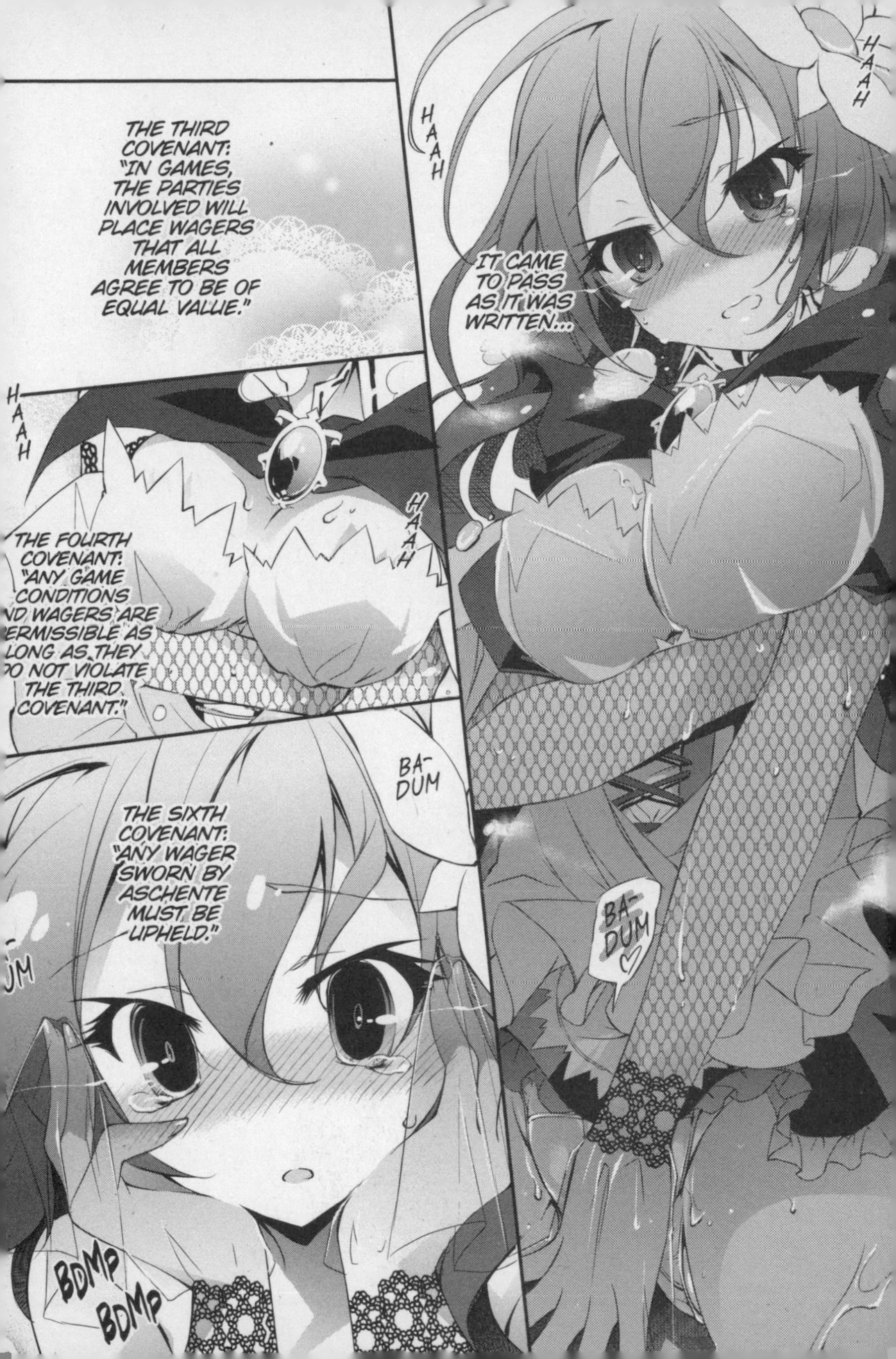
HAAAH
HAAAH
IT CAME TO PASS AS IT WAS WRITTEN...
BA-DUM ♡
THE THIRD COVENANT: "IN GAMES, THE PARTIES INVOLVED WILL PLACE WAGERS THAT ALL MEMBERS AGREE TO BE OF EQUAL VALUE."
HAAAH
HAAAH
THE FOURTH COVENANT: "ANY GAME CONDITIONS ND WAGERS ARE ERMISSIBLE AS LONG AS THEY O NOT VIOLATE THE THIRD COVENANT."
BA-DUM
THE SIXTH COVENANT: "ANY WAGER SWORN BY ASCHENTE MUST BE UPHELD."
BDMP
BDMP

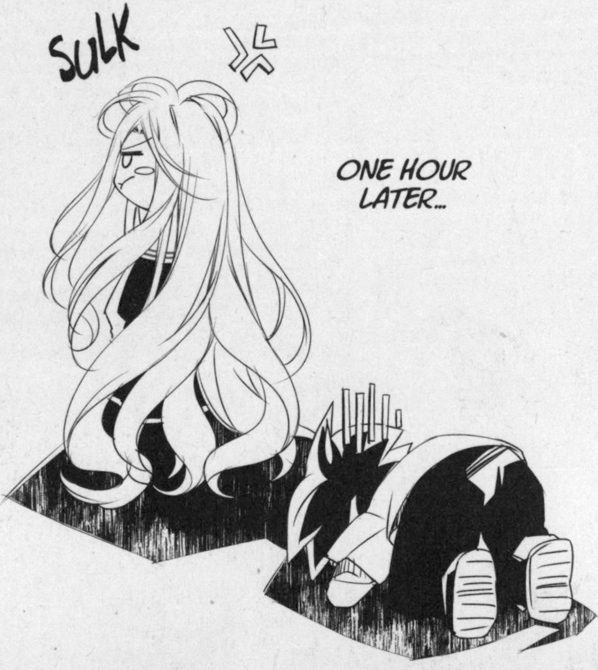
ONE HOUR LATER...
SULK

No Game No Life

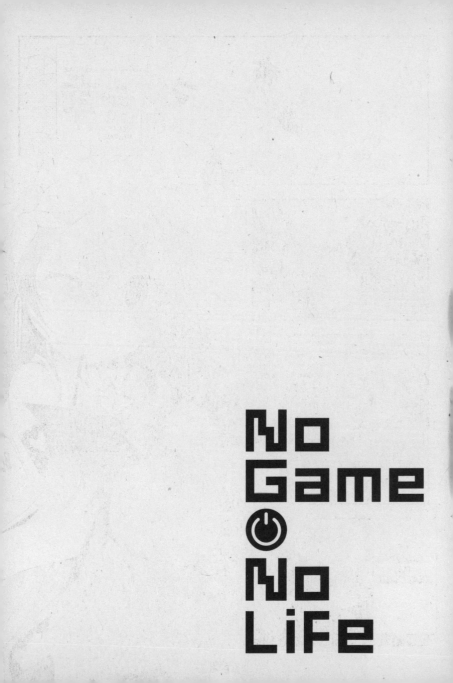

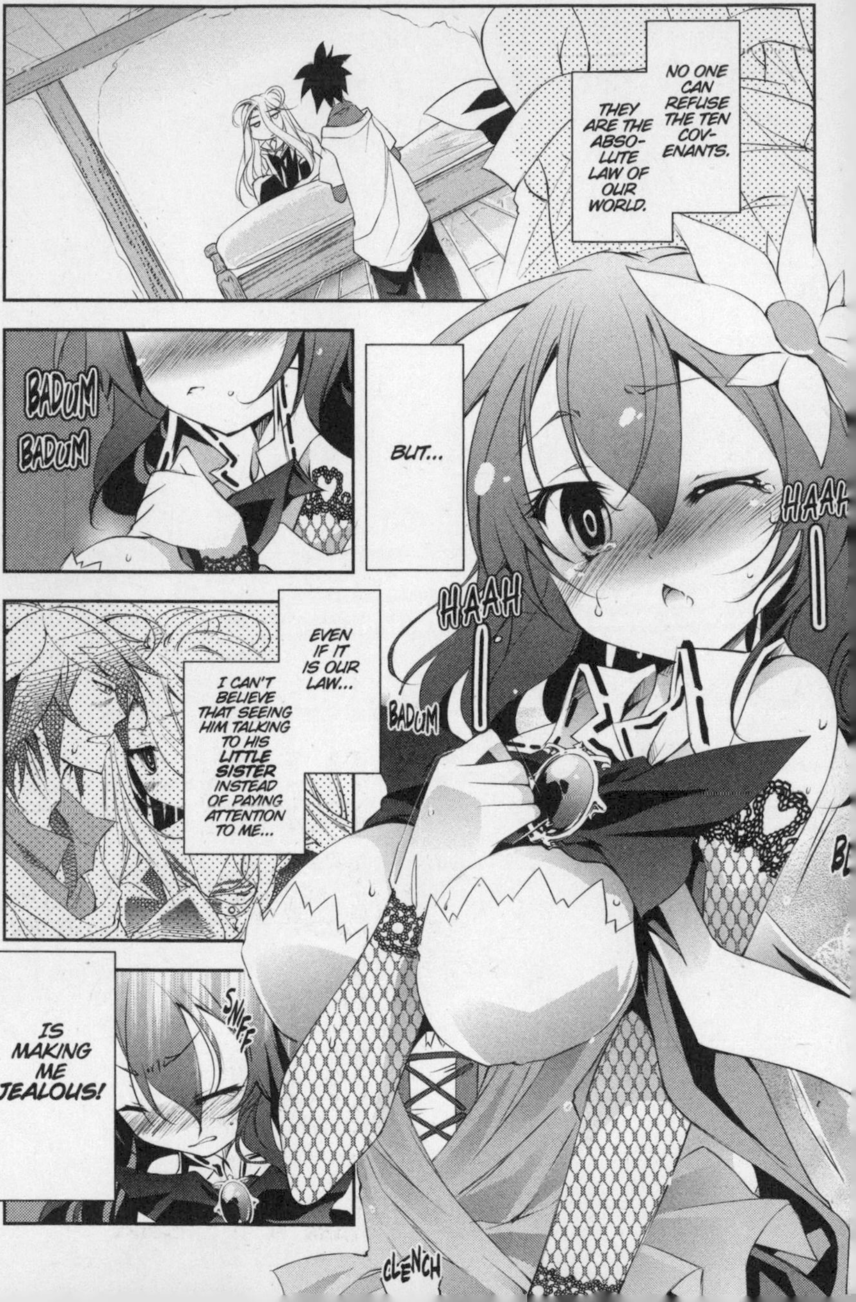
NO ONE CAN REFUSE THE TEN COVENANTS.
THEY ARE THE ABSOLUTE LAW OF OUR WORLD.
BUT...
HAAH
HAAH
BADUM
BL
CLENCH
BADUM
BADUM
EVEN IF IT IS OUR LAW...
I CAN'T BELIEVE THAT SEEING HIM TALKING TO HIS LITTLE SISTER INSTEAD OF PAYING ATTENTION TO ME...
IS MAKING ME JEALOUS!
SNIFF

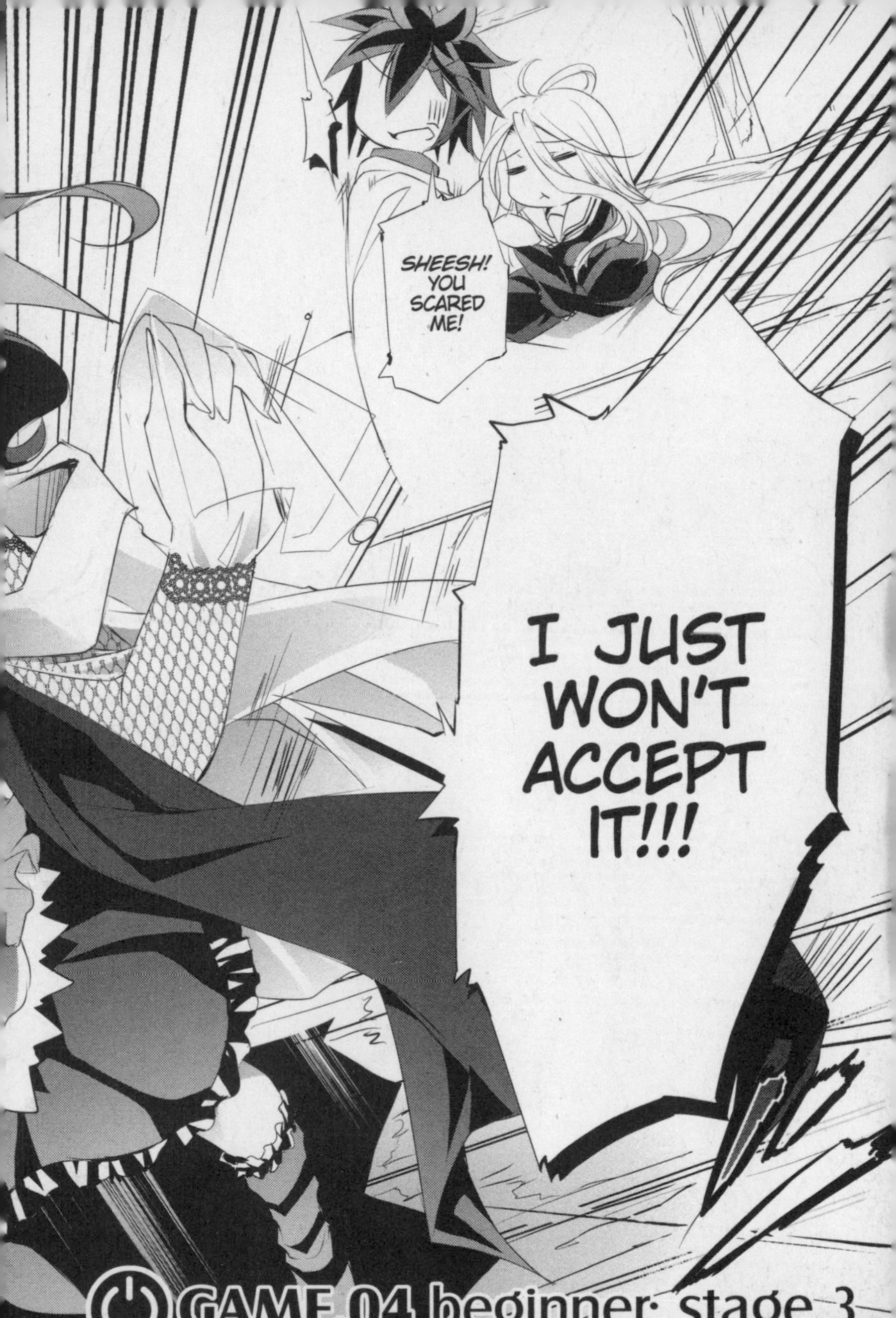
I JUST WON'T ACCEPT IT!!!
SHEESH! YOU SCARED ME!

GAME.04 beginner: stage 3

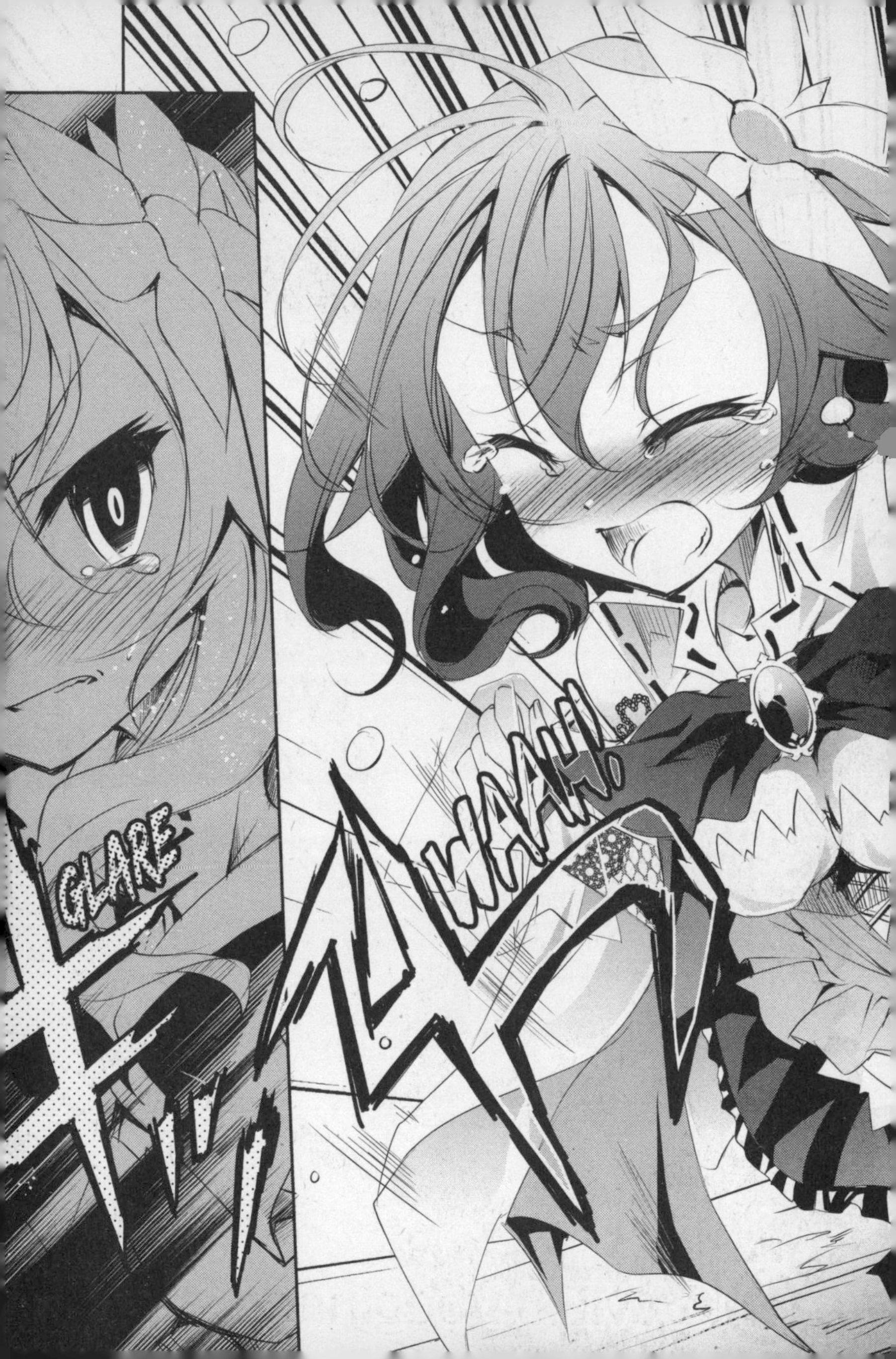
WAAH!
GLARE

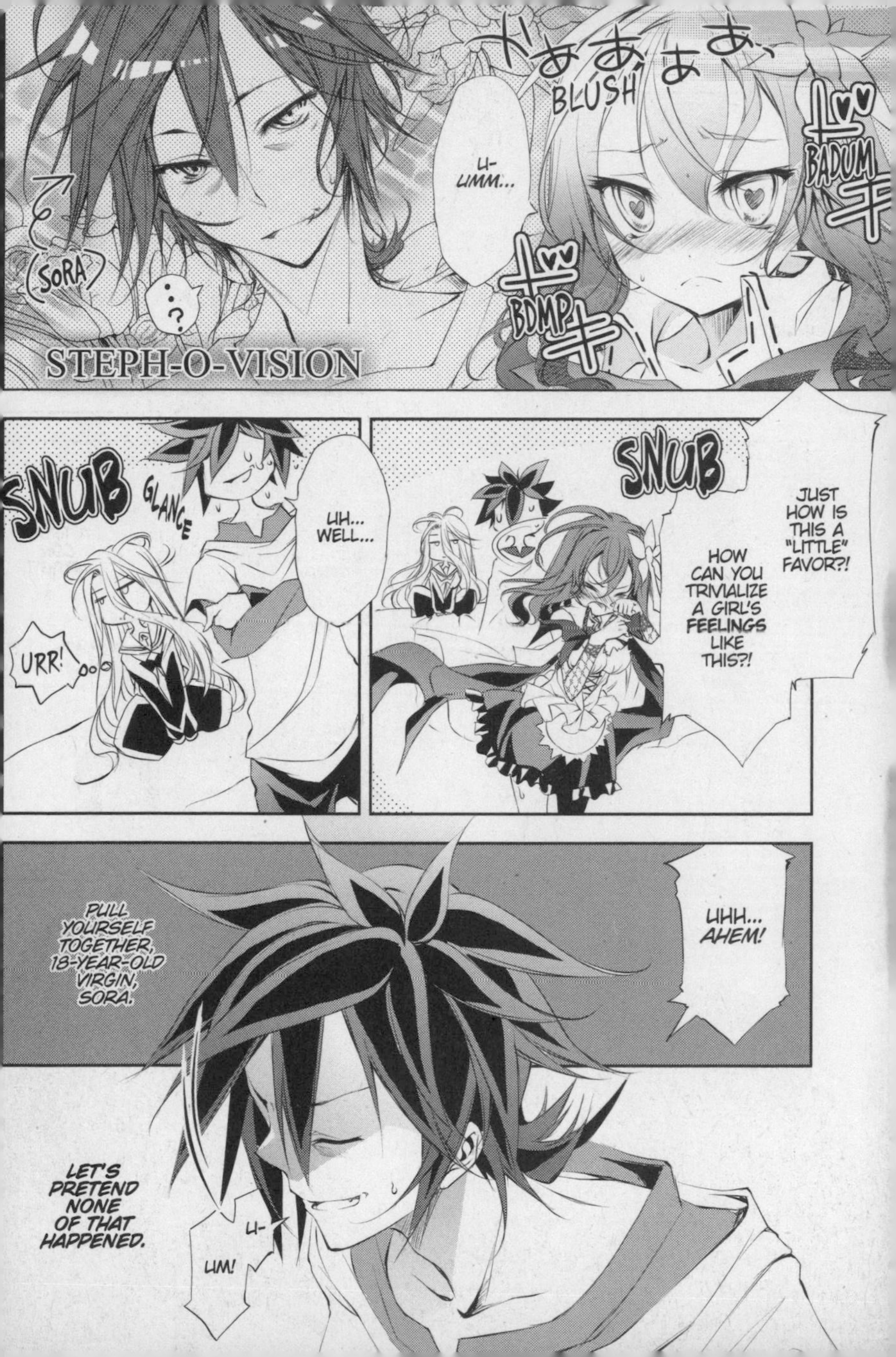
BADUM
BLUSH
U-UMM...
BDMP
...?
SORA
STEPH-O-VISION
JUST HOW IS THIS A "LITTLE" FAVOR?!
HOW CAN YOU TRIVIALIZE A GIRL'S FEELINGS LIKE THIS?!
SNUB
UH... WELL...
GLANCE
SNUB
URR!
UHH... AHEM!
PULL YOURSELF TOGETHER, 18-YEAR-OLD VIRGIN, SORA.
LET'S PRETEND NONE OF THAT HAPPENED.
U- UM!

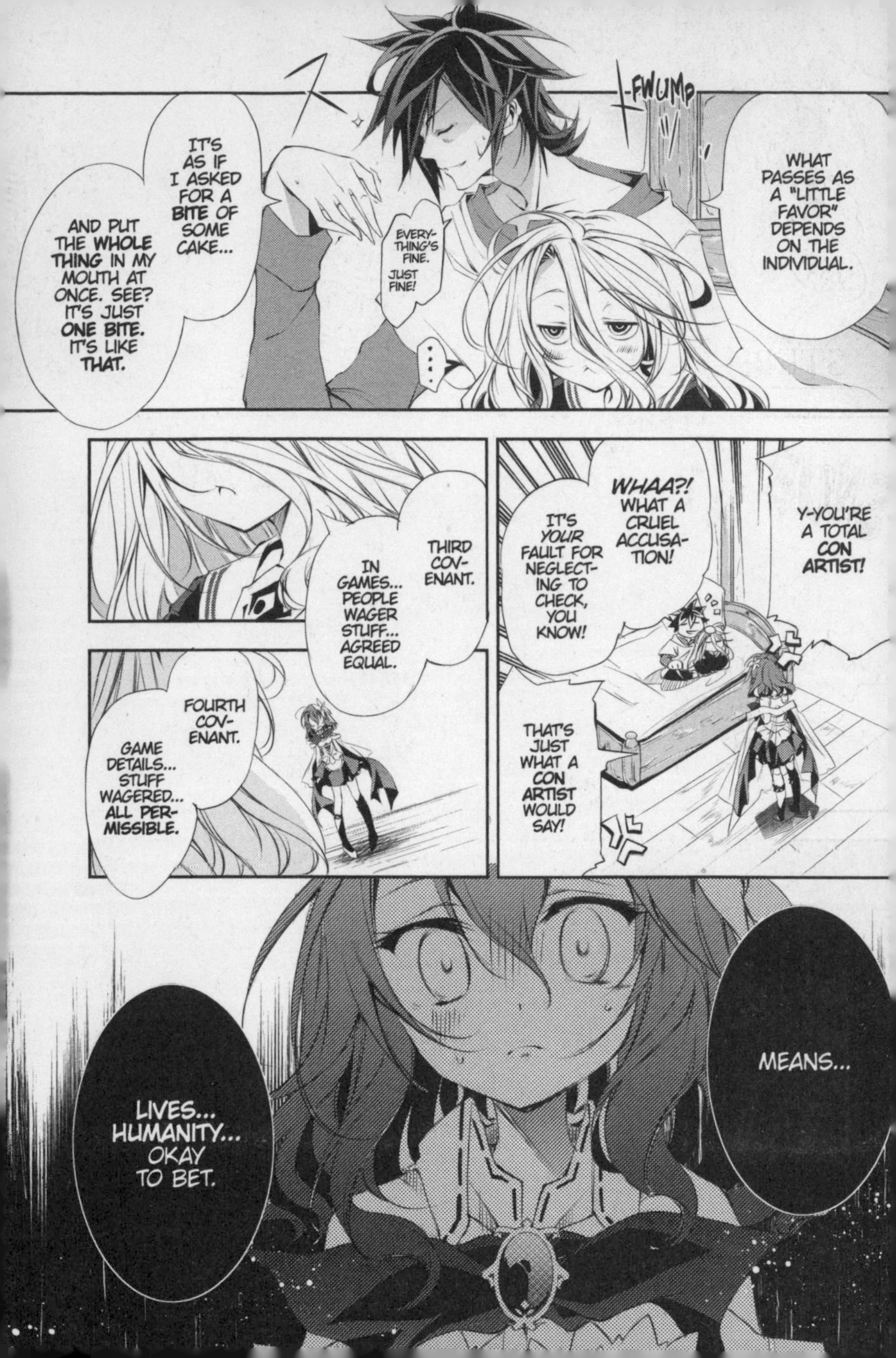
WHAT PASSES AS A "LITTLE FAVOR" DEPENDS ON THE INDIVIDUAL.
FWUMP
EVERYTHING'S FINE. JUST FINE!
IT'S AS IF I ASKED FOR A BITE OF SOME CAKE...
AND PUT THE WHOLE THING IN MY MOUTH AT ONCE. SEE? IT'S JUST ONE BITE. IT'S LIKE THAT.
...
Y-YOU'RE A TOTAL CON ARTIST!
WHAA?! WHAT A CRUEL ACCUSATION!
IT'S YOUR FAULT FOR NEGLECTING TO CHECK, YOU KNOW!
THAT'S JUST WHAT A CON ARTIST WOULD SAY!
THIRD COVENANT.
IN GAMES... PEOPLE WAGER STUFF... AGREED EQUAL.
FOURTH COVENANT.
GAME DETAILS... STUFF WAGERED... ALL PERMISSIBLE.
MEANS...
LIVES... HUMANITY... OKAY TO BET.

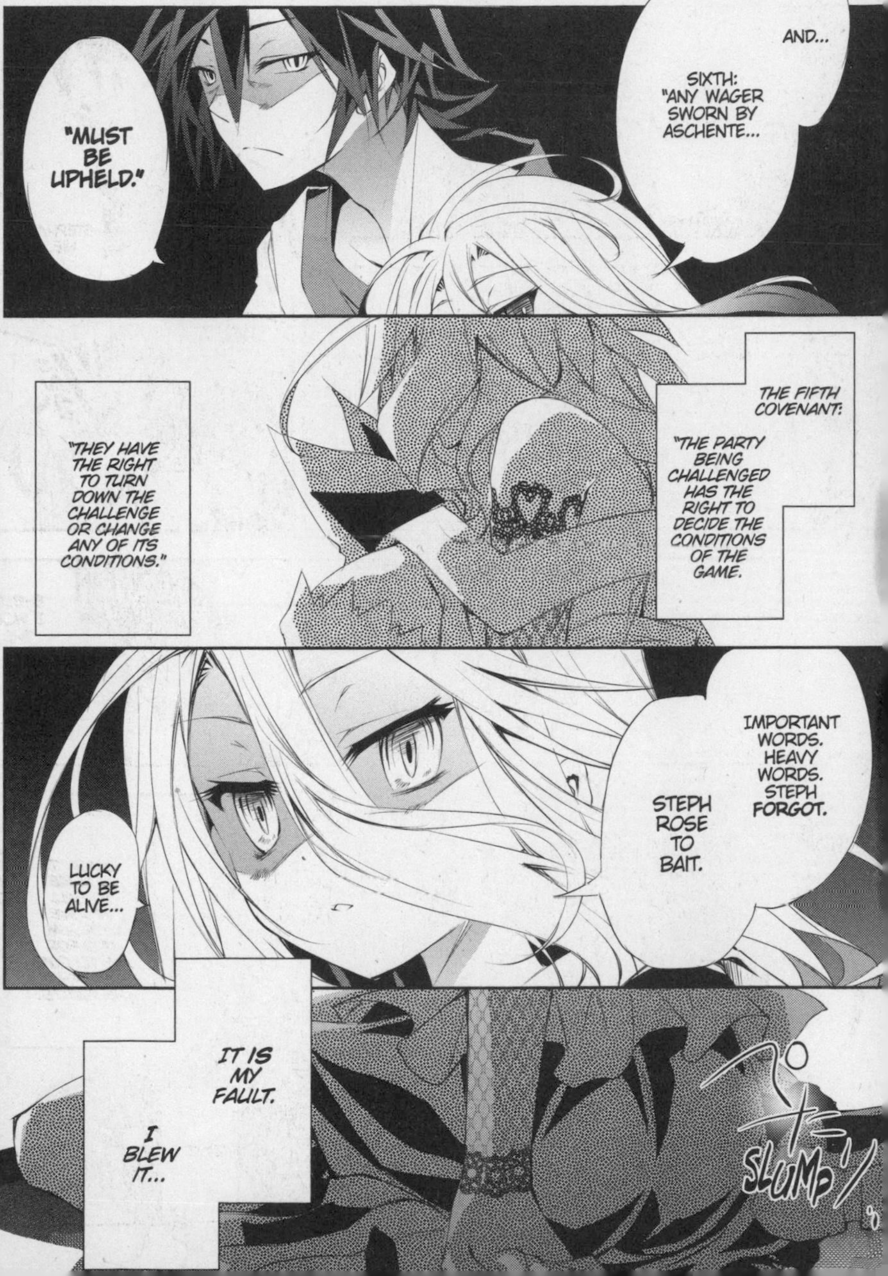

AND...
SIXTH: "ANY WAGER SWORN BY ASCHENTE...
"MUST BE UPHELD."
THE FIFTH COVENANT:
"THE PARTY BEING CHALLENGED HAS THE RIGHT TO DECIDE THE CONDITIONS OF THE GAME.
"THEY HAVE THE RIGHT TO TURN DOWN THE CHALLENGE OR CHANGE ANY OF ITS CONDITIONS."
IMPORTANT WORDS. HEAVY WORDS. STEPH FORGOT.
STEPH ROSE TO BAIT.
LUCKY TO BE ALIVE...
SLUMP!
IT IS MY FAULT.
I BLEW IT...

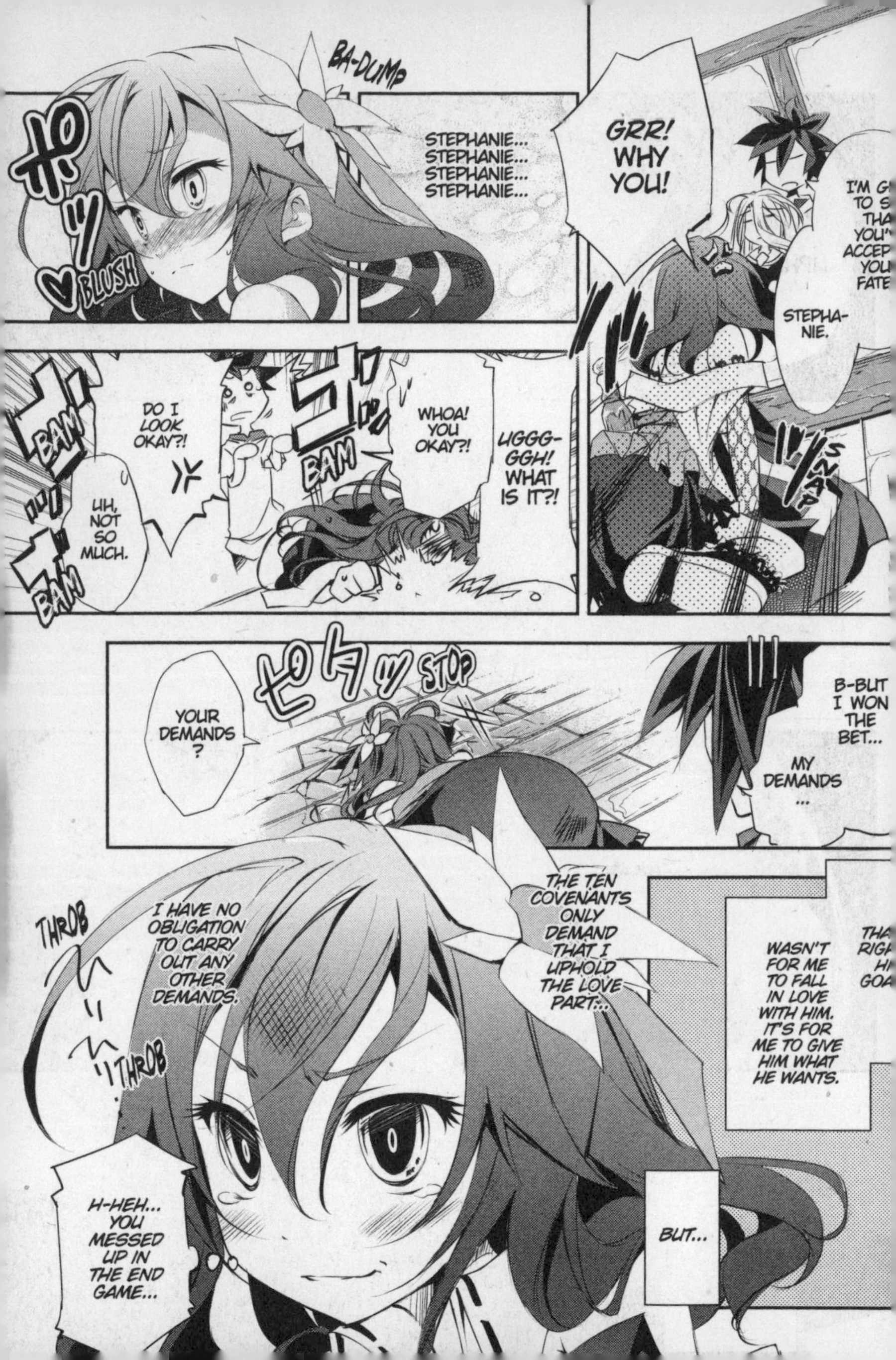
GRR! WHY YOU!
I'M G TO S THA YOU' ACCEP YOU FATE
STEPHA-NIE.
SNAP
STEPHANIE... STEPHANIE... STEPHANIE... STEPHANIE...
BA-DUMP
BLUSH
UGGG-GGH! WHAT IS IT?!
WHOA! YOU OKAY?!
BAM
DO I LOOK OKAY?!
UH, NOT SO MUCH.
BAM
BAM
B-BUT I WON THE BET...
MY DEMANDS...
STOP
YOUR DEMANDS?
THA RIG HI GOA
WASN'T FOR ME TO FALL IN LOVE WITH HIM. IT'S FOR ME TO GIVE HIM WHAT HE WANTS.
THE TEN COVENANTS ONLY DEMAND THAT I UPHOLD THE LOVE PART...
I HAVE NO OBLIGATION TO CARRY OUT ANY OTHER DEMANDS.
THROB
THROB
BUT...
H-HEH... YOU MESSED UP IN THE END GAME...

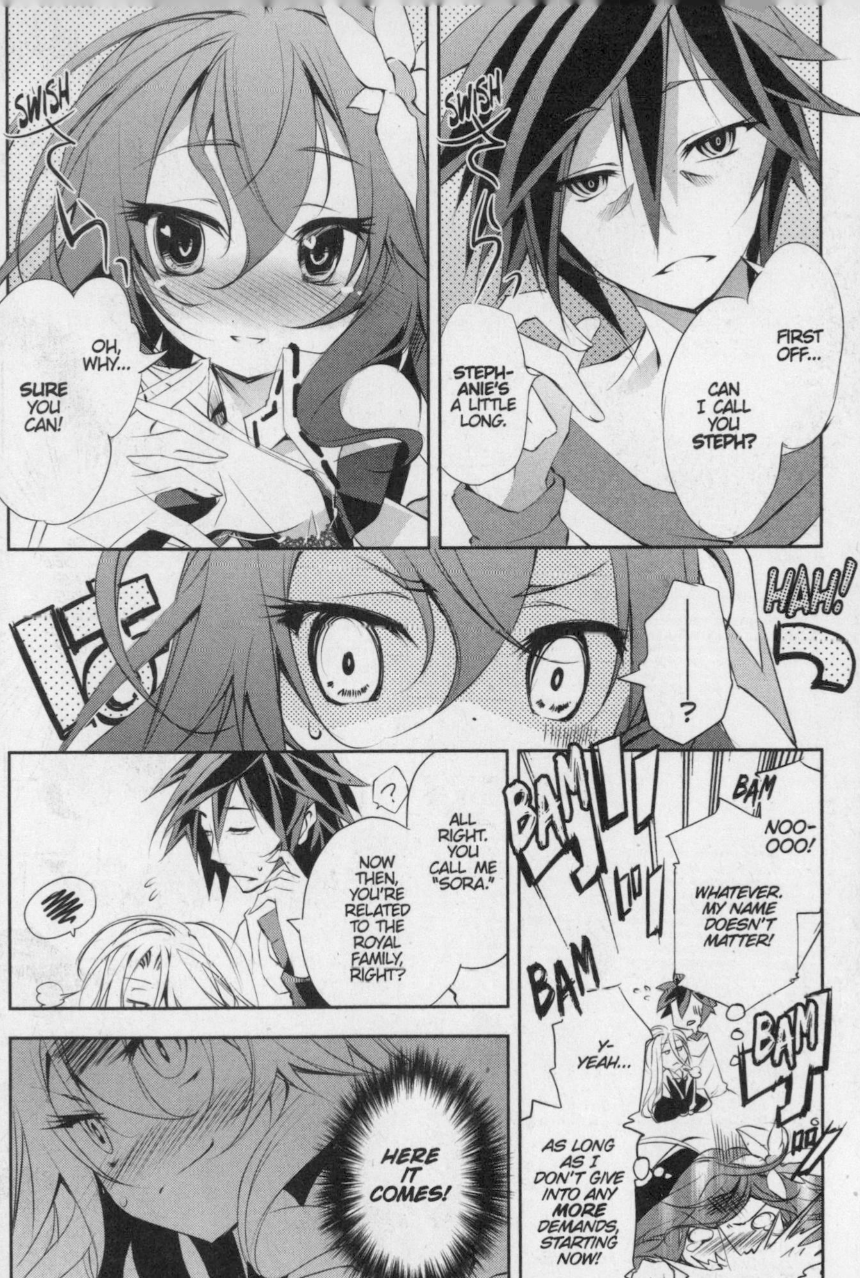
SWISH
FIRST OFF...
CAN I CALL YOU STEPH?
STEPH-ANIE'S A LITTLE LONG.
SWISH
OH, WHY...
SURE YOU CAN!
HAH!
...?
BAM
BAM
NOO-OOO!
WHATEVER. MY NAME DOESN'T MATTER!
BAM
BAM
Y-YEAH...
AS LONG AS I DON'T GIVE INTO ANY MORE DEMANDS, STARTING NOW!
?
ALL RIGHT. YOU CALL ME "SORA."
NOW THEN, YOU'RE RELATED TO THE ROYAL FAMILY, RIGHT?
HERE IT COMES!

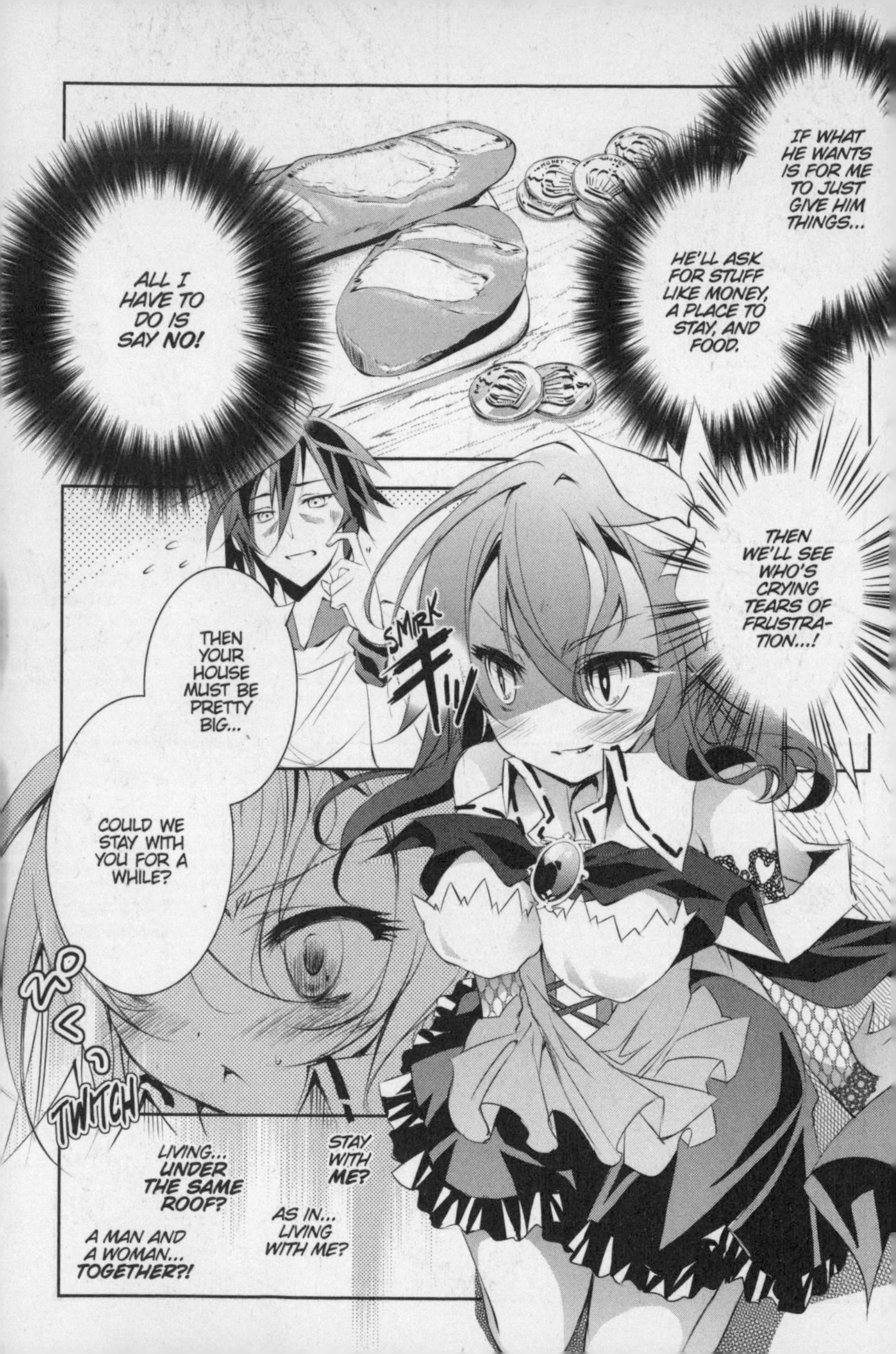
IF WHAT HE WANTS IS FOR ME TO JUST GIVE HIM THINGS...
HE'LL ASK FOR STUFF LIKE MONEY, A PLACE TO STAY, AND FOOD.
ALL I HAVE TO DO IS SAY NO!
THEN WE'LL SEE WHO'S CRYING TEARS OF FRUSTRATION...!
SMIRK
THEN YOUR HOUSE MUST BE PRETTY BIG...
COULD WE STAY WITH YOU FOR A WHILE?
TWITCH
STAY WITH ME?
AS IN... LIVING WITH ME?
LIVING... UNDER THE SAME ROOF?
A MAN AND A WOMAN... TOGETHER?!

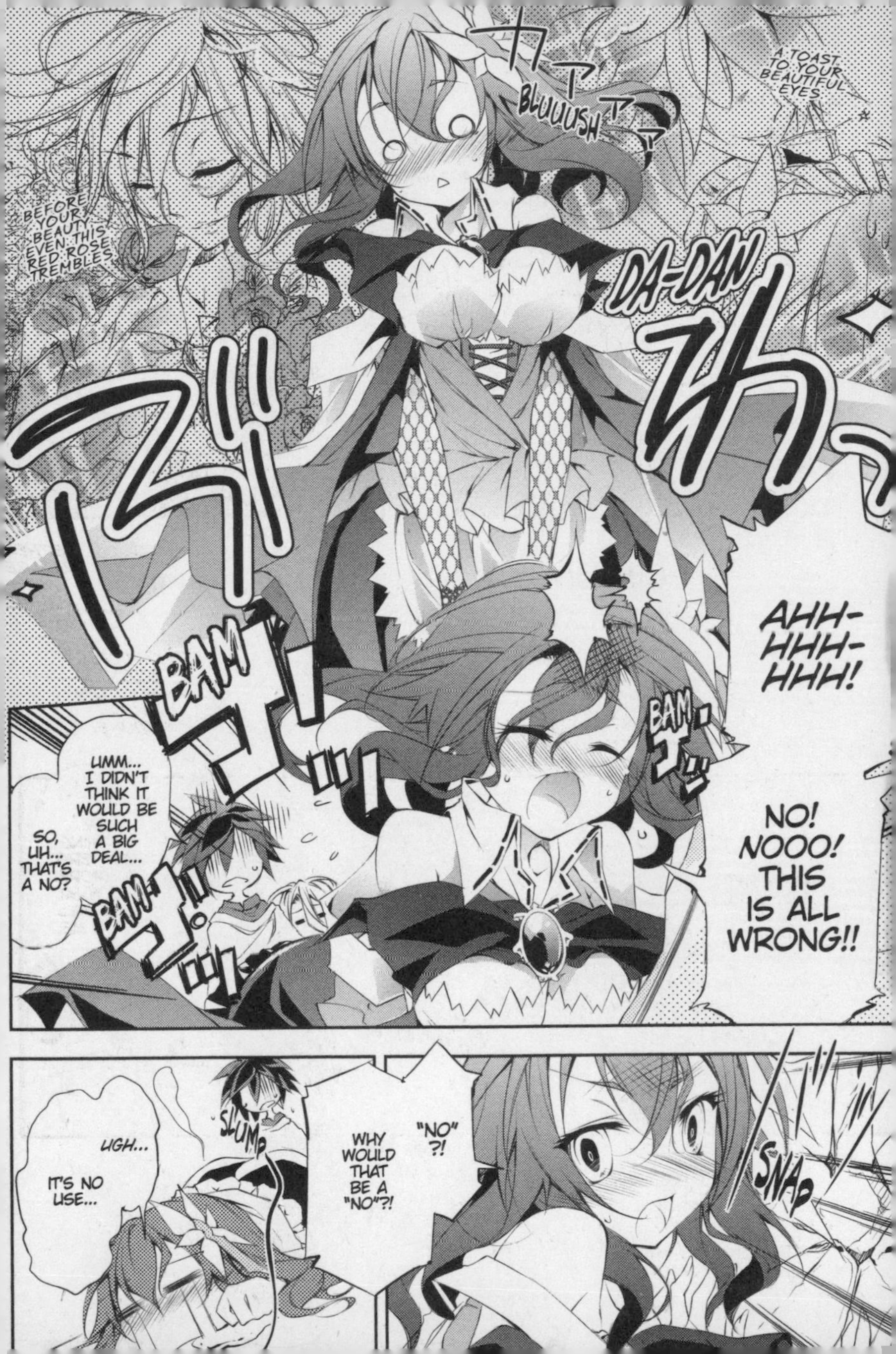

A TOAST TO YOUR BEAUTIFUL EYES
BLUUUSH
BEFORE YOUR BEAUTY EVEN THIS RED ROSE TREMBLES
DA-DAN
AHHHHHHHHH!
BAM
NO! NOOOO! THIS IS ALL WRONG!!
BAM
UMM... I DIDN'T THINK IT WOULD BE SUCH A BIG DEAL...
SO, UH... THAT'S A NO?
BAM
SNAP
"NO"?!
WHY WOULD THAT BE A "NO"?!
SLUMP
UGH...
IT'S NO USE...

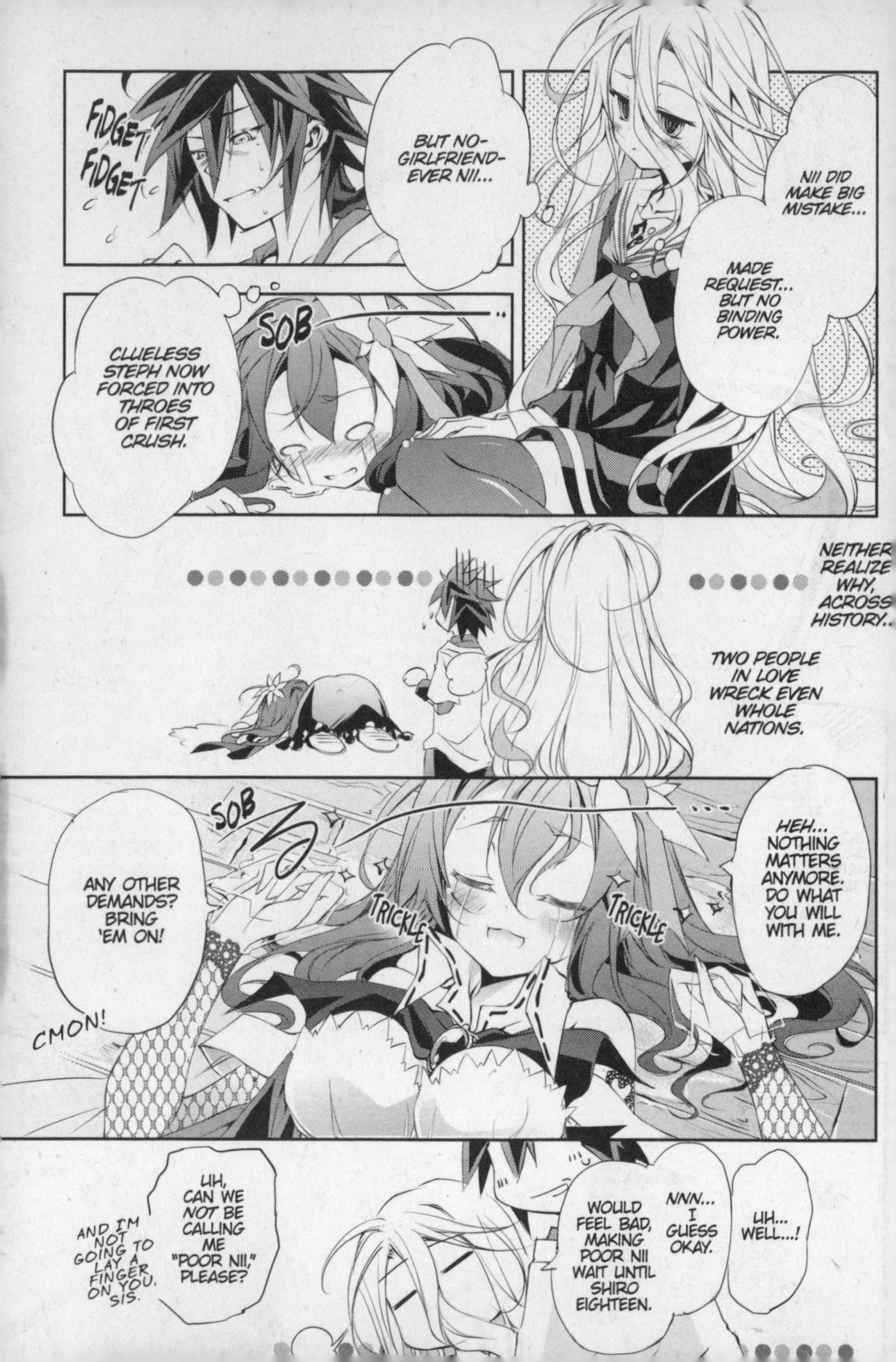
NII DID MAKE BIG MISTAKE...
MADE REQUEST... BUT NO BINDING POWER.
FIDGET FIDGET
BUT NO-GIRLFRIEND-EVER NII...
SOB
CLUELESS STEPH NOW FORCED INTO THROES OF FIRST CRUSH.
NEITHER REALIZE WHY, ACROSS HISTORY..
TWO PEOPLE IN LOVE WRECK EVEN WHOLE NATIONS.
HEH... NOTHING MATTERS ANYMORE. DO WHAT YOU WILL WITH ME.
TRICKLE
TRICKLE
SOB
ANY OTHER DEMANDS? BRING 'EM ON!
CMON!
UH... WELL...!
NNN... I GUESS OKAY.
WOULD FEEL BAD, MAKING POOR NII WAIT UNTIL SHIRO EIGHTEEN.
UH, CAN WE NOT BE CALLING ME "POOR NII," PLEASE?
AND I'M NOT GOING TO LAY A FINGER ON YOU, SIS.

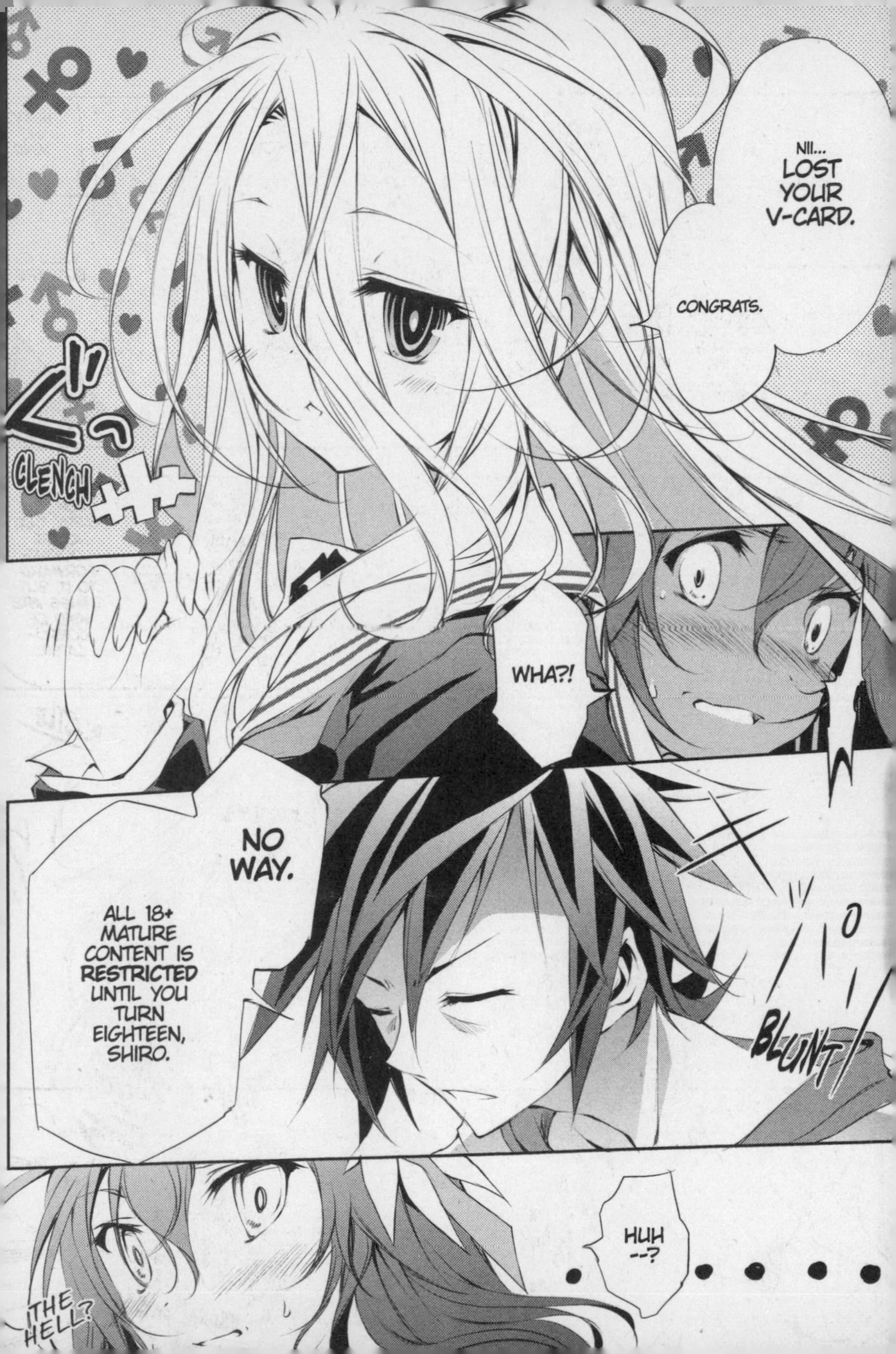
NII... LOST YOUR V-CARD.
CONGRATS.
CLENCH
WHA?!
NO WAY.
ALL 18+ MATURE CONTENT IS RESTRICTED UNTIL YOU TURN EIGHTEEN, SHIRO.
BLUNT
. . . . .
HUH --?
THE HELL?

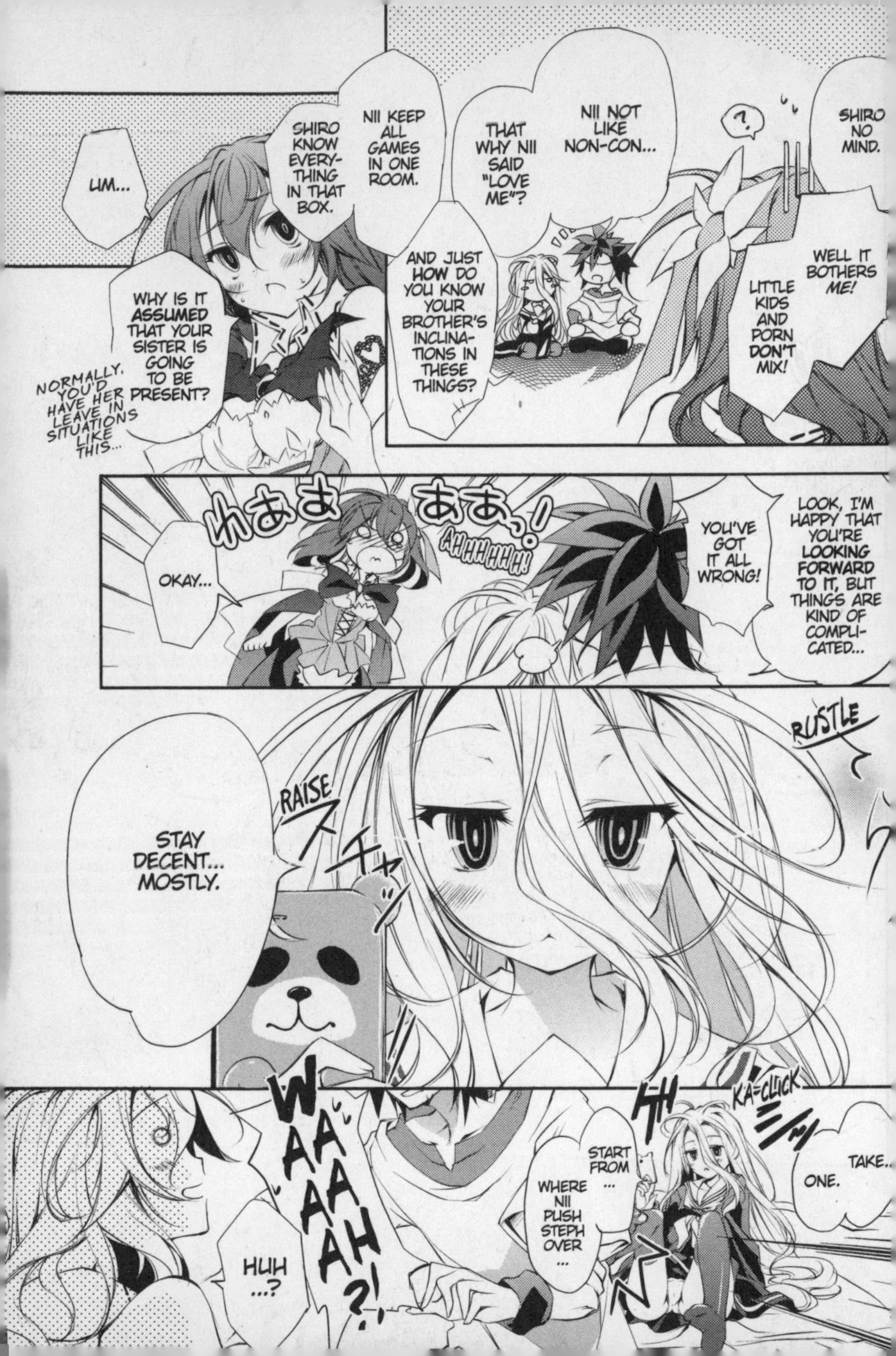
SHIRO NO MIND.
?
WELL IT BOTHERS ME!
LITTLE KIDS AND PORN DON'T MIX!
NII NOT LIKE NON-CON...
THAT WHY NII SAID "LOVE ME"?
NII KEEP ALL GAMES IN ONE ROOM.
SHIRO KNOW EVERY-THING IN THAT BOX.
AND JUST HOW DO YOU KNOW YOUR BROTHER'S INCLINA-TIONS IN THESE THINGS?
UM...
WHY IS IT ASSUMED THAT YOUR SISTER IS GOING TO BE PRESENT?
NORMALLY, YOU'D HAVE HER LEAVE IN SITUATIONS LIKE THIS...
LOOK, I'M HAPPY THAT YOU'RE LOOKING FORWARD TO IT, BUT THINGS ARE KIND OF COMPLI-CATED...
YOU'VE GOT IT ALL WRONG!
AHHHHHHH!
OKAY...
RUSTLE
STAY DECENT... MOSTLY.
RAISE
TAKE..
ONE.
KA-CLICK
START FROM ...
WHERE NII PUSH STEPH OVER ...
WAAAAAH?!
HUH ...?

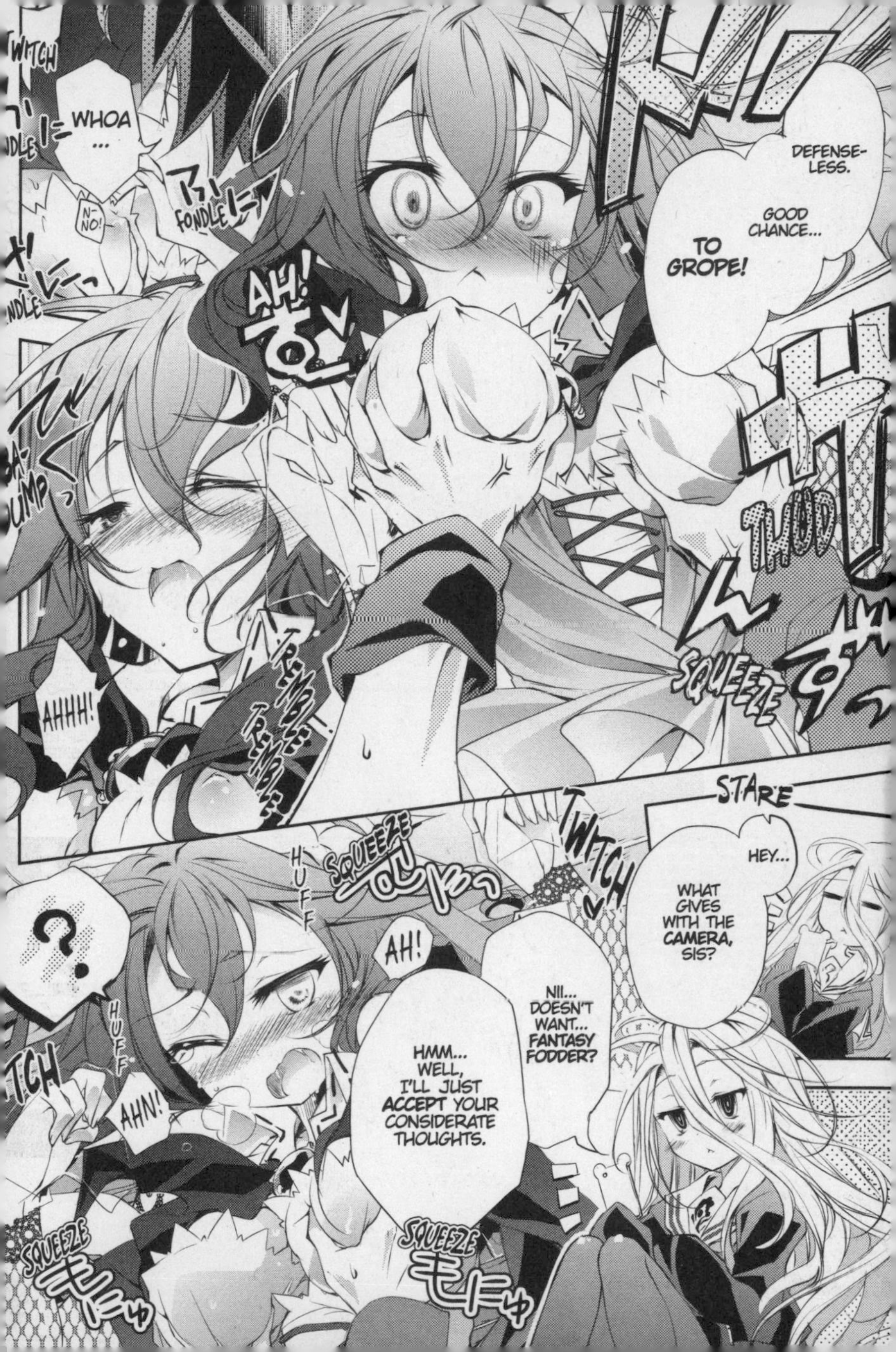
DEFENSE-LESS.
GOOD CHANCE...
TO GROPE!
THUD
SQUEEZE
AH!
TREMBLE
TREMBLE
AHHH!
WHOA ...
N-NO!
FONDLE
TWITCH
STARE
HEY...
WHAT GIVES WITH THE CAMERA, SIS?
NII... DOESN'T WANT... FANTASY FODDER?
HMM... WELL, I'LL JUST ACCEPT YOUR CONSIDERATE THOUGHTS.
TWITCH
SQUEEZE
HUFF
AH!
?
HUFF
AHN!
SQUEEZE
SQUEEZE

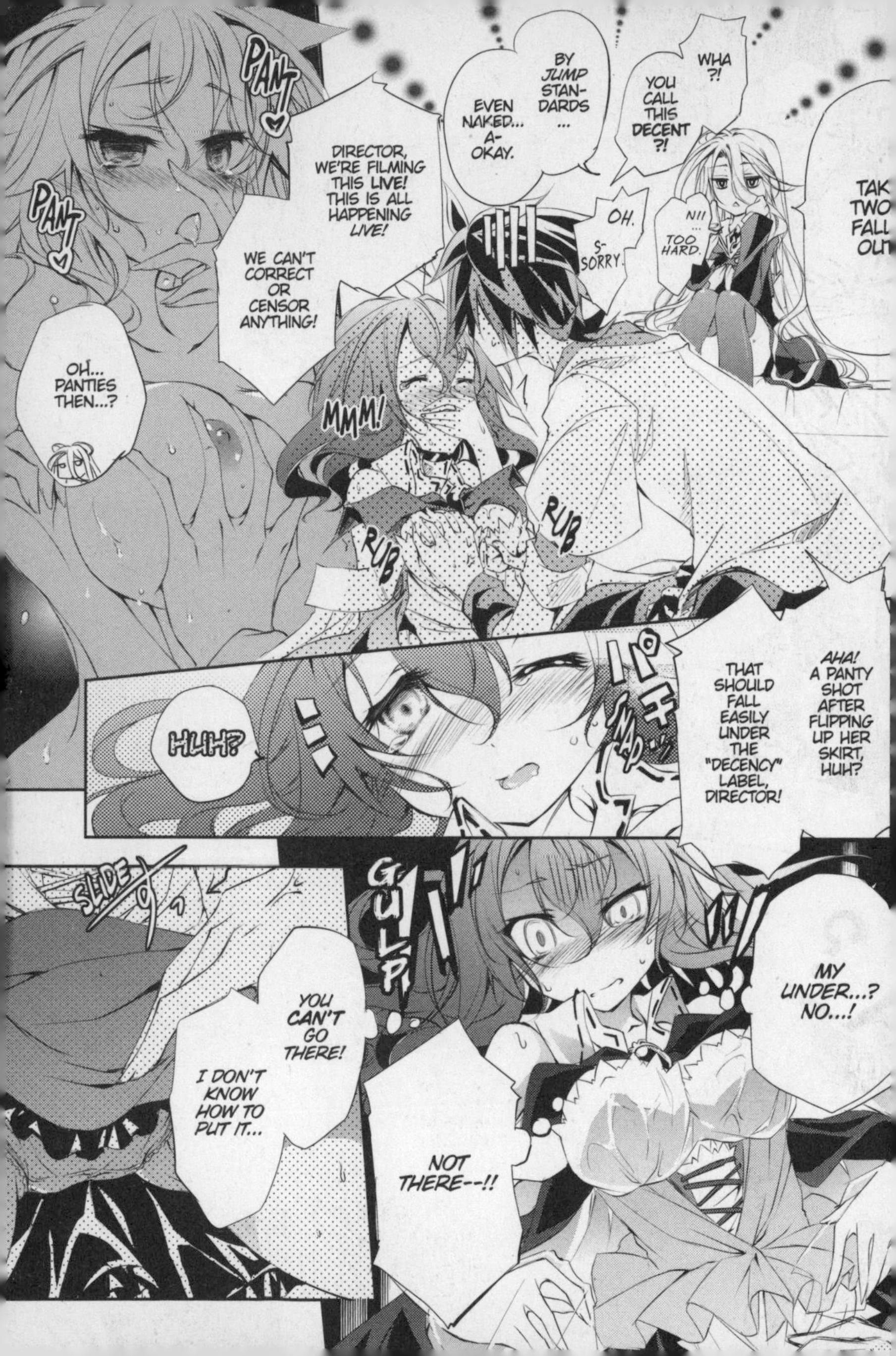
TAK TWO FALL OUT
WHA?! YOU CALL THIS DECENT?!
BY JUMP STANDARDS... EVEN NAKED... A-OKAY.
NI!... TOO HARD.
OH. S-SORRY.
DIRECTOR, WE'RE FILMING THIS LIVE! THIS IS ALL HAPPENING LIVE!
WE CAN'T CORRECT OR CENSOR ANYTHING!
MMM!
RUB
RUB
PANT
PANT
OH... PANTIES THEN...?
AHA! A PANTY SHOT AFTER FLIPPING UP HER SKIRT, HUH?
THAT SHOULD FALL EASILY UNDER THE "DECENCY" LABEL, DIRECTOR!
パチ
SNAP
HUH?
MY UNDER...? NO...!
GULP
YOU CAN'T GO THERE!
I DON'T KNOW HOW TO PUT IT...
NOT THERE--!!
SLIDE

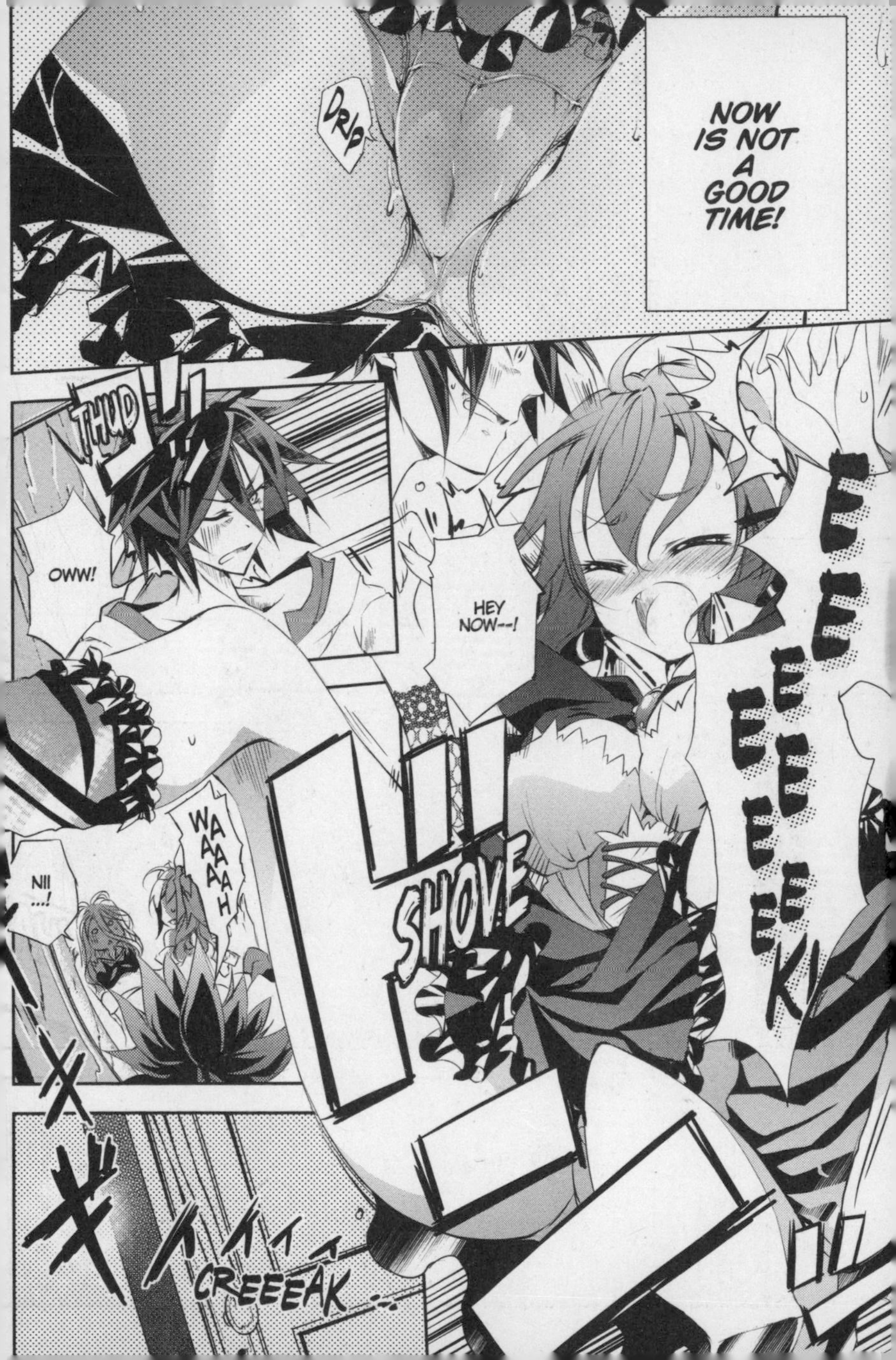

NOW IS NOT A GOOD TIME!
DRIP
EEEEEEEEEEK!
HEY NOW--!
SHOVE
THUD
OWW!
WAAAAAH
NII ...!
CREEEEAK ...

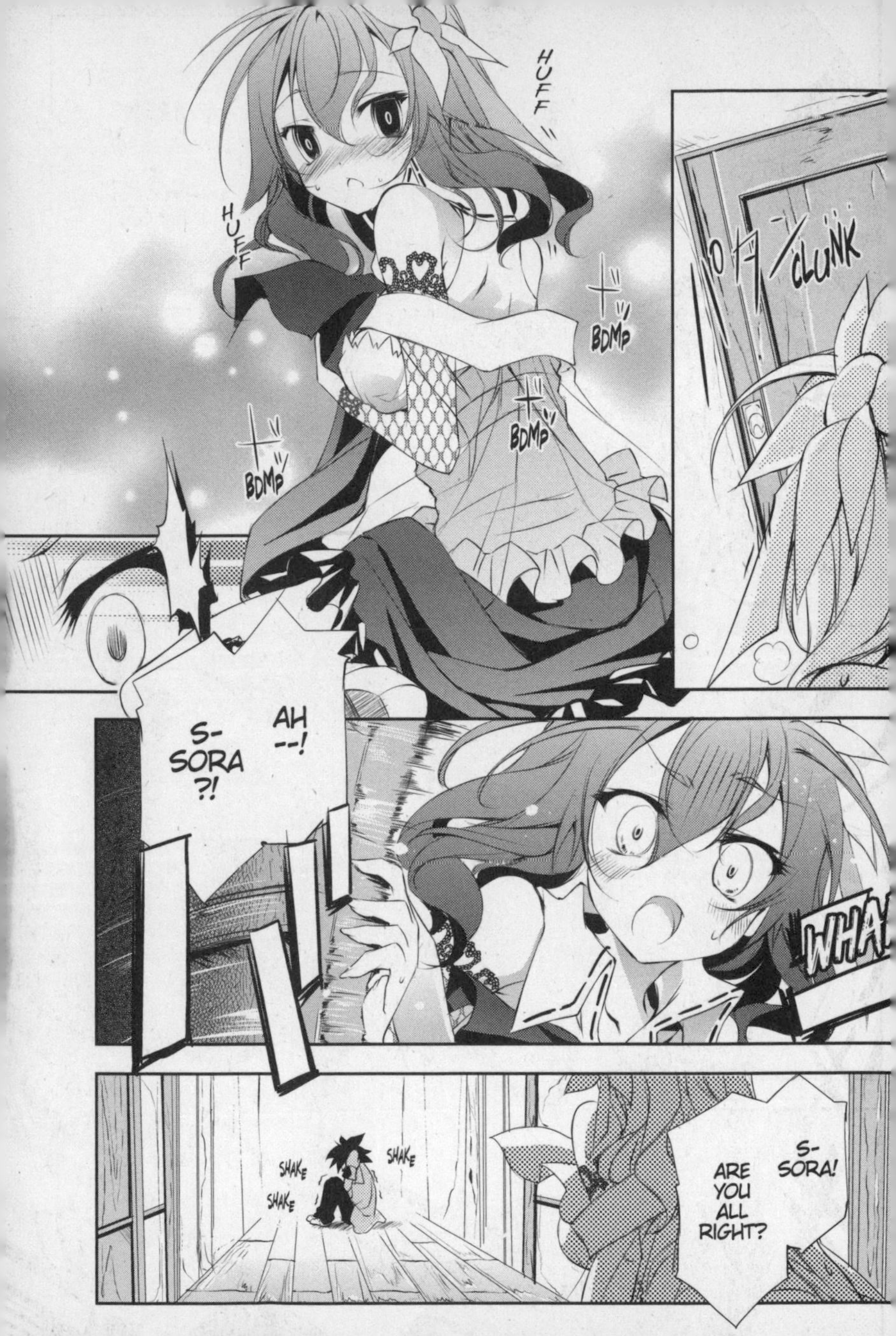
CLUNK
HUFF
HUFF
BDMP
BDMP
BDMP
WHA
AH--!
S-SORA?!
S-SORA!
ARE YOU ALL RIGHT?
SHAKE
SHAKE
SHAKE

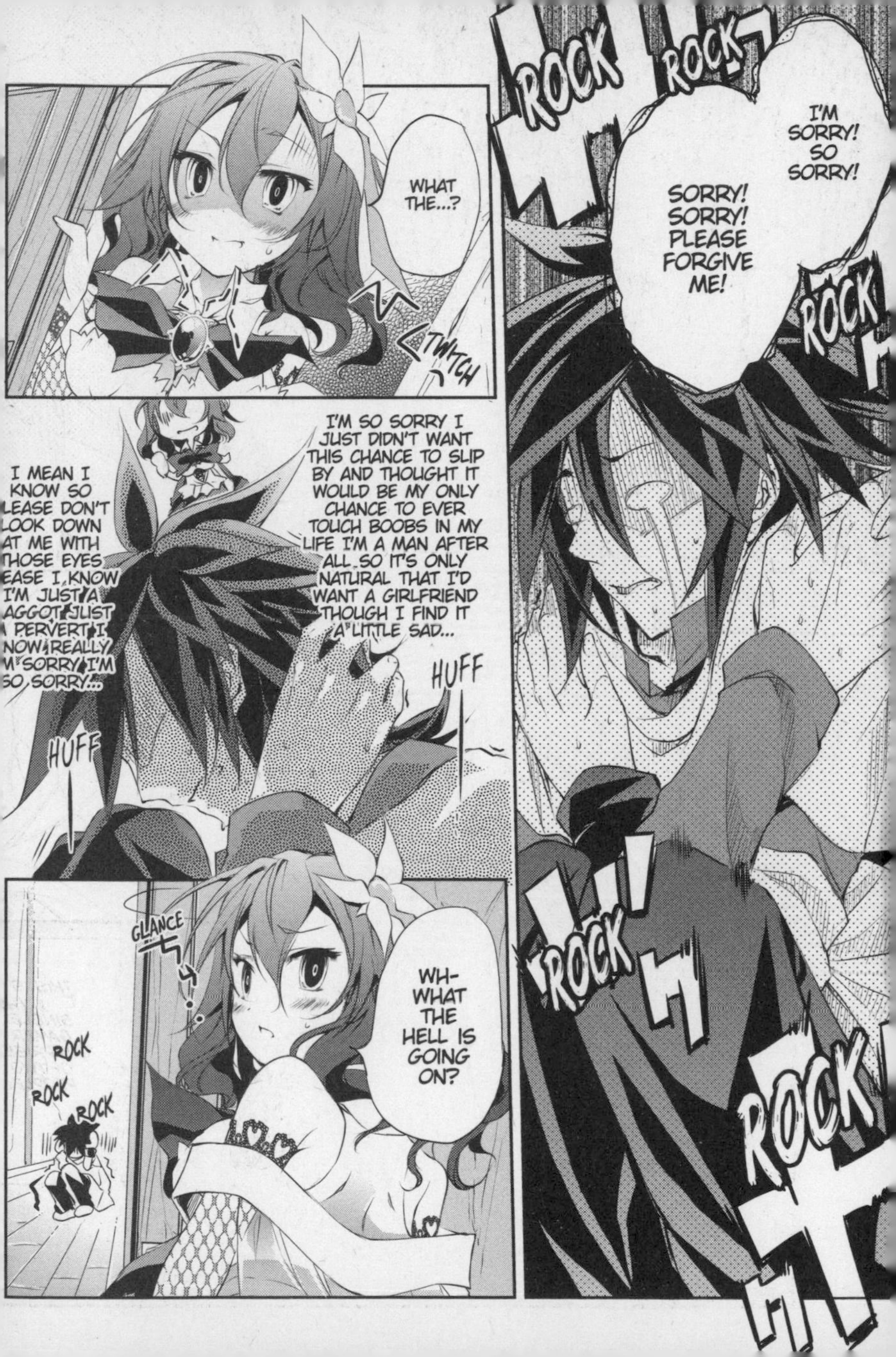
ROCK
ROCK
I'M SORRY! SO SORRY!
SORRY! SORRY! PLEASE FORGIVE ME!
ROCK
ROCK
ROCK
WHAT THE...?
TWITCH
I'M SO SORRY I JUST DIDN'T WANT THIS CHANCE TO SLIP BY AND THOUGHT IT WOULD BE MY ONLY CHANCE TO EVER TOUCH BOOBS IN MY LIFE I'M A MAN AFTER ALL SO IT'S ONLY NATURAL THAT I'D WANT A GIRLFRIEND THOUGH I FIND IT A LITTLE SAD...
I MEAN I KNOW SO LEASE DON'T LOOK DOWN AT ME WITH THOSE EYES EASE I KNOW I'M JUST A AGGOT JUST PERVERT I NOW REALLY M SORRY I'M SO SORRY...
HUFF
HUFF
GLANCE
WH- WHAT THE HELL IS GOING ON?
ROCK
ROCK
ROCK

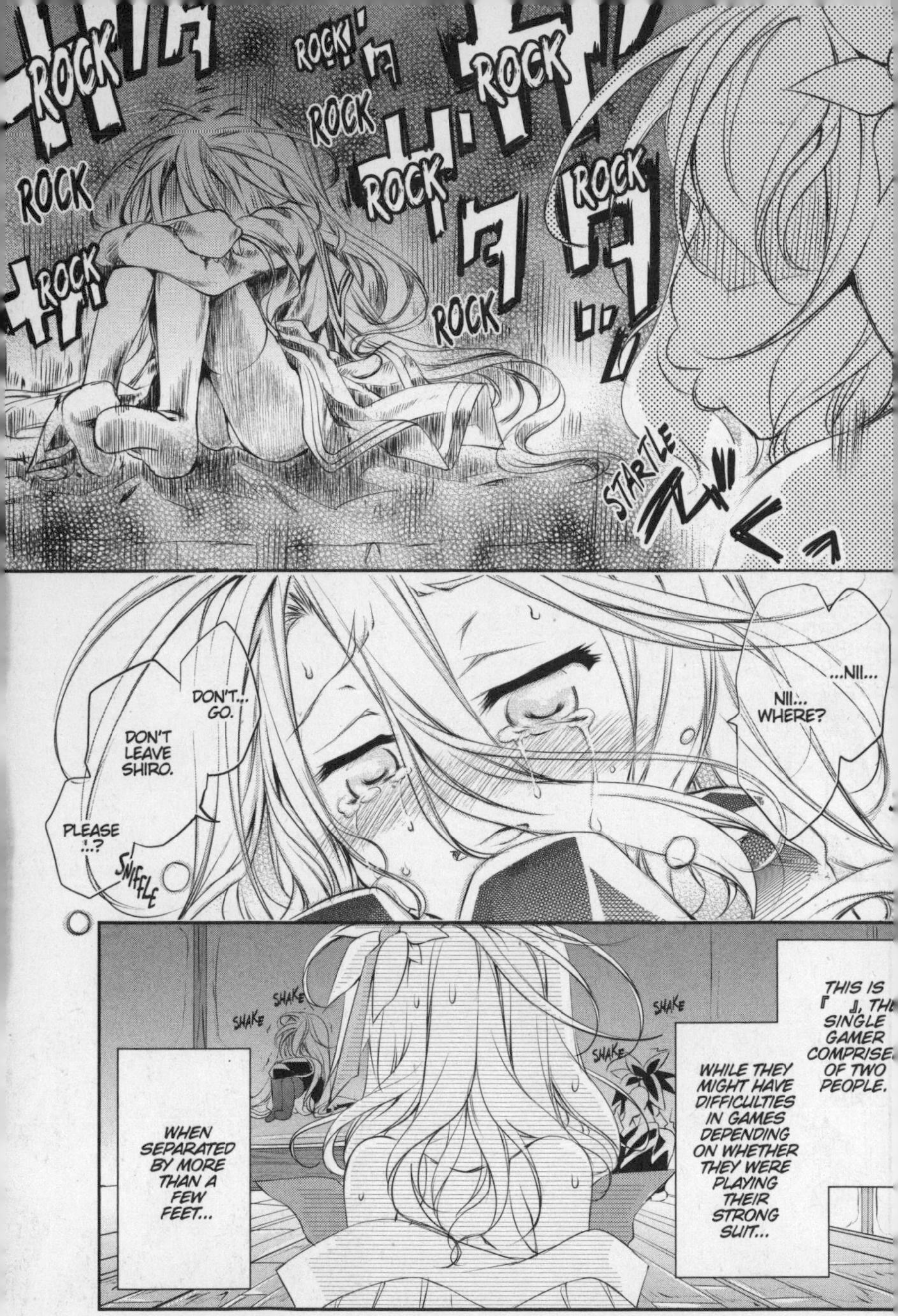
ROCK
ROCK
ROCK
ROCK
ROCK
ROCK
ROCK
ROCK
ROCK
STARTLE
...NII...
NII... WHERE?
DON'T... GO.
DON'T LEAVE SHIRO.
PLEASE !..?
SNIFFLE
SHAKE
SHAKE
SHAKE
SHAKE
THIS IS 『 』, THE SINGLE GAMER COMPRISED OF TWO PEOPLE.
WHILE THEY MIGHT HAVE DIFFICULTIES IN GAMES DEPENDING ON WHETHER THEY WERE PLAYING THEIR STRONG SUIT...
WHEN SEPARATED BY MORE THAN A FEW FEET...

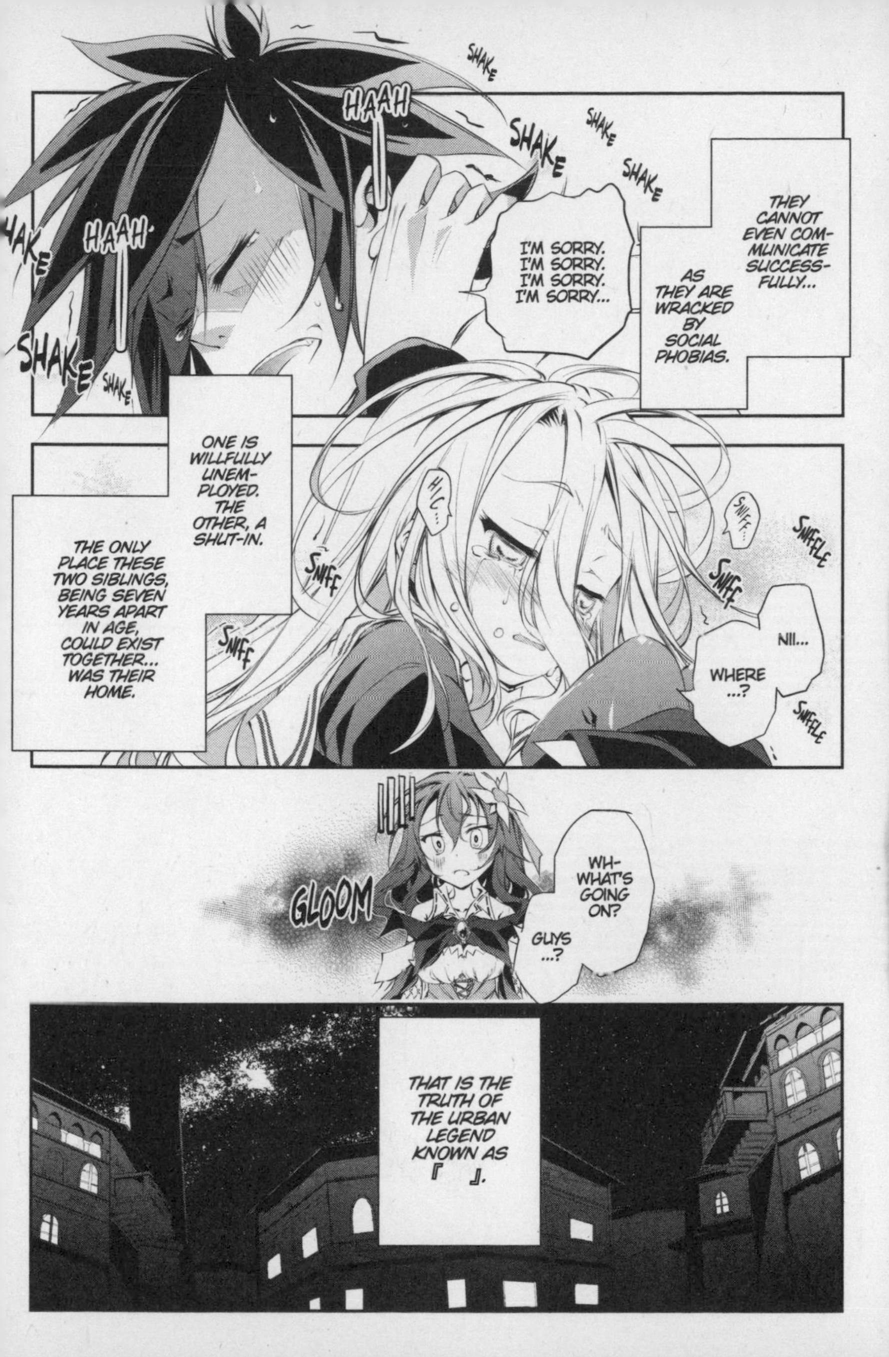
THEY CANNOT EVEN COMMUNICATE SUCCESSFULLY...
AS THEY ARE WRACKED BY SOCIAL PHOBIAS.
SHAKE
SHAKE
SHAKE
SHAKE
I'M SORRY. I'M SORRY. I'M SORRY. I'M SORRY...
HAAH
HAAH
SHAKE
SHAKE
SHAKE
SNIFFLE
SNIFF...
SNIFF
NII...
WHERE ...?
SNIFFLE
HIC...
SNIFF
SNIFF
ONE IS WILLFULLY UNEMPLOYED. THE OTHER, A SHUT-IN.
THE ONLY PLACE THESE TWO SIBLINGS, BEING SEVEN YEARS APART IN AGE, COULD EXIST TOGETHER... WAS THEIR HOME.
WH-WHAT'S GOING ON?
GUYS ...?
GLOOM
THAT IS THE TRUTH OF THE URBAN LEGEND KNOWN AS 『 』.

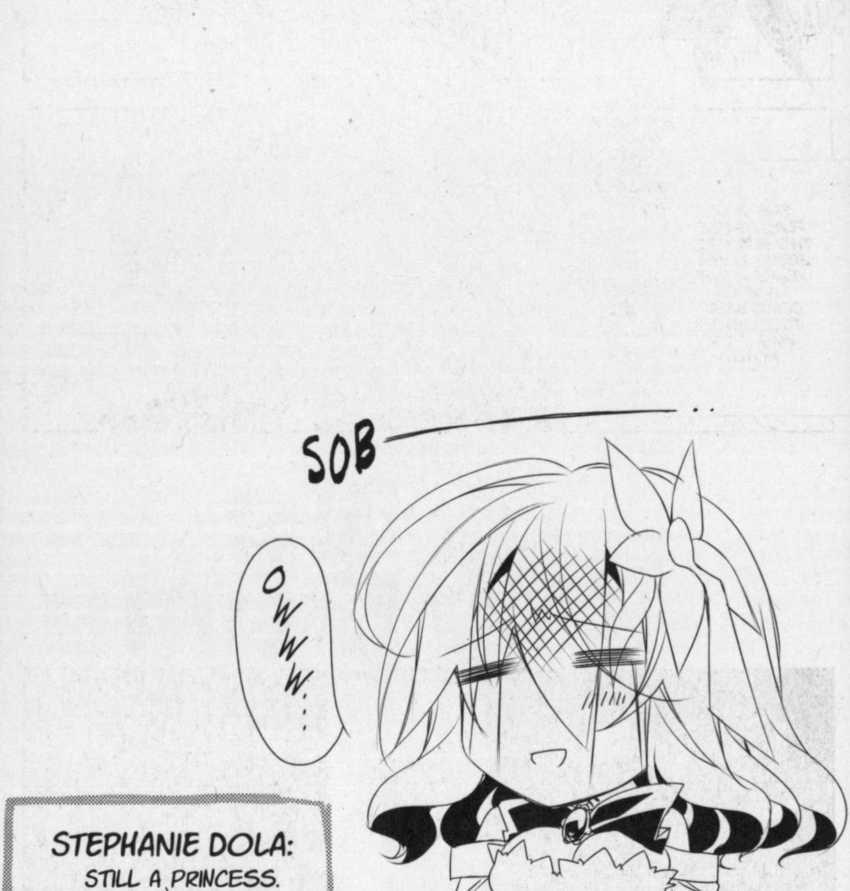
SOB......
OWWW...
STEPHANIE DOLA:
STILL A PRINCESS.
FORMER

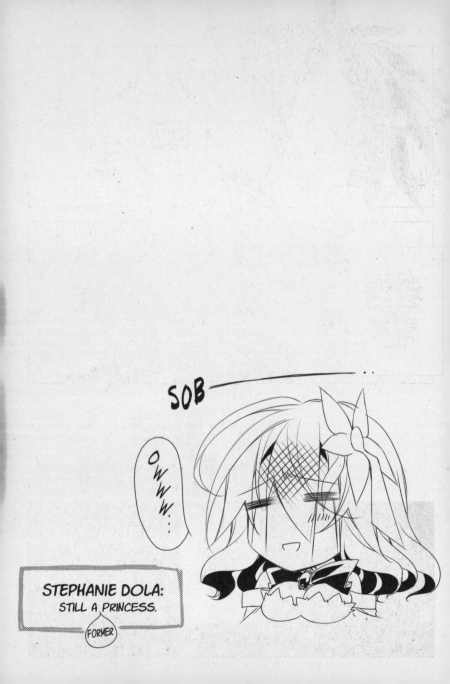

No
Game
No
LiFe

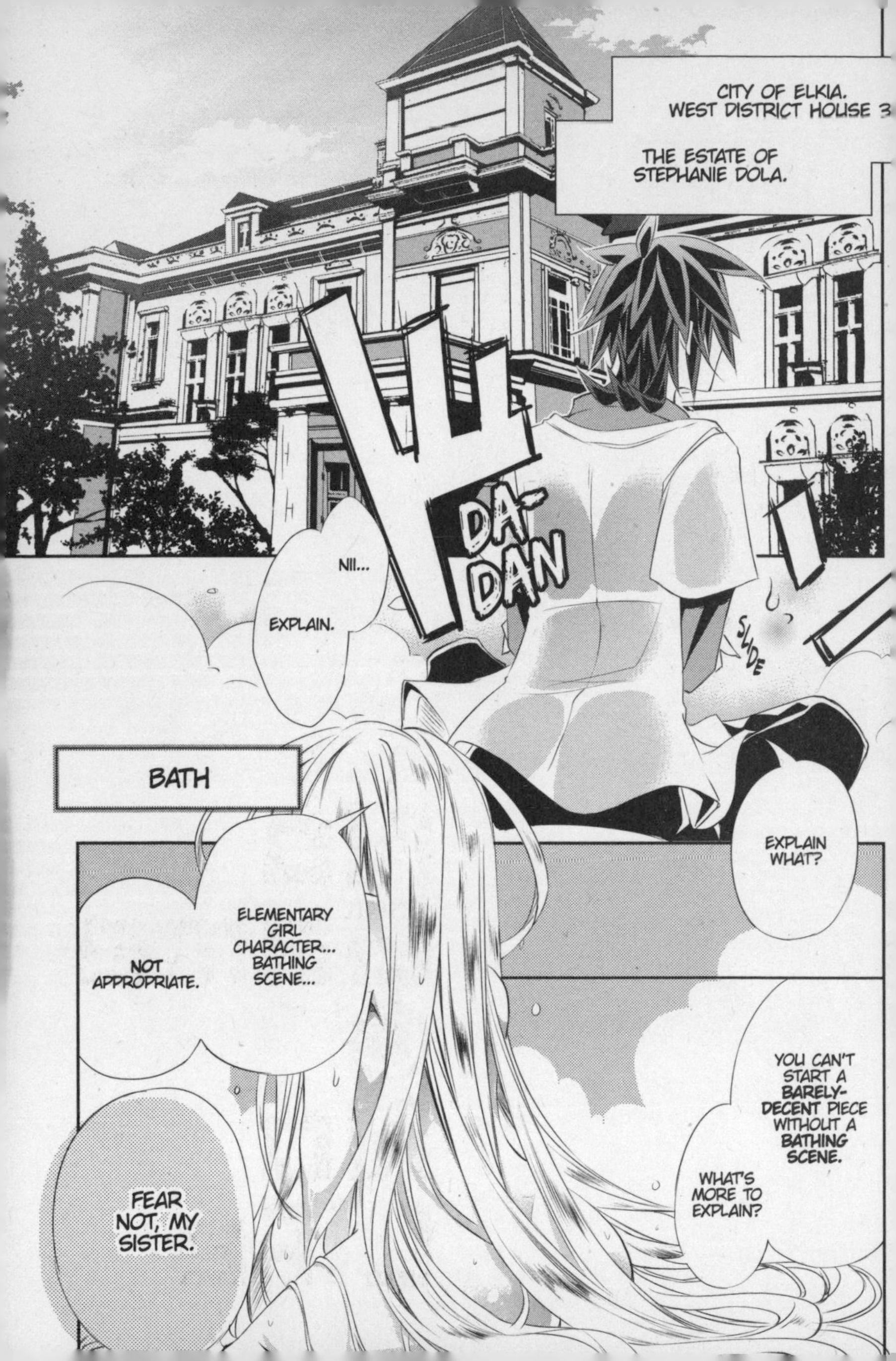
CITY OF ELKIA. WEST DISTRICT HOUSE 3
THE ESTATE OF STEPHANIE DOLA.
DA-DAN
SLIDE
BATH
NII...
EXPLAIN.
EXPLAIN WHAT?
ELEMENTARY GIRL CHARACTER... BATHING SCENE...
NOT APPROPRIATE.
YOU CAN'T START A BARELY-DECENT PIECE WITHOUT A BATHING SCENE.
WHAT'S MORE TO EXPLAIN?
FEAR NOT, MY SISTER.

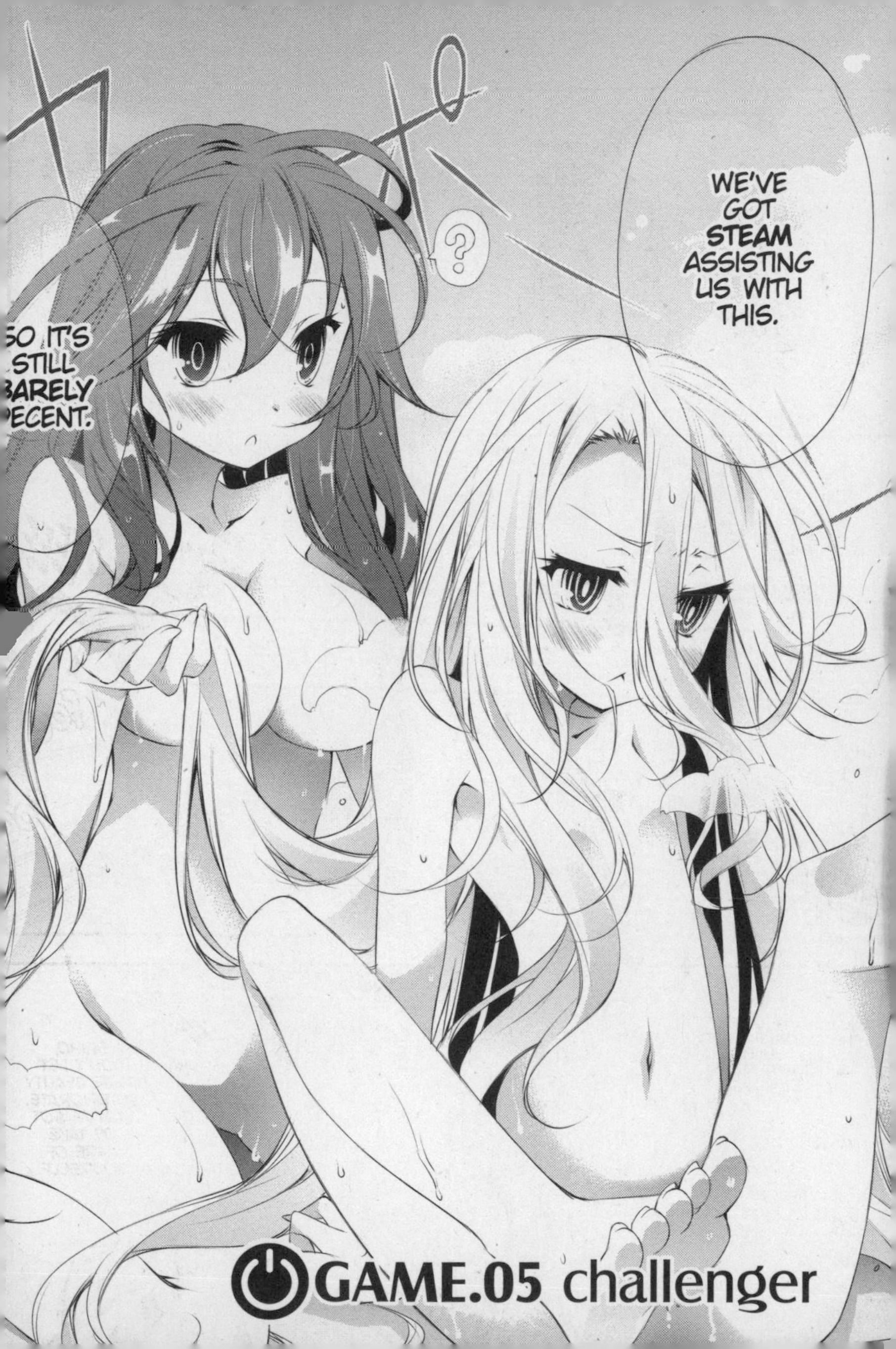
WE'VE GOT STEAM ASSISTING US WITH THIS.
?
SO IT'S STILL BARELY DECENT.
GAME.05 challenger

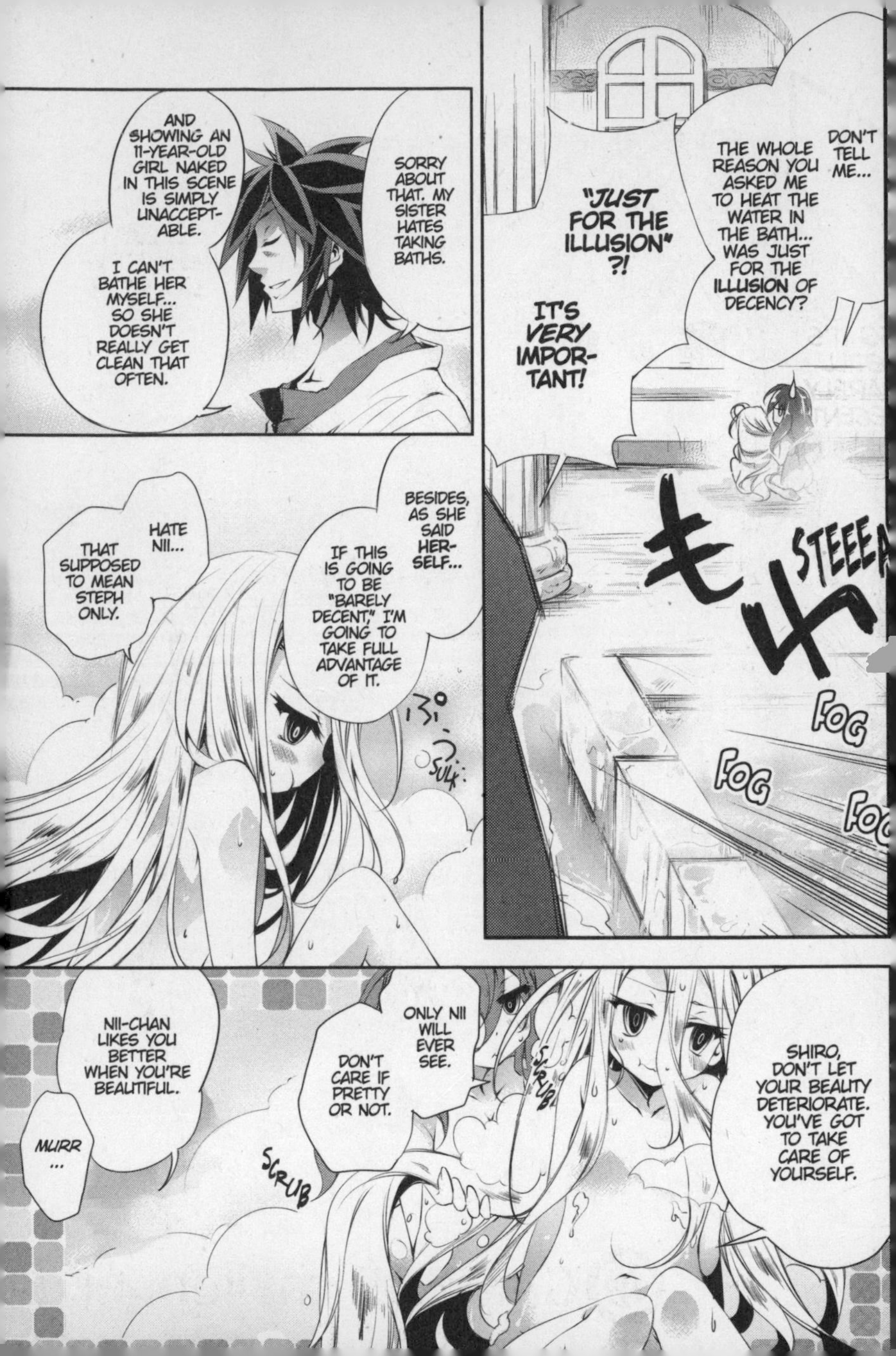
DON'T TELL ME...
THE WHOLE REASON YOU ASKED ME TO HEAT THE WATER IN THE BATH... WAS JUST FOR THE ILLUSION OF DECENCY?
"JUST FOR THE ILLUSION" ?!
IT'S VERY IMPORTANT!
STEEEA
FOG
FOG
FOG
SORRY ABOUT THAT. MY SISTER HATES TAKING BATHS.
AND SHOWING AN 11-YEAR-OLD GIRL NAKED IN THIS SCENE IS SIMPLY UNACCEPTABLE.
I CAN'T BATHE HER MYSELF... SO SHE DOESN'T REALLY GET CLEAN THAT OFTEN.
BESIDES, AS SHE SAID HERSELF...
IF THIS IS GOING TO BE "BARELY DECENT," I'M GOING TO TAKE FULL ADVANTAGE OF IT.
HATE NII...
THAT SUPPOSED TO MEAN STEPH ONLY.
SULK
SHIRO, DON'T LET YOUR BEAUTY DETERIORATE. YOU'VE GOT TO TAKE CARE OF YOURSELF.
SCRUB
ONLY NII WILL EVER SEE.
DON'T CARE IF PRETTY OR NOT.
SCRUB
NII-CHAN LIKES YOU BETTER WHEN YOU'RE BEAUTIFUL.
MURR ...

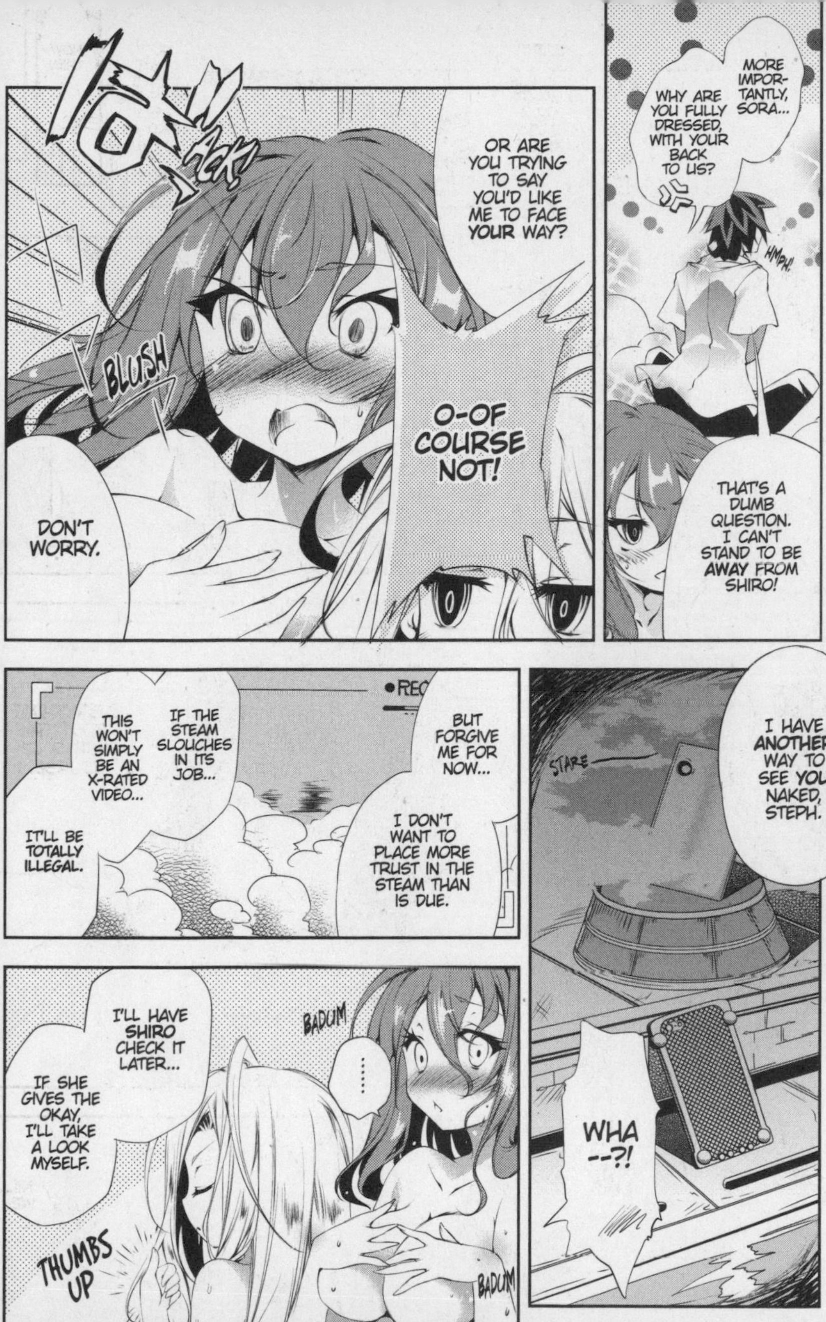

MORE IMPORTANTLY, SORA...
WHY ARE YOU FULLY DRESSED, WITH YOUR BACK TO US?
HMPH!
THAT'S A DUMB QUESTION. I CAN'T STAND TO BE AWAY FROM SHIRO!
OR ARE YOU TRYING TO SAY YOU'D LIKE ME TO FACE YOUR WAY?
ACK!
O-OF COURSE NOT!
BLUSH
DON'T WORRY.
I HAVE ANOTHER WAY TO SEE YOU NAKED, STEPH.
STARE
WHA--?!
REC
BUT FORGIVE ME FOR NOW...
I DON'T WANT TO PLACE MORE TRUST IN THE STEAM THAN IS DUE.
IF THE STEAM SLOUCHES IN ITS JOB...
THIS WON'T SIMPLY BE AN X-RATED VIDEO...
IT'LL BE TOTALLY ILLEGAL.
BADUM
......
I'LL HAVE SHIRO CHECK IT LATER...
IF SHE GIVES THE OKAY, I'LL TAKE A LOOK MYSELF.
THUMBS UP
BADUM

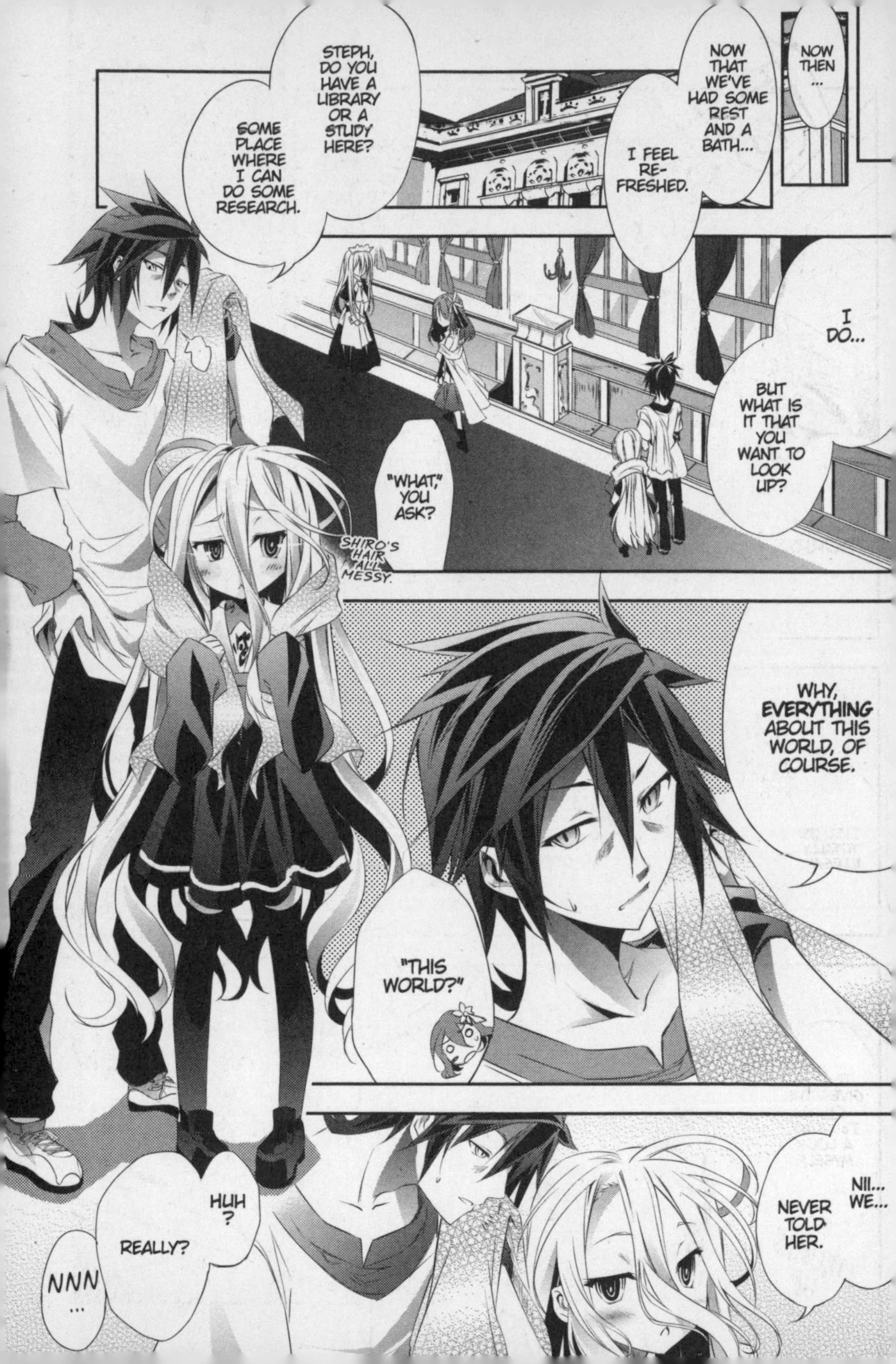
NOW THEN...
NOW THAT WE'VE HAD SOME REST AND A BATH...
I FEEL RE-FRESHED.
STEPH, DO YOU HAVE A LIBRARY OR A STUDY HERE?
SOME PLACE WHERE I CAN DO SOME RESEARCH.
I DO...
BUT WHAT IS IT THAT YOU WANT TO LOOK UP?
"WHAT," YOU ASK?
SHIRO'S HAIR ALL MESSY.
WHY, EVERYTHING ABOUT THIS WORLD, OF COURSE.
"THIS WORLD?"
NII... WE...
NEVER TOLD HER.
HUH?
REALLY?
NNN...

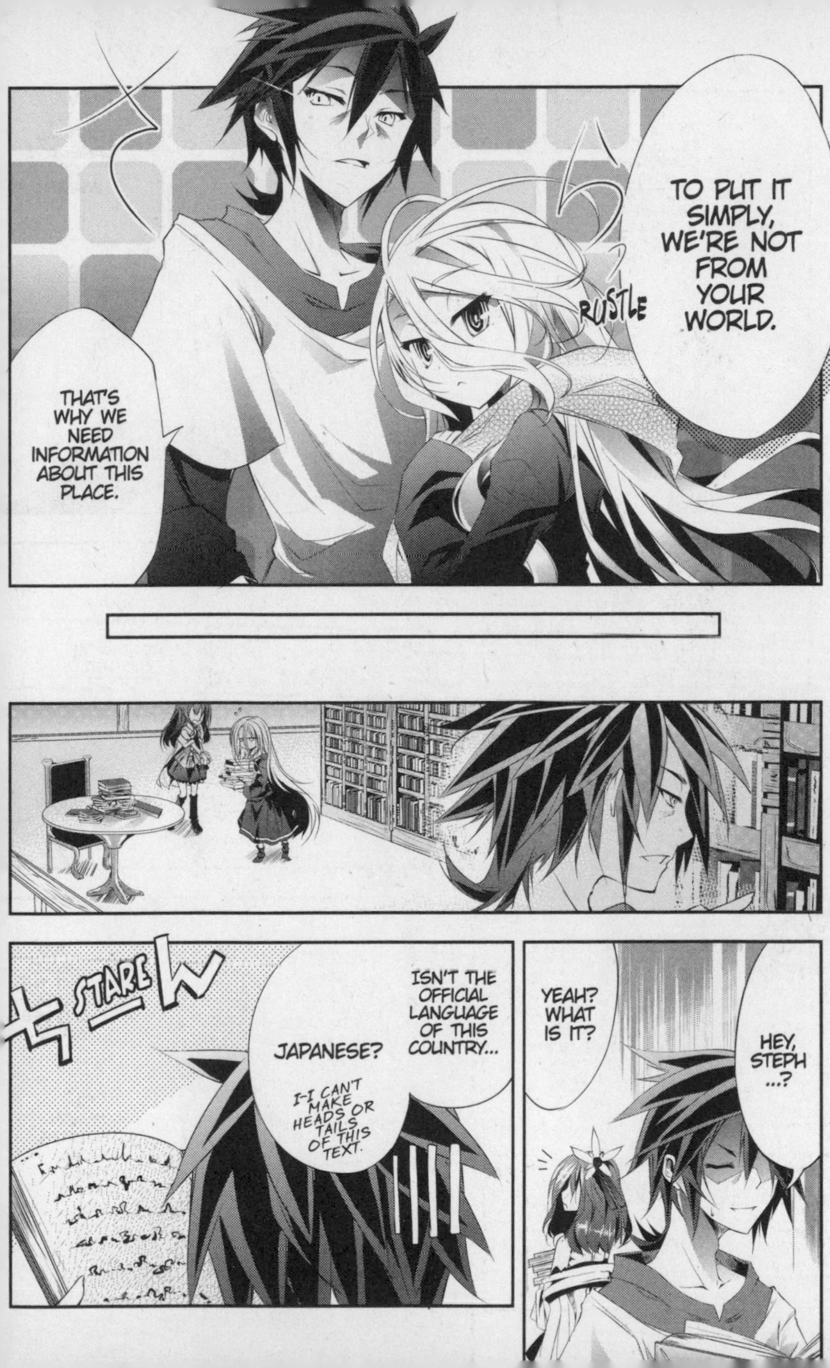
TO PUT IT SIMPLY, WE'RE NOT FROM YOUR WORLD.
RUSTLE
THAT'S WHY WE NEED INFORMATION ABOUT THIS PLACE.
HEY, STEPH ...?
YEAH? WHAT IS IT?
ISN'T THE OFFICIAL LANGUAGE OF THIS COUNTRY...
JAPANESE?
I-I CAN'T MAKE HEADS OR TAILS OF THIS TEXT.
STARE

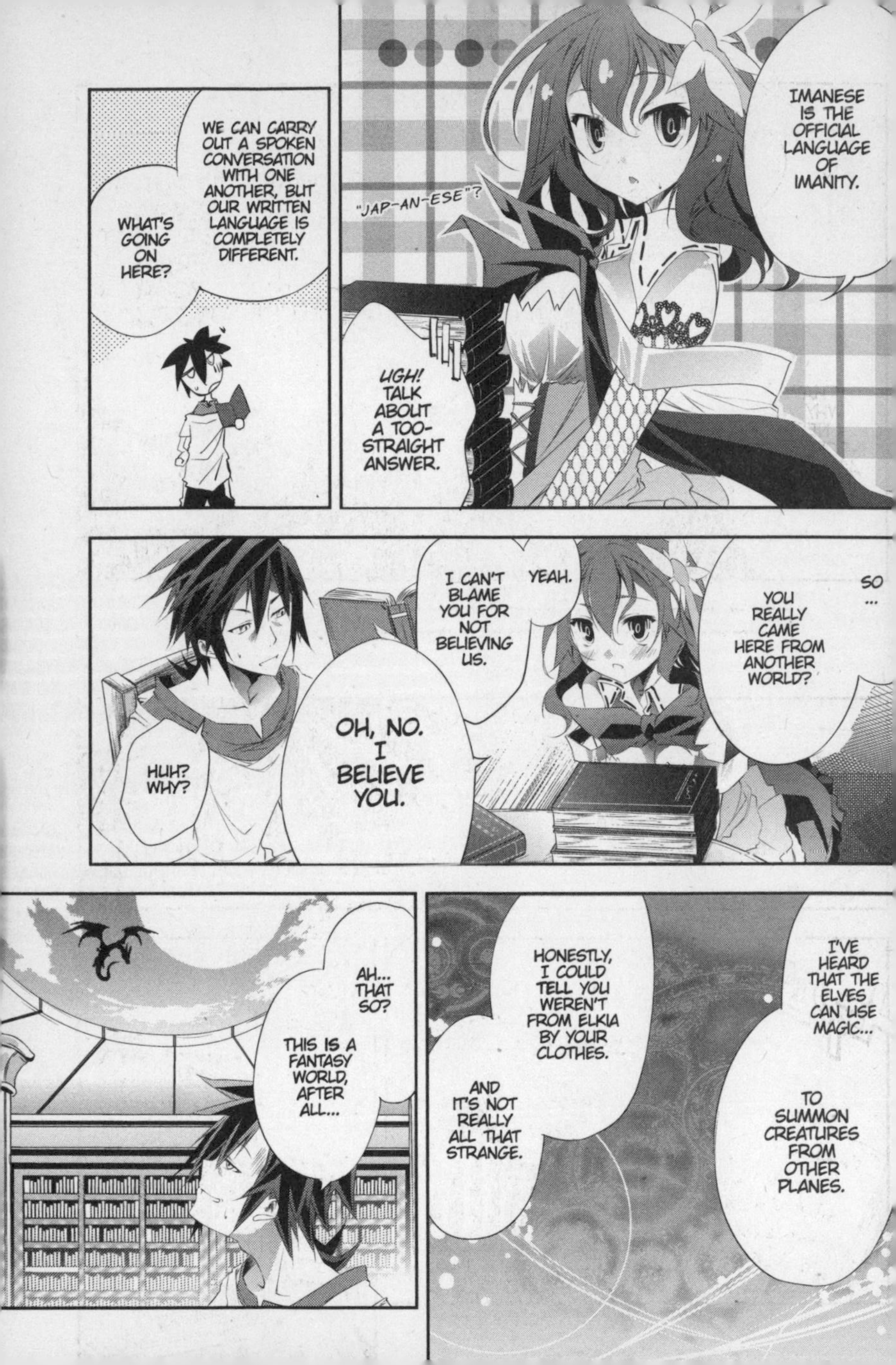
IMANESE IS THE OFFICIAL LANGUAGE OF IMANITY.
"JAP-AN-ESE"?
UGH! TALK ABOUT A TOO-STRAIGHT ANSWER.
WE CAN CARRY OUT A SPOKEN CONVERSATION WITH ONE ANOTHER, BUT OUR WRITTEN LANGUAGE IS COMPLETELY DIFFERENT.
WHAT'S GOING ON HERE?
SO ...
YOU REALLY CAME HERE FROM ANOTHER WORLD?
YEAH.
I CAN'T BLAME YOU FOR NOT BELIEVING US.
OH, NO. I BELIEVE YOU.
HUH? WHY?
I'VE HEARD THAT THE ELVES CAN USE MAGIC...
TO SUMMON CREATURES FROM OTHER PLANES.
HONESTLY, I COULD TELL YOU WEREN'T FROM ELKIA BY YOUR CLOTHES.
AND IT'S NOT REALLY ALL THAT STRANGE.
AH... THAT SO?
THIS IS A FANTASY WORLD, AFTER ALL...

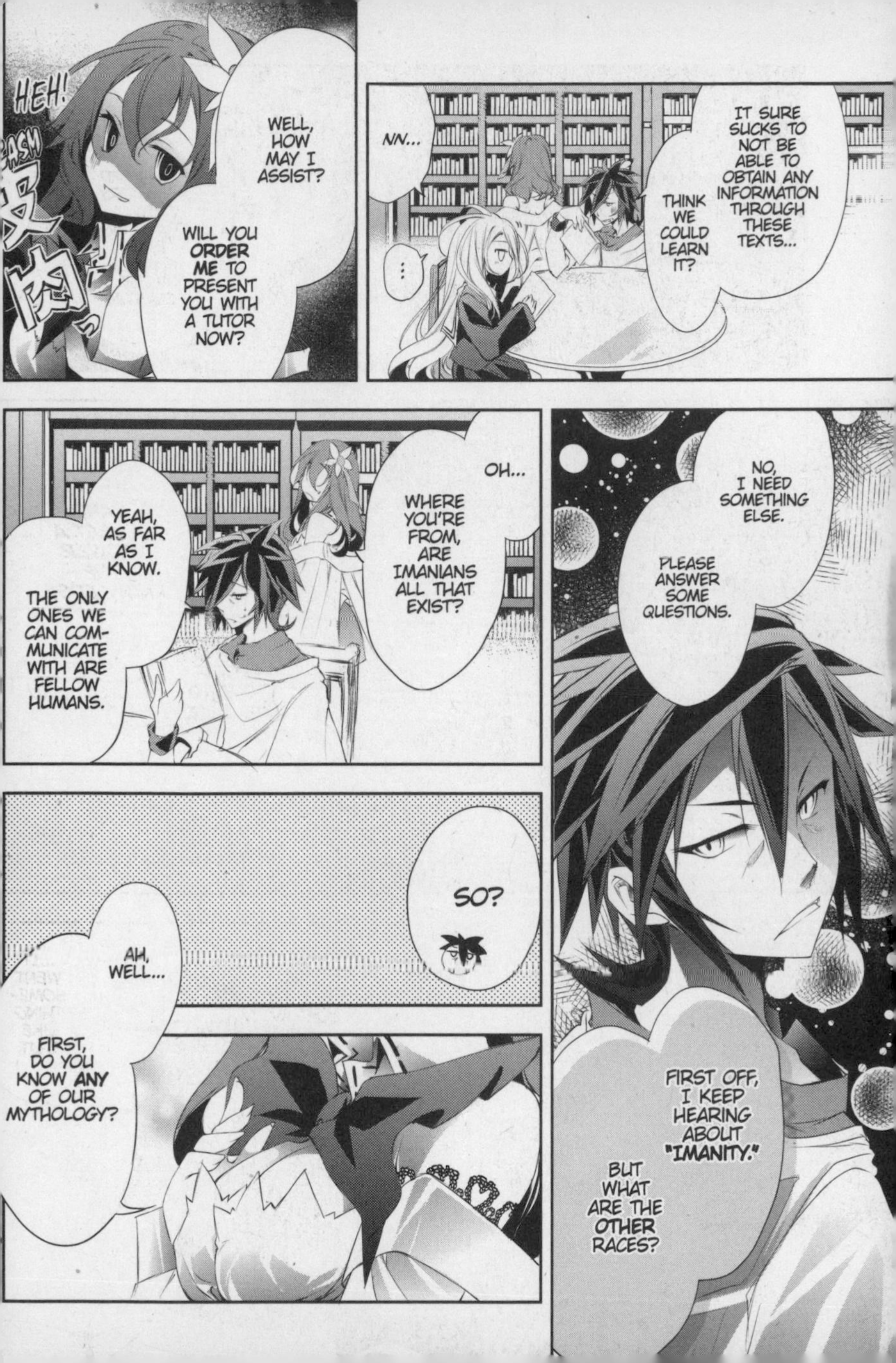
IT SURE SUCKS TO NOT BE ABLE TO OBTAIN ANY INFORMATION THROUGH THESE TEXTS...
NN...
THINK WE COULD LEARN IT?
...
HEH!
WELL, HOW MAY I ASSIST?
WILL YOU ORDER ME TO PRESENT YOU WITH A TUTOR NOW?
NO, I NEED SOMETHING ELSE.
PLEASE ANSWER SOME QUESTIONS.
FIRST OFF, I KEEP HEARING ABOUT "IMANITY."
BUT WHAT ARE THE OTHER RACES?
OH...
WHERE YOU'RE FROM, ARE IMANIANS ALL THAT EXIST?
YEAH, AS FAR AS I KNOW.
THE ONLY ONES WE CAN COMMUNICATE WITH ARE FELLOW HUMANS.
SO?
AH, WELL...
FIRST, DO YOU KNOW ANY OF OUR MYTHOLOGY?

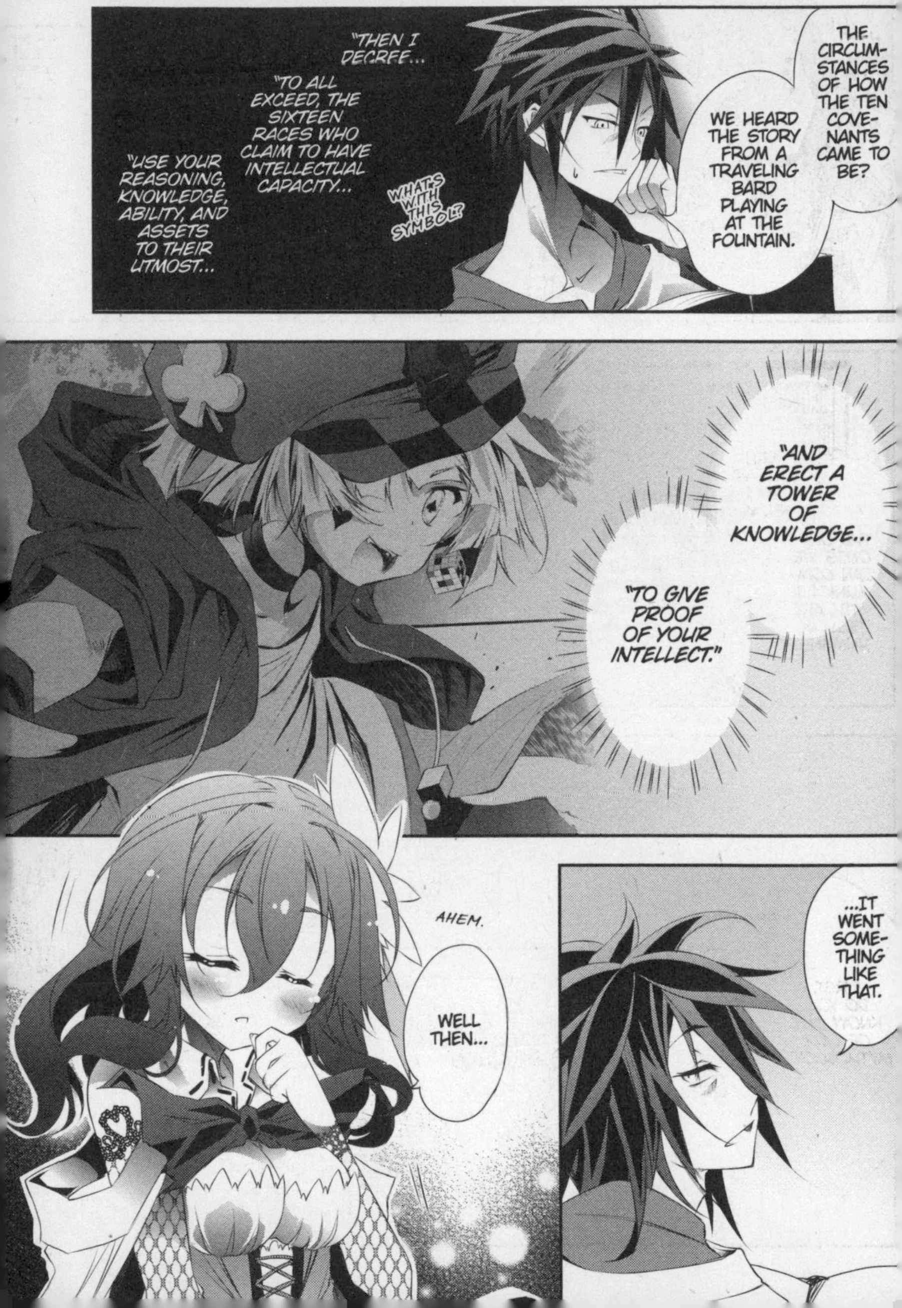
THE CIRCUMSTANCES OF HOW THE TEN COVENANTS CAME TO BE?
WE HEARD THE STORY FROM A TRAVELING BARD PLAYING AT THE FOUNTAIN.
WHAT'S WITH THIS SYMBOL!?
"THEN I DECREE...
"TO ALL EXCEED, THE SIXTEEN RACES WHO CLAIM TO HAVE INTELLECTUAL CAPACITY...
"USE YOUR REASONING, KNOWLEDGE, ABILITY, AND ASSETS TO THEIR UTMOST...
"AND ERECT A TOWER OF KNOWLEDGE...
"TO GIVE PROOF OF YOUR INTELLECT."
...IT WENT SOMETHING LIKE THAT.
AHEM.
WELL THEN...

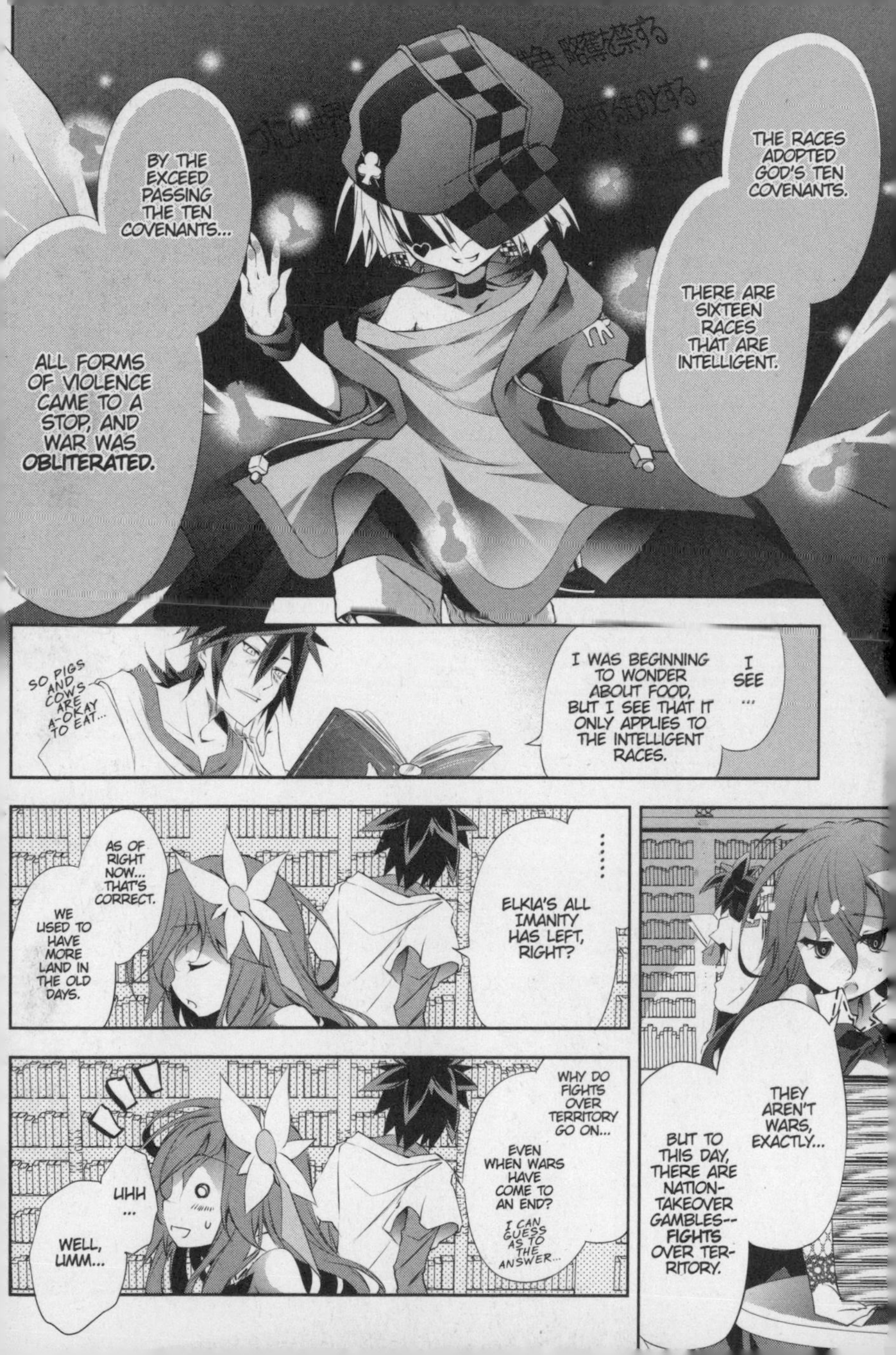
THE RACES ADOPTED GOD'S TEN COVENANTS.
THERE ARE SIXTEEN RACES THAT ARE INTELLIGENT.
BY THE EXCEED PASSING THE TEN COVENANTS...
ALL FORMS OF VIOLENCE CAME TO A STOP, AND WAR WAS OBLITERATED.
I SEE...
I WAS BEGINNING TO WONDER ABOUT FOOD, BUT I SEE THAT IT ONLY APPLIES TO THE INTELLIGENT RACES.
SO PIGS AND COWS ARE A-OKAY TO EAT...
THEY AREN'T WARS, EXACTLY...
BUT TO THIS DAY, THERE ARE NATION-TAKEOVER GAMBLES--FIGHTS OVER TERRITORY.
......
ELKIA'S ALL IMANITY HAS LEFT, RIGHT?
AS OF RIGHT NOW... THAT'S CORRECT.
WE USED TO HAVE MORE LAND IN THE OLD DAYS.
WHY DO FIGHTS OVER TERRITORY GO ON...
EVEN WHEN WARS HAVE COME TO AN END?
I CAN GUESS AS TO THE ANSWER...
UHH...
WELL, UMM...

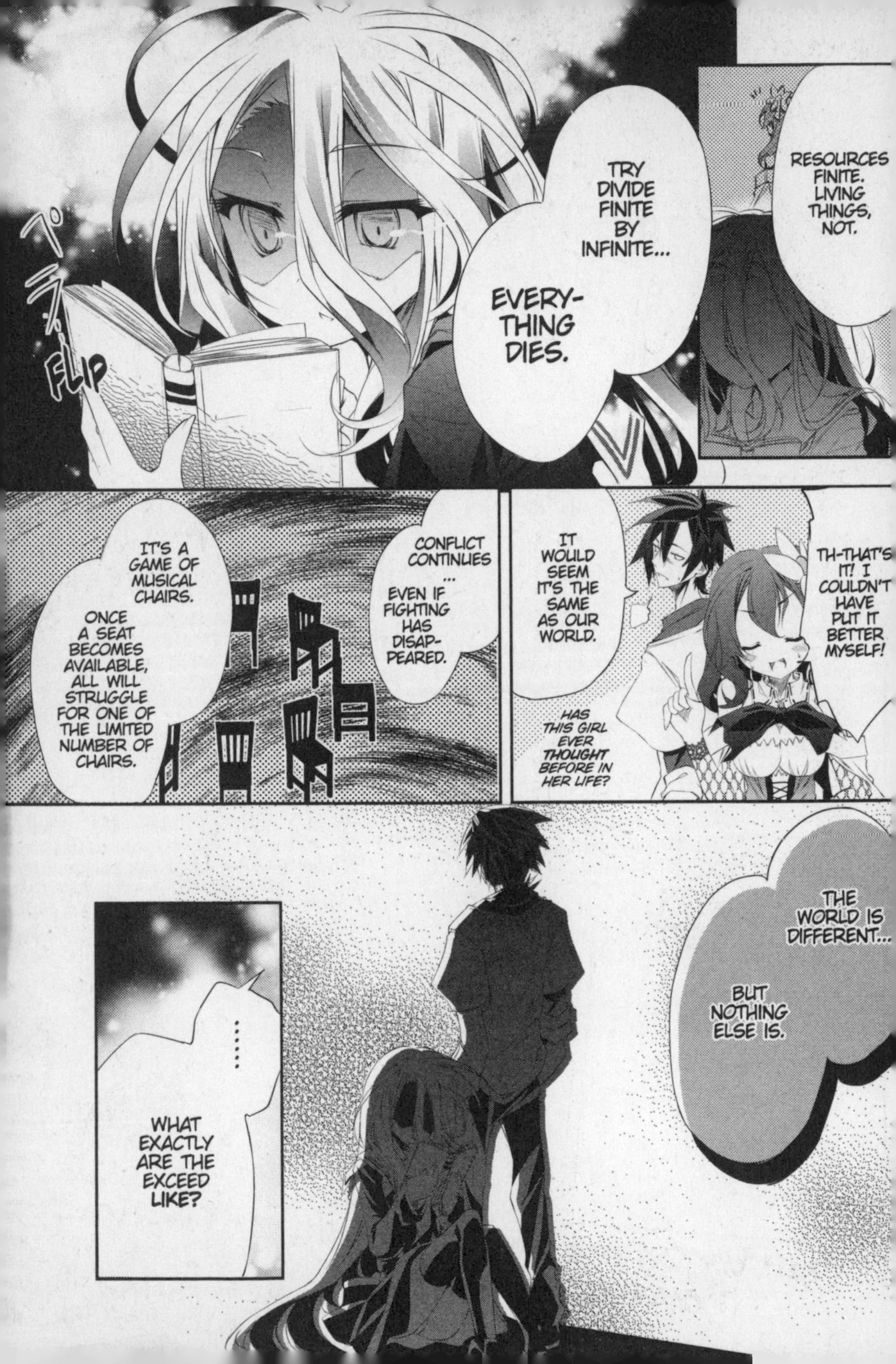

RESOURCES FINITE. LIVING THINGS, NOT.
TRY DIVIDE FINITE BY INFINITE...
EVERY-THING DIES.
FLIP
IT WOULD SEEM IT'S THE SAME AS OUR WORLD.
TH-THAT'S IT! I COULDN'T HAVE PUT IT BETTER MYSELF!
HAS THIS GIRL EVER THOUGHT BEFORE IN HER LIFE?
CONFLICT CONTINUES ... EVEN IF FIGHTING HAS DISAPPEARED.
IT'S A GAME OF MUSICAL CHAIRS.
ONCE A SEAT BECOMES AVAILABLE, ALL WILL STRUGGLE FOR ONE OF THE LIMITED NUMBER OF CHAIRS.
THE WORLD IS DIFFERENT...
BUT NOTHING ELSE IS.
......
WHAT EXACTLY ARE THE EXCEED LIKE?

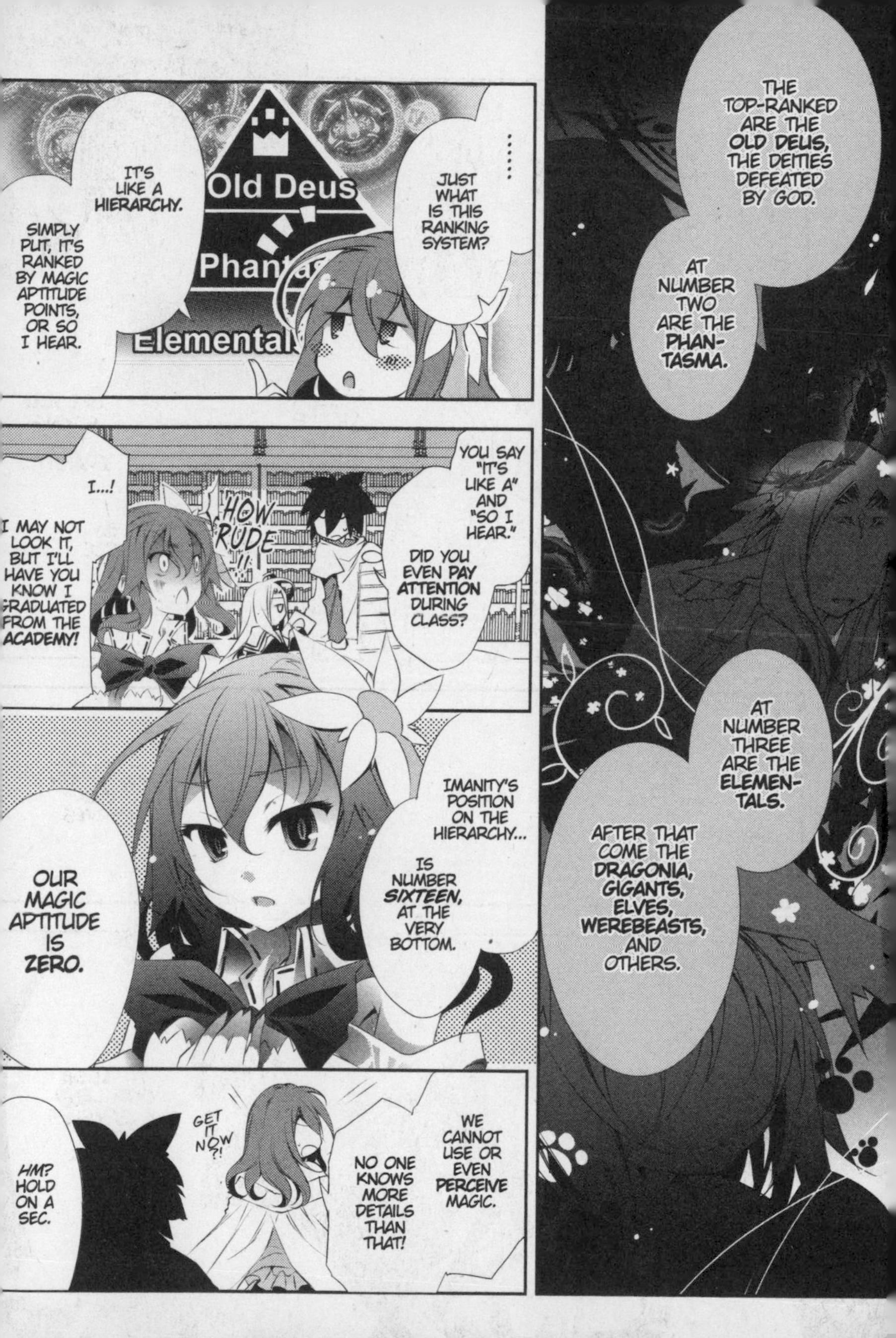

THE TOP-RANKED ARE THE OLD DEUS, THE DEITIES DEFEATED BY GOD.
AT NUMBER TWO ARE THE PHANTASMA.
AT NUMBER THREE ARE THE ELEMENTALS.
AFTER THAT COME THE DRAGONIA, GIGANTS, ELVES, WEREBEASTS, AND OTHERS.
......
JUST WHAT IS THIS RANKING SYSTEM?
Old Deus
Phantas
Elemental
IT'S LIKE A HIERARCHY.
SIMPLY PUT, IT'S RANKED BY MAGIC APTITUDE POINTS, OR SO I HEAR.
YOU SAY "IT'S LIKE A" AND "SO I HEAR."
DID YOU EVEN PAY ATTENTION DURING CLASS?
HOW RUDE!!
I...!
I MAY NOT LOOK IT, BUT I'LL HAVE YOU KNOW I GRADUATED FROM THE ACADEMY!
IMANITY'S POSITION ON THE HIERARCHY...
IS NUMBER SIXTEEN, AT THE VERY BOTTOM.
OUR MAGIC APTITUDE IS ZERO.
WE CANNOT USE OR EVEN PERCEIVE MAGIC.
NO ONE KNOWS MORE DETAILS THAN THAT!
GET IT NOW?!
HM? HOLD ON A SEC.

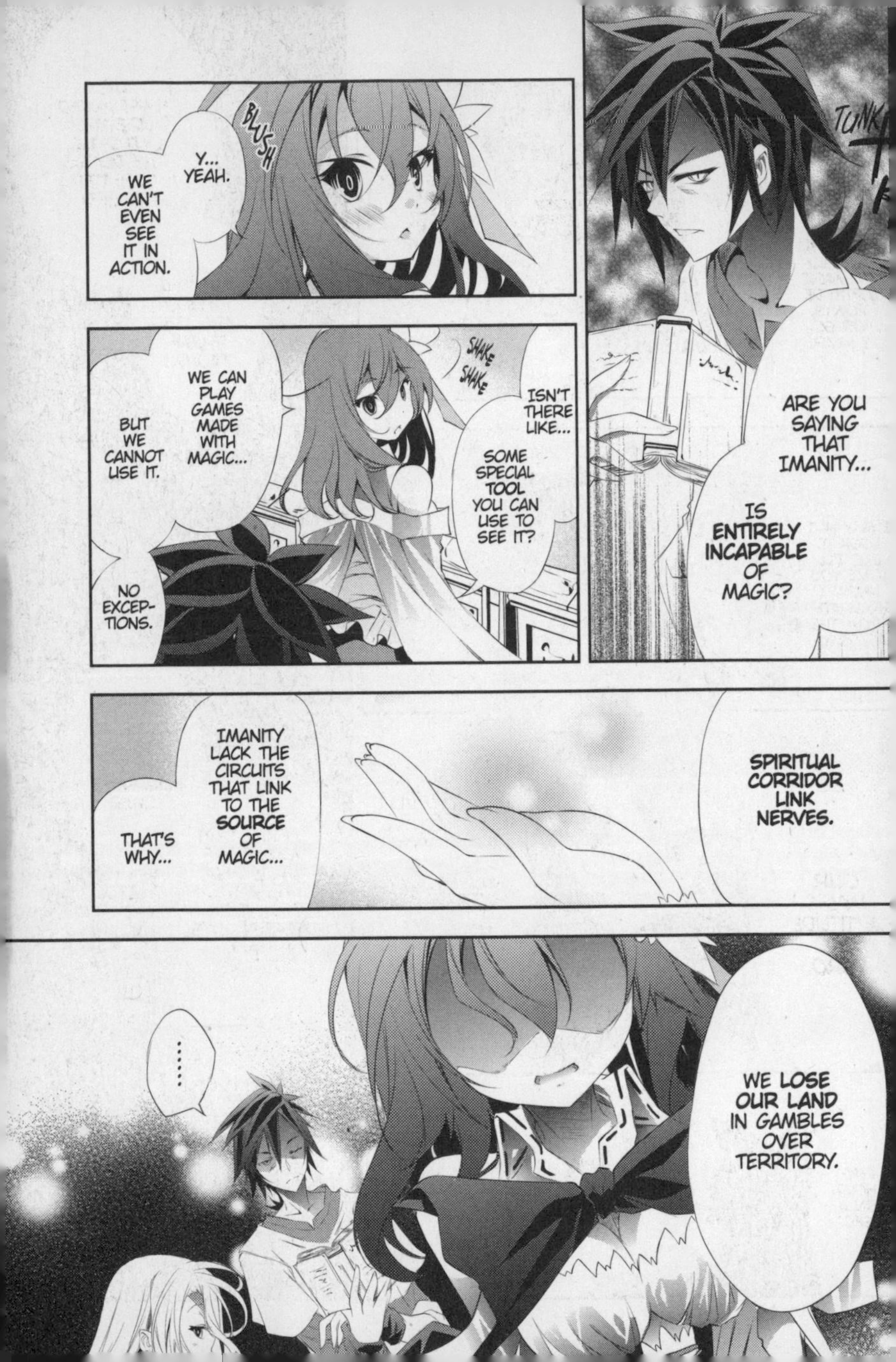
TUNK
ARE YOU SAYING THAT IMANITY...
IS ENTIRELY INCAPABLE OF MAGIC?
BLUSH
Y... YEAH.
WE CAN'T EVEN SEE IT IN ACTION.
SHAKE SHAKE
ISN'T THERE LIKE...
SOME SPECIAL TOOL YOU CAN USE TO SEE IT?
WE CAN PLAY GAMES MADE WITH MAGIC...
BUT WE CANNOT USE IT.
NO EXCEPTIONS.
SPIRITUAL CORRIDOR LINK NERVES.
IMANITY LACK THE CIRCUITS THAT LINK TO THE SOURCE OF MAGIC...
THAT'S WHY...
WE LOSE OUR LAND IN GAMBLES OVER TERRITORY.
......

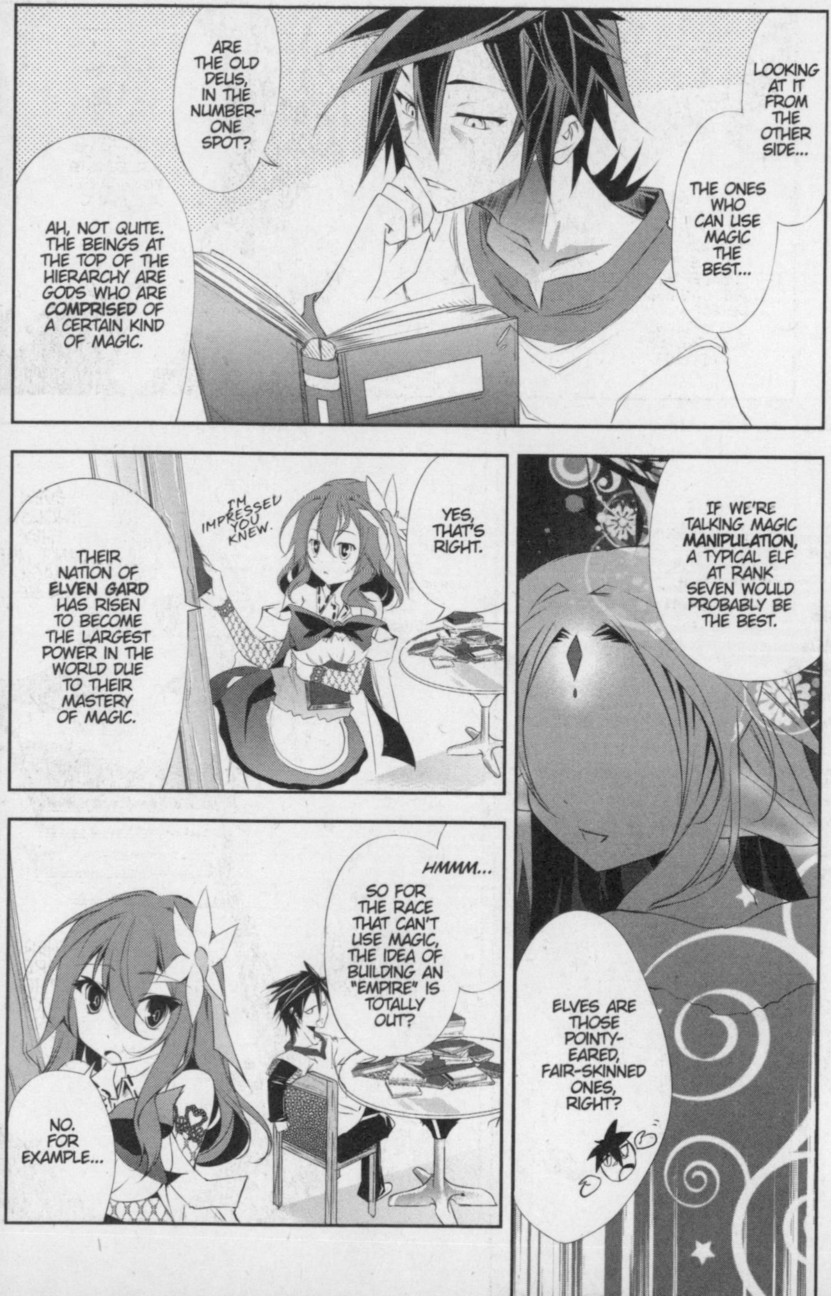
LOOKING AT IT FROM THE OTHER SIDE...
THE ONES WHO CAN USE MAGIC THE BEST...
ARE THE OLD DEUS, IN THE NUMBER-ONE SPOT?
AH, NOT QUITE. THE BEINGS AT THE TOP OF THE HIERARCHY ARE GODS WHO ARE **COMPRISED OF** A CERTAIN KIND OF MAGIC.
IF WE'RE TALKING MAGIC **MANIPULATION**, A TYPICAL ELF AT RANK SEVEN WOULD PROBABLY BE THE BEST.
ELVES ARE THOSE POINTY-EARED, FAIR-SKINNED ONES, RIGHT?
YES, THAT'S RIGHT.
I'M IMPRESSED YOU KNEW.
THEIR NATION OF **ELVEN GARD** HAS RISEN TO BECOME THE LARGEST POWER IN THE WORLD DUE TO THEIR MASTERY OF MAGIC.
HMMM...
SO FOR THE RACE THAT CAN'T USE MAGIC, THE IDEA OF BUILDING AN "EMPIRE" IS TOTALLY OUT?
NO. FOR EXAMPLE...

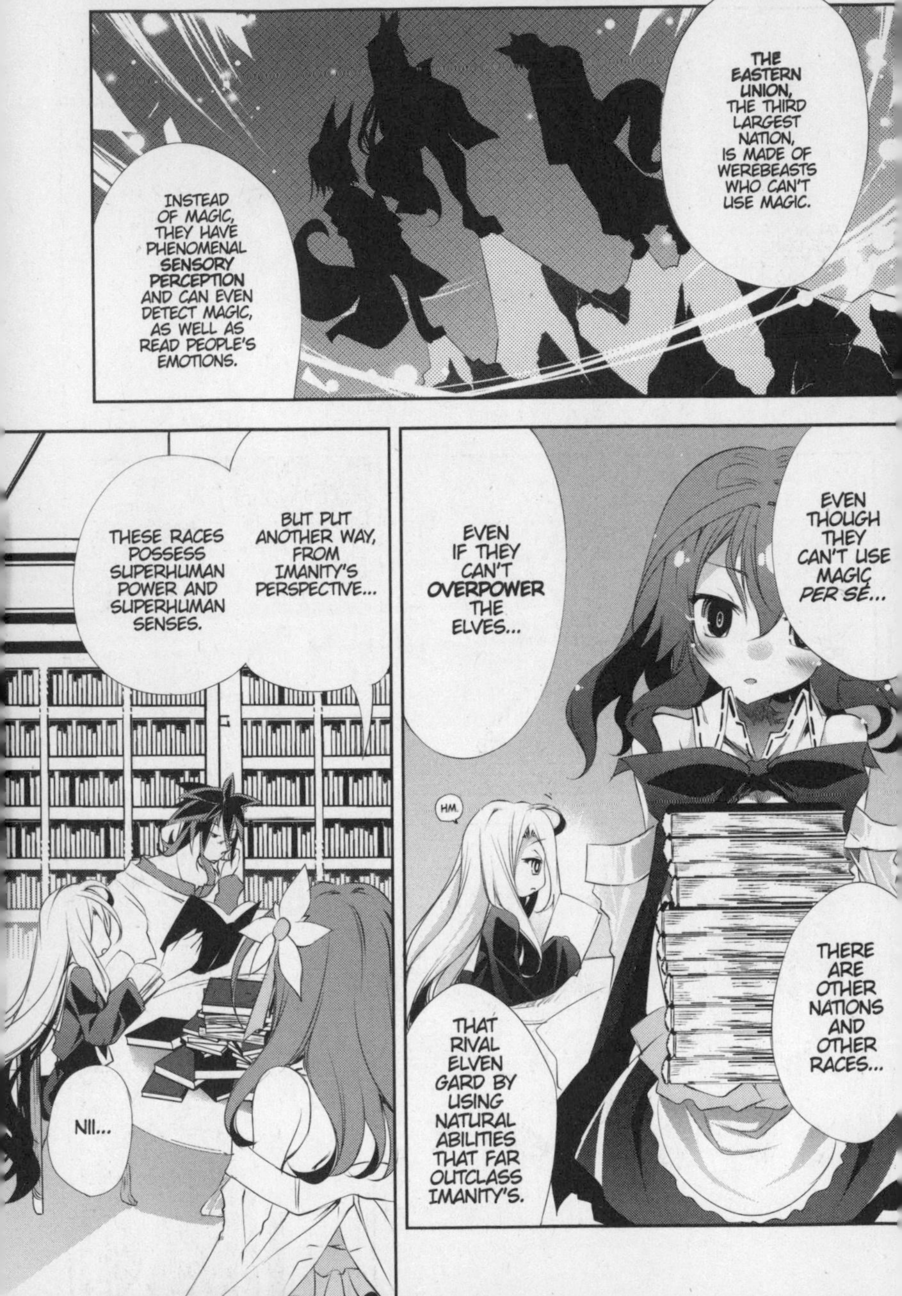
THE EASTERN UNION, THE THIRD LARGEST NATION, IS MADE OF WEREBEASTS WHO CAN'T USE MAGIC.
INSTEAD OF MAGIC, THEY HAVE PHENOMENAL **SENSORY PERCEPTION** AND CAN EVEN DETECT MAGIC, AS WELL AS READ PEOPLE'S EMOTIONS.
EVEN THOUGH THEY CAN'T USE MAGIC *PER SE*...
EVEN IF THEY CAN'T **OVERPOWER** THE ELVES...
THERE ARE OTHER NATIONS AND OTHER RACES...
HM.
THAT RIVAL ELVEN GARD BY USING NATURAL ABILITIES THAT FAR OUTCLASS IMANITY'S.
BUT PUT ANOTHER WAY, FROM IMANITY'S PERSPECTIVE...
THESE RACES POSSESS SUPERHUMAN POWER AND SUPERHUMAN SENSES.
NII...

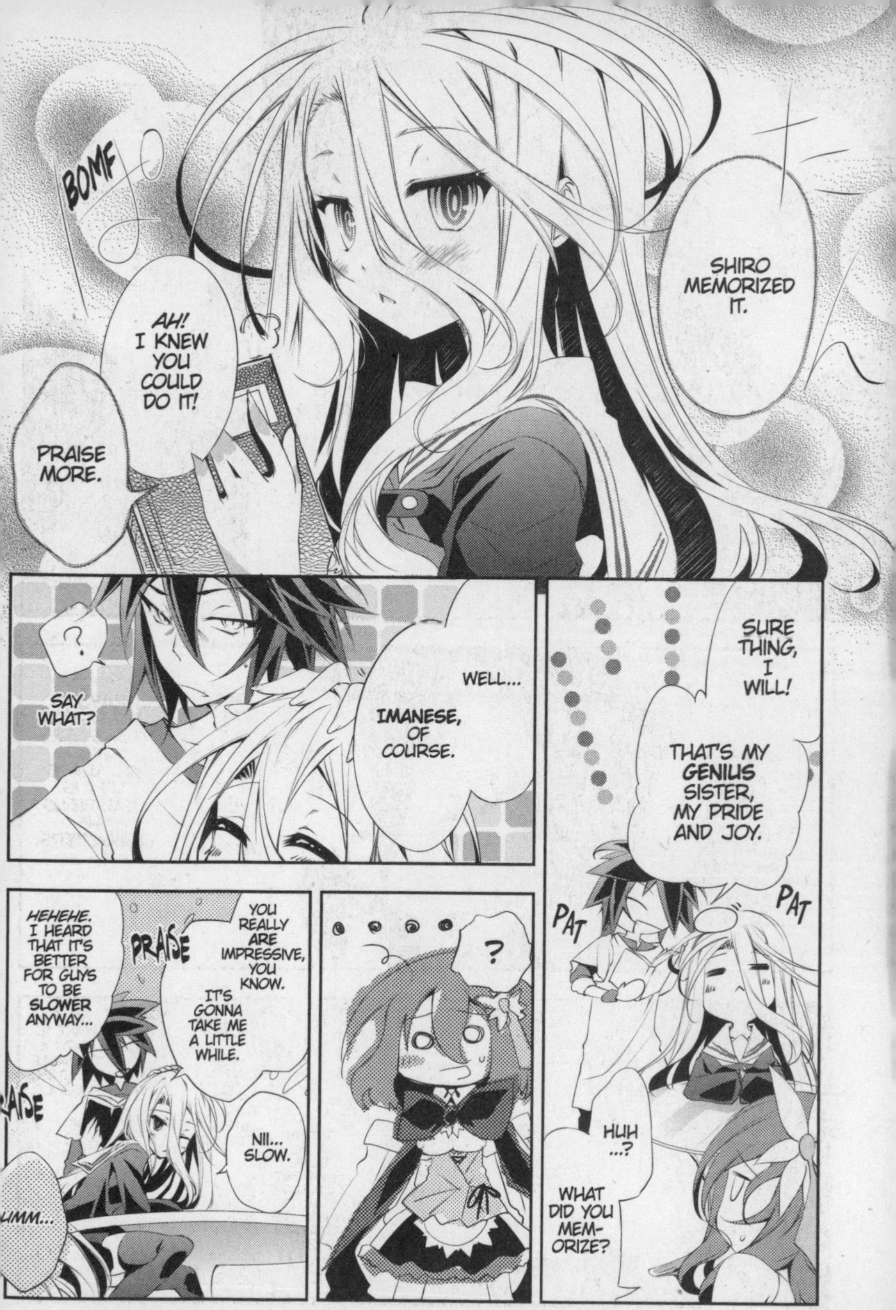
SHIRO MEMORIZED IT.
BOMF
AH! I KNEW YOU COULD DO IT!
PRAISE MORE.
SURE THING, I WILL!
THAT'S MY GENIUS SISTER, MY PRIDE AND JOY.
PAT
PAT
HUH ...?
WHAT DID YOU MEM-ORIZE?
WELL...
IMANESE, OF COURSE.
?
SAY WHAT?
?
YOU REALLY ARE IMPRESSIVE, YOU KNOW.
IT'S GONNA TAKE ME A LITTLE WHILE.
PRAISE
HEHEHE. I HEARD THAT IT'S BETTER FOR GUYS TO BE SLOWER ANYWAY...
NII... SLOW.
UMM...

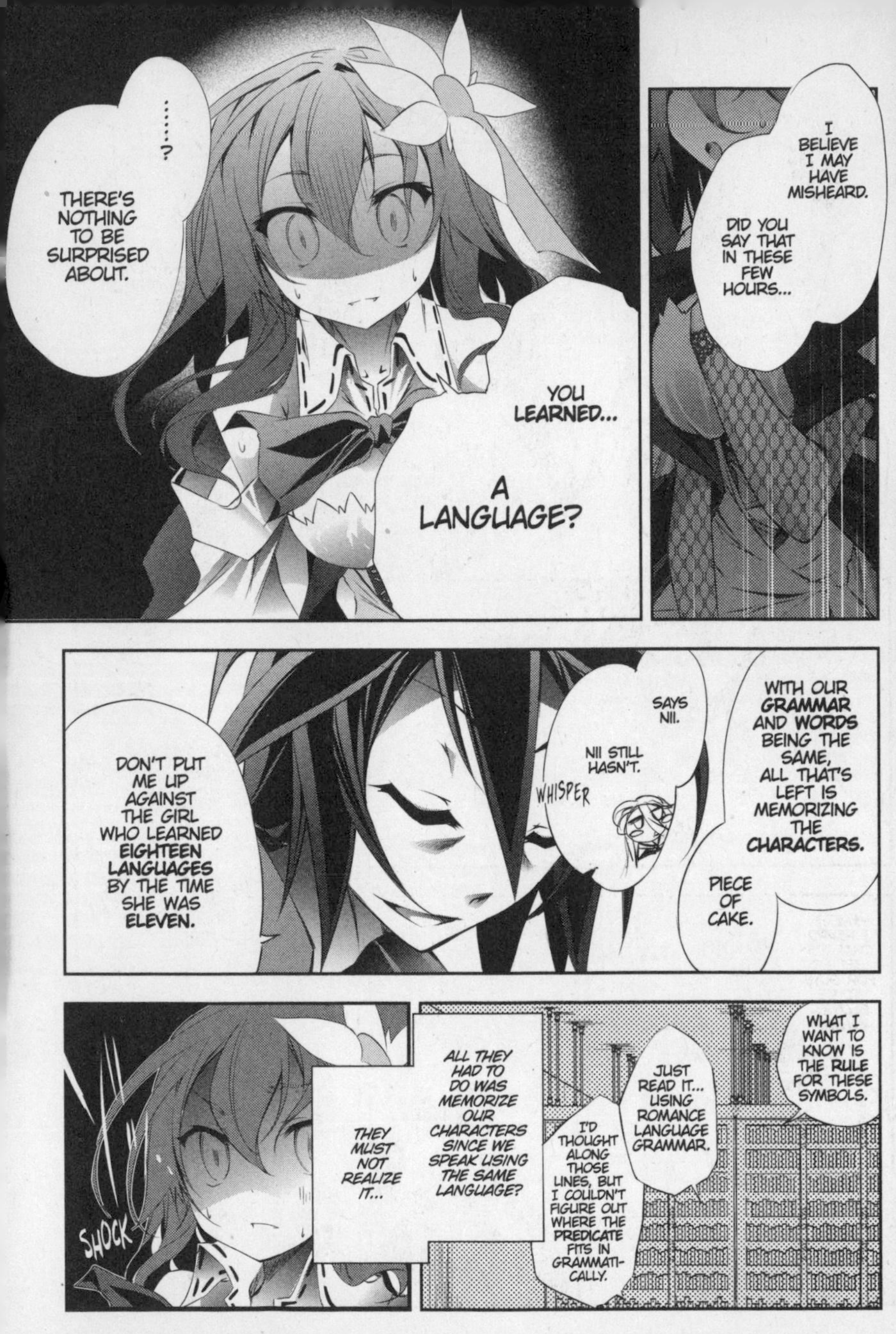

I BELIEVE I MAY HAVE MISHEARD.
DID YOU SAY THAT IN THESE FEW HOURS...
YOU LEARNED...
A LANGUAGE?
......?
THERE'S NOTHING TO BE SURPRISED ABOUT.
WITH OUR GRAMMAR AND WORDS BEING THE SAME, ALL THAT'S LEFT IS MEMORIZING THE CHARACTERS.
PIECE OF CAKE.
SAYS NII.
NII STILL HASN'T.
WHISPER
DON'T PUT ME UP AGAINST THE GIRL WHO LEARNED EIGHTEEN LANGUAGES BY THE TIME SHE WAS ELEVEN.
WHAT I WANT TO KNOW IS THE RULE FOR THESE SYMBOLS.
JUST READ IT... USING ROMANCE LANGUAGE GRAMMAR.
I'D THOUGHT ALONG THOSE LINES, BUT I COULDN'T FIGURE OUT WHERE THE PREDICATE FITS IN GRAMMATICALLY.
ALL THEY HAD TO DO WAS MEMORIZE OUR CHARACTERS SINCE WE SPEAK USING THE SAME LANGUAGE?
THEY MUST NOT REALIZE IT...
SHOCK

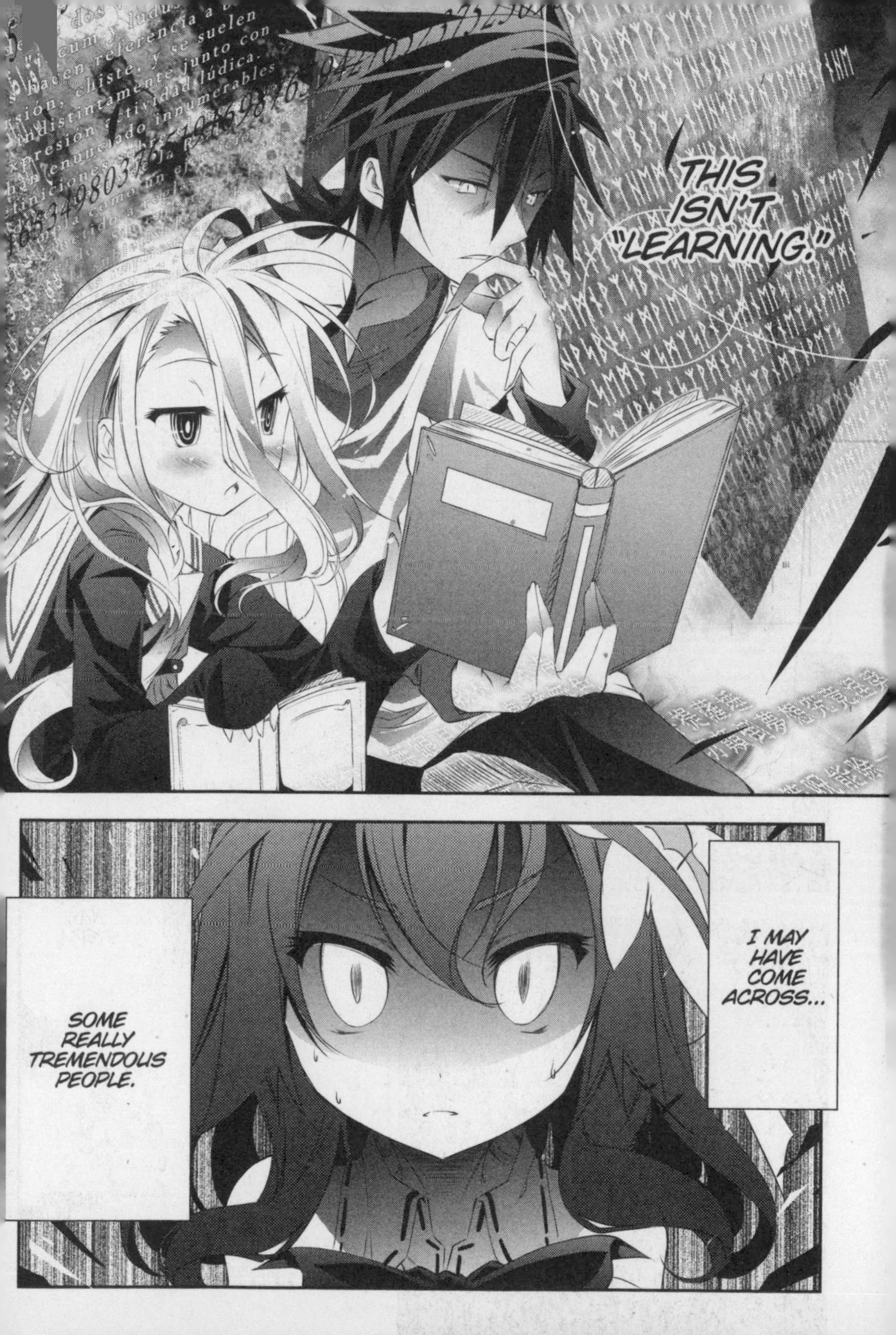
THIS ISN'T "LEARNING."
I MAY HAVE COME ACROSS...
SOME REALLY TREMENDOUS PEOPLE.

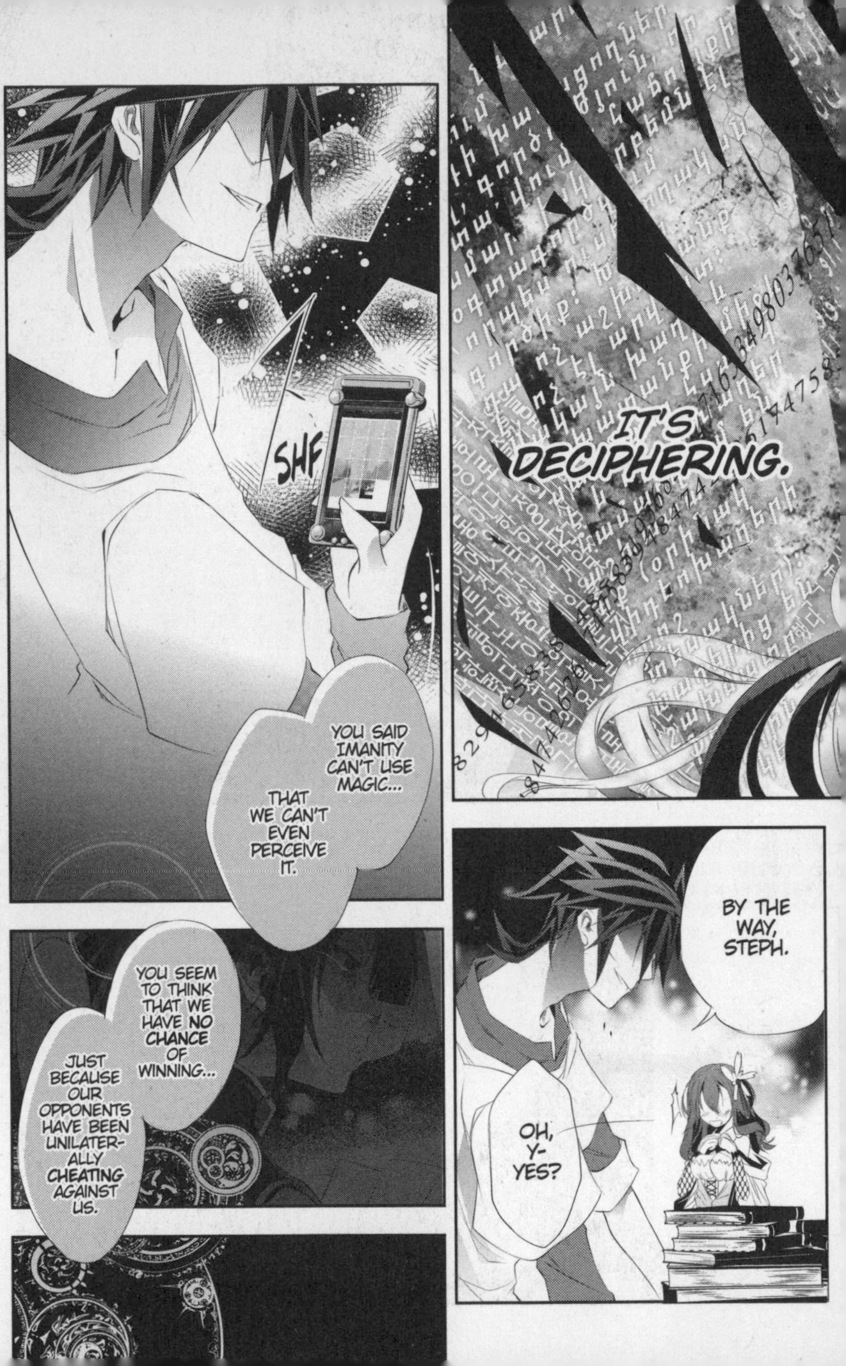
IT'S DECIPHERING.
BY THE WAY, STEPH.
OH, Y-YES?
SHF
YOU SAID IMANITY CAN'T USE MAGIC...
THAT WE CAN'T EVEN PERCEIVE IT.
YOU SEEM TO THINK THAT WE HAVE NO CHANCE OF WINNING...
JUST BECAUSE OUR OPPONENTS HAVE BEEN UNILATER-ALLY CHEATING AGAINST US.

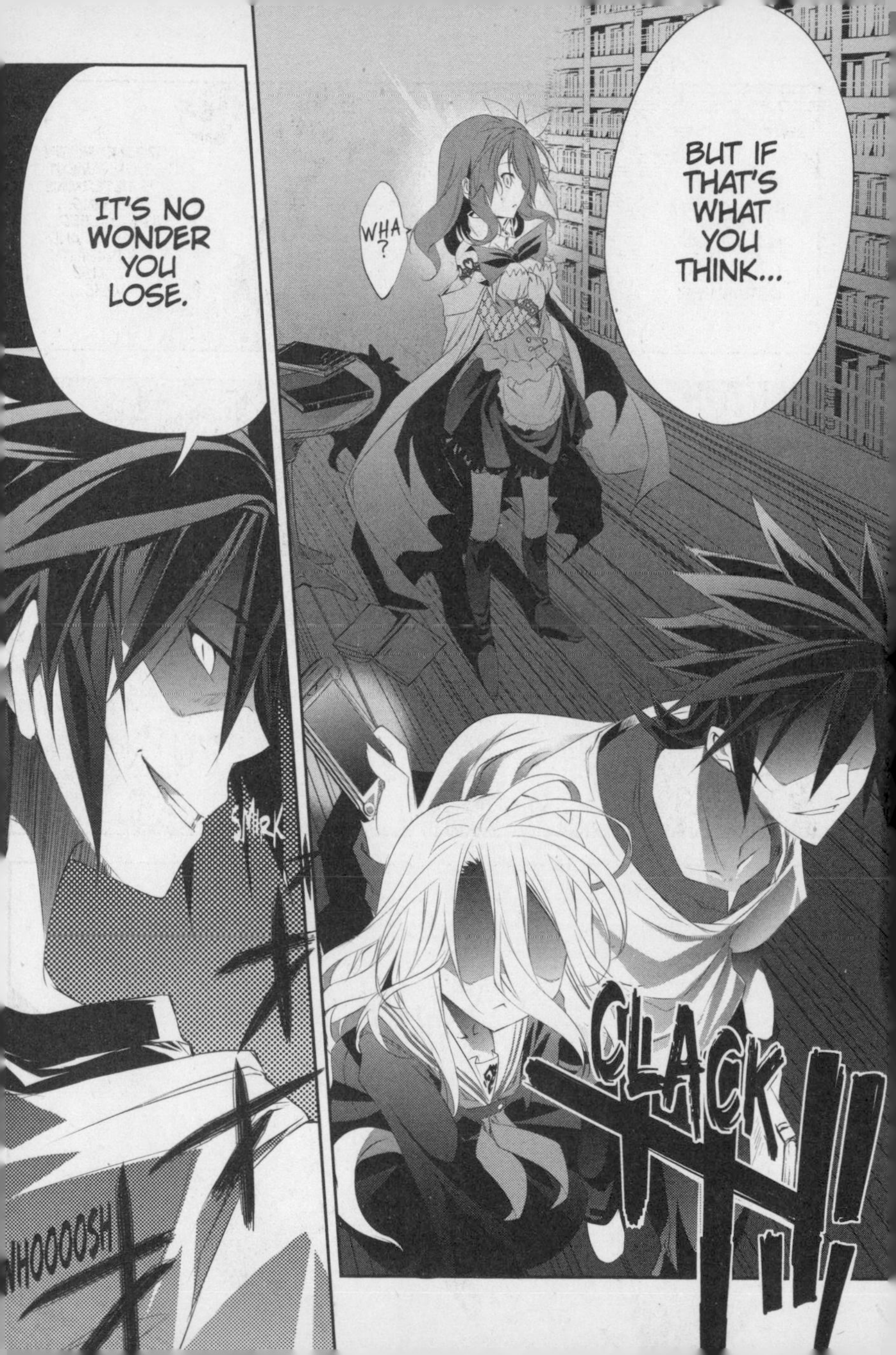

BUT IF THAT'S WHAT YOU THINK...
WHA?
CLACK
IT'S NO WONDER YOU LOSE.
SMIRK
WHOOOOSH

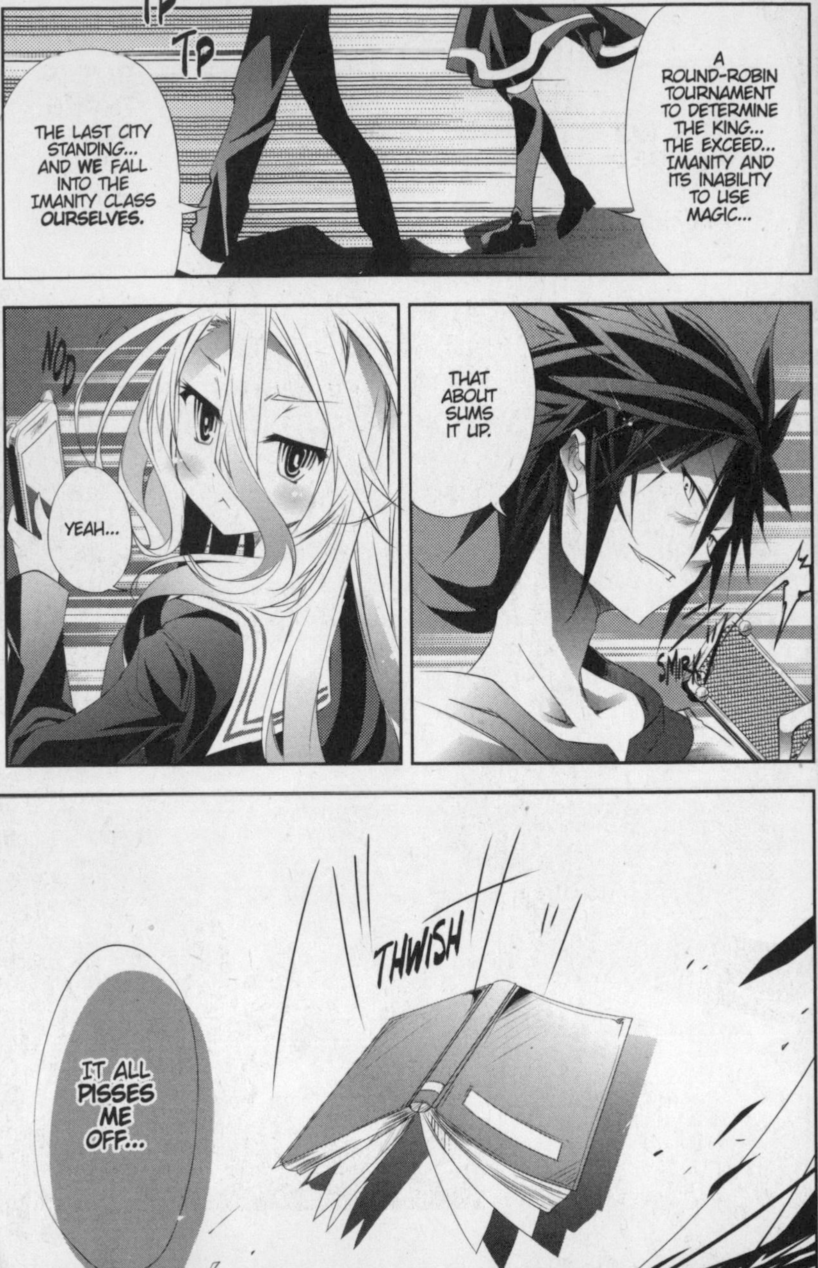
A ROUND-ROBIN TOURNAMENT TO DETERMINE THE KING... THE EXCEED... IMANITY AND ITS INABILITY TO USE MAGIC...
Tp
Tp
THE LAST CITY STANDING... AND WE FALL INTO THE IMANITY CLASS OURSELVES.
THAT ABOUT SUMS IT UP.
SMIRK
NOD
YEAH...
THWISH
IT ALL PISSES ME OFF...

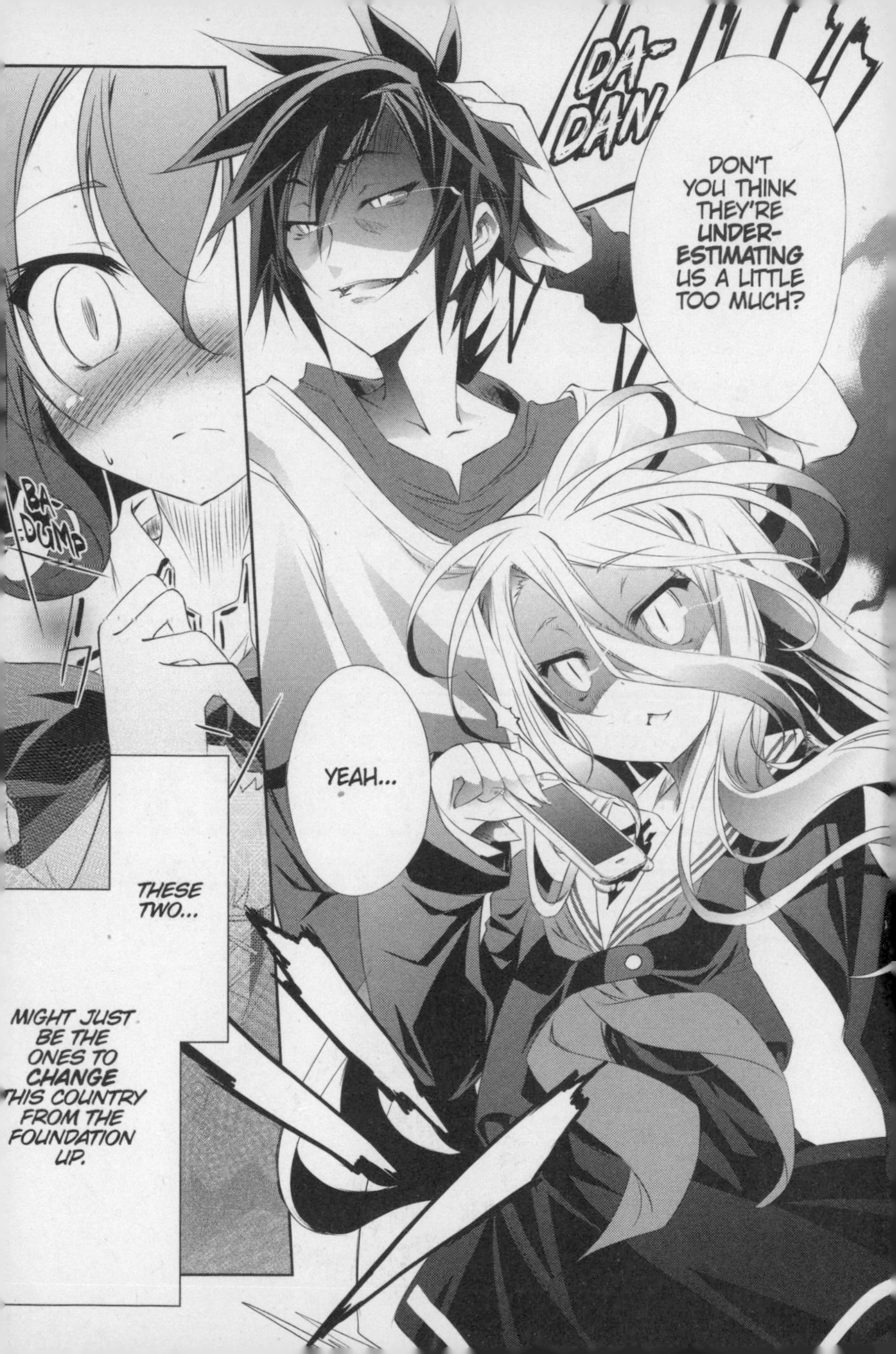
DA-DAN
DON'T YOU THINK THEY'RE UNDER-ESTIMATING US A LITTLE TOO MUCH?
YEAH...
BA-DUMP
THESE TWO...
MIGHT JUST BE THE ONES TO CHANGE THIS COUNTRY FROM THE FOUNDATION UP.

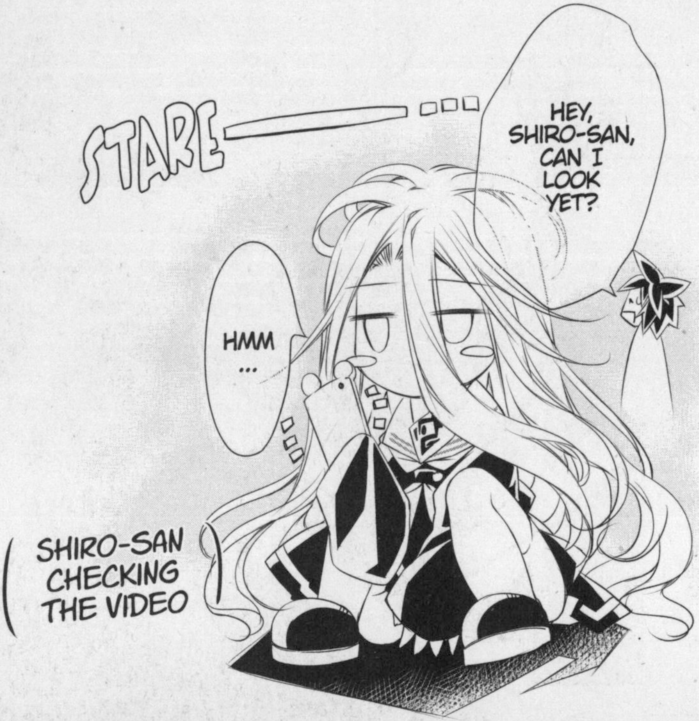
HEY, SHIRO-SAN, CAN I LOOK YET?
STARE—...
HMM ...
(SHIRO-SAN CHECKING THE VIDEO)

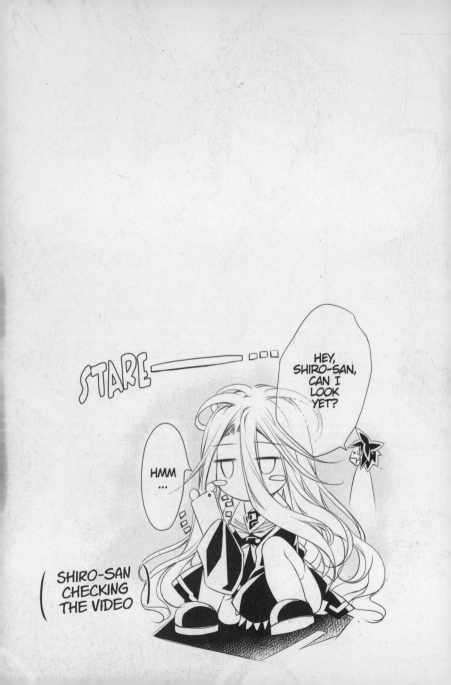

No Game No Life

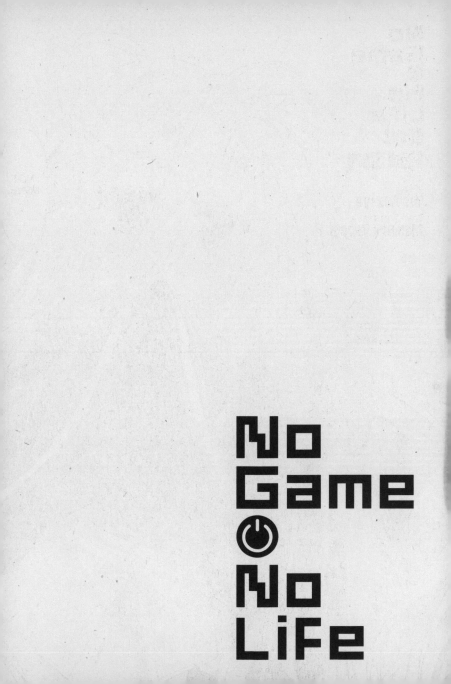

No Game No Life
Bonus Short Story

Written By:
Yuu Kamiya

Cover Illustration:
Mashiro Hiiragi

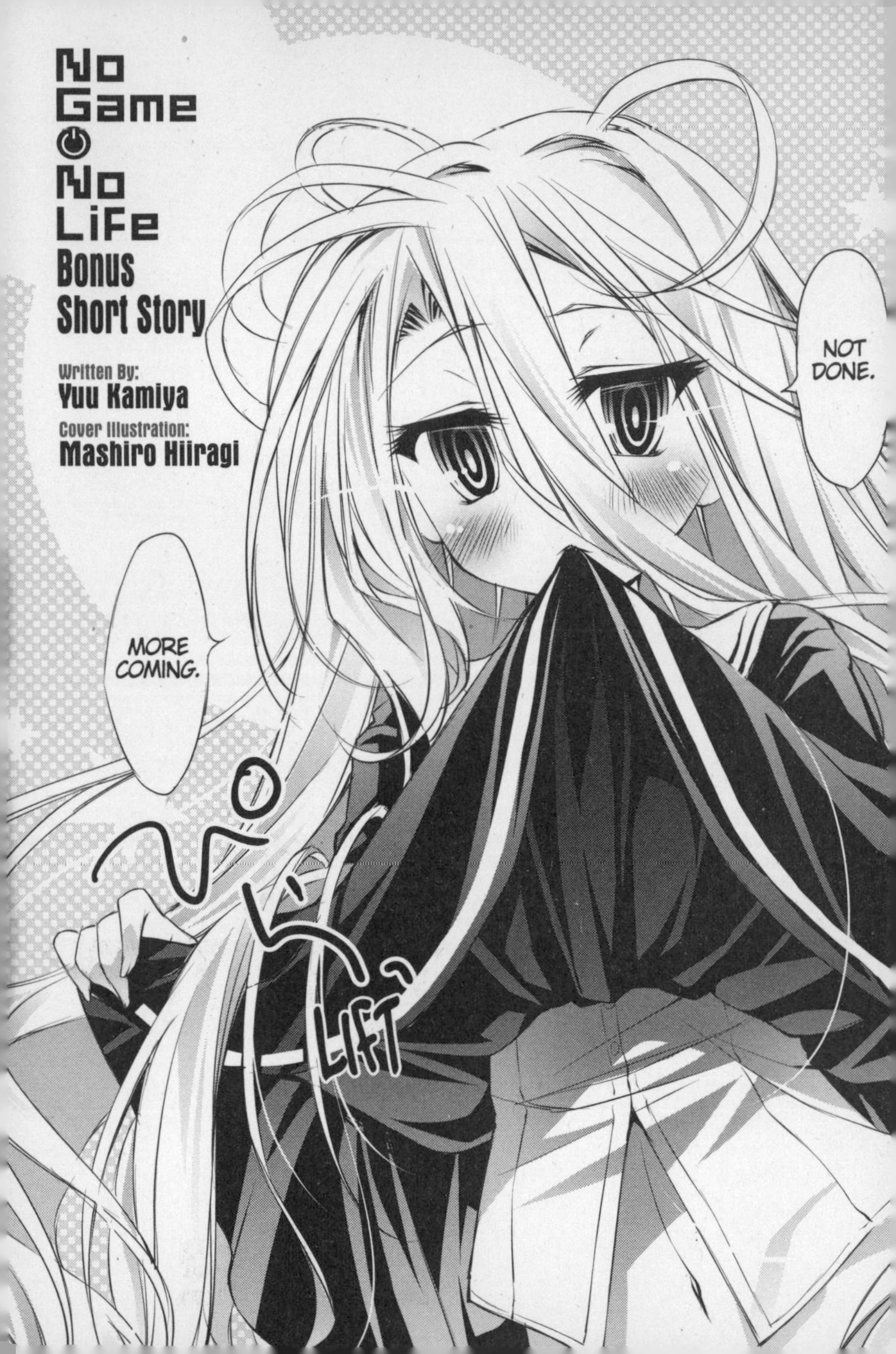
NOT DONE.
MORE COMING.
LIFT

Five Years Ago

*K*ingdom *of Elkia, Steph's Mansion.*

As the two siblings pored through copious piles of books in her library, Stephanie Dola stared on in wonderment. "You guys came from another world, right?"

"Yeah. What of it?" Sora responded, not taking his eyes off of his book.

"Well, don't you want to go back to your home world?"

Steph asked this question out of concern, imagining how she would feel about suddenly finding herself in a strange world. To Sora and Shiro, Steph's world was entirely new—even the writing

needed deciphering! This world offered no place for them to call home, and common sense was scarce and underrated. She was certain that, were she in their position, she would be aching to return home.

However, to Steph's surprise, both siblings responded instantly:

"Never even crossed my mind."

"Nope…"

"May I ask why not?" Steph tried to picture herself in a completely foreign land. She thought of how terrified and lonely she would feel. What horrors had these two witnessed in their former home that would make them so hesitant to return? Steph was taken aback by the siblings' complete lack of lingering attachment to their former world, and she asked timidly, unsure of whether it was really safe to raise the question.

"Hmm…" Sora closed his book with a clap, his gaze somewhere far away. "Our home world isn't nice like it is here."

Shiro remained silent, as she often did.

Sora continued, "We went through some awful times. It was so miserable that it still hurts to think

about it. One event in particular will haunt me until the day that I die." He paused. "Anyway, I suppose that's why we've got no love for our home world."

"…What Nii said," Shiro confirmed quietly.

It was a memory that the two siblings shared, and a day they would never forget.

From the look on Sora's face, Steph could tell that this was a bitter and painful memory. "Well, if doesn't bother you, you can talk about it," she urged gently. "We've got time to kill, anyway."

Sorrowfully, Sora cast his eyes downward. Bit by bit, he began to talk about what happened that day.

Five Years Ago—
Sotokanda, Chiyoda-ku, Tokyo, Japan.
Akihabara, fondly referred to as the Mecca of Geekiness.

In an arcade, just off the overpass over the landmark Central Street, stood a brother and sister who looked as different as night and day. One was a middle-school-aged boy with black hair and a

fiendish look in his black eyes. The other was a young girl with white hair and red eyes, clearly still in elementary school. For the last two hours, these two had remained glued in place in front of the arcade's crane game cabinet.

To win the crane game, a player must use simple controls to position a small crane directly above the prize he seeks. Many believe that there is no further depth to the game, but these two young siblings knew better. They knew, in truth, that the crane game is a *fighting* game.

It is a battle between the customer and the store, and allowance money and store profits are the resources each side brings to the fight. With its steep difficulty and tangible rewards at stake, it is the single most serious, hardcore game at the arcade. If the customers go home empty-handed, they may never return. But if the highly-coveted prizes were easy to win, the arcade would lose money. Therefore, the store clerk must use every measure at his disposal—from simple adjustments to the angle of the crane's claw or the strength of the spring, all the way to more advanced considerations, such as

ensuring that it takes a higher number of tries (and consequently more money) to move desirable prizes into catching range—all the while keeping in mind how much money the customer is willing to spend beyond the original cost of the prize. The store clerk uses all of the knowledge and know-how he's cultivated over the years to produce this challenge.

On the other hand, for the player, it is a challenge of the highest degree to determine if he can see through the store's schemes, thwart the multitude of traps, and coax out the prize in the fewest possible number of turns.

All the same, many believe that the store clerk will give them the prize after enough tries if they only ask.

What a charming, heart-warming thought. Think back again on this story, and see the folly of this thinking. The arcade wants the customer to continue playing, even after investing past the actual value of the prize. Indeed, the true identity of the crane game is a shameless farce—a seemingly innocent and earnest game that turns a profit after absorbing the price of the treasures inside. Behind the scenes, it's

nothing more than money-grubbing capitalists out to create a zombie-like horde of repeat customers!

And yet…

"Nii…done," spoke the young girl. Dozens of plush toys lay scattered around her feet. Shiro stood before a totally empty crane game cabinet.

At the tender age of six, Shiro commanded a pinpoint accuracy that let her weave between the threads and seams of the plush toys, hooking multiple prizes every time. With three tries costing 500 yen per set, she had spent a scant 2000 yen and twelve turns to extract every prize in the cabinet. The arcade had lost a substantial amount. But the issue at hand was something else entirely…

"Then would you mind helping me out, here? This one's pretty tough," young Sora called, wiping the sweat from his brow. Sora had already emptied a second crane cabinet of its contents, and with his own mountain of prizes piled near his feet, he had started on a third machine. However, he had already lost five coins to this cabinet, leaving him shaking in his boots.

"Nii struggling…? Weird…"

"Yeah, every time I think I'm getting close, I wind up missing. This store clerk knows what he's doing!" Sora muttered, gritting his teeth.

The store clerk responsible for the machine and its prizes observed them from the shadows, pleased that his tactics were working against his adversary.

Sora was after a limited edition figure from a popular anime. With its rarity, it was a prize that would sell for double—no—*ten* times its original price on the secondhand market. Truly, it was intended as bait to attract customers. It wouldn't be at all surprising for a treasure like this to be physically impossible to obtain.

Sora shifted his gaze. Just as the store clerk had noticed Sora, so too had Sora noticed the store clerk. The clerk flashed a triumphant glare at Sora, his face showing no concern. The clerk's eyes were not those of a man who would resort to cheap tricks, such as making the prize physically impossible to win. They were the eyes of a gambler...the eyes of a man full of confidence, experience, and pride. The eyes of this clerk spoke without words: "Catch it if you can."

"That's just the way I wanted it," Sora's eyes retorted sharply. "That means there's a weak point somewhere!"

Shiro crunched numbers like a madwoman, taking the cabinet's unique characteristics into consideration. Sora ran vigorous strategies through his head based on the prize's position. At a glance, it would seem that there was no opening to be found. With ten or twenty turns, one could create an opening, but then the investment would exceed the cost of the prize.

In other words, this was a battle against the clerk.

"I don't necessarily need to *catch* the prize…I just need it to fall through the chute and into the hatch… If only…" muttered Sora, biting his nails as he tried to figure out just how to execute this plan. If only…

"Nii! Try…there?" Detecting something from Sora's murmurs, Shiro ran complex calculations in her head and pointed her finger. In the area that she pointed, a plan came into focus in Sora's mind.

"Ah! Just leave it to me." With these words, Sora inserted a sixth coin into the machine. He had spent 3000 yen so far, which seemed like a small fortune

to a child. With the insertion of the 500 yen coin, the cabinet made a clink as it gobbled up the money. Music began to play, and the machine came alive.

Sora controlled the vertical axis while Shiro was in charge of horizontal, with each sibling's finger placed on top of his respective button. Without any signal or either starting first, the two naturally moved as one gamer, as 『　　』.

The store clerk's confident expression remained undisturbed, but there was no hesitation in the siblings' movements. Sora stopped the crane with laser precision as it headed inward to a spot notably further in than the prize he sought.

"Heh." The store clerk unconsciously let out a sarcastic snicker at Sora's mishandling.

But still, Shiro continued on moving the crane right until it very precisely clutched a box much lighter than the prize they were after. It was clear that it had been calculated to land directly in front of the prize chute, almost as if it were a bridge.

"Wha…?!" A gasp of surprised horror escaped the lips of the stunned clerk. Now it was the siblings' turn to smirk.

"*Hehehe.* Sorry, guy. The owner's gonna chew you out."

"『　　』...cannot be defeated," affirmed the two young siblings in unison.

The clerk made a fiendish growl, which didn't seem to match his appearance at all.

The inside of the arcade buzzed with the chirps and bleeps of the games. A fierce but silent battle waged indirectly between the trio. Then came the ringing sound that heralded the end of the conflict: the sound of the cabinet eating Sora's seventh coin. Sora and Shiro smoothly worked their hands without a moment's hesitation. The crane grazed the box of the figure they desired. And that was that. The box fell over and slid down the bridge they had built...

"Sorry, guy."

"You were a good foe..."

The prize headed straight for the chute. At the sight of this spectacle, the siblings thrust their fists to the sky, a gesture of victory for the customer and a sign of loss for the arcade. Meanwhile, their opponent against whom they had used all their might had a smile on his face as he hung up the phone.

"What the heck are you two doing here?! Why aren't you sweeties at school?!"

"Uh…"

"Eek…!"

It was a weekday morning. The two truant minors, riddled with social phobias, had come this early to avoid dealing with a crowd. Upon hearing the question, the pair jumped and bolted, leaving behind on the arcade floor the numerous prizes that they couldn't hope to carry.

In his sad state of flight, Sora turned back and yelled, "You bastard! Where's your pride?!"

But the clerk who had called for the truancy officer simply responded with a silent, twisted smile and a happy sigh, revealing to Sora that the man was a true gambler. True gamblers do whatever it takes to win.

"Sorry, kid. That's life for you. Winning's all that matters." The clerk had managed to avoid being docked any pay and, heaving a deep sigh of relief, he began to pick up the prizes spread all over the ground.

"……"

This is the story of a young Sora and Shiro—the siblings who would later become an urban legend—the two who would be summoned by God to Disboard, a world where everything is determined by games.

The siblings who would one day rise to the stuff of myths. Imanity's strongest gamer, 『　』—and the one game they didn't win.

"Nii… Shiro's plushies…"

"God dammit! How long is that old hag going to chase us?! Oh, don't worry about the toys. I'm gonna do whatever it takes to get them back…"

"Wait up, sweeties! Don't run from me, hun!" As the grating voice of the officer loomed ever closer, Sora consoled his weeping sister and, clicking his tongue with a magnificent tick, yelled, "DAMMIT! GROWN-UPS ARE CROOKED!!!"

The one game they didn't win. That was the day they learned of the game called "life."

The end of Sora's story was met with utter stillness. The two siblings broke the silence. Sora took a

deep breath. "…Well, now you can see why we feel that way."

"Shiro hurt. Deeply hurt…" Shiro added.

Steph responded with a narrowed, steely gaze. "I didn't understand even half of your story, but what I *did* get is that it's an astonishingly stupid reason."

As if he hadn't heard her retort at all, Sora opened his book anew and resumed reading, his chin resting on his hands.

"Well, we did go back on a later date and took every last one of the arcade's prizes," Sora muttered. Shiro nodded in agreement.

"They removed that crane game cabinet after we pillaged their prizes every day for a week. I wonder if that arcade's still around…"

"Revenge… gotten." Upon saying this, a fiendish smile erupted across the siblings' faces.

Dejected, Steph gave voice to her feelings. "Don't you think *you two* are the ones who are vicious?"

Steph decided that for the time being, she didn't want to get on their bad side.

No Game No Life – "Five Years Ago" [End]

No
Game
No
Life

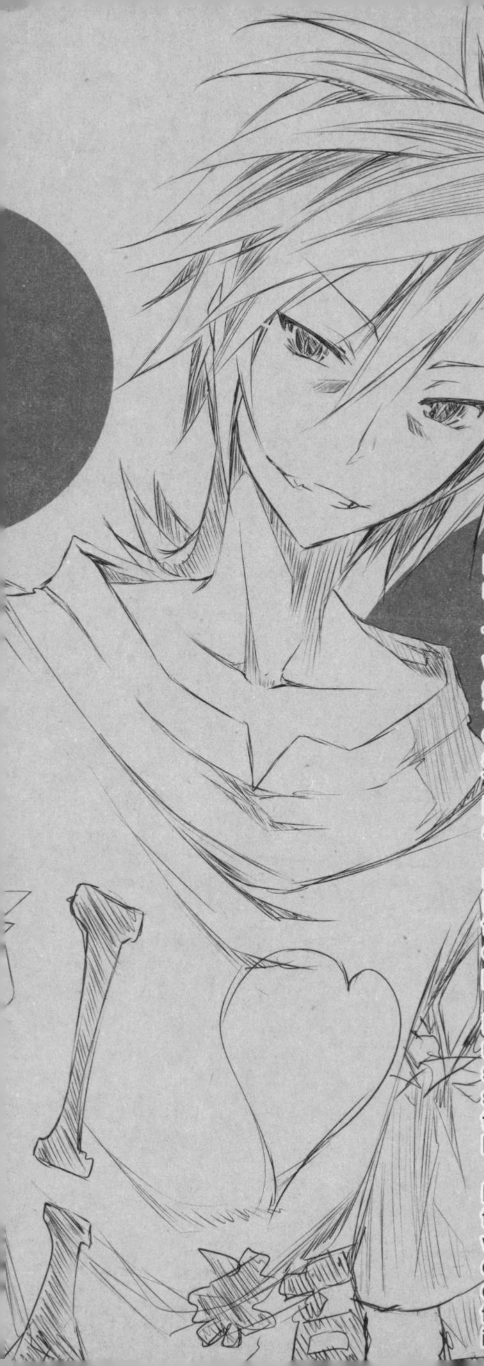

YUU KAMIYA

Hello, sorry to interrupt here in the manga, too. I'm Yuu Kamiya.

The idea was proposed to us as if we were asked to pick up an extra pack of gum on the way back from the store: "Since you already write the story and draw the art for *No Game No Life*, how about you make a manga version, too?" Thus began this totally reckless foray into the manga world between husband and wife.

Now that we've gained some popularity, I've begun to worry about releasing both the light novels and manga simultaneously. We work at such a murderous pace to finish everything in time!

I'd taken a break from working as a manga artist due to health problems, so I told them that there would be several conditions if I were to accept this project. In any case, life just can't be too easy, can it? T.T

Perhaps it'll be fun for you try and figure out which of us is in charge of what with the particular differences in our art styles, panel placement, and composition habits. But first and foremost, I hope you enjoy the work itself...

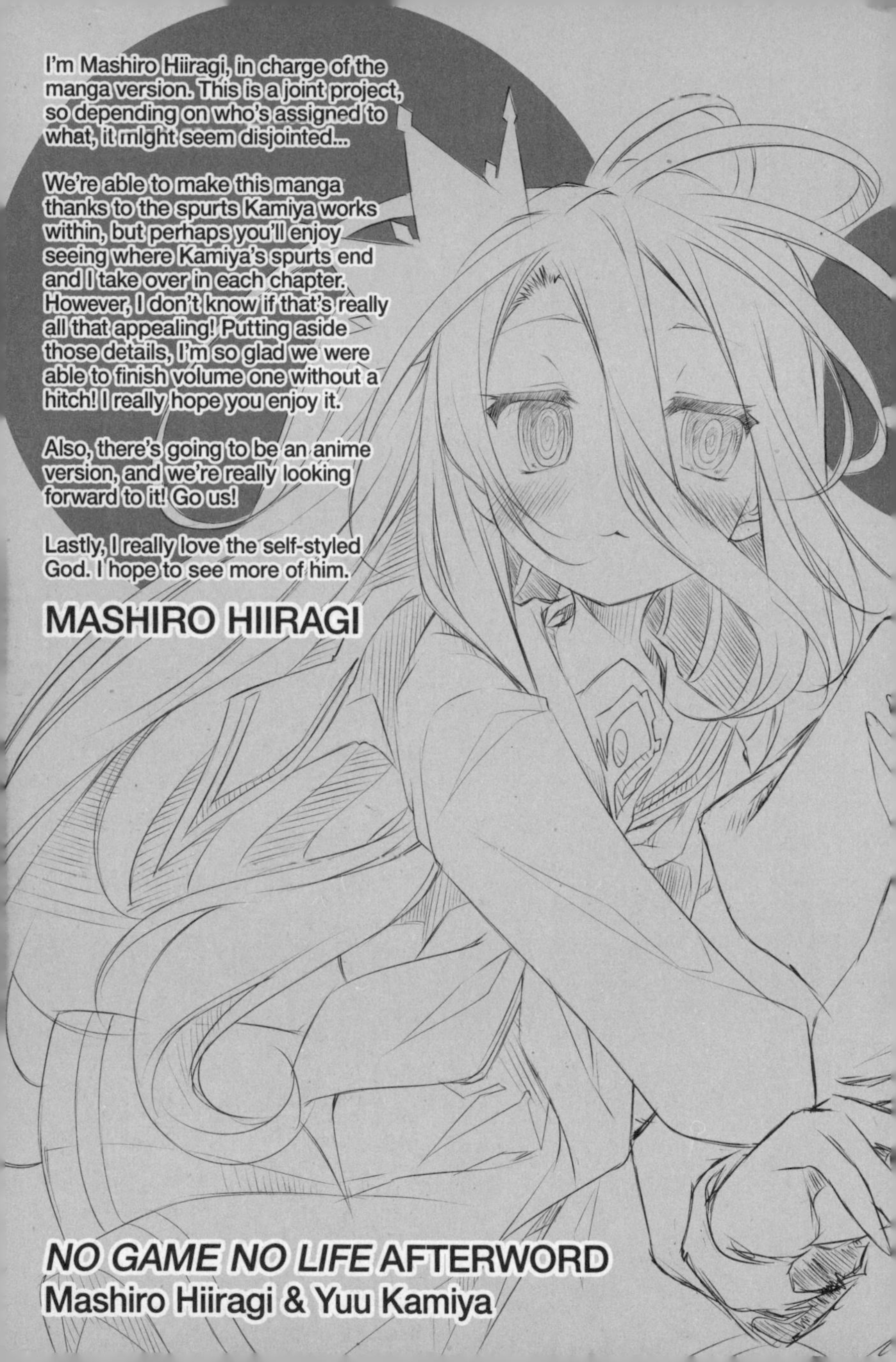

I'm Mashiro Hiiragi, in charge of the manga version. This is a joint project, so depending on who's assigned to what, it might seem disjointed...

We're able to make this manga thanks to the spurts Kamiya works within, but perhaps you'll enjoy seeing where Kamiya's spurts end and I take over in each chapter. However, I don't know if that's really all that appealing! Putting aside those details, I'm so glad we were able to finish volume one without a hitch! I really hope you enjoy it.

Also, there's going to be an anime version, and we're really looking forward to it! Go us!

Lastly, I really love the self-styled God. I hope to see more of him.

MASHIRO HIIRAGI

NO GAME NO LIFE AFTERWORD

Mashiro Hiiragi & Yuu Kamiya

PREVIEW

No Game No Life
Volume 2

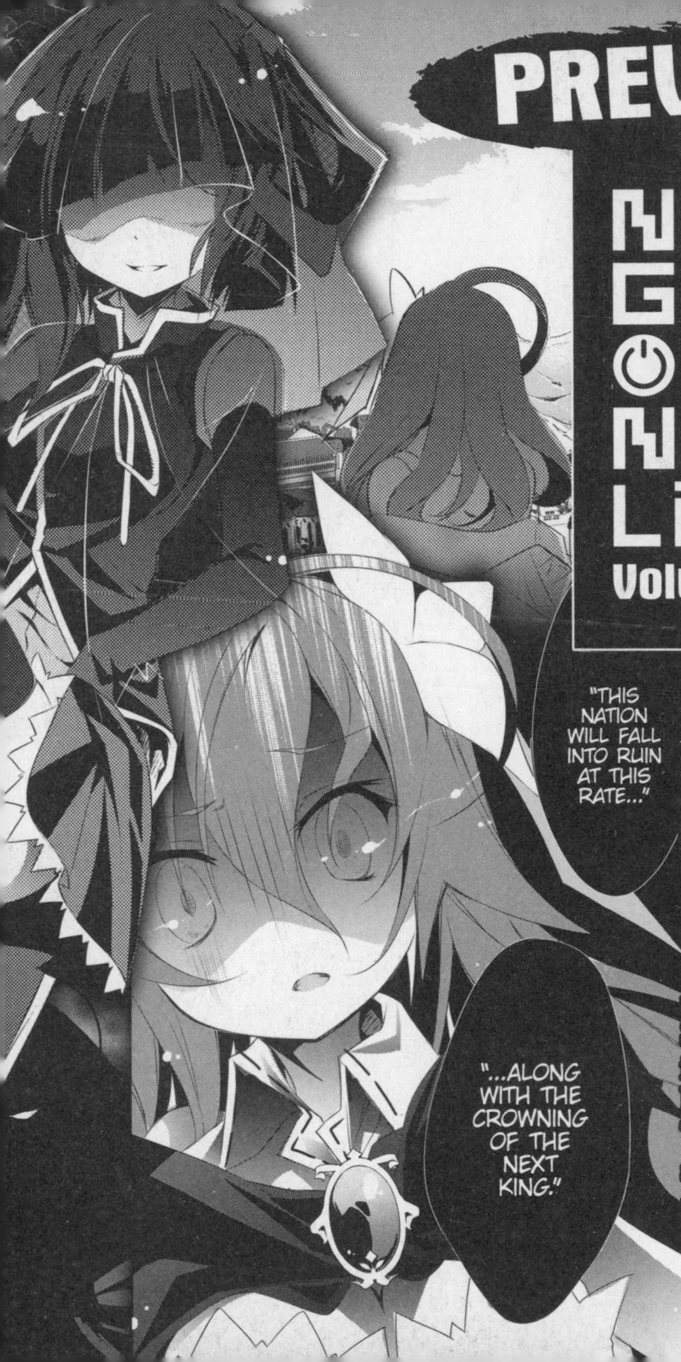
"THIS NATION WILL FALL INTO RUIN AT THIS RATE..."
"...ALONG WITH THE CROWNING OF THE NEXT KING."

After the formation of the Ten Covenants, Imanity's king seemed unable to win any of the games he attempted. Steph's faith in the former king survived. The sky suddenly spoke to her:

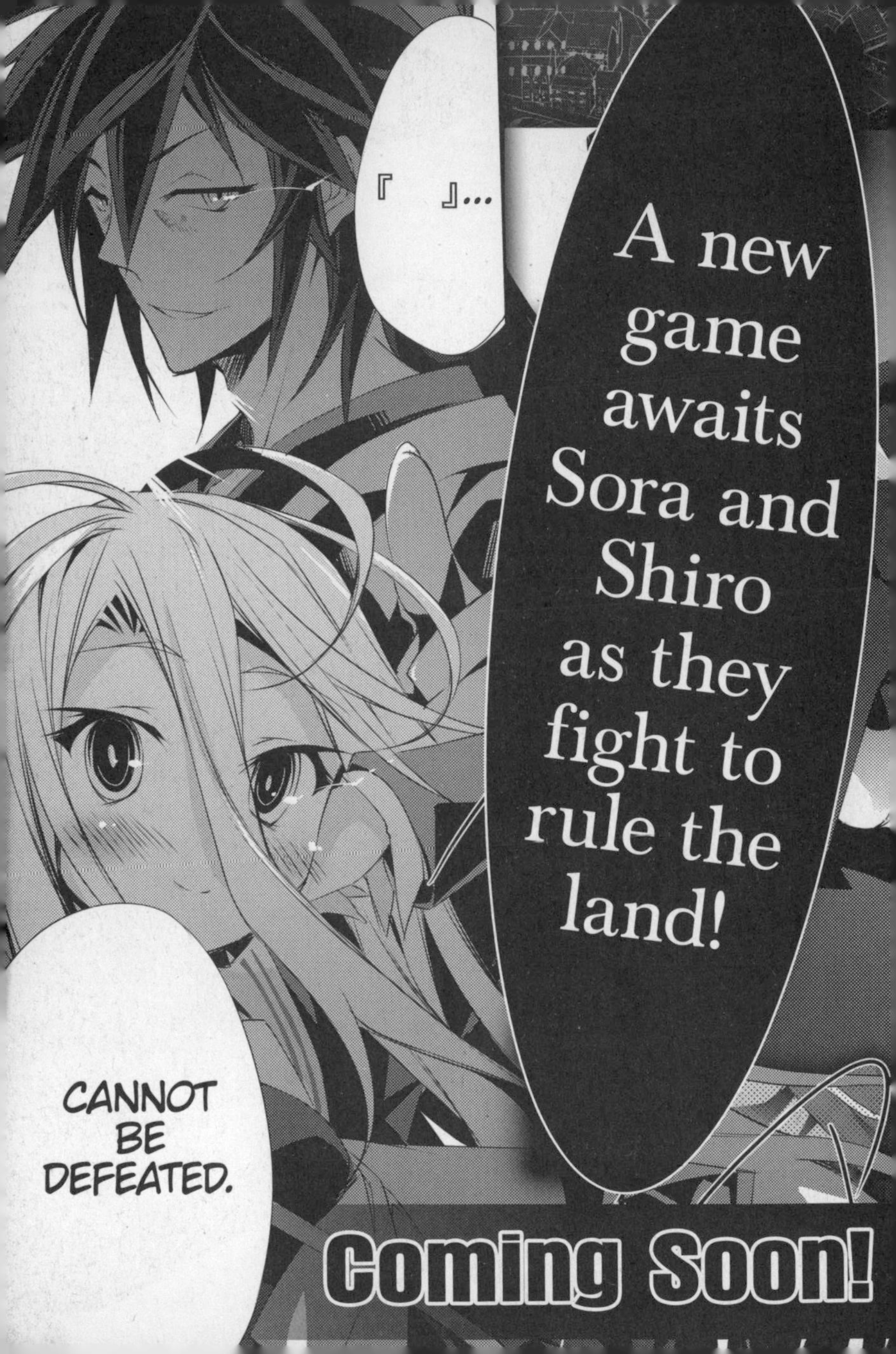
『　』...
A new game awaits Sora and Shiro as they fight to rule the land!
CANNOT BE DEFEATED.
Coming Soon!

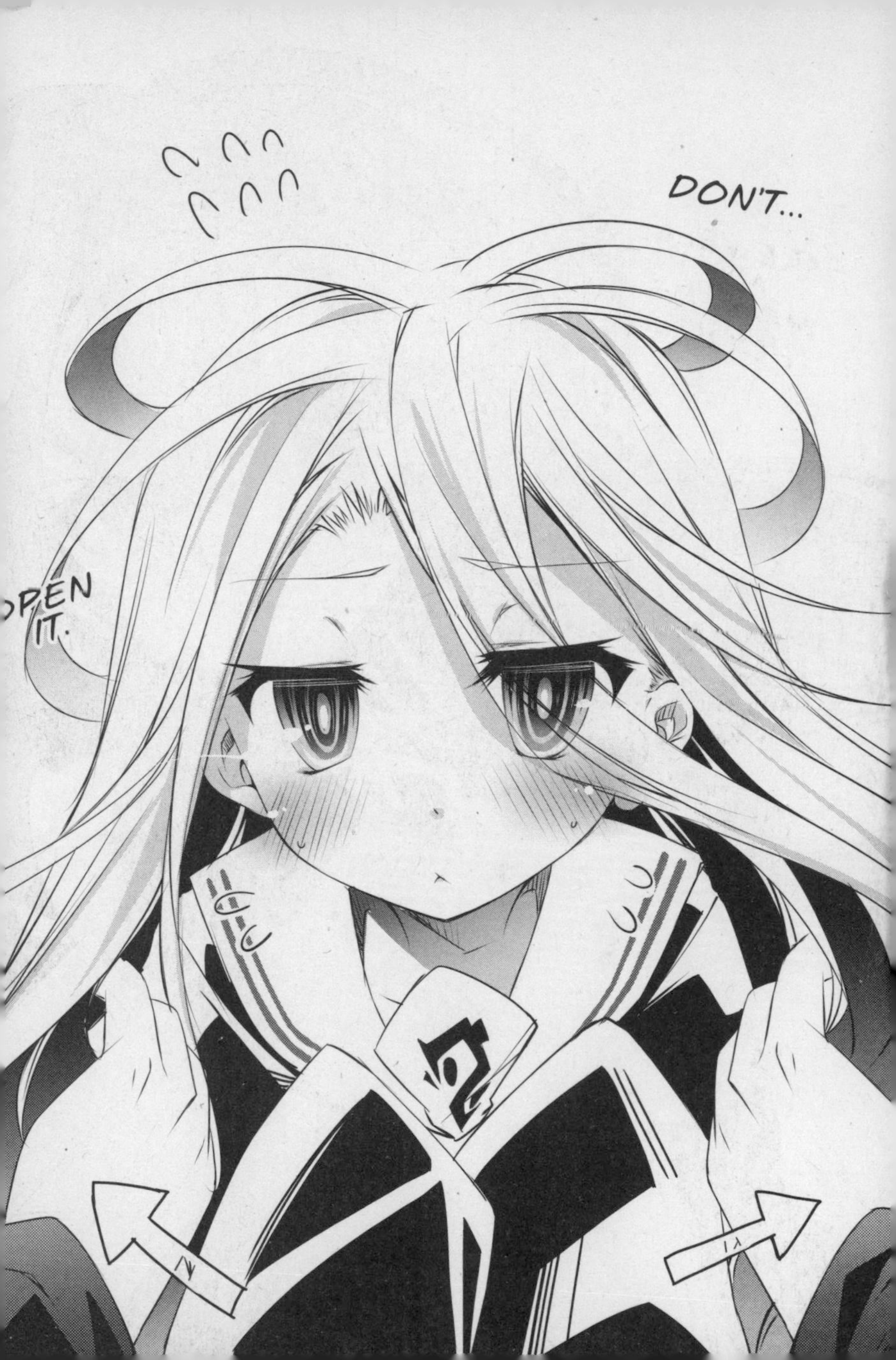
DON'T...
OPEN IT.

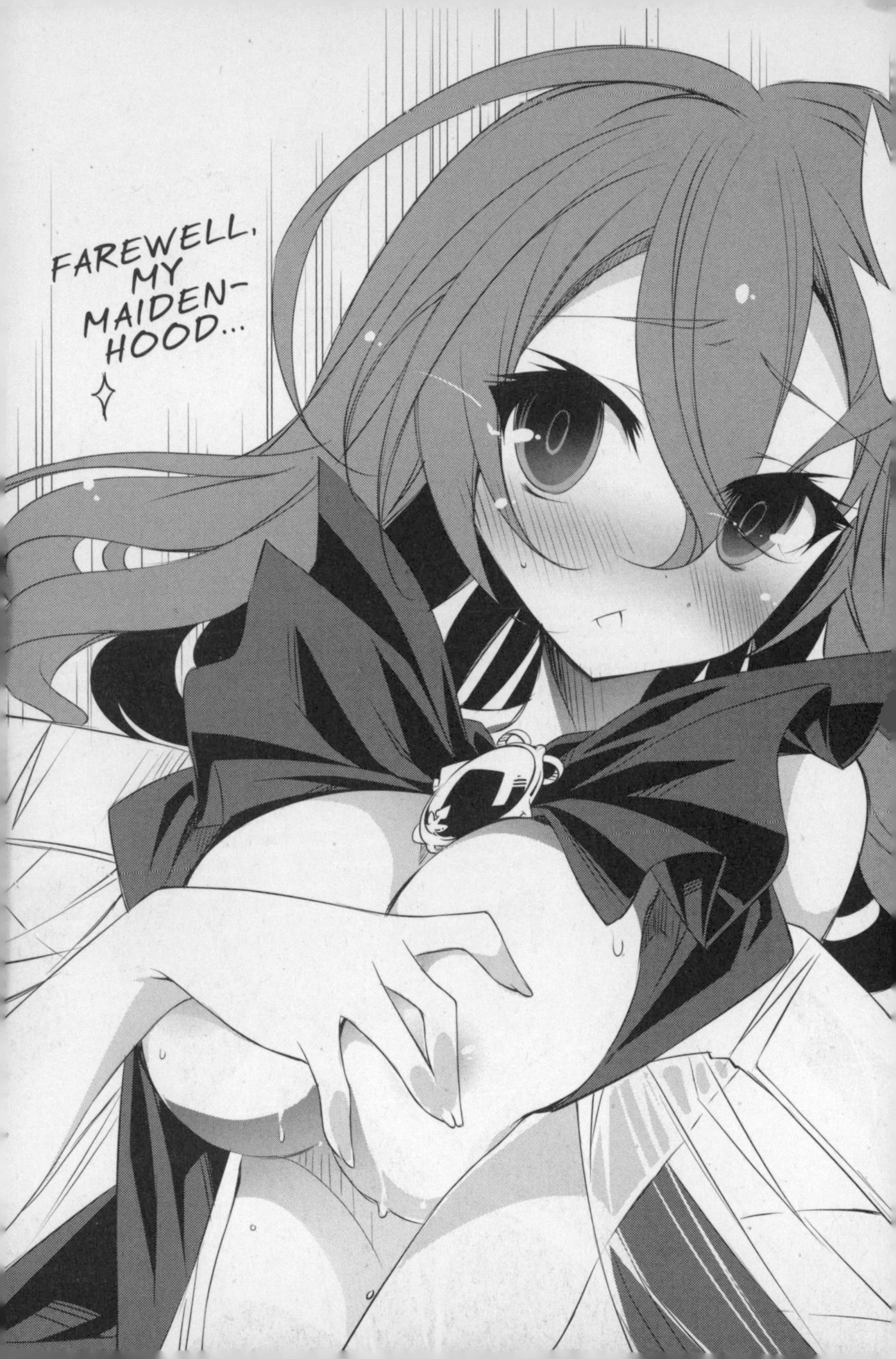
FAREWELL, MY MAIDEN-HOOD...

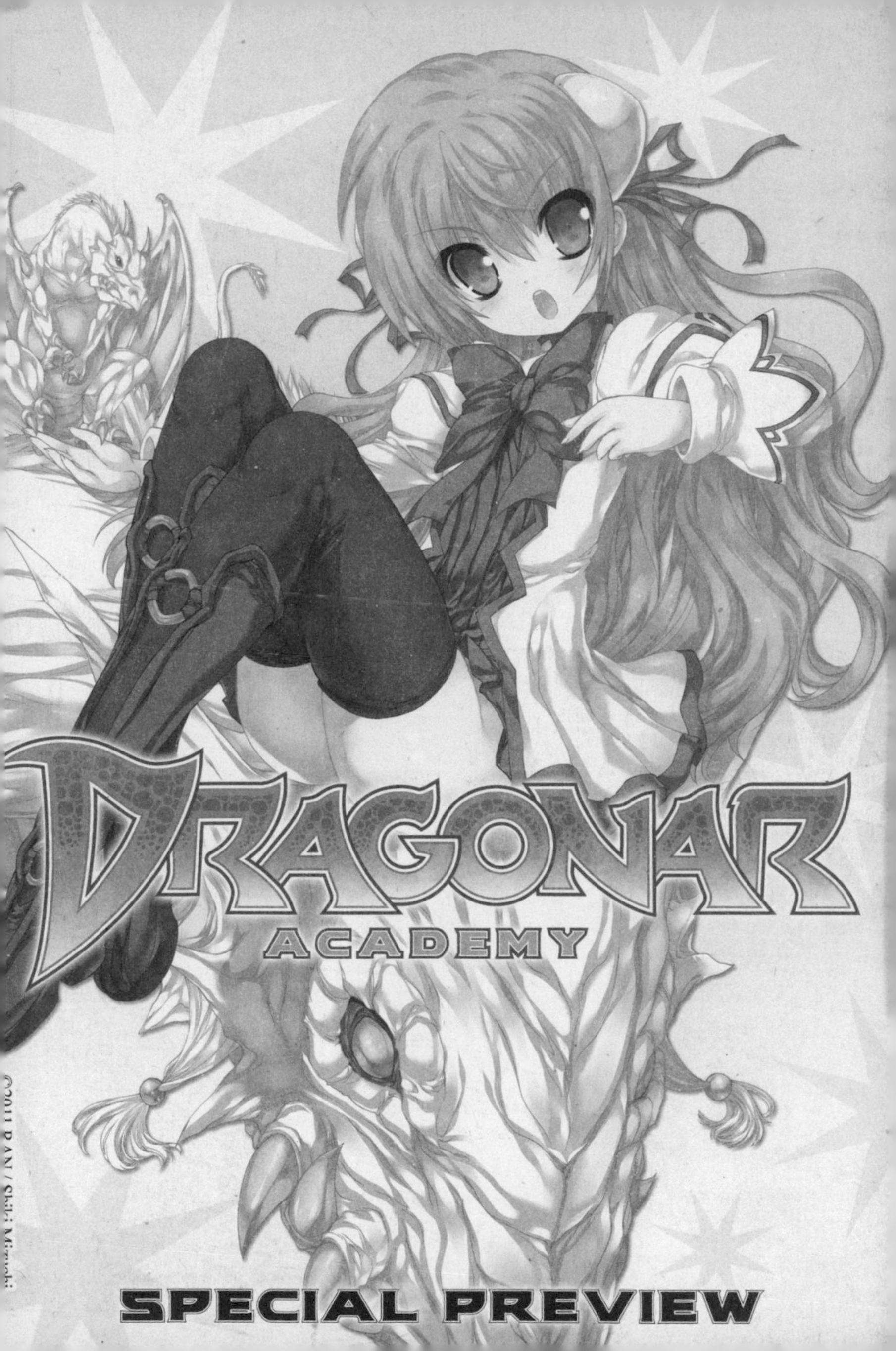
DRAGONAR
ACADEMY
SPECIAL PREVIEW

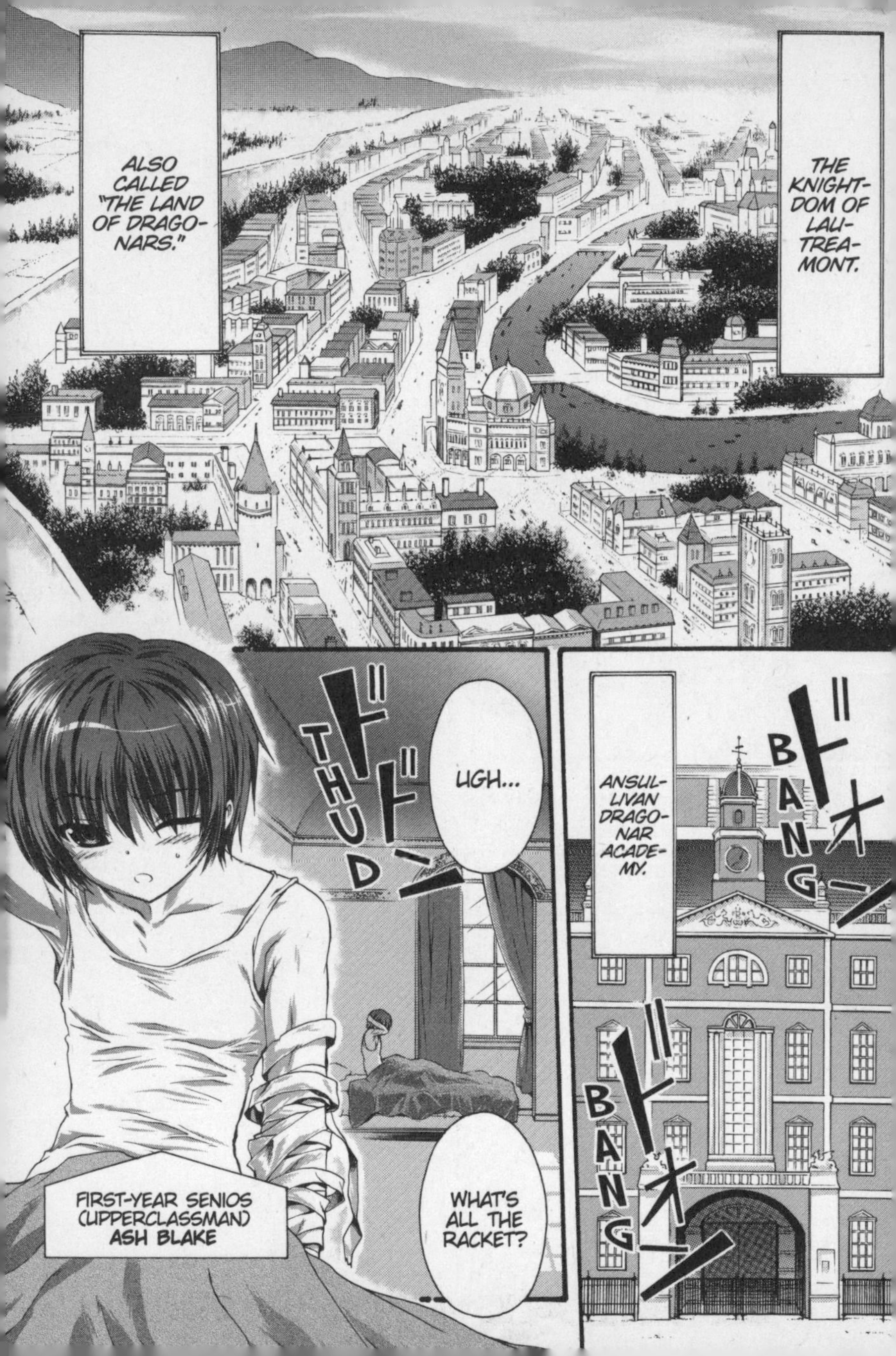
THE KNIGHT-DOM OF LAU-TREA-MONT.
ALSO CALLED "THE LAND OF DRAGO-NARS."
ANSUL-LIVAN DRAGO-NAR ACADE-MY.
BANG
BANG
THUD
UGH...
WHAT'S ALL THE RACKET?
FIRST-YEAR SENIOS (UPPERCLASSMAN) ASH BLAKE

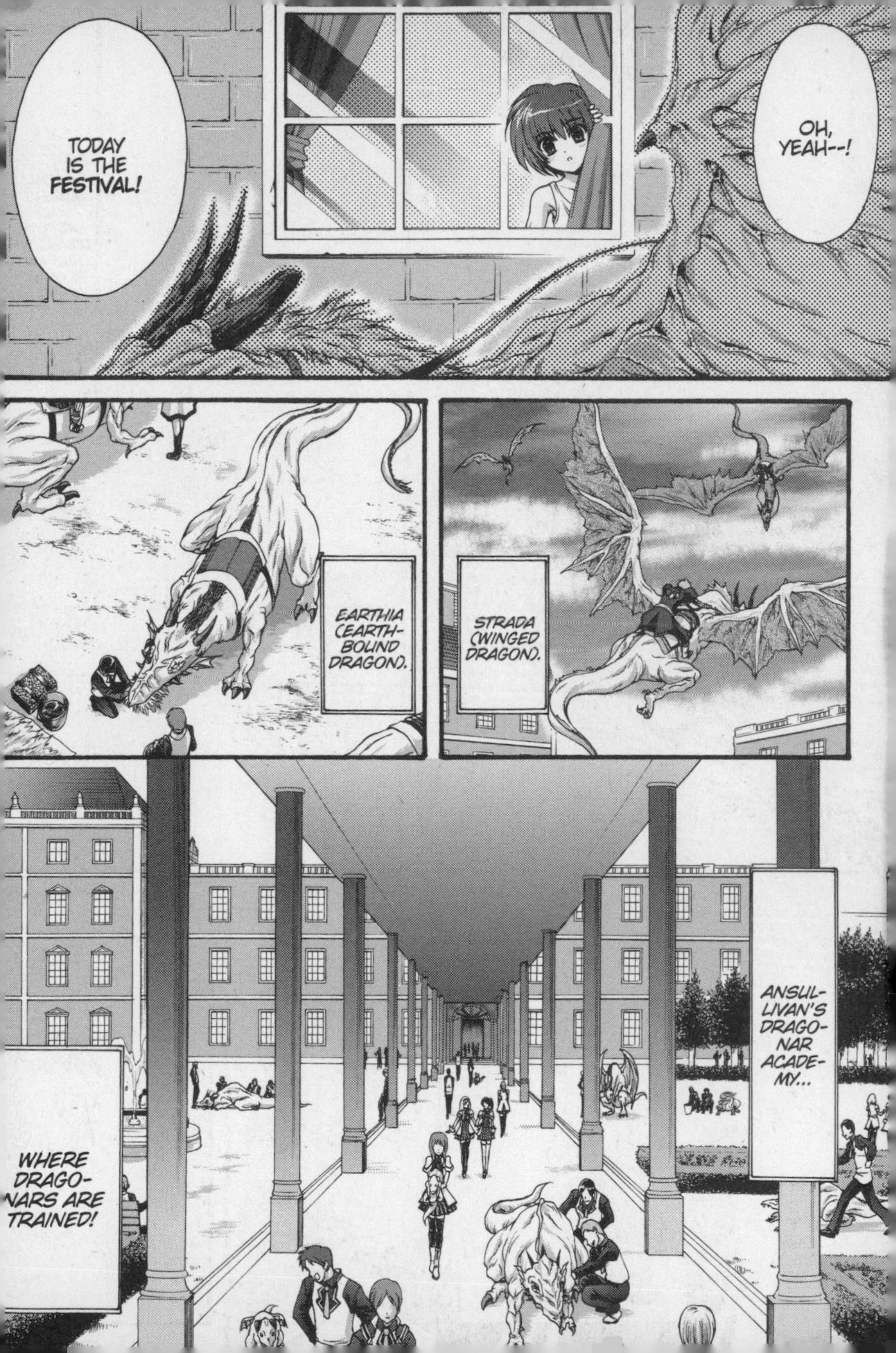

OH, YEAH--!
TODAY IS THE FESTIVAL!
STRADA (WINGED DRAGON).
EARTHIA (EARTH-BOUND DRAGON).
ANSULLIVAN'S DRAGONAR ACADEMY...
WHERE DRAGONARS ARE TRAINED!

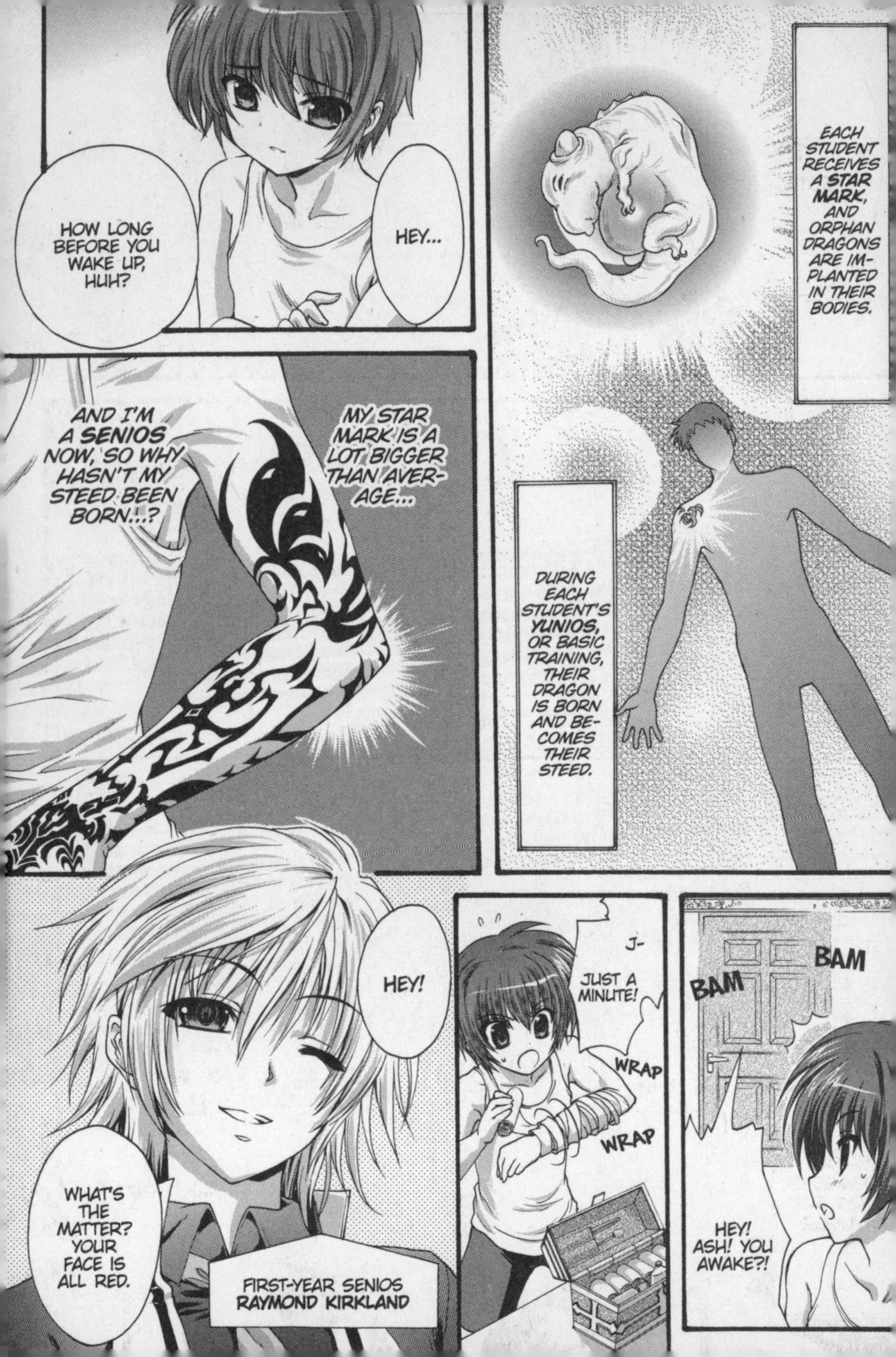
EACH STUDENT RECEIVES A STAR MARK, AND ORPHAN DRAGONS ARE IMPLANTED IN THEIR BODIES.
DURING EACH STUDENT'S YUNIOS, OR BASIC TRAINING, THEIR DRAGON IS BORN AND BECOMES THEIR STEED.
HEY...
HOW LONG BEFORE YOU WAKE UP, HUH?
MY STAR MARK IS A LOT BIGGER THAN AVERAGE...
AND I'M A SENIOS NOW, SO WHY HASN'T MY STEED BEEN BORN...?
BAM
BAM
HEY! ASH! YOU AWAKE?!
J-
JUST A MINUTE!
WRAP
WRAP
HEY!
WHAT'S THE MATTER? YOUR FACE IS ALL RED.
FIRST-YEAR SENIOS RAYMOND KIRKLAND

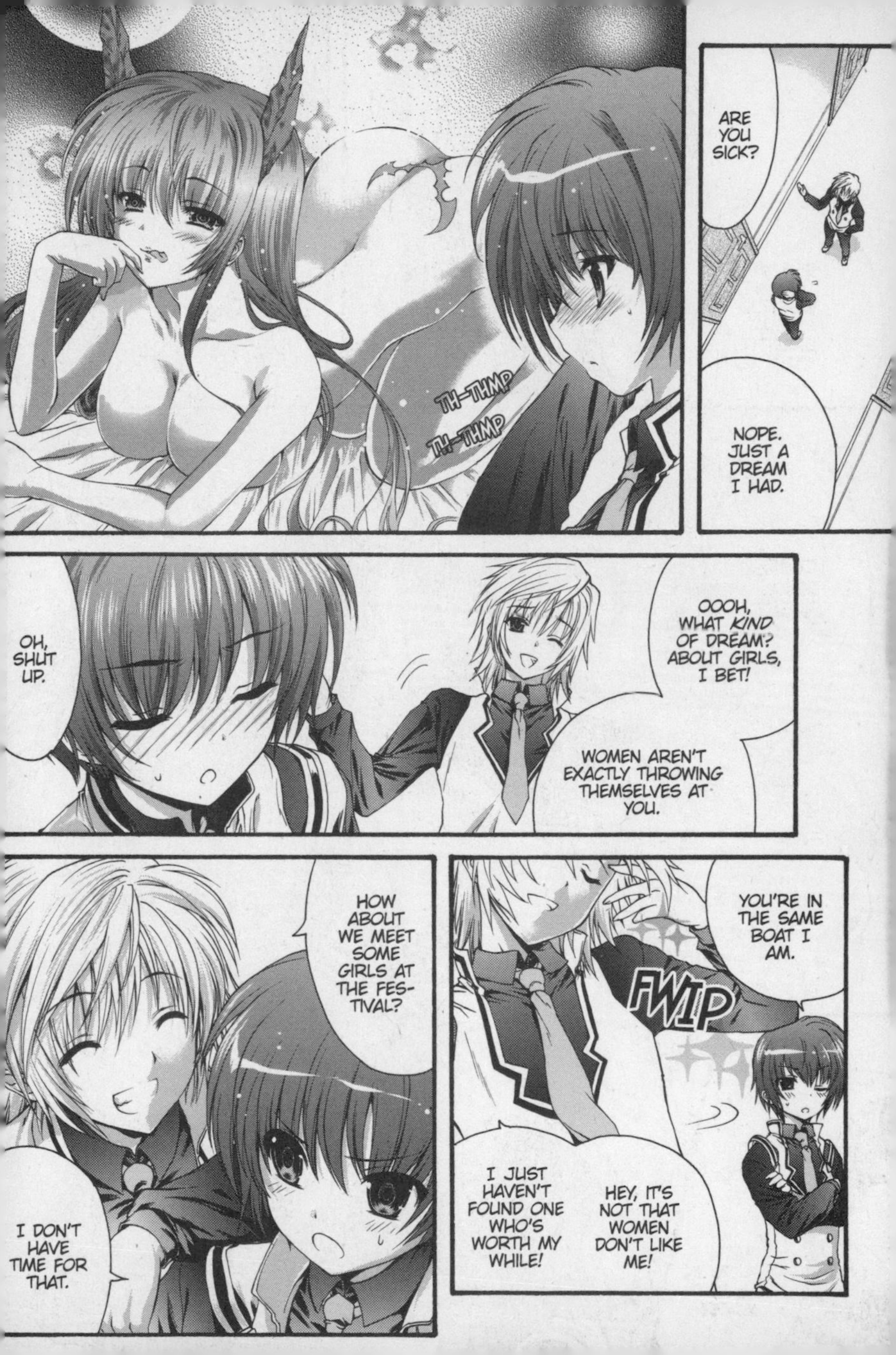
ARE YOU SICK?
NOPE. JUST A DREAM I HAD.
TH-THMP
TH-THMP
OOOH, WHAT KIND OF DREAM? ABOUT GIRLS, I BET!
WOMEN AREN'T EXACTLY THROWING THEMSELVES AT YOU.
OH, SHUT UP.
YOU'RE IN THE SAME BOAT I AM.
FWIP
HEY, IT'S NOT THAT WOMEN DON'T LIKE ME!
I JUST HAVEN'T FOUND ONE WHO'S WORTH MY WHILE!
HOW ABOUT WE MEET SOME GIRLS AT THE FES-TIVAL?
I DON'T HAVE TIME FOR THAT.

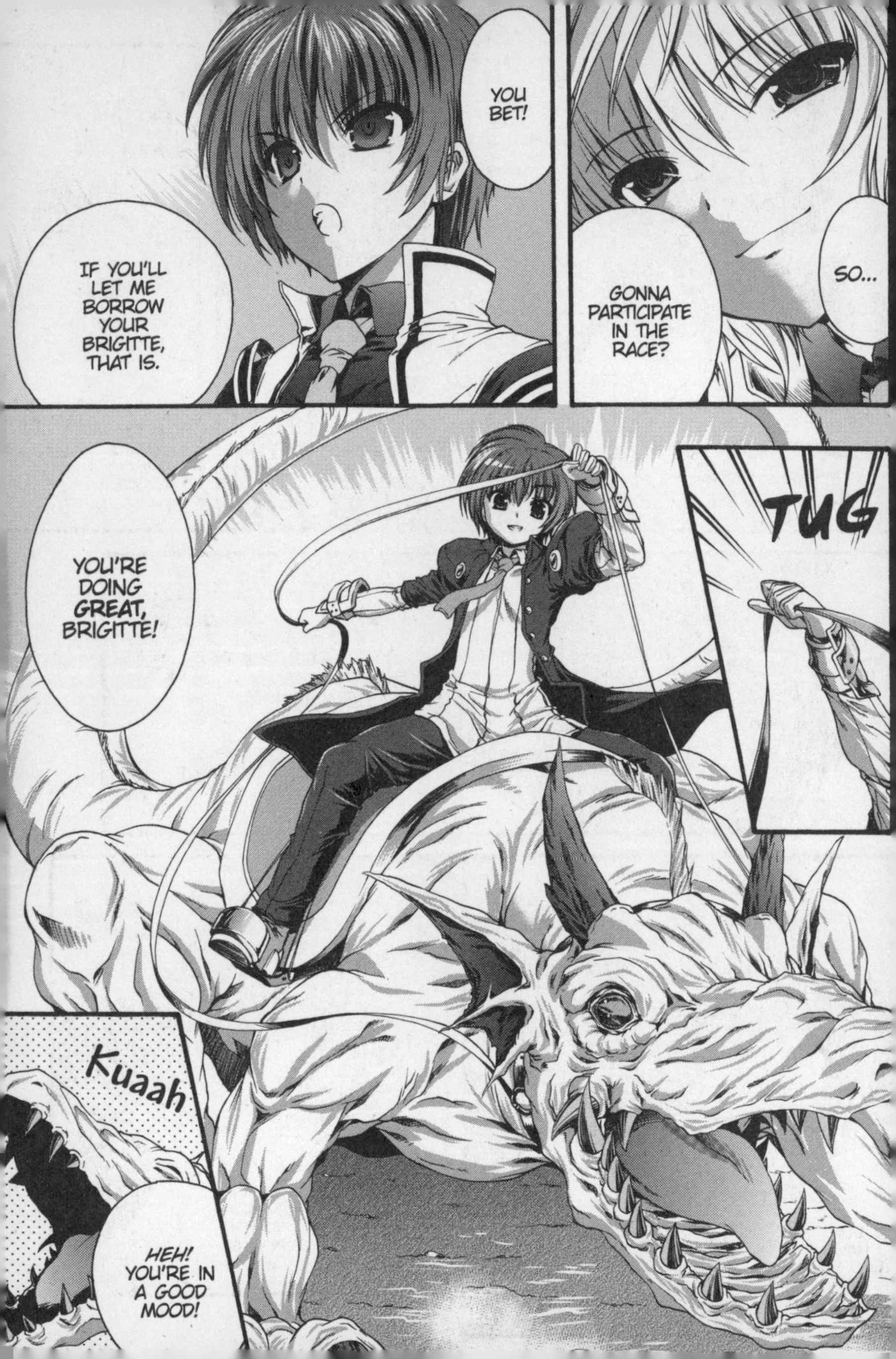
SO...
GONNA PARTICIPATE IN THE RACE?
YOU BET!
IF YOU'LL LET ME BORROW YOUR BRIGITTE, THAT IS.
TUG
YOU'RE DOING GREAT, BRIGITTE!
Kuaah
HEH! YOU'RE IN A GOOD MOOD!

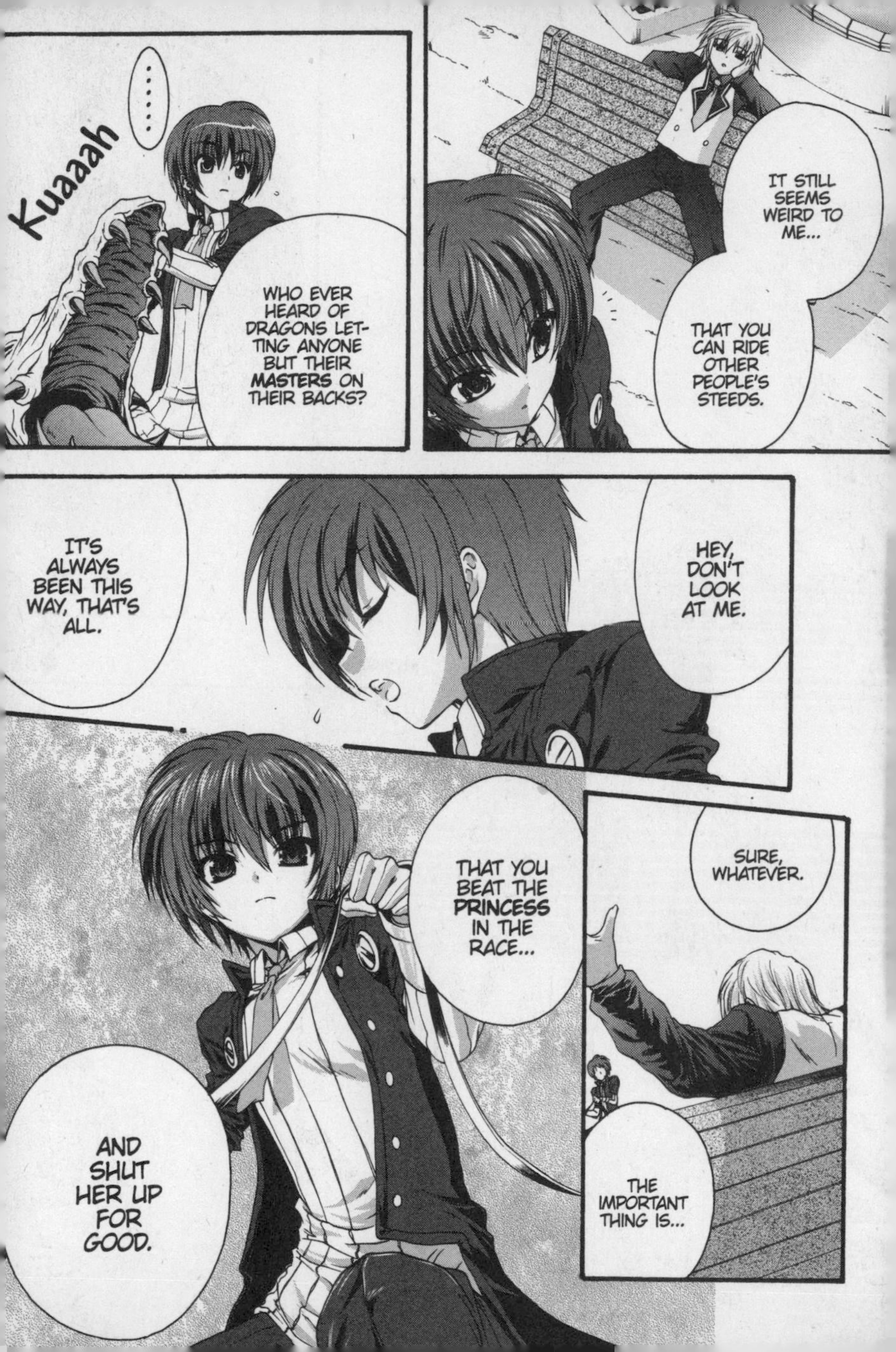
IT STILL SEEMS WEIRD TO ME...
THAT YOU CAN RIDE OTHER PEOPLE'S STEEDS.
......
Kuaaah
WHO EVER HEARD OF DRAGONS LETTING ANYONE BUT THEIR MASTERS ON THEIR BACKS?
HEY, DON'T LOOK AT ME.
IT'S ALWAYS BEEN THIS WAY, THAT'S ALL.
SURE, WHATEVER.
THE IMPORTANT THING IS...
THAT YOU BEAT THE PRINCESS IN THE RACE...
AND SHUT HER UP FOR GOOD.

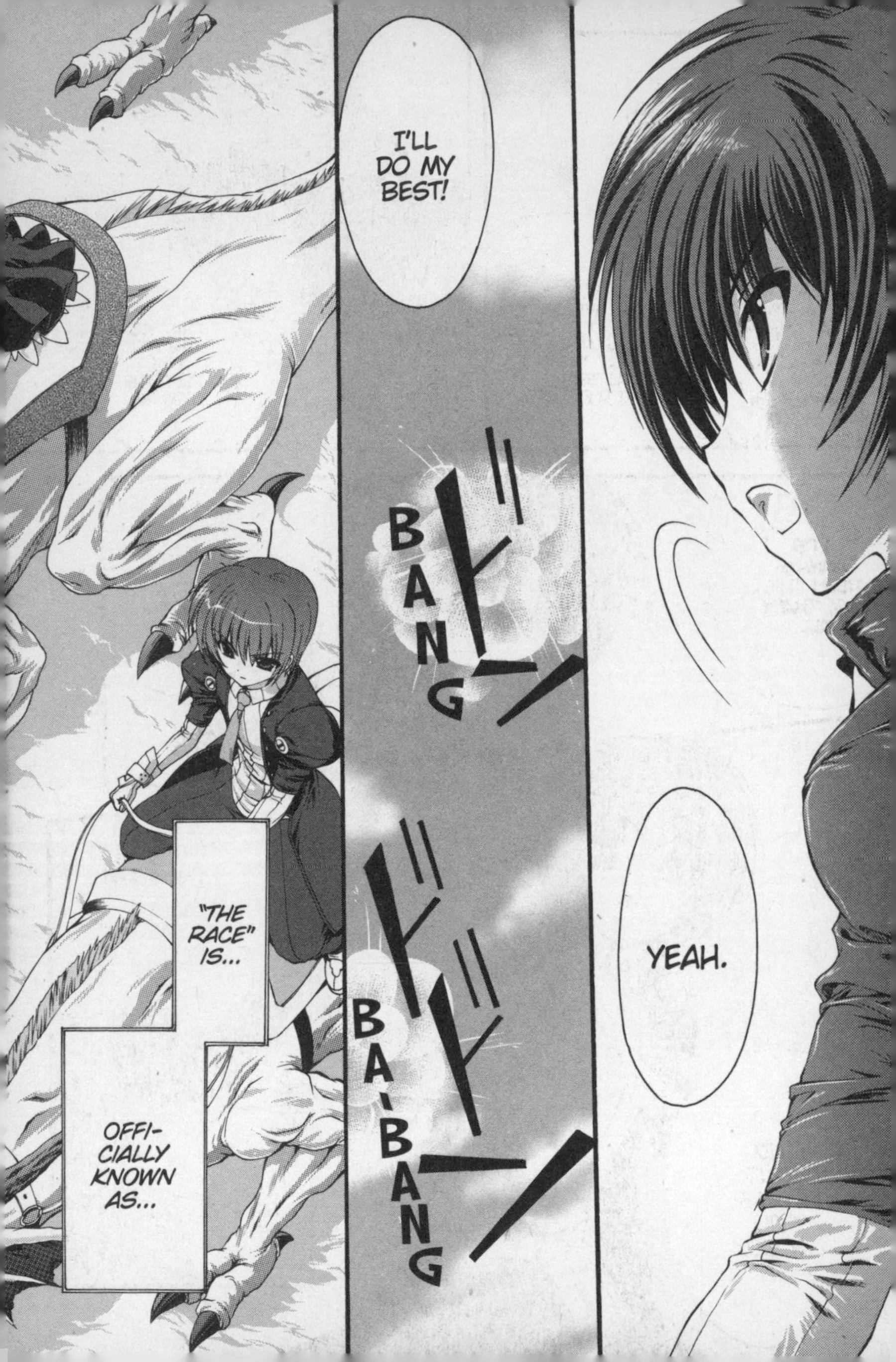
YEAH.
I'LL DO MY BEST!
BANG
BA-BANG
"THE RACE" IS...
OFFI-CIALLY KNOWN AS...

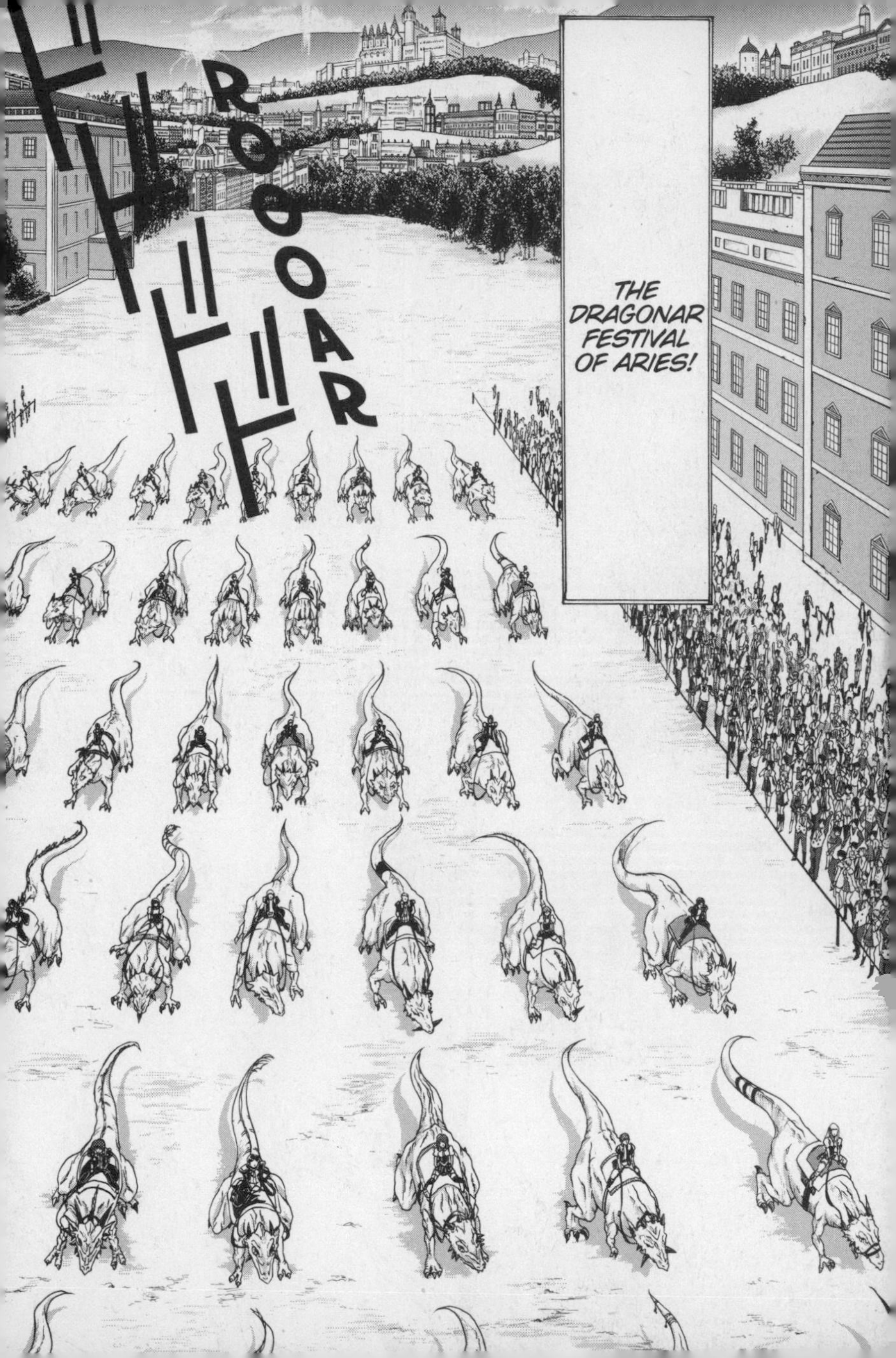
ROOOAR
THE DRAGONAR FESTIVAL OF ARIES!

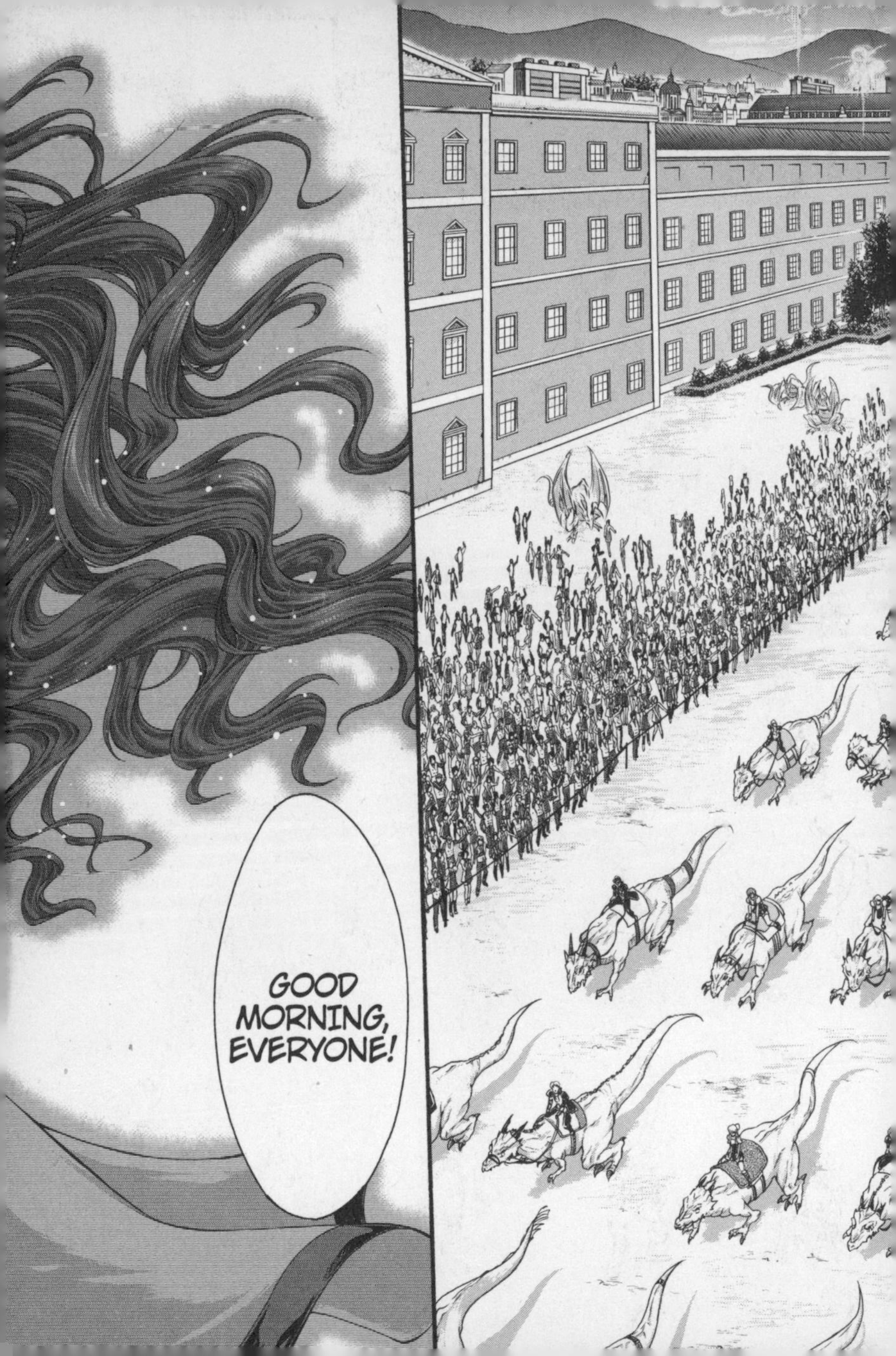
GOOD MORNING, EVERYONE!

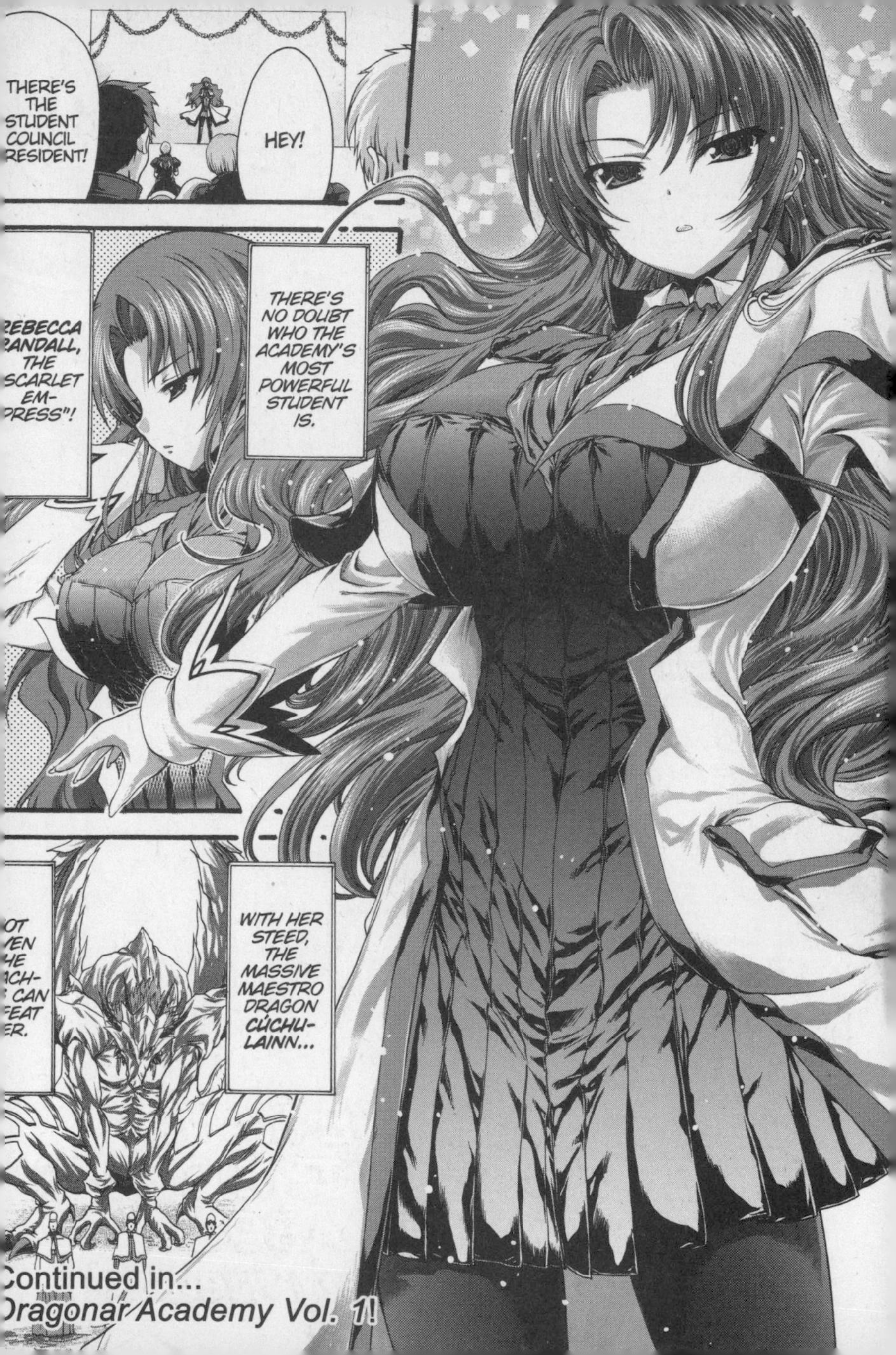
HEY!
THERE'S THE STUDENT COUNCIL RESIDENT!
THERE'S NO DOUBT WHO THE ACADEMY'S MOST POWERFUL STUDENT IS.
REBECCA RANDALL, THE SCARLET EM-PRESS"!
WITH HER STEED, THE MASSIVE MAESTRO DRAGON CÚCHULAINN...
OT VEN HE ACH- CAN FEAT ER.

Continued in...
Dragonar Academy Vol. 1!

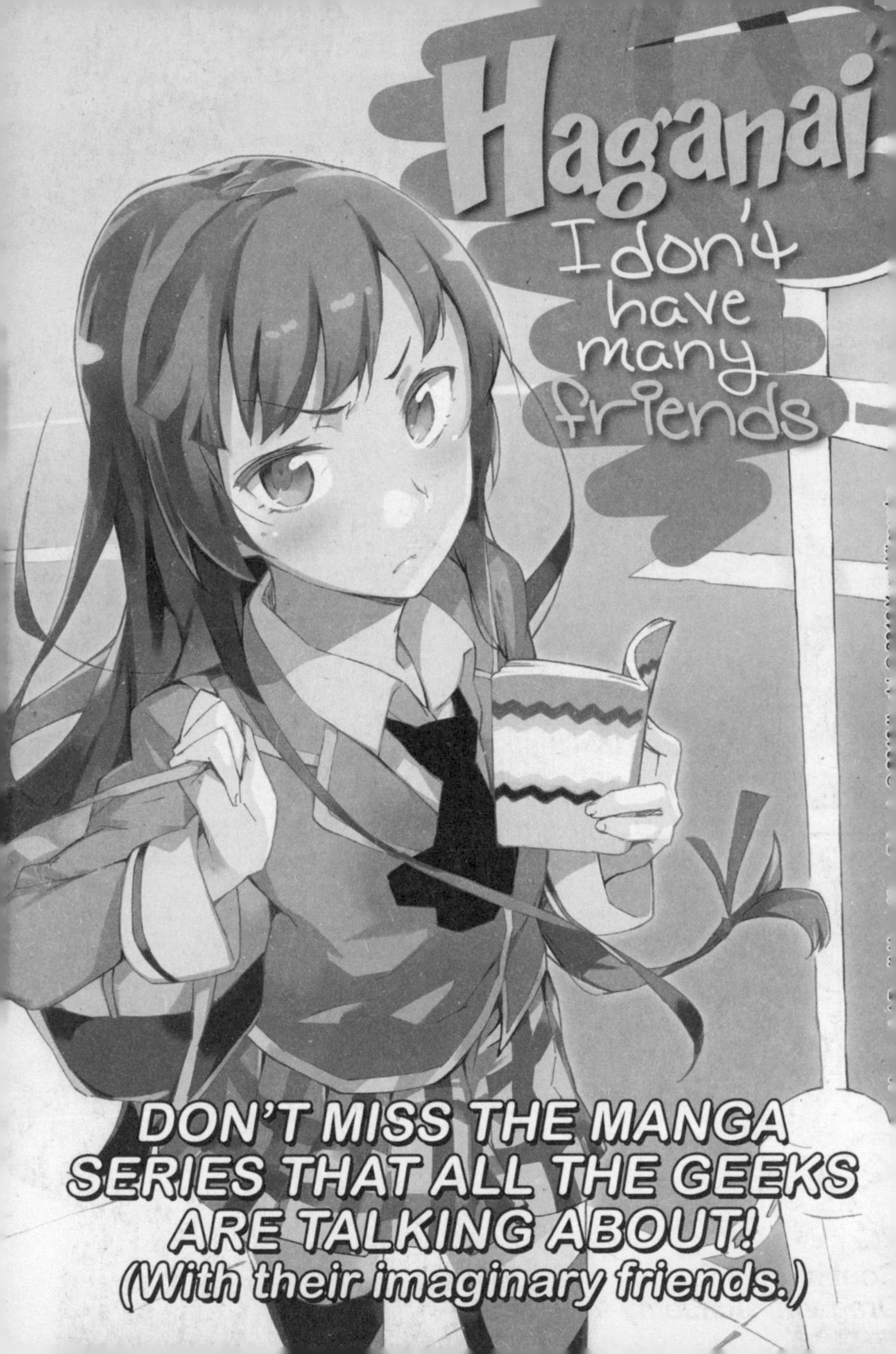
Haganai
I don't have many friends
DON'T MISS THE MANGA SERIES THAT ALL THE GEEKS ARE TALKING ABOUT!
(With their imaginary friends.)

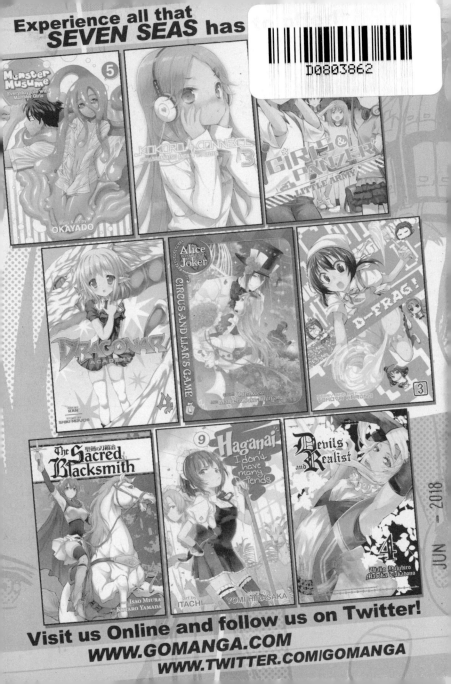